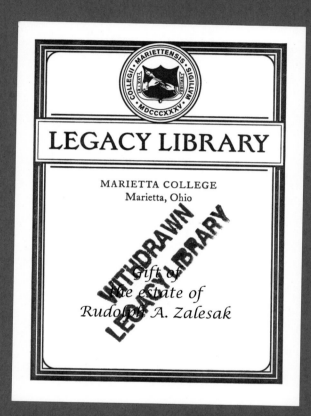

Figure Drawing
the structure, anatomy, and expressive design of human form

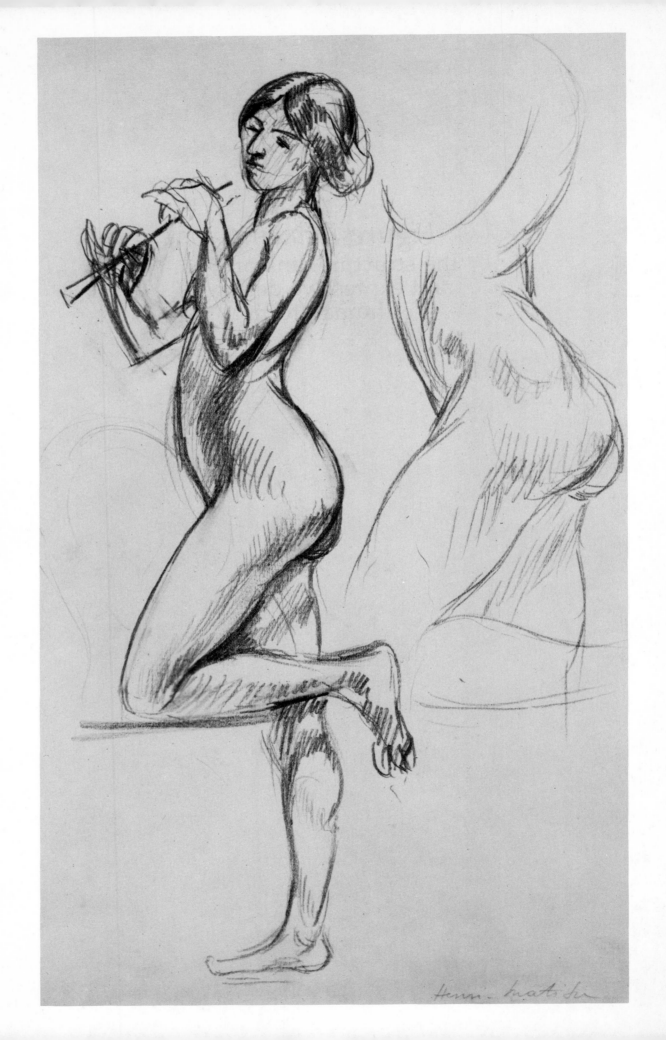

Figure Drawing

the structure, anatomy,
and expressive design
of human form

Nathan Goldstein

Prentice-Hall, Inc., Englewood Cliffs, New Jersey

Library of Congress Cataloging in Publication Data

GOLDSTEIN, NATHAN.
  Figure drawing: the structure, anatomy, and
expressive design of human form.

  Bibliography: p. 285
  Includes index.
  1. Figure drawing.   I. Title.
NC765.G64   743'.4   75-17786
ISBN 0-13-314765-7

10   9   8   7   6   5   4   3   2   1

Printed in the United States of America

Prentice-Hall International, Inc., *London*
Prentice-Hall of Australia, Pty. Ltd., *Sydney*
Prentice-Hall of Canada, Ltd., *Toronto*
Prentice-Hall of India Private Limited, *New Delhi*
Prentice-Hall of Japan, Inc., *Tokyo*
Prentice-Hall of Southeast Asia (Pte.), *Singapore*

Frontispiece:
HENRI MATISSE, *Two Sketches of a Nude Girl
Playing a Flute.* Fogg Art Museum, Harvard
University.

Contents

3

The Anatomical Factor

part one: the skeleton

4

The Anatomical Factor

part two: the muscles

5

The Design Factor

the relational content of figure drawing

6

The Expressive Factor

the emotive content of figure drawing

7

The Factors Interworking

some examples

Bibliography

Index

For Renee, Sarah, and Hilly,
and in memory of my mother and father

Love's mysteries in souls do grow
But yet the body is his book.

JOHN DONNE
The Ecstasy, 1,7

Preface

This book is designed to assist the art student, the interested amateur, the art teacher, and the practicing artist in developing a more extensive understanding of the figurative and dynamic considerations of drawing observed or envisioned human forms.

I began with the single assumption that the artist-reader's interest in expanding his or her understanding is motivated more by a wish to embrace those universal facts and forces present in the best examples of figure drawing by old and contemporary masters alike, rather than by a wish for ready-made techniques and solutions. Although five of the seven chapters provide suggested exercises, they are intended to clarify and reinforce the particulars and potentialities of the chapter's subject, and not to suggest canons of figure drawing. The exercises may be simplified, embellished, or otherwise varied, or may be bypassed without interrupting the flow of the text.

The term *figure drawing* as used here refers to drawings of the draped as well as nude figure, and drawings of parts of the figure or, where the figure represents only a small segment, of the configuration. Very often the beginner is too much in awe of the figure to utilize those skills he or she does possess, and which are more readily applied to still life and landscape subjects. This broader view, in regarding the figure among the multitude of things that make up our physical world, helps us to recognize that many of the concepts and skills we call on in responding to the objects and organisms that surround us, apply just as much to the figure's form and spirit.

For the same reason I have abandoned the traditional approach to anatomy, which is isolated from the figure's dynamic and humanistic qualities and often seems clinical and remote from the living individuals around us. Instead I have tried to integrate with master drawings creative applications of the various parts of anatomy under discussion, and to show anatomy's role as both servant and source of structural and dynamic inventions.

In this book anatomy is regarded as only one of the four basic factors of figure drawing. The best figure drawings always reveal a congenial interaction among the factors of structure, anatomy, design, and expression. The best teachers, sensitive to this interplay, try to show students the mutually reinforcing behavior of these factors, both in their teaching and in their own creative efforts.

To my knowledge no one has previously written a comprehensive discussion of the ways in which the four factors assist each other. If this formulation of the concepts at work (and at play) in the figure helps the reader to better focus on the options and obstacles of figure drawing, or even if in contesting aspects of this presentation the reader is aided in forming a pattern of issues more suited to his or her views, I will have achieved my goal. In any case, I cannot cite a fifth factor, and in good conscience I could not restrict myself to any three. This, then, is a discussion of the figure as a construction, a machine, a harmony, and a voice.

I would like to acknowledge my debt to the writings of Rudolf Arnheim, whose important contributions to the psychology of perception frequently clarified and occasionally confirmed my views on various aspects of perception as it applies to figure drawing.

I wish to express my gratitude and thanks to the many students, artists, and friends whose needs, advice, and interest helped to shape and test the views presented in this book. I wish also to thank the many museums and individuals for granting permission to reproduce works in their collections; Charles D. Wise, of Medical Plastics Laboratory, Gatesville, Texas, for his cooperation in providing the skeleton replica reproduced in Chapter Three; David Yawnick, whose excellent photographs are matched only by his patience and good will; Walter R. Welch, of Prentice-Hall, whose cooperation and generosity in numerous ways have made working with him as rewarding as on my previous book; and Marvin Warshaw, Lorraine Mullaney, and Hilda Tauber, for their gifted efforts in helping to give the book its present form. Special thanks go to Sally Lesser for her time and effort in helping me to state my thoughts.

I owe the deepest gratitude in equal measure to my wife Renee, for the considerable gift of her time and for her invaluable assistance and counsel, and to my daughter Sarah who, now an old hand at enduring her father's pace and preoccupation, helped by making her understanding and affection so evident.

NATHAN GOLDSTEIN

Figure Drawing
the structure, anatomy, and expressive design of human form

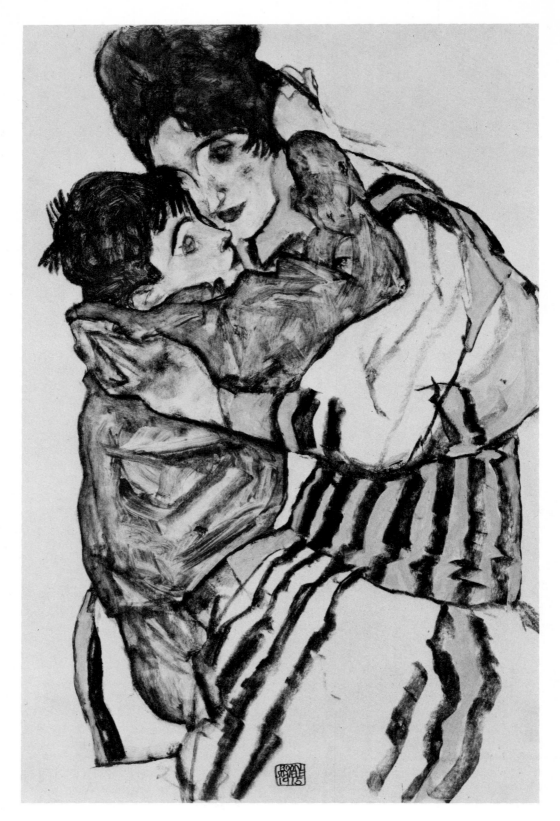

Figure 1.1
EGON SCHIELE (1890–1918)
Mother and Child
Black crayon, watercolor, gouache. 7 x 9 1/4 in.
Courtesy Museum of Fine Arts, Boston.
Edwin E. Jack Fund.

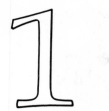

The Evolution of Intent

major factors
and concepts of figure drawing

SOME COMMON DENOMINATORS

Some figure drawings have the power to affect and involve us deeply. The reasons why this is so have little to do with the artist's facility, objective accuracy, or choice of subject. Nor is time a factor, for some of these drawings have been with us for centuries, while others are very recent. What all seem to possess are certain extraordinary though hard to define energies and meanings that make them important creative statements for many people—connoisseurs and laymen alike. Naturally, not every one of these drawings appeals in the same way to every viewer, but each has its admirers, and many enjoy universal esteem.

Other figure drawings, though deftly stated, anatomically correct, and fascinating in subject matter, do not have these special qualities. They lack any interest beyond their descriptive content. Indeed, drawings preoccupied merely with facility, accuracy, or "story-telling" usually go no further than these dubious goals.

They lack the vitality and the lasting power found in master figure drawings.

What is there about the figure drawings of Michelangelo, Rembrandt, Matisse, and other old and contemporary masters that makes them alive and lasting, that attracts and engages us so? It is not their success as faithful documents of observed individuals or situations, for many are wholly invented images. Nor are they the most thoroughly researched, scientifically detailed accounts. Sometimes, as in Schiele's drawing *Mother and Child* (Figure 1.1), such works are strikingly subjective interpretations. Often they make a boldly concise statement, as in Kollwitz's drawing *Woman Weeping* (Figure 1.2). It is not that the best figure drawings exemplify some cultural standard of beauty, for many do not meet even minimal standards of attractive human proportions. Still no matter how plain or misshapen the forms, the best figure drawings always impart some degree of psychological or spiritual attraction, as in Grünewald's study *An Old Woman with Closed Eyes* (Figure 1.3). Fi-

3

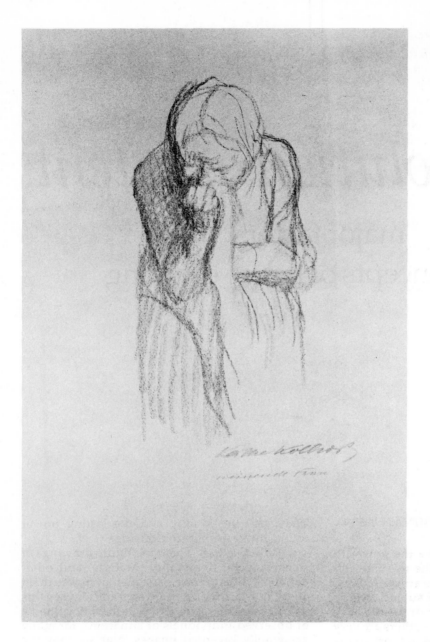

Figure 1.2
KÄTHE KOLLWITZ (1867–1945)
Woman Weeping
Charcoal on blue paper. 24 x 19 in.
National Gallery of Art, Washington, D.C.

nally, the appeal of master drawings doesn't depend on their overall composition. Many are unfinished preparatory studies, for example, del Sarto's sketch *Red Chalk Drawing* (Figure 1.4). Yet even an abbreviated sketch by a master shows a tasteful placement of the figure on the page and a sensitive order among the parts.

It would seem, then, that the impact of master figure drawings cannot be explained solely in terms of aesthetics, accuracy, or depictive theme. To understand why certain works have the power to hold our attention, to please, provoke, and inform us, we must begin with

the recognition that we respond to more than their representational, or what we call *figurative*, content. All such drawings possess a "plastic life"—a network of visual relationships and energies between the marks employed and the forms they create. This network of activities— suggestions of movements, rhythms, tensions, of similarities and contrasts—generates forces and feelings that the visually sensitive viewer apprehends. Those activities which issue from the interactions of the lines and tones themselves, we should understand to be a drawing's *abstract design*; those inherent in a drawing's recognizable forms, its *figurative design*. In master drawings these two design aspects are inseparable and mutually supportive.

Additionally, these interacting design themes, by the nature of their activities, convey expressive meanings. Hence, in the best figure drawings expressive meanings exist at both the figurative and abstract levels. For example, in Figure 1.2, both the woman *and* the lines and tones that shape her reveal similar expressive qualities. Notice how the downward flow of the lines, like the "lines" of a weeping willow tree, complement and intensify the expressive mood of the figure. Such lines are rarely the result of conscious choice alone. Rather, their character reflects the artist's intuitive as well as empathic feelings about the subject. The artist feels his subjects at both the conscious and subconscious levels. The best figure drawings are never merely descriptions of people, places, and things. They emerge from the negotiations between the subject's *measurable* actualities and the artist's relational and empathic interests in those actualities—his interpretation of the subject's design and expression, that is, its *dynamics*.

The figure's measurable qualities—its differing masses and their various shapes, planes, values, textures, and locations in space—like the figure's dynamics, can also be reduced to two fundamental considerations: its general structural nature, and its specific anatomical one. We will refer to these as the *structural factor* and the *anatomical factor*. Although these factors are always interdependent aspects of a figure's draped or undraped forms, in the next three chapters we will consider them separately so as to better examine the nature of each and see how they may interwork. Likewise for discussion, we will divide the figure's *dynamic* properties—its potential for order and impact—into the *design factor* and the *expressive factor*. These two factors are also interdependent, but by separating them (in Chapters Five and Six) we can explore each more fully. Because we make these arbitrary divisions, it is important to bear in mind that a drawing's design and expression are really understood by the artist as aspects of the same phenomenon in the subject: its allusions to emotive order. Furthermore, in practice, both pairs of factors are interrelated. One of the major themes of this book is to call attention to the high degree of interdependence of the measurable and dynamic factors.

Thus, in the best figure drawings, representational content not only coexists, but interacts with a system of abstract relational and expressive content. A drawing's figurative and abstract content issues from the behavior of the *visual elements*—the six basic visual tools of graphic communication. These elements are: line, shape, value, volume, space, and texture. Chapters Five and Six examine these visual tools and the energies they release. Here, it is important to recognize that this first and universal common denominator of creative figure drawing—the presence of an interworking abstract and figurative expressive order—is a fundamental, given responsibility of the artist. All drawn marks relate in *some* way. Left unregarded, the abstract behavior of a drawing's elements will produce confusing discords and inconsistencies—a kind of visual "noise" that obscures figurative meanings. The best exponents of figure drawing have always understood that the organizational and emotive powers of the visual elements affect the clarity of the representational forms they denote; that the dynamic nature of the marks and of the recognizable forms they produce are interdependent considerations.

Figure 1.3
MATTHIAS GRÜNEWALD (1470?–1528)
An Old Woman with Closed Eyes
Black chalk. 22.8 x 28.9 cm.
Cabinet des Dessins. Musée du Louvre, Paris.

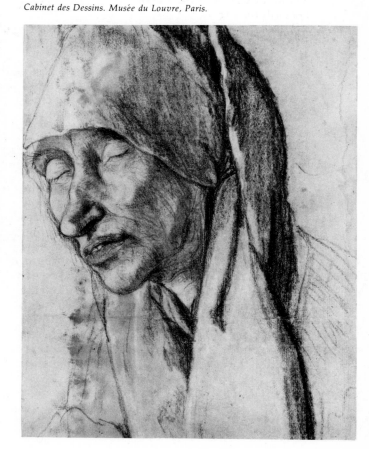

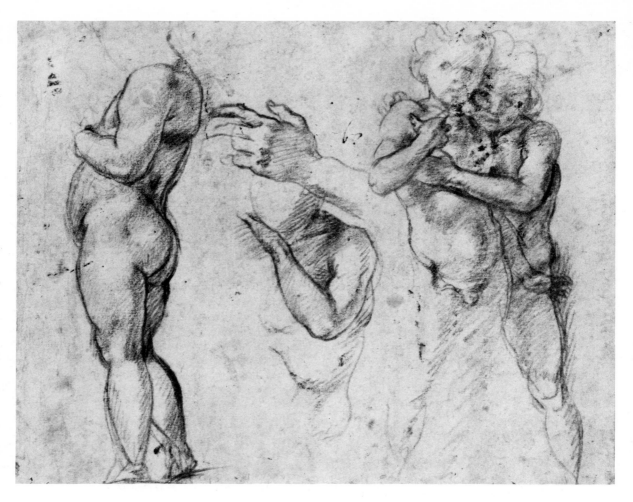

Figure 1.4
ANDREA DEL SARTO (1486–1530)
Red Chalk Drawing
Red chalk. 14 7/8 x 8 in.
Trustees of the British Museum, London.

In creative figure drawing, then, the marks not only define, they enact and evoke the character of the subject, bringing the image to life. And master drawings are always "alive." In Rembrandt's drawing *Bearded Oriental* (Figure 1.5), the animated quality of the figure *and* of the lines and tones suggest vigorous life. The man's confident stance is intensified by the artist's swift but certain strokes. Notice how the fan-like radiation of the rhythmic lines emerging from the arms and waist further heighten the figure's barely contained energy. Even in the more specifically stated forms of the head: the beard, eyes, and nose are developed with authoritative force. Despite the small scale of the drawing in the man's head, the forms and the lines and tones that comprise them are powerfully alive. Again, in Matisse's lithograph *Crouching Nude with Black Hair* (Figure 1.6), the assured and nimble character of the lines helps to enact the figure's dance-like gesture. Her forms, although anatomically inexact, are expressively right. Their spirited and supple nature amplifies those qualities in the figure itself.

Although the Rembrandt drawing asserts a sense of elegant strength, while the Matisse conveys a gentle pliancy, both artists share a common enthusiasm for lively, graceful forms. The marks in both drawings tell us that. But aliveness in drawing doesn't always depend on graceful harmonies. The goal in Hokusai's drawing *Wrestlers* (Figure 1.7) seems to be to depict the ruggedly potent, even awkward character of the two struggling figures. Their gnarled and straining forms contrast with the more graceful ones of the man observing on the right. He serves as a visual-expressive counterpoint against which the tensions and stresses of the struggling wrestlers gain greater impact. Note that the wrestlers are drawn with lines that are rather deliberate, even crabbed, suggesting the tension of the forms they depict, while those of the third figure are more rhythmic and flowing. This contrast can also be seen in the difference between the shapes of the wrestlers' feet (and the lines used to form them) and the feet of the onlooker. Likewise, the more or less angular shapes of the wrestlers' muscular forms, and their strong directions and interlockings, are in marked contrast to the gentler shapes and volumes of the third figure. Hokusai even manages to extract a heightened sense of drama (while simultaneously balancing the masses of the entire drawing) by emphasizing the leftward lurching of the wrestlers with an opposing tilt in the figure on the right.

Note that Hokusai, like Rembrandt and Matisse, has altered anatomical fact in order to strengthen dynamic interests. For example, by sacrificing anatomical accuracy in the placement of the feet of the foreground wrestler (which would show them foreshortened and hence, small) Hokusai gains an expressive "rightness" by providing a more stable base for the weight of the upper body's leftward thrust. The best figure draughtsmen *utilize* rather than eulogize anatomical facts. Likewise,

Figure 1.5
REMBRANDT VAN RIJN (1606–1669)
Bearded Oriental in a Turban, Half Length
Pen and wash. 11.7 x 11.4 cm
Staatliche Museen Preussischer Kulturbesitz.
Kupferstichkabinett. West Berlin.

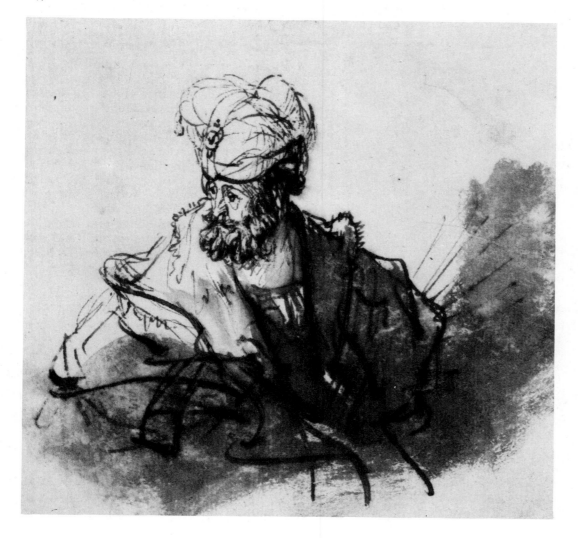

artists exploit the laws of perspective and the "rules" that have accumulated around the uses of line or value, compositional order, or the various drawing media only insofar as these laws and rules support their creative intentions. Drawings by such artists tell us that these authors place their desire for honest and free inquiry, experience, and interpretation ahead of conformity to any convention or system. Although widely separated in time, place, and culture, Rembrandt, Matisse, and Hokusai show their understanding of how abstract meanings augment, and in turn gain from, representational meanings.

Another common denominator of master exponents of figure drawing is the economy and directness with which the artist establishes the drawing. Invariably, master drawings are as directly stated as the artist's intent, understanding, and tools—his media and the surfaces he draws on—permit. In fact, one of the most engaging qualities of great drawings is the great amount of figurative and dynamic content present in a concise statement. The choice of a medium that permits a succinct graphic statement is important. All master drawings demonstrate a sensitive interaction between the meanings and the means used.

Still another important common denominator is that the best drawings convey a discernable and unique attitude, a temperament. This quality stems partly from the character of the interplay of the figurative and plastic considerations and partly from the artist's overall temperament—his general likes and dislikes—both as an artist and as an individual. A discussion of the psychological and social forces that shape an artist's point of view—how he arrives at his particular aesthetic and temperamental persuasion—is beyond the scope of this book, but we should recognize that an artist's temperament definitely determines the kinds of perceptions and responses he makes. What is perhaps less obvious is that the artist's ability to assert his attitude clearly is crucial to the drawing's success as a work of art. For genuine creativity demands genuinely personal interpretations, as little deflected by outside influences as possible. The best figure drawings always strongly show the artist's unwavering and uninhibited insistence on a frank declaration of his interests—his aesthetic and temperamental judgments. Such works are always eloquent in the clarity of their intent. They are keenly bold or delicate, schematic or sensual, animated or stilled. In other words, great figure drawings always incisively affirm the artist's felt convictions about the subject's important human and dynamic conditions.

The best figure drawings also reveal the artist's knowledge of the structural and anatomical nature of human form. But, as noted earlier, in master drawings it is always evident that anatomy is the artist's servant, not his master. In studying anatomy it is important to make many drawings that are precise and thorough; some artists, such as Michelangelo (Figure 1.14), elevate their anatomical studies to the level of art. When this is the case, artists have integrated their interest in anatomy with their awareness of the figure's dynamic potential. Such drawings are never merely anatomical

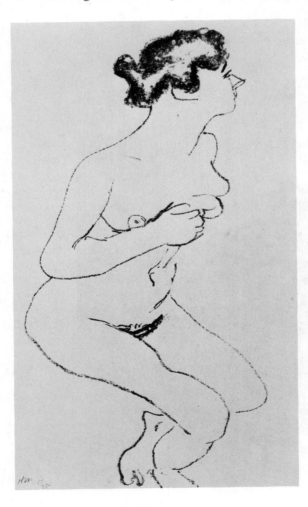

Figure 1.6
HENRI MATISSE (1869–1954)
Crouching Nude with Black Hair
Lithograph, printed in black. 16 5/8 x 8 3/4 in.
Collection, The Museum of Modern Art, New York.
Larry Aldrich Fund.

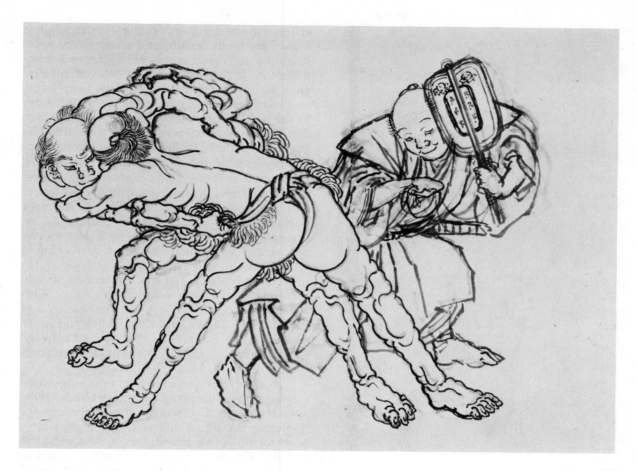

Figure 1.7
KATSUSHIKA HOKUSAI (1760–1849)
Wrestlers
Brush and sumi ink. 12 x 16 1/2 in.
Trustees of the British Museum, London.

inventories. Structure and anatomy are essential as liberating, not restricting, factors. And whether we accentuate or subdue their role in our drawings, we must do so with the quality of judgment and the degree of, authority that only a genuine understanding of these factors makes possible.

One of the most important realizations of such understanding is that structural and anatomical considerations, in addition to clarifying figurative conditions, can participate in a drawing's dynamic meanings; they can both stimulate and strengthen relational and emotive ideas. In Lachaise's drawing *Back of a Nude Woman* (Figure 1.8), the design strategy exists among the marks *and* the human forms they denote. Here, the "beat" of ovoid shapes and the rhythmic undulations of contour lines are the abstract counterpart of the pattern and ripple of the figure's forms. It is impossible to view La-

chaise's drawing without responding to the dynamic nature of the lines and shapes that express in abstract terms the same activities and sensual tone of the drawing's figurative character. It is apparent that the structural aspects of Lachaise's drawing, as shown in the solid, interjoining masses and his use of anatomy to simplify some forms and to amplify others, are the product of sound knowledge, and that they interrelate with the drawing's design and expression. Here, all four factors interwork to advance the same theme.

This leads us to the last common denominator. Great figure drawings reveal an authoritative and personal solution to the universal challenge that all serious figure draughtsmen face: the governance between the factors of structure, anatomy, design, and expression, inherent in human form. Although the degree to which each factor participates in a drawing's

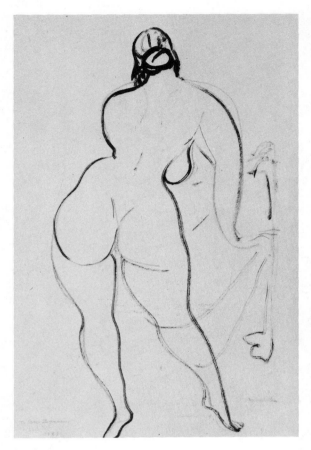

Figure 1.8
GASTON LACHAISE (1882–1935)
Back of a Nude Woman (1929)
Pencil, quill pen, and india ink. 45.5 x 30.9 cm.
The Brooklyn Museum.
Gift of Carl Zigrosser.

creation is determined by perception and intent, *all four* must be inventively integrated in forming the image. Because these four elements are the *given conditions* in figure drawing, and each is dependent on the others, none can be disregarded without weakening the quality of the rest.

THE EMERGENCE OF INTERPRETIVE FIGURE DRAWING

Interpretive figure drawing, in the sense described earlier as conveying the felt convictions of an individual temperament, was a relatively late arrival in the history of art. But when it arrived on the scene, structure, anatomy, design, and expression were all interacting prop-

erties of the best figure drawings. Perhaps figure drawing's main feature and strength, namely, its ability as a direct means of inquiry and interpretation, is the reason for its delayed appearance as a major means of creative expression.

Artistic imagery from the dawn of history to the late Middle Ages (if such a sweep of time can be summarized) was largely determined by highly formalized, collective conventions. Representations of the figure, human or animal, conformed to these rigid schemas. The earliest representations of the human figure are fewer and rather crude when compared to the cave paintings of bison and horses of that period. By the neolithic era, man had begun to leave a visual record of human activities conveying a spritely charm and even a sense of design (Figure 1.9), but these pictures conformed strictly to formula and were simple in concept. With the emergence of the Egyptian civilization and those of the Tigris-Euphrates valley, far more sophisticated, but still rigidly stylized conventions developed for representing human form (Figure 1.10).

Although impressive humanistic developments occurred in many aspects of Greek civilization, in early Greek art formula solutions for depicting the figure showed only slight allowance for objective investigation. Not until 550 B.C. did Greek art begin to develop its grand aesthetic concepts based on objective visual inquiry and a collective ideal concerning human form. It was an ideal that saw Man as physically and spiritually perfected according to Greek societal standards. This classic style was to have a great impact on most artists of the Renaissance, and, periodically, on many artists throughout the world, especially in the West. But despite the great heights that idealized representations of the figure—owing much to a profound understanding of human form—attained in later Greek sculpture and painting, drawings of the figure—done almost exclusively as vase decorations—generally show a still markedly conventionalized treatment (Figure 1.11). This is not to suggest that these drawings are less aesthetically valid or pleasing; indeed, many are of outstanding artistic merit. But they are less the result of inquiry and response than of a collective system, a cultural schema for depicting human forms. Virtually no drawings on flat, bounded surfaces emerged from Greek, or still later, Roman art. And, with the exception of a small number of sculptors, no tradition of art done in a spirit of personal interpretation developed from these cultures.

During the Middle Ages a highly symbolic

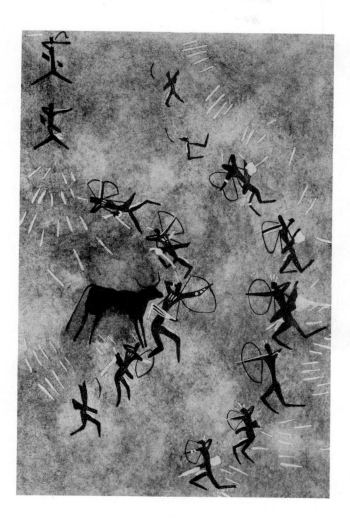

Figure 1.9
Facsimile of rock painting: A fight, apparently for possession of a bull. Khargur Tahle, Libyan Desert.
Frobenius-Institut, Frankfort am Main.

Figure 1.10
Hieratic, Late Period
Papyrus of Ta-Amon. *Book of the Dead*
Courtesy Museum of Fine Arts, Boston.
Gift of Martin Brimmer.

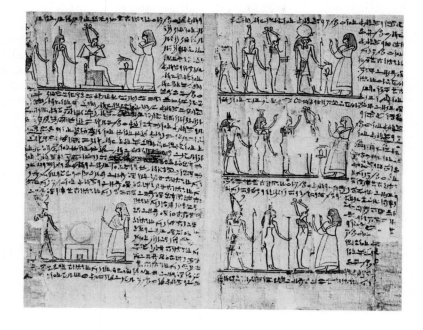

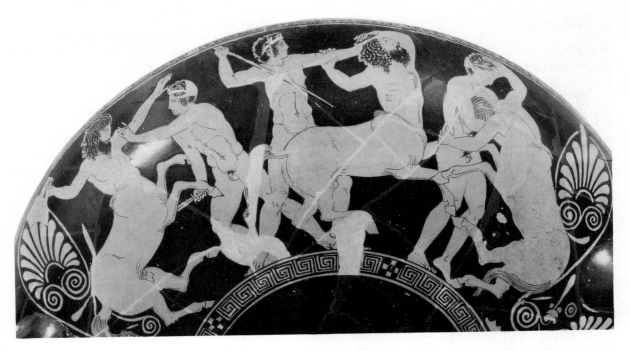

Figure 1.11
Attic Red-Figured Style (c. 490–480 B.C.)
Battle of Centaurs and Lapiths
Kylix (exterior). Terracotta and brush.
Courtesy Museum of Fine Arts, Boston.
H. L. Pierce Fund.

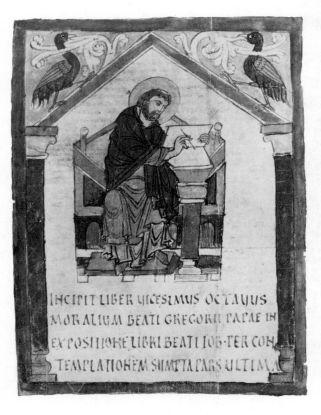

convention arose in the art of manuscript illumination, which became somewhat more observational and interpretive with time. Occasionally, as in Figure 1.12 such manuscript art reached an interpretive level of drawing, but such works were the exception.

Drawing, and especially figure drawing, resulting from an investigative, humanistic, and personally interpretive attitude didn't begin to appear as a serious creative activity until the Renaissance. With the emergence of a sense of individuality, a thirst for scientific and philosophical knowledge, and a desire to understand the nature of the world and of man, drawing became an efficient and even necessary mode of exploration and expression. In this climate of inquiry, earlier, collective conventions of art

Figure 1.12
Carolingian Illumination, 10th Century
St. Gregory
Manuscript.
Courtesy Museum of Fine Arts, Boston.
William Francis Warden Fund.

quickly gave way to individual interpretation, and a powerful interest in drawing burst forth. Not only did this emancipation from the restrictions of formal schemas dramatically alter the motives and meanings for works in painting and sculpture. The spirit of the Renaissance can also be credited with the birth of interpretive drawing—especially figure drawing—as a serious form of creative expression.

The engraving *Battle of Nudes* (Figure 1.13), by the fifteenth century Italian sculptor Pollaiuolo, provides an example of the emerging interest in human form during the early Renaissance period. The artist's observant attention to anatomical facts and his sensitivity to the supple, rhythmic nature of human forms represent a new level of interest and understanding in the art of figure drawing. Although the drawing's overall style is one of deliberate, refined delineation—characteristics which typify earlier artistic attitudes—its dynamic nature shows

a sensitive, if muted, reciprocity between structure, anatomy, design, and expression.

By the sixteenth century the tendencies toward a calculated elegance in figure drawing had been largely superseded by more uninhibited attitudes of inquiry and response. This change resulted from a growing perceptual sophistication nurtured by cross-influences between artists, the value that patrons of the arts placed on original concepts, and the ready market for major projects in painting and sculpture which required many investigative, preparatory drawings. Additionally, sixteenth century drawing, especially in Italy, was concerned with a sense of drama and, often, monumentality, qualities that prompted bolder approaches to the act of drawing. These qualities also reflected the strong attraction that Renaissance artists felt for the humanism and grandeur of Greek and Roman art. A comparison of Pollaiuolo's drawing of the male figure with Michel-

Figure 1.13
ANTONIO POLLAIULO (c. 1430–1498)
Battle of Nudes
Engraving. 40 x 57 cm.
Courtesy The Fogg Art Museum, Harvard University.
Francis Bullard Bequest.

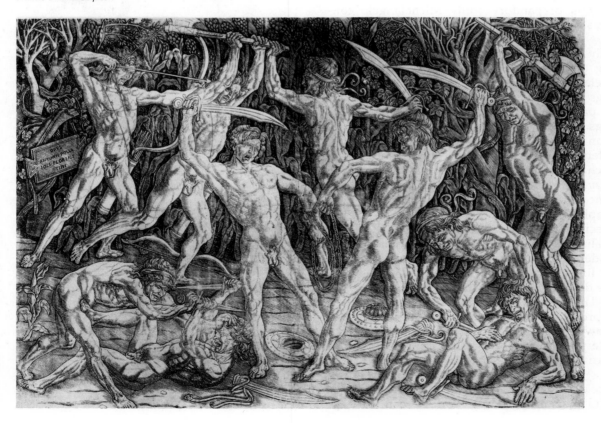

Figure 1.14
MICHELANGELO BUONARROTI (1475–1564)
Study of Adam for "The Creation of Adam"
in the Sistine Chapel
Chalk on tan paper. 9 5/8 x 15 in.
Trustees of the British Museum, London.

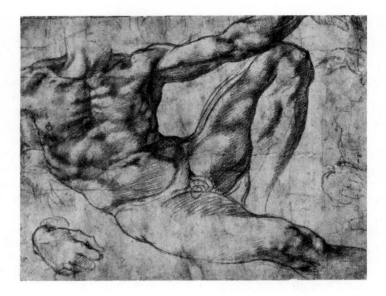

angelo's treatment of it (Figure 1.14) shows the high degree of understanding of, and feeling for, human forms that was to develop in Renaissance drawing. What prompts Pollaiuolo to a somewhat demure use of structural and anatomical matters moves Michelangelo to an almost sculptural and dramatic expression. Even in this preparatory study Michelangelo conveys a sense of Adam's power and grace.

Throughout the Renaissance, especially in Italy and Northern Europe, an interest in drawing the human form flourished. Like the Michelangelo drawing, many of these figure drawings represent preparatory sketches for works in painting and sculpture. Many other drawings, like da Vinci's study of the shoulder region of a male (Figure 1.15), resulted from the intense investigatory spirit of the time. Some, such as *Portrait of Anna, the Daughter of Jakob Mayer* (Figure 1.16), by the Northern Renaissance artist Holbein, *were* intended as final graphic statements. In Holbein's drawing the precise and subtle fluctuations of volume-revealing edges and surfaces, and his sympathetic understanding of the young woman conveyed by lines and tones as gentle as the subject and the design, provide a striking contrast with Michelangelo's dramatic and structurally rugged approach to human form. Seen together, these drawings suggest something of the range of interpretation made possible by the liberating spirit of the Renaissance.

A sensitive interest in the figure's structure and anatomy as capable of conveying powerful dynamic meanings continued to flourish

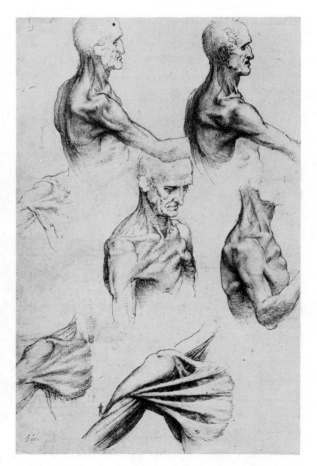

Figure 1.15
LEONARDO DA VINCI (1452–1519)
Myology of the Shoulder Region
Pen and ink, some gray washes. 19 x 24 cm.
Windsor Castle, Royal Library.
By gracious permission of Her Majesty the Queen.

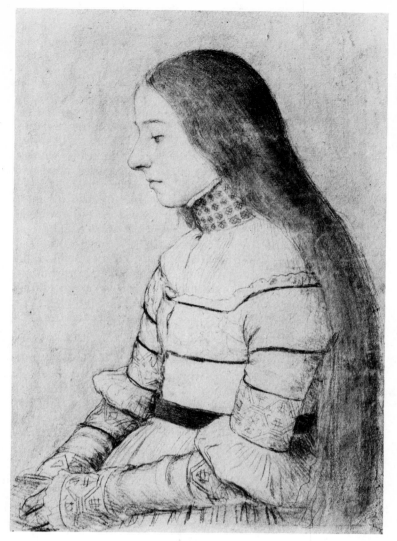

Figure 1.16
HANS HOLBEIN the Younger (1497–1543)
Portrait of Anna, Daughter of Jakob Meyer
Colored chalks. 39 x 27.4 cm.
Kupferstichkabinett, Basel, Switzerland.

in the seventeenth century. Often, drawings showed a more daring search for the spirit, rather than the letter, of an action. Rosa's drawing *Youth Pulling off His Shirt* (Figure 1.17) illustrates this more interpretive concept. It is immediately apparent that Rosa has intensified the flow of the figure's forms into a fluid ripple, creating a strong sense of animation and vitality. Such rhythmic movement and energy demand more than an understanding of anatomical facts. They demand an awareness of the abstract possibilities—the expressive design—of human forms, and an empatic response to their behavior and *feel* in various physical activities. Whether Rosa observed or imagined this figure, he had to feel the weight and effort of the upraised arms, the fullnesses and hollows of the forms, *as if they were his own.* Only a total identification with the figure's forms could have

prompted the selections and the handling of the lines and tones that convey this action with such economy, clarity, and impact.

Another seventeenth century artist, the great Flemish painter Rubens, was an enthusiastic student of Renaissance attitudes and techniques, but brought to them an individual stamp of vigor and tactile sensitivity. In his drawing *Study for the Figure of Christ on the Cross* (Figure 1.18), there is the same high degree of knowledge about, and empathy with, human form that we see in the Michelangelo and Rosa drawings. Rubens's emphasis on the figure's action, masses, design, and character, rather than on "finished surfaces," suggests the artist's need to identify with the effort and strain of the figure, to feel as well as to visualize the experience he depicts.

If the Renaissance artists were attracted to

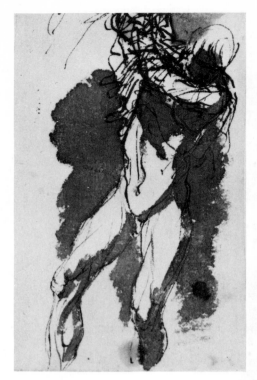

Figure 1.17
SALVATOR ROSA (1615–1673)
Youth Pulling off His Shirt, Full Figure
Pen and brown ink, brown wash. 2 3/8 x 3 1/2 in.
The Art Museum, Princeton University.

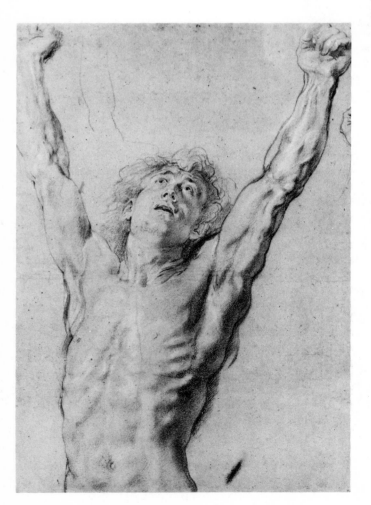

the idealized forms of antiquity, seventeenth century artists were usually more impelled toward encounters with human forms as they found them. And, as Figures 1.17 and 1.18 show, they drew them with more tumultuous energy. But if some traces of the Renaissance interest in an idealized, heroic interpretation of man lingered on (as in the Rosa and Rubens drawings), this influence is wholly absent in the drawings of the greatest seventeenth century artist, Rembrandt.

Rembrandt's drawings depict individuals realistically. That is, they seek to evoke humanistic and dynamic meanings through accurately observed or envisioned subjects. No one, until Rembrandt, focused as intensively or with such penetrating clarity upon the introspective nature of ordinary people, and few have ever expressed such insights more engagingly and with greater force. Although drawings in a realistic manner and with a sensitivity to psychological subtleties had appeared earlier (Figure 1.16), few approach the power in Rembrandt's drawings to transcend their figurative content, to imply universal truths. In Rembrandt's drawings even simple domestic scenes are transformed into moments that suggest deeper significance. A drawing by Rembrandt, whether of a child, a cripple, or a wealthy burgher, is at once a penetrating human statement and a daring system of expressive design.

His figure drawings are more than an integration of abstract and psychological expressions with figurative matter. There is instead a nearly total fusion of these qualities. In his drawing *Saskia Sick in Bed* (Figure 1.19), the lines and tones are simultaneously engaged in establishing the design and the mood, as well as the forms in space. Each mark is engaged in all of these functions. For example, the value, shape, and overall activity of the broad strokes of the background complement the value, shape, and activity of the blanket, and by their airy nature, reinforce the figure's substantiality. Additionally, these strokes, representing a large cast shadow, explain the light source and, by their agitated nature, serve to underscore the figure's stillness. The figure's hand is at once an expression of relaxation and a member of the finger-like curved lines, large and small, that

Figure 1.18
PETER PAUL RUBENS (1577–1640)
Study for the Figure of Christ on the Cross
Charcoal, heightened by white. 15 1/2 x 20 1/4 in.
Trustees of the British Museum, London.

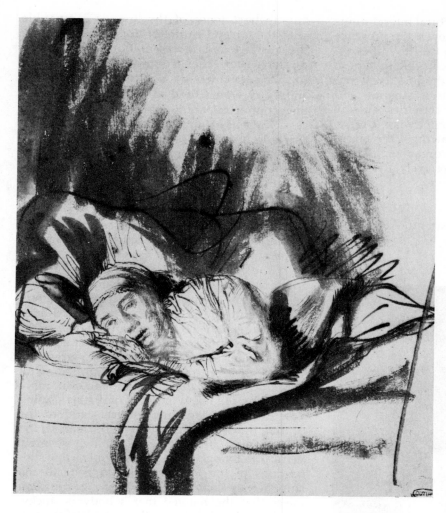

Figure 1.19
REMBRANDT VAN RIJN (1606–1669)
Saskia Sick in Bed
Pen, washes of tone. 16.3 x 13.5 cm.
Musée du Petit Palais, Paris. Photo Bulloz.

appear in the clothing and surrounding bedding. The large, dark tone on the far left acts as a necessary "containing wall" for the vigorous undulations that course through the image, and by its dry, "abrasive" passages, "calls" to similar tones in the background and on the bedding.

Again, Rembrandt's drawings are almost always imbued with the power to transcend the particulars of their figurative theme. Even his interpretation of an old woman bathing becomes transformed into a universally understood expression of dignity and grace. In his etching *Old Woman Bathing Her Feet* (Figure 1.20), Rembrandt approaches his theme with empathy, not pity, with respect, not sentimentality. Here, the measurable factors and the dynamic ones merge to form an affirmation of human strength and nobility, and to tell of spiritual, not physical, beauty.

The eighteenth century brought a subtle but steady increase in the dynamic aspects of figure drawing. A growing interest in design

and expression, and a deepening need to make drawings reflect a more personal point of view continued to spur the exploration for new approaches to figure drawing.

This trend can be seen in the study for *Jupiter et Antioche* (Figure 1.21), by the eighteenth century artist Watteau. In this continuing climate of self-search, Watteau accepts and utilizes his sensitivity to inflections of movement and modelling, revealed by the confident, supple lines, and by his emphasis on the gestural nature of his subject. Rhythmic, searching lines often weave through large segments of the figure, their character and action relating even distant parts to each other. For example, some of the lines in the figure's right arm move along its entire length and appear to continue down the left arm, giving evidence of the relatedness of the two limbs. (How often, in student drawings, are limbs drawn without reference to each other!) Note how these tactile lines grow thicker and thinner as they ride upon the forms, suggesting volume, areas of structural interjoinings and muscular tensions, and even the presence of a light source. As they do this, the lines establish a visual theme—a discernible pattern of light and heavy stresses—of the line itself, and of curving movements. These stresses and curves, in addition to the activities already noted, give the image an overall dynamic force. Here, as in Rembrandt's drawings, the marks that form the image depict, organize, and express, at the same time. Expressively, the vigor-

ous abstract tenor of the lines is compatible with the forceful nature of the figure's gesture; the abstract and representational expressions reinforce each other. To draw a figure engaged in such spontaneous action in a slow and deliberate way would tend to diminish the feel of the action (compare Figure 1.13).

The eighteenth century Spanish artist Goya, in his series of etchings *The Disasters of War*, effectively communicates his outrage through powerful systems of expressive design. In the etching *"Tampoco"* or *No More* (Figure 1.22), the atrocity described relies for its impact on more than accurate recollections of the grim event. Goya has feelingly devised dynamic activities that intensify our reaction to the barbaric scene.

The entire configuration describes a large triangular shape interrupted only by the "softer" shape of the lounging French officer, a wry visual counterpoint to the severe vertical lines of the hanged men. Goya's knowledge of structure and anatomy, and of the abstract energies of the visual elements helps him to stress the weight of the centrally placed victim. The awful forward thrust of the head is made even more terrible by the heavy mass of dark hair sloping downward. Fast-moving verticals add to the central figure's weight. Even the man's long shirt is simplified, its edges drawn severely vertical. Although Goya gives us only a few suggestions of the body's presence beneath the shirt, we are convinced it is there; we can even guess that the hanged man's body is stocky. The fallen leggings, even the fast fall of the cast shadow below the victim's arm add to our feeling as well as seeing what has happened here. Goya further adds to the sense of vertically dropping forms by the repetition of the vertical lines of the foliage in the distance, and by the vertical edge of the block against which the officer relaxes. Goya increases our initial shock of recognition by harshly contrasting the stark white of the victim's shirt and the dark tones that surround him. Note that the only lines suggesting animation are those more gestural ones enacting the lounging pose of the officer. In this way, too, Goya conveys the tragic stillness of the hanged men.

Despite the deepening interest in such dynamically reinforced and more subjectively interpreted figure drawings, there were some who held to a more objective, reportorial approach to the figure's actualities, and to an interest in the aesthetics of earlier periods. The nineteenth century artists Ingres (Figure 1.23)

Figure 1.20
REMBRANDT VAN RIJN (1606–1669)
Old Woman Bathing Her Feet
Etching. 16.2 x 8 cm.
Courtesy Museum of Fine Arts, Boston.

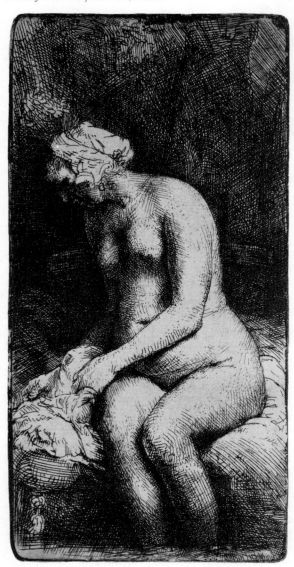

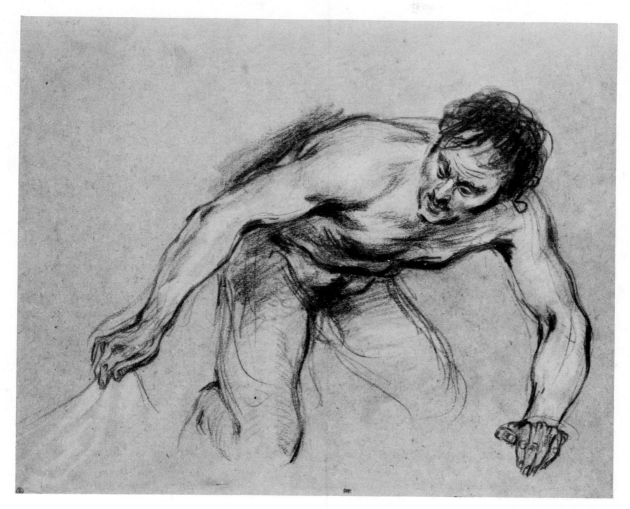

Figure 1.21
ANTOINE WATTEAU (1684–1721)
Study for "Jupiter et Antioche"
Conté crayon on toned paper. 9 5/8 x 11 5/8 in.
Cabinet des Dessins, Musée du Louvre, Paris.

and Delacroix (Figure 1.24) show two extremes of aesthetic persuasion that occupied the attention of many artists of that time.

Ingres, the older of the two artists, held that "the simpler the lines and forms, the more effectively they reveal beauty and power." Figure 1.23 shows his dedication to the concept of contour—the linear, volume-informing delineation of forms—as the desired means by which to draw. In this drawing, Ingres reveals an interest in the style of ancient Greek and Roman art. The forms are shaped by the same concern for the classic standards of beauty that attracted such Renaissance masters as Raphael (Figure 1.25). In both works elegant and precise contours create figures of somewhat idealized pro-

portions. In both, general structural facts and specific anatomical ones are as important as an overall graceful design of the forms. Ingres' lines, like Raphael's, are easy-paced and serenely harmonious, always engaged in subtle dynamic as well as volume-informing activities, and attracted to the graceful order of even small anatomical details.

By contrast, Delacroix abhorred the idea of patient and deliberate contour drawing, although he too aimed for the impression of convincing volumes in space. But for Delacroix, emphasizing a volume's edges by contour lines only serves to weaken the sense of three-dimensional mass by calling forward those most distant parts of human forms—their outlines. He

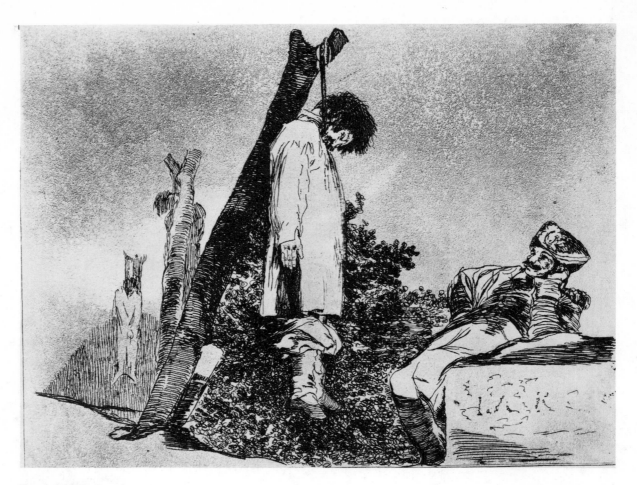

Figure 1.22
FRANCISCO DE GOYA (1746–1828)
No More, from "The Disasters of War"
Aquatint and etching. 7 1/4 x 5 1/2 in.
Courtesy The Fogg Art Museum, Harvard University.
Bequest of Francis Calley Gray.

advised that forms should be grasped "by their centers, not by their lines of contour." Nor did Delacroix possess the temperament that could devote itself to explicit nuances and little harmonies. His interests lay in capturing fleeting actions by direct means. One of the boldest Romantics of nineteenth century art, he sought the gestural, sensual qualities of the figure. In René Huyghe's view, "It is not form he studies, but rather its animating principle, its living essence that he transcribes." That a passionate search for essence was an important theme in Delacroix's drawings is borne out by his advice to a student: "If you are not skillful enough to sketch a man jumping out of a window in the time it takes him to fall from the fourth story to the ground, you will never be able to produce great works."

These opposing attitudes of Ingres and Delacroix: deliberate, measured delineation versus spontaneous, gestural attack, have to some degree continued to contest with each other to this day. Indeed, these differing dispositions toward the act and purpose of drawing existed long before the 1800s. They are, after all, as much determined by individual temperament as by the stylistic trends of a particular period or country. We have only to compare the drawing by Veronese (Figure 1.26) with that of a contemporary Renaissance artist, Vaga (Figure 1.27), to recognize the fundamental differences between an explicit and a gestural approach.

Other artists, however, saw the desirable qualities of the two approaches not as opposing but actually as complementing each other. In fact, embracing both ideas, these artists emphasized at times the "letter" and at times the "spirit" of their subjects. Michelangelo, Rubens, and Rembrandt are a few of the artists for whom the seeming conflicts between the prose of delineation and the poetry of evocation are not only resolved, but become necessary, reciprocal concepts that permit a more encompassing and

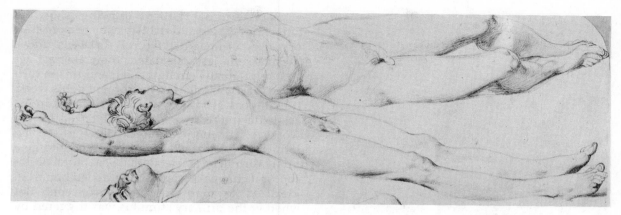

Figure 1.23
DOMINIQUE INGRES (1780–1867)
Three Studies of a Male Nude (detail)
Pencil.
The Metropolitan Museum of Art, New York
Rogers Fund, 1919.

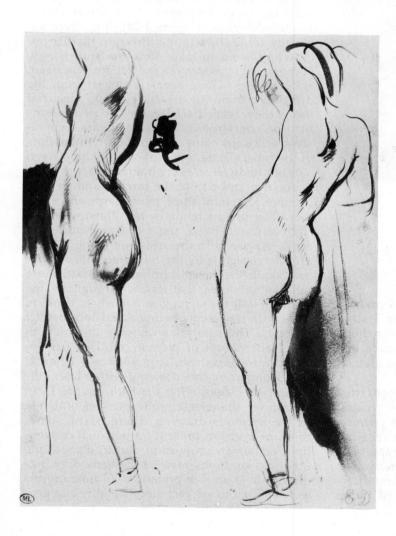

Figure 1.24
EUGÈNE DELACROIX (1798–1863)
Two Nude Studies
Pen and ink, washes of color. 19 x 14.8 cm.
Cabinet des Dessins, Musée du Louvre, Paris.

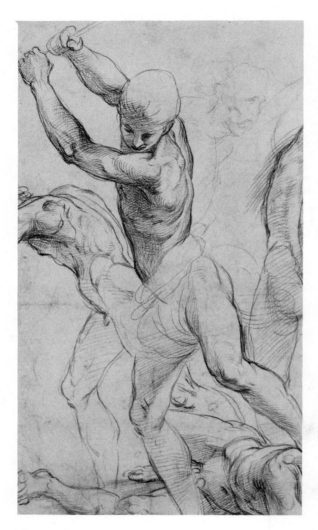

Figure 1.25
RAPHAEL (1483–1520)
Combat of Nude Men (detail)
Red chalk over preliminary stylus work.
14 13/16 x 11 1/8 in. (entire)
Ashmolean Museum, Oxford.

profound apprehension of human form and spirit. Such artists cannot accept the restrictions of either precision or gesture. For them, the freedom to range between exactitude and impression was an essential condition of creativity.

The figure drawings of the French artist Degas, regarded by many as one of the greatest figure draughtsmen of the nineteenth century, offer an interesting example of an artist's change, over the years, from a deliberate, linear approach to a strongly animated, almost painterly one. Early Degas figure drawings show his attraction to precise delineations influenced by an

envisioned ideal. The later drawings show his attraction to bold and richly plastic responses to perceived or imagined figures. As Degas' drawings became less calculated, their abstract activities gradually strengthened, and this in turn led to drastic changes in the content of his work. It is impossible to say whether a change in his aesthetic interests, perhaps influenced by the works of his impressionist fellow-artists, led him from calculated, "quiet" drawings to gestural, turbulent ones. Perhaps a more philosophical change toward the figure led him from idealized to more responsive concepts. But whether the primary stimulus was triggered by aesthetic or human considerations, both of these qualities changed together. That is, his abstract and figurative interests were always congenially suited to each other.

As a young man, Degas was attracted to the classical views of artists such as Raphael, and was an admirer of his near-contemporary, Ingres. These influences are evident in an early drawing, *Study of a Nude for "The Sorrows of the Town of Orleans"* (Figure 1.28). But, there are already some clues to the direction that Degas' drawings were to take. Note the surprisingly "reportorial" passages in the left arm, the head, and the legs. These seem to depart from the drawing's main theme of elegant, idealized form; they seem based more on perceptions than on conceptions. These segments seem almost awkward compared to the rhythmic flow of the torso. There is a hint of conflict between a desire to dwell on every nuance of edge, every gentle dip and rise of the terrain, and an urge to more forcefully stress movements and energies. The urgent tenor in the drawing of the right arm and hand; the frequent gestural accents, especially in the arms and along the figure's lower left side; the heavy accents of charcoal along the raised arm; and the fast, more calligraphic lines that occur throughout the drawing—all these suggest a wish to come to grips with issues concerning actual and abstract energies. The result is a drawing in which an idealized concept of Woman, and felt perceptions of *a* woman coexist in a tenuous alliance.

Comparing this drawing with a later lithograph by Degas, *After the Bath* (Figure 1.29), we can see the release of the energies hinted at in the previous drawing. There is still something of a vision present—a personal convention for human proportion. But in place of the lithe and sensuous ideal of the early drawings there is here an interpretation of human forms as simplified to suggest more weighty and geo-

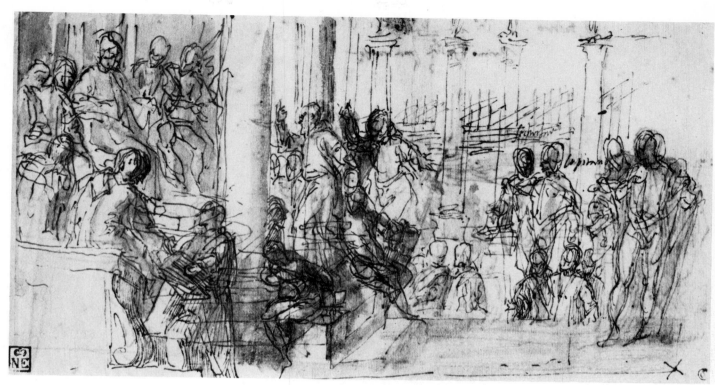

Figure 1.26
PAOLO VERONESE (1528–1588)
Peter of Amiens before The Doge Vitale Michele
Pen and wash. 19 x 27.3 cm.
Budapest Museum of Fine Arts.
Collection: Poggi Estethary

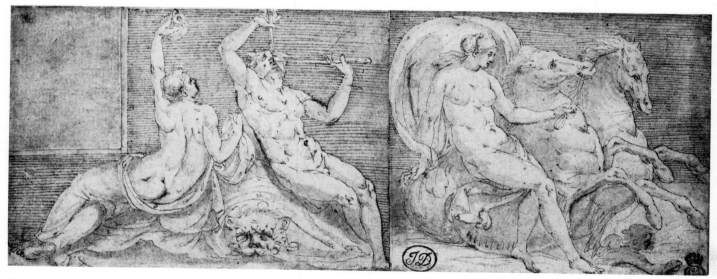

Figure 1.27
School of PERINO DEL VAGA (1500–1547)
Nereids and Sea Horses
Pen and ink. 10.1 x 28 cm.
Courtesy The Fogg Art Museum, Harvard University.
Bequest of Charles Alexander Loesser.

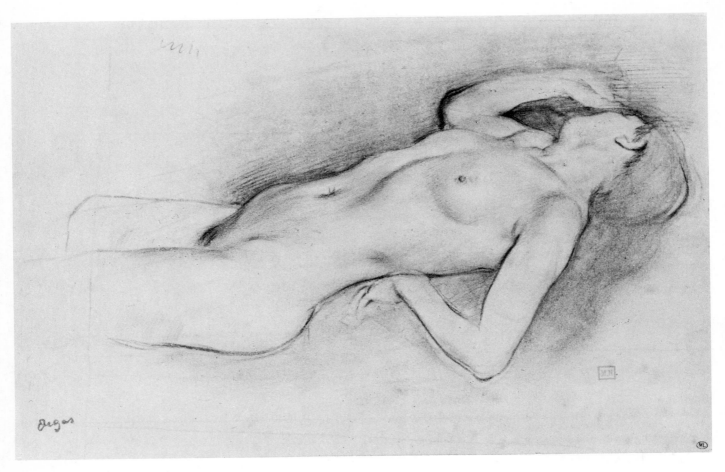

Figure 1.28
EDGAR DEGAS (1834–1917)
Study of a Nude for "The Sorrows of the
Town of Orleans"
Charcoal. 35.6 x 23.2 cm.
Cabinet des Dessins, Musée du Louvre, Paris.

metrically pure forms. The drawing's dominant plastic theme is movement. The hair, the curving torso, the towel, even the pattern of the background all exhibit a sense of motion. There is a kind of candid camera effect—a frozen moment—in what we feel is a continuing sequence of movements. "Catching" the woman in the act of drying herself, Degas gives us a sense of what her prior actions were, and foretells the action to come. Notice how much stronger the abstract activities become when Degas shifts from an emphasis on denoting the figure's specifics, as in Figure 1.28, to evoking its essential structure and spirit. Degas, like Rosa, Delacroix, and Veronese, intensifies the relational play among the elements to create this more dynamically energetic graphic and human statement. In Chapters Five and Six we will explore

the relational and emotive dynamics of figure drawing to see what creative possibilities they hold. Here, it is important to emphasize again that in all great figure drawings, every mark contributes to the figural content, the order, and to the expression of the image. In these two Degas drawings the four factors interwork differently, but in each they succeed in shaping forms that live.

So far, in broadly tracing the emergence of interpretive approaches to figure drawing, we have observed a fluctuation in emphasis between the depictive and the abstract. During the early Renaissance, emphasis focused on depiction. During the nineteenth century (and earlier), artists differed in their choice of emphasis but, as we have seen, for some of them both qualities were (or in the case of Degas, became) equally attractive. Much twentieth century figure drawing continues to move in the direction of subjective interpretation and drawing's abstract potentialities. But, as in earlier periods, the strongest drawings, both in creative and human terms, seem to be those which reveal a sensitive interworking between the four basic factors, and between the figurative and abstract meanings they generate. The best exponents of figure drawing have always understood that each factor inevitably affects—and is affected by—the other three.

From what has been said it should not be inferred that artists favoring figurative matters are necessarily less sensitive to dynamic ones, or that artists who emphasize plastic and emotive matters are less concerned with depictive issues. In his choice of emphasis the artist cannot disregard either aspect. When he does,

however realistic or abstract the drawing may be, it usually lacks the impact of drawings in which the depictive and the dynamic reinforce one another. Although Goya's etching (Figure 1.22) emphasizes the figurative whereas de Kooning's drawing (Figure 1.30) stresses the abstract, both are integrated systems of depictive *and* dynamic themes. Their differences of emphasis are based on their different creative and temperamental needs. Similarly, although all are highly figurative statements, the emphasis on gestural and emotive energies in Rosa's drawing, on harmonious design in Raphael's, and on an integration of both of these themes in Rembrandt's drawing of Saskia shows how a drawing's representational content can be clarified and enhanced by different dynamic stresses.

Later nineteenth century figure drawings and those of the twentieth century are char-

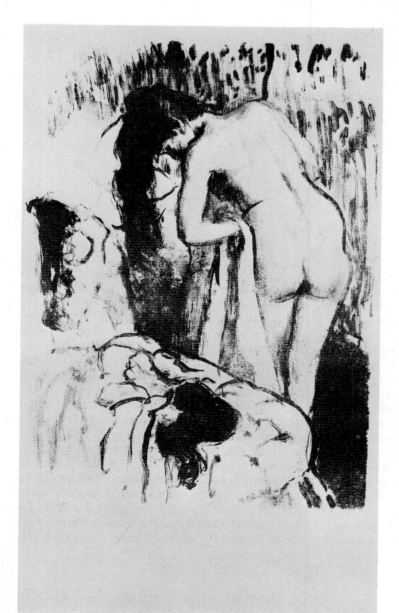

Figure 1.29
EDGAR DEGAS (1834–1917)
After the Bath
Lithograph. 14 3/4 x 11 in.
Courtesy The Fogg Art Museum, Harvard University.
Bequest of Francis Calley Gray.

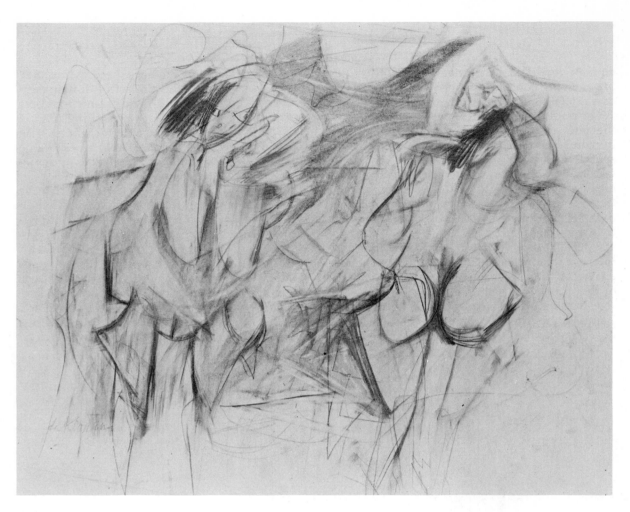

Figure 1.30
WILLEM DE KOONING (1904–)
Two Women III (1952)
Pastel and charcoal on paper. 14 3/8 x 18 1/2 in.
Allen Art Museum, Oberlin College, Ohio.
Friends of Art Fund.

acterized by their general tendency toward more daring, direct, and ever more subjective points of view, and by their broad range of interests and goals. In Schiele's drawing (Figure 1.1) the animated swirl of the figures and the bolder, abstract life of the elements that form them are dynamic intensifications of both considerations. Again, in Matisse's drawing (Figure 1.6) the dual life of the drawing's figurative and abstract aspects is vigorously active.

This tendency toward more personal and inventive approaches to figure drawing encouraged artists to explore new ways of interpreting the human figure, and of communicating ideas and feelings. For the German artist Kollwitz, the figure became a vehicle for expressing her (and everyman's) anguish at the pain and bereavement that war brings. As noted earlier, her drawing of a weeping woman (Figure 1.2) is a deeply moving expression of sorrow.

The wavering flow that envelops the figure suggests the movements we associate with weeping. In contrast to the soft, downward fall of the lines of the drapery and kerchief, the angular arms, the strong action of the fist pressed to the face, the sudden tonal contrast between the woman's right shoulder and head, and even her scale and placement on the page, all serve to intensify our understanding of the drawing's message of grief.

Some artists have always been motivated by the need to convey a moving, provocative, or perhaps amusing message. Their theme might be compassion, as in the drawing by the Northern Renaissance artist Grünwald (Figure 1.3); it might be sensuality, as in the drawing by the late nineteenth century artist Rodin (Figure 1.31); or rage and protest, as in the drawings by the twentieth century artists de Kooning (Figure 1.30) and Rothbein (Figure 1.36). Such artists are impelled as much by human as by dynamic themes. Unlike artists for whom figure drawing is first of all an act of inquiry and analysis, artists oriented toward expression are motivated by the need to feel as well as to find.

In the twentieth century the factor of design in figure drawing has become increasingly important. This interest in the formal, relational ordering of the elements and of the figurative forms they produce has led to a notable characteristic of many contemporary artists: the emphasis on the two-dimensional aspects of the figure and of its environment. Although the best figure draughtsmen have always been

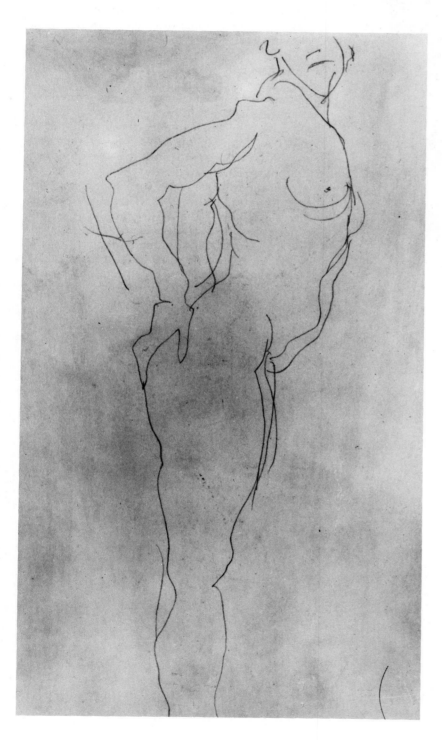

Figure 1.31
AUGUSTE RODIN (1840–1917)
Study of a Standing Nude
Pencil. 23.8 x 16.7 cm.
National Gallery, Prague.

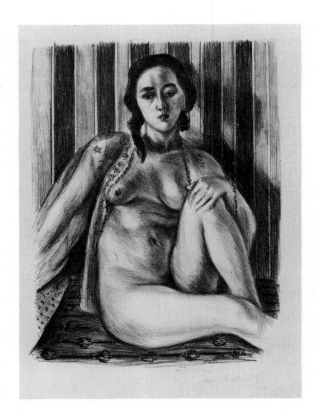

Figure 1.32
HENRI MATISSE (1869–1954)
Odalisque
Lithograph. 12 x 16 in.
National Gallery of Art, Washington, D.C.
Rosenwald Collection.

sensitive to a drawing's two-dimensional design—to the relational interactions of the visual elements within the flat, bounded area of the page, or *picture plane*—such relational activities were generally subordinated to those of the third-dimension. This should not suggest that the two-dimensional designs of earlier drawings are necessarily less fully considered or sophisticated, but that their impact—their ability to attract and dominate our attention—is intentionally reduced to avoid muffling the drawing's volumetric and spatial order.

For many recent and contemporary artists, expanding the abstract activities upon the picture plane has permitted new graphic ideas and experiences. In Matisse's lithograph *Odalisque* (Figure 1.32), bold systems of straight and curved lines, textural and tonal contrasts, and shape variations call our attention to the draw-

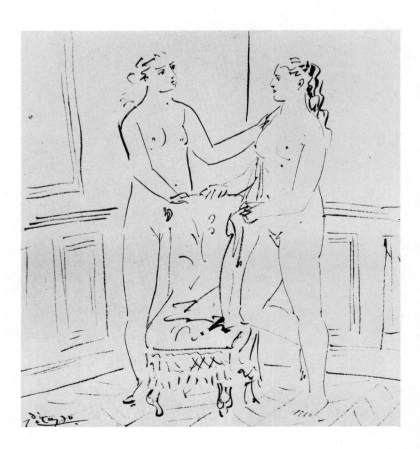

Figure 1.33
PABLO PICASSO (1881–1973)
Two Nudes (1923)
Pen and ink. 8 1/4 x 7 13/16 in.
Museum of Art, Rhode Island School of Design.
Gift of Paul Rosenberg.

ing's surface-state. There are equally strong clues to these forms as volumes in space, but these structural and spatial statements share in, rather than dominate, the drawing's overall design. This allows us to "read" the drawing in two compatible and interesting ways. No sooner do we experience an ordering of two-dimensional conditions than volumes emerge to offer an ordering of masses in space. This impression, in turn, subsides into the matrix of picture-plane activities to start the cycle over again. This creates an engaging, pulsating ambiguity between flat and deep space, where the contrasts between geometric and organic areas, and among the variously patterned textures take on different visual meanings.

Picasso's drawing *Two Nudes* (Figure 1.33) is another example of a design-oriented drawing. In contrast to the Matisse drawing, which relies for its design strategy on strong patterns and heavily defined, enclosed shapes, Picasso's drawing is a design based on subtle tensions. There is tension in the broken lines, in the lines that strongly suggest but never actually enclose shapes, in the lines and shapes that suggest vertical and horizontal directions but are themselves always diagonal, and in the overall fluctuation between the depictive and plastic nature of the lines. Additionally, small "bursts" of textural activity in the hair of both figures, the chair, and the floor contrast with the austere character of the two figures and their surroundings.

In Picasso's drawing, as in Matisse's, the visual impact of its two- and three-dimensional activities are roughly equal. This is not the case in de Kooning's drawing *Two Women III* (Figure 1.30), which is conceived in a way that sharply restricts the sense of volumes in space. Here, the tempestuous life of the elements, occasionally breaking free of any depictive role, accomplishes two things: it creates a predominantly two-dimensional drawing, and it conveys a powerfully aggressive statement about the subject matter. De Kooning relies on the expressive nature of the elements' abstract state to convey the drawing's mood; here, evocation largely replaces denotation.*

We have seen that in figure drawing a concern with abstract considerations is not new. However, recent artists have made daring advances in extracting new visual and expressive meanings from the relational interactions of the elements. We have also seen that a sound under-

*See Nelson Goodman, *Language of Art* (New York and Indianapolis: Bobbs-Merrill, 1968), chap. 1.

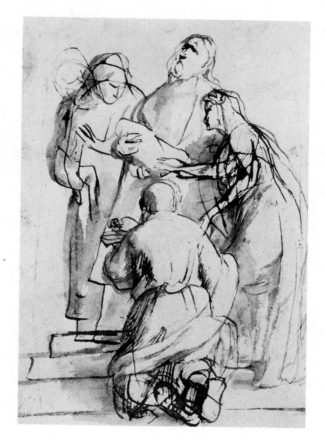

Figure 1.34
PETER PAUL RUBENS (1577–1640)
Studies for "The Presentation in the Temple"
Brown ink and wash. 21.4 x 14.2 cm.
The Metropolitan Museum of Art, New York
Gift of Mr. and Mrs. Janos Scholz.

standing of structure and anatomy has informed and influenced the best figure drawings. Whether it is a dominant theme, as in Figure 1.14, a spur to gestural activity, as in Figure 1.24, or a guideline to expressive summaries of human forms, as in Figure 1.30, it is apparent that structural and anatomical knowledge participated in the choices and judgments that shaped these drawings.

Sometimes, structural issues have provided themes for figure drawings, as in Figures 1.14 and 1.32, where the figure's constructional, often planar, aspects are strongly in evidence. Sometimes, as in Figures 1.6 and 1.33, they are only felt, rather than seen; gentle nuances instead of bold carvings. That both Figures 1.6 and 1.32 are by the same person indicates the differing attitudes toward structure that may interest a single artist. For many artists structural matters are important in the early

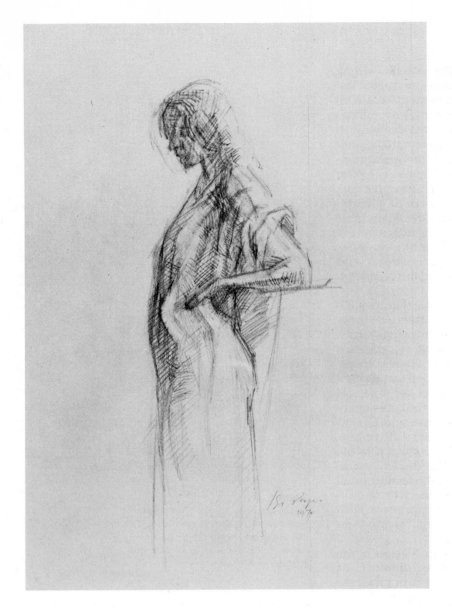

Figure 1.35
ISO PAPO (1925–   )
Standing Figure
Pencil. 13 x 18 in.
Collection of Rachel Papo, Newton, Mass.

stages of developing their figure drawings. In Rubens's preparatory sketch *Studies for the Presentation in the Temple* (Figure 1.34), we can follow the artist's thinking about the placement and general character of volumes. Many of the lines, especially in the three standing figures, are primarily investigative probes to establish masses. Note how some of these lines are drawn through forms, as if they were transparent, enabling Rubens to understand the forms in more sculptural terms.

Similarly, Papo, in his drawing *Standing Figure* (Figure 1.35), uses "ranks" of schematic lines to establish the subject's major planes and masses. Papo's concern for understanding the architectural character of these forms can be seen in the way the lines measure them, how lines are drawn through some forms to locate their far sides and to interjoin forms, and are

made to explore their terrain. Note the surprisingly curvilinear movements among these incisively summarized and mainly angular masses. In Chapter Two we will examine this analytical, planar approach to the figure's forms. Although such structural considerations are only sometimes, as here a dominant theme, in all good figure drawings they are always in evidence, however subtly, interworking with the other factors.

Every age re-defines humankind. The artists of the twentieth century, creating with a greater sense of freedom, inquiry, and dedication to personal response, have come forward with a multitude of definitions. This wide diversity of approaches to figure drawing, whether they tend toward an expressionistic, design-oriented, or realistic persuasion, have to con-

30

tend with the same forms that confronted Michelangelo, Rembrandt, Picasso, and all the other great exponents of the figure. And this common challenge—the figure—has imposed *its* conditions on artists of every age, as they have imposed their modes of order and expression on it. The figure demands perceptive investigation, empathy, and imagination before it will reveal to the artist a personally satisfying basis for interpretation.

In this broad review, anatomy and the underlying factor of structure have been only briefly commented on. Their importance in figure drawing cannot be overemphasized. But, it should again be noted that structure and anatomy are tools to be controlled, not concepts to be worshipped to the exclusion of the figure's dynamic aspects. Our purpose in understanding these systems is to broaden, not restrict, choice; to enhance, not diminish, abstract meanings. This is the case even when anatomical forms are themselves the subject, as in Rothbein's drawing *Study for the Nazi Holocaust* (Figure 1.36). In this drawing both the skulls *and* the eruptive fury of the dynamic forces cry out. To lose sight of anatomy's function as both a source and agent of dynamic inventions is to replace felt perceptions and insights with unselective scrutiny. Such an attitude tends toward taxidermy, not life.

Art is not science. The young artist today who wishes to draw the figure cannot pick up the trail where Degas or Matisse stopped. He cannot begin by building upon the achievements of these artists, not only because he lacks their vast factual knowledge about human form, but also because he lacks the penetrating perceptual comprehension and informed intuition that all great artists evolve over a lifetime of encountering human form and spirit. We cannot (and should not want to) adopt another's sensibility.

We must form our own interests and insights by a dedicated study of the basic factors of figure drawing and by a searching examination of what these factors demand of us as art-

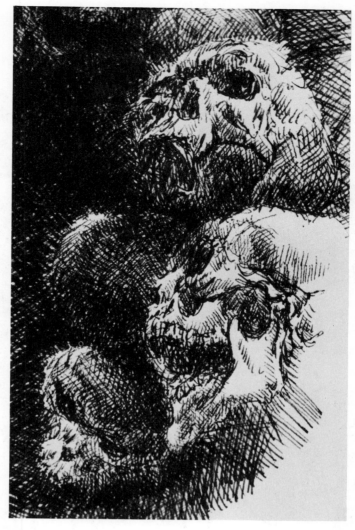

Figure 1.36
RENEE ROTHBEIN (1924–   )
Study for the Nazi Holocaust Series
Pen and ink. 5 x 7 1/2 in.
Courtesy of the artist.

ists and as members of the human family. Thus our interests (a) in the figurative—the inquiring, analytical, and interpretive responses to salient actualities; (b) in design—the selecting, governing, and unifying of relational forces; and (c) in expression—the desire to heighten, provoke, and release, all require that we undertake a "four-dimensional" study of the figure: as a construction, a machine, a harmony, and a voice.

(3 ?)
4 cluster-relates
nec. approach
to a good
drawing!

1. Structure
2. anatomy
3. design
4. expression

31

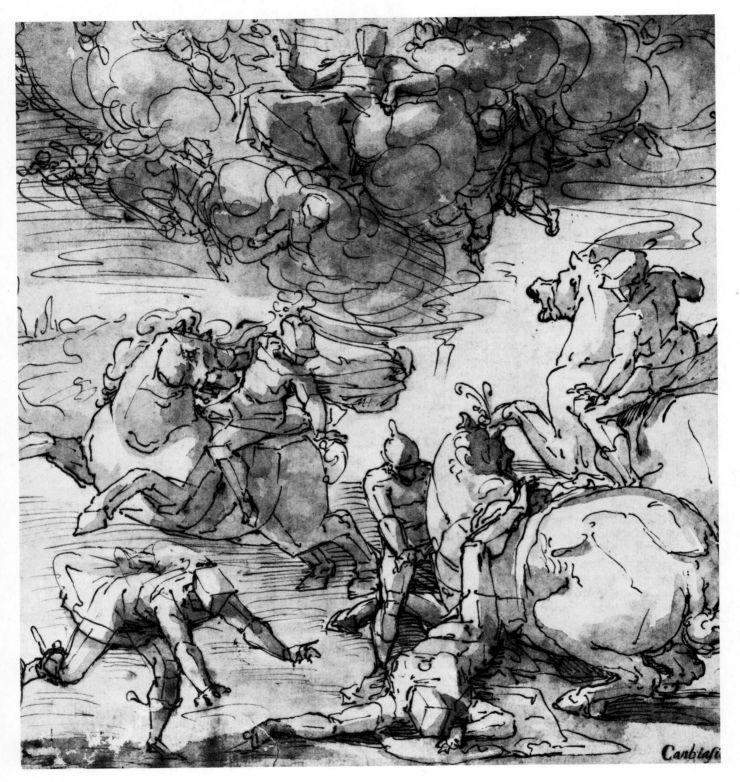

Figure 2.1
LUCA CAMBIASO (1527–1585)
Conversion of St. Paul (detail)
Pen and brown ink, brown wash.
The Art Museum, Princeton University.

2

The Structural Factor

the figure
as a constructional system

SOME GENERAL OBSERVATIONS

Paul Cézanne had this advice for the art student: "Treat nature by the cylinder, the sphere, the cone. . . ." In other words, become aware of the basic geometric volumes that underlie all forms. This is easy to do with some objects. For example, we recognize the cylindrical nature of a cigar or a silo, and can readily see a Christmas tree as conical or a barn as block-like. But we may at first have difficulty in seeing these and other geometric solids as underlying the human figure. There are several reasons for this. The beginner is preoccupied with the challenge of depicting the figure's surface textures and the light playing across its forms. His attempt to *re-present* the observed actualities in detail often blinds him to the geometric "core" forms. Moreover, the beginner's awe of the figure, which he rightly regards as complex, beautiful, and important; and the subtlety with which the figure suggests its pure solids make an analytical search for them diffi-

cult. Finally, the beginner's tendency to assemble his image in a series of mostly unrelated segments makes a search for the figure's essential form-character impossible. As with the traveler who "can't see the forest for the trees," the beginner, in concentrating on a sequence of details, misses the figure's fundamental masses. One of the primary insights to sound figure drawing, then, is the need to understand the figure's forms as reducible to simple geometric summaries.

Seen this way, human forms can be reduced to such geometric solutions as shown in Figure 2.2. As this illustration shows, most of the figure's forms yield to more than one kind of geometric interpretation. Some artists, such as Cambiaso (Figures 2.1, 2.5, 2.31), favor block-like solutions; others, such as Picasso (Figure 2.7) and Tintoretto (Figure 2.19), often reduce the figure to cylinders, spheres, and ovoids. As Figure 2.2 shows, some form-summaries are not, strictly speaking, purely geometric. So we must expand on Cézanne's list of simple forms.

33

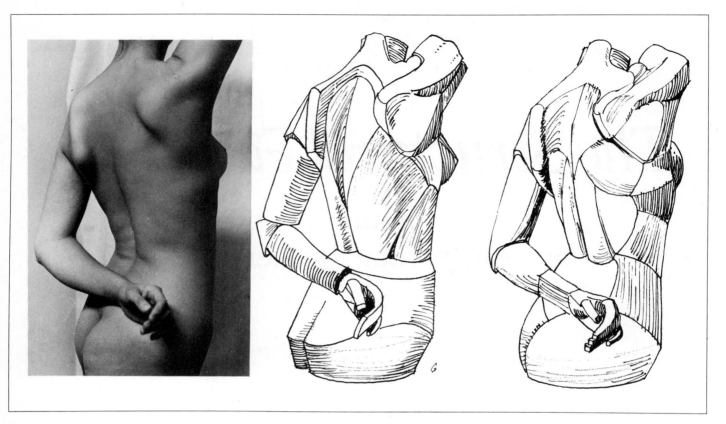

Figure 2.2

In the human figure we can find underlying forms that suggest the pyramid, the egg-like or ovoid forms, and the bent or twisted block, as well as several variants and combinations of these and other simple forms (Figure 2.3). All of these simple forms are useful in helping us better understand the structural nature of the figure.

But simple solids can also be understood as *emerging from* human forms. In Figure 2.2 segments of the figure are seen as reduced to the simple forms in the analyses, but in Figure 2.4 we sense these segments to have been formed by smaller versions and variants of the masses in Figures 2.2 and 2.3.

Once we understand the figure as both reducible to and emerging from simple geometric volumes, we have the reciprocal concepts that help in understanding the figure's forms in various positions in space. As we have seen, in his drawing *The Conversion of St. Paul,* Cambiaso relies on just such simple masses to clarify the structure and positions of complex human and animal forms. In this preparatory sketch the artist is exploring the structure and illumination of a proposed painting theme.

Logically enough, he reduces his subject matter to its volumetric essentials. Notice how in this envisioned scene Cambiaso calls on his store of anatomical knowledge to help shape the simple volume-summaries. As Figure 2.1 clearly shows, the foreshortened upper and lower segments of the fallen rider's torso, despite their blocky simplifications, strongly suggest the rib cage and pelvis.

Cambiaso's use of a light source also helps clarify the volume-summaries. Light coming from a single source will most strongly illuminate those flat or curved surface-segments, or *planes* directly facing it, leaving those planes turned away from the light source darker. Cambiaso's consistency in illuminating all the planes facing the light, which here falls from a point just over our left shoulder, provides us with an additional means for interpreting the structure and placement of these forms.

But this strong emphasis on structural simplicity and clarity is often present in works that intend more than exploratory study. For many artists the figure's architectural aspects are important matters, as Michelangelo's drawing *Adam* (Figure 1.14) clearly shows. But for some, these constructional aspects are expressed even more by frankly stressing the geometric masses that human forms hint at. In Dürer's etching *Man in Despair* (Figure 2.6), we find strong suggestions of cylinders, cones, ovoids, and only slightly less evident hints of block forms, as in the left arm and leg of the central figure. Again, in Picasso's drawing *Woman Seated and Woman Standing* (Figure 2.7), the forms boldly show their geometric origins.

Other artists, such as Whistler (Figure 2.8), or Pascin (Figure 2.9), although they hold these form simplifications in mind, emphasize instead the figure's pliant, serpentine character. For such artists, structural deductions are still necessary (though largely unseen) guides in suggesting volume in forms primarily concerned with movement and rhythm. These energies and tensions existing among a drawing's forms—the drawing's abstract, dynamic life (to be explored in later chapters), can always be inferred, can be felt, in the observed or imagined figure.

Although the need to see the structural, stable aspects of mass is fundamental to good figure drawing, it should be recognized that perception doesn't begin or end with the noting of planes and values. We must discover our ability to respond to the abstract meanings in our subject matter *and* in the emerging drawing —the rhythms, tensions, contrasts, and affinities that constitute the dynamics of perception. Once we do, these inferences become as visually evident as the stable, measurable aspects of perception. Thus, the criteria that determine sound responses in drawing the figure (or anything else) must embrace a comprehension of the subject's structural qualities *and* an apprehension of its plastic, expressive ones. They are, in fact, interdependent perceptual considerations. In failing to see the interdependence between the measurable and dynamic components of perception we fail to fertilize our constructions. When this occurs, the resulting drawings are dead blueprints rather than living graphic inventions.

Accentuating either a subject's structure or its plastic life is a valid and necessary theme for many artists. For others—among them some of the best figure draughtsmen—the structural and dynamic essentials are equally important. For these artists the figure's solid geometry is both a goal and a tool. Their drawings reflect the view that a subject's structure is an important key to its dynamics, and its dynamics a key to its structure. These artists realize that in disregard-

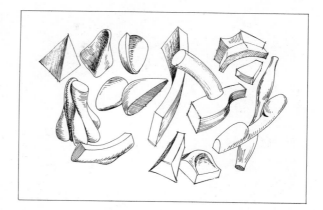

Figure 2.3

Figure 2.4

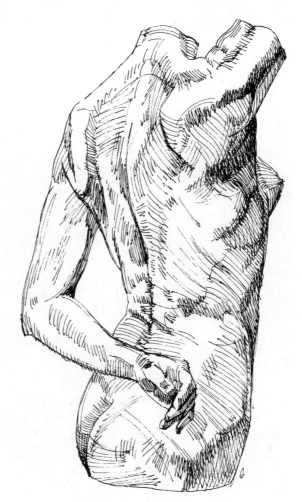

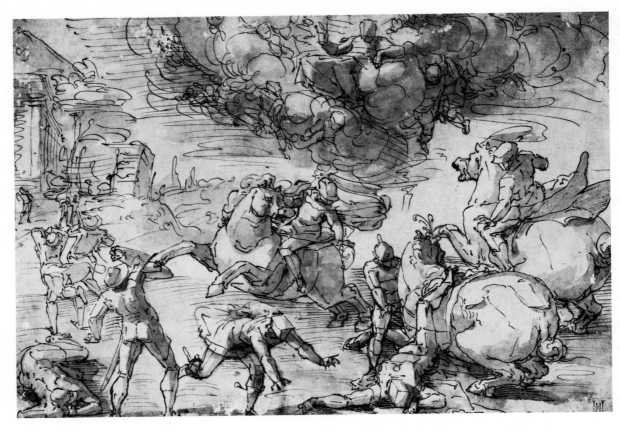

Figure 2.5
LUCA CAMBIASO (1527–1585)
Conversion of St. Paul
Pen and brown ink, brown wash. 27.7 x 40.7 cm.
The Art Museum, Princeton University.

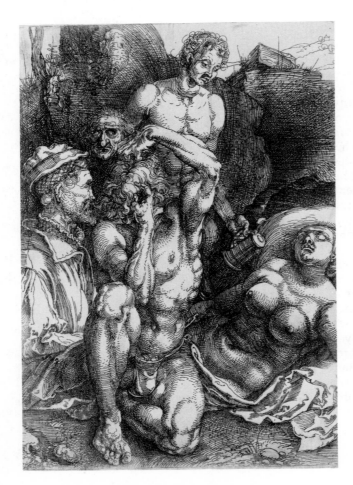

Figure 2.6
ALBRECHT DÜRER (1471–1528)
Man in Despair
Etching. 7 3/8 x 5 3/8 in.
National Gallery of Art, Washington, D.C.
Rosenwald Collection.

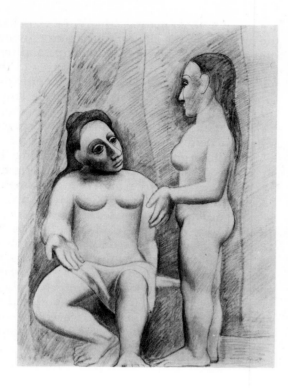

Figure 2.7
PABLO PICASSO (1881–1973)
Woman Seated and Woman Standing (1906)
Charcoal. 24 1/8 x 18 1/4 in.
Philadelphia Museum of Art.
Louise and Walter Arensberg Collection.

ing a figure's plastic character they fail to grasp important structural traits. For, in any pose, the effects of weight, the tension and pressure between parts, and the sense of forms being strained or limp are all *felt* as well as observed realities. An exclusive concern with structural analysis can seriously intrude on the emotive realities. Likewise, in failing to respond to a figure's structural essentials, much of a drawing's dynamic potential is lost. Structural considerations provide a powerful stimulus to graphic invention. A drawing of the figure is not the figure itself but a graphic equivalent. If this equivalent is to convey the artist's truest total response he will need to negotiate between fact and feeling, between analysis and empathy.

Rembrandt does this in his drawing *Female Nude Asleep* (Figure 2.10). The figure's limp weight is conveyed by simple, blocky forms that are, considering the urgent spontaneity of Rembrandt's handling, remarkably convincing volumes. But these forms do much more than convey structural essentials. By their weight and pliancy, by the emphatic overlappings, and by their rhythmic harmony, they *enact* as well as define the pose. They do still more. Note how Rembrandt draws the billowing forms of the bedding to emphasize the "crescendo" of the design; a great burst of dynamic force at the head. Note, too, that Rembrandt further underscores this center of activity by placing the drawing's largest tones on and below the head, by the scale of the pillows, and by the bold lines that radiate from them. The design builds in weight and tension to the left, enacting the character of the figure's forms. By their similarity of handling and direction, the lines that "roll" around the figure's forms and those which express the bedding's mass as well as the weight of the figure upon it, serve both structural and dynamic functions. These lines act as a kind of visual meter—a beat—that unites forms as it defines them.

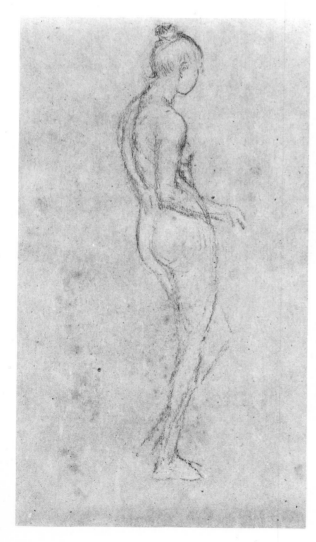

Figure 2.8
JAMES McNEIL WHISTLER (1834–1903)
Standing Female Figure
Crayon, pastel on brown paper. 10 3/4 x 6 5/16 in.
Courtesy The Fogg Art Museum, Harvard University.
The David and Lucie Stone Collection.

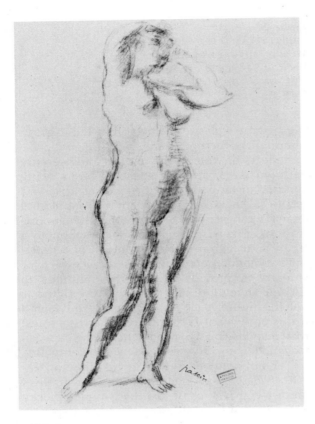

Figure 2.9
JULES PASCIN (1885–1930)
Nude
Pencil. 9 x 11 3/4 in.
Courtesy The Fogg Art Museum, Harvard University.
The David and Lucie Stone Collection.

are stated with animating drive. For Kokoschka, the analysis of the subject's structure provides him with strong plastic relationships and tensions. In the same way, his responses to the woman's gestural and plastic character provides him with motives for emphasizing the structure in some areas and subduing it in others. Here, as mentioned earlier, structural discoveries stimulate dynamic ones, and vice versa.

In these general remarks concerning the structural factor, we have been examining the artist's need to see the underlying geometric basis of the figure's forms. Comprehending a subject's fundamental masses serves as a tool, a theme, and as a stimulus and carrier of the dynamic energies that make drawings come alive. To better understand how the artist extracts the structural character from the raw material of the figure—often obscured by conflicting light sources and always somewhat camouflaged by color, texture, and minor surface effects—we must now turn to those issues that activate these perceptions.

A PLANAR APPROACH TO HUMAN FORM

For the artist the basic structural unit is the plane. Planes can here be further defined as flat or curved surfaces, or facets of a surface whose boundaries can be described by lines. Usually these boundaries are determined by the shape of a surface, or by changes in the terrain of a form's surface. For example, in Figure 2.12, the three planes (a) represent three separate surfaces which, by their positions in space, collectively suggest a cube. But in (b) the six upper planes are more readily understood as changes in the direction of a single, roof-like surface. When planes group together to form solids, they suggest other, unseen planes, as in (c).

Just as planes always result from the shape of, or changes in, a form's surface, so do we, in nature, always see planes as separated from each other by changes in value and color. The use of lines to separate adjacent planes is a convenient graphic convention that rarely exists in nature, and not at all in the figure. In human forms even the finest creases are actually narrow valleys and fine trenches.

Examining your hand from several angles will show that very few planes are easily visible as neat, bounded facets. Most of the planes of the hand, like those of the rest of the human

This brief analysis only touches on some of the ways in which Rembrandt understands the interdependence of his subject's structure and design. There are other ways. For example, the dual role of the various types of edges throughout the drawing—their depictive *and* plastic activities—also show the artist's grasp of the interplay of architectural and abstract matters. But here we have seen that much of the sleeping figure's compelling presence is due to dynamic activities, and that much of the drawing's dynamics issue from intensifications of the figure's structural nature.

This fusion of analytical and empathic interests is also apparent in Kokoschka's drawing *Trudl Wearing a Straw Hat* (Figure 2.11). As in Rembrandt's drawing, we sense the artist's understanding of perception to be more a dynamic than a static phenomenon. Not only do lines and shapes imply sweeping movements in the hair, hat, and background, but even the planes that construct the young woman's forms

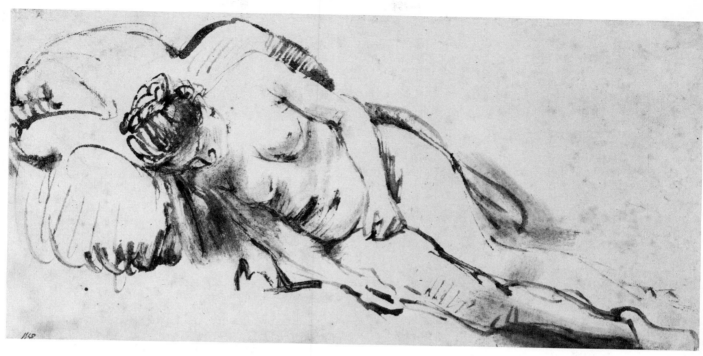

Figure 2.10
REMBRANDT VAN RIJN (1606–1669)
Female Nude Asleep
Pen and brush in bistre ink. 13.5 x 28.3 cm.
Rijksmuseum, Amsterdam.

Figure 2.11
OSKAR KOKOSCHKA (1886–   )
Trudl Wearing a Straw Hat
Black crayon. 33.3 x 47.8 cm.
Rijksmuseum, Amsterdam.

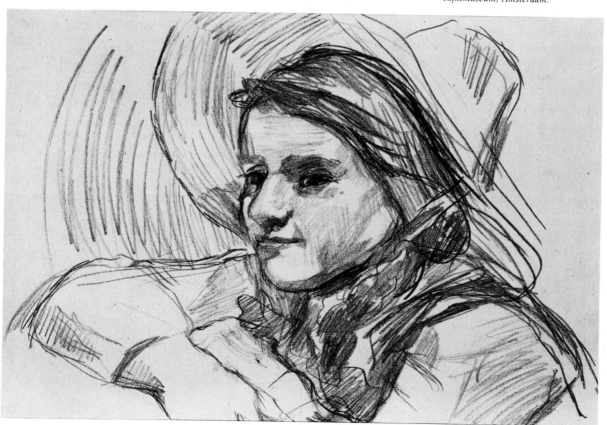

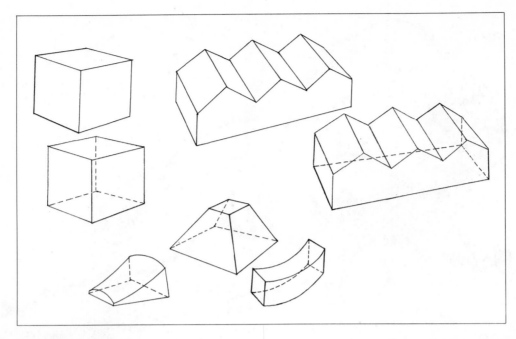

Figure 2.12

figure, are small, often curved, and generally tend to flow into each other. In analyzing or inventing a figure's masses, the artist must train himself to see groups of these small planes as forming larger ones when they are roughly alike in their general direction in relation to other groups of small planes. For example, examining our hand held in a fist, as in Figure 2.13, we see that the four fingers suggest a block-like mass, and that the thumb and palm also offer similar block-like masses. But to see these blocky forms we must disregard the little planar surface changes that each part of the fist is comprised of. They obscure our recognition of the large planes they collectively form.

Like these large, general planes of the fist, large planes exist throughout the figure, as we saw in Cambiaso's drawing. For convenience, we will refer to any form's largest planar summaries as *major planes*. Examining these major planes we find that they subdivide into somewhat smaller ones; the *secondary planes*. Secondary planes modify the major ones to provide more specific, but still simplified, versions of the figure's actual forms. These major and secondary planes are well illustrated in Cretara's drawing *Seated Figure, Back View* (Figure 2.14). The artist clarifies the planes by group-

Figure 2.13

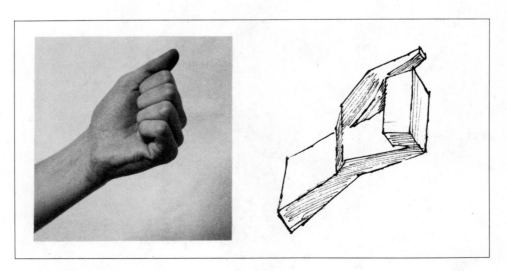

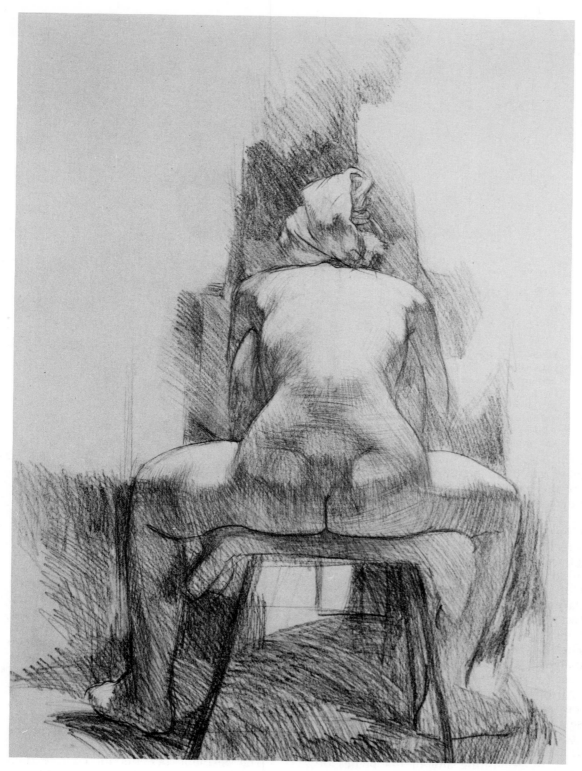

Figure 2.14
DOMENIC CRETARA (1946–   )
Seated Figure, Back View
Pencil. 18 x 24 in.
Courtesy of the artist.

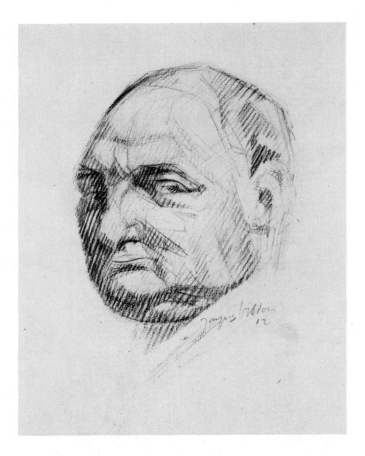

Figure 2.15
JACQUES VILLON (1875–1963)
Portrait of Félix Barré
Black chalk over traces of blue pencil.
14 3/4 x 13 15/16 in.
The Metropolitan Museum of Art, New York.
Purchase, 1963 Rogers Fund.

ing them into three tonal divisions: white (the tone of the paper), light gray, and dark gray. Note that the crosshatched lines creating these planes are usually drawn in the direction of a plane's position on the figure's surface, and show its flat or curved state. Even in the head-dress these line groups turn with the form. Cretara is sensitive to the abstract possibilities of such line groups. He unifies those of the figure with a network of similar but darker lines in the background, simultaneously creating a field of spatial depth and a handsome design of tonal "patches." As this drawing amply demonstrates, an analytical approach to the figure's planar character can result in compelling graphic ideas.

All of the figure's forms, large or small, can be reduced to simpler, more manageable masses. Looking again at our fist we see that each of the four clenched fingers is, in each segment, as block-like as the fist they collectively produce. In examining any of the planes of these smaller forms we find they subdivide into still smaller planes. It seems the closer we look, the more aware we become of these tiny variations and the less aware we are of a form's major and secondary planes. Learning to see the larger

planes that groups of small planes "belong to" is fundamental to understanding any form's structural essentials. Overlooking this analytical stage is one of the common pitfalls of the beginner. In analyzing the figure's forms we should avoid drifting too far from the mainstreams of its major and secondary planes down the tributaries of superficial detail.

Comparing the female figure in Dürer's etching (Figure 2.6) with Rembrandt's drawing of a woman in a similar pose (Figure 2.10), shows that although Dürer has gone further in explaining the figure's structure, he does not go much beyond the major and secondary planes in doing so. Where Dürer does become engrossed with surface niceties, as in the side view of the head on the left, the head just above it and, though to a lesser extent, the right foot of the central figure, the structural character of the forms is less clearly stated.

The aesthetic benefits that derive from analyzing the figure's planes are highly regarded by many artists. For such artists the benefits are not so much the result of an intention to present a system of planes as they are the dividends—the "rewards" of inquiry and invention. But other artists do intend to interpret the figure in these prismatic terms, not for purposes of study and preparation, as Cambiaso does, but for creative purposes. In Villon's drawing *Portrait of Félix Barré* (Figure 2.15), the artist's intent appears to be the realization of the psychological as well as the architectural character of the sitter through a reliance on the emotive and explanatory power of planes. Planar analysis, then, is more than a necessary tool for understanding a subject's construction; it is one of the more important sources of creative insight.

THE INTERJOINING OF PLANES AND MASSES

Some parts of the figure appear to interlock and some to fuse. Again, our hands provide a useful example for study. Looking at your partially open hand, palm side up, notice

that the thumb and its fleshy heel seem to be deeply rooted in the palm and wrist. As you bring the thumb and fingers together a bit more, each segment of the fingers, the fleshy pads of the palm, and the thumb more strongly show these embedding, interlocking, and overlapping characteristics. Opening the hand wide, each finger stretched to its limits greatly reduces this type of structural arrangement. In this position the fingers seem fused with the palm; a five-lane continuation of the major plane of the palm.

In analyzing the figure's forms we must decide when parts seem to interlock and when they seem to fuse. Here, the term *form* defines the figure's major segments (arm, head, foot, etc.), and the smaller segments of which they are comprised. For example, the features of the head (eyes, nose, lips, ears) and the often overlooked features that separate them (chin, cheek, forehead, etc.) can all be regarded as interjoinings and fusions of small *form-units*.

The way parts appear to interjoin is, of

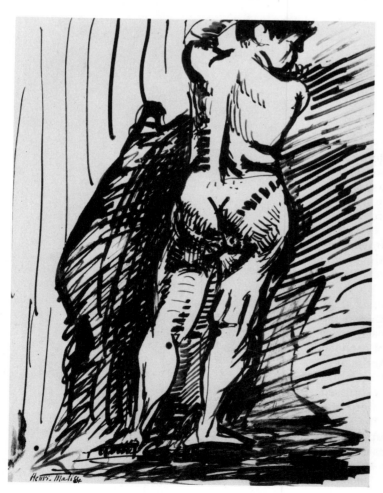

Figure 2.16
HENRI MATISSE (1869–1954)
Nude Study
India ink with quill pen. 26.4 x 20.2 cm.
National Gallery, Prague.

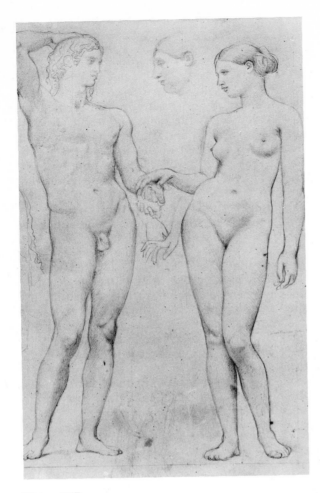

Figure 2.17
DOMINIQUE INGRES (1780–1867)
Two Nudes, study for "The Golden Age"
Pencil. 16 3/8 x 12 7/16 in.
Courtesy The Fogg Art Museum, Harvard University.
Bequest of Granville L. Winthrop.

Nude Men (Figure 2.18), there is a balance between abrupt and fluid unions. Although each figure clearly shows the deep roots of the limbs in the torso, and many other forms such as those in the left arm and leg of the central figure are vigorously structured, Raphael keeps a graceful flow moving throughout the drawing. He does this by stressing curved, rather than flat planes, by simply omitting some interjoinings, as along the left side of the central figure's raised leg, and by a delineating edge as rich in rhythmic flow as it is in volume-informing fact.

Tintoretto merges the concepts of strong and subtle interjoinings by strong interlockings of graceful forms. His powerful drawing *Study of a Model for the "Giuliano de' Medici" of Michelangelo* (Figure 2.19), is a system of exaggerated interjoinings of ovoid rather than block-like form-units. This study of a work by Michelangelo, itself a heightened interpretation of idealized forms boldly interjoined, conveys a

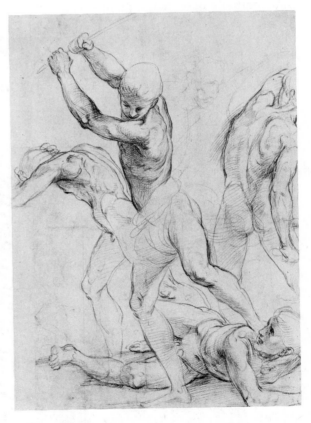

Figure 2.18
RAPHAEL (1483–1520)
Combat of Nude Men
Red chalk over preliminary stylus work.
14 13/16 x 11 1/8 in.
Ashmolean Museum, Oxford.

course, largely determined by our anatomy and, as we have seen, by the particular arrangement of the forms. But there remains a considerable degree of freedom to interpret the interjoining of forms according to personal preference and graphic intent. Some artists emphasize the wedging, overlapping, and embedding characteristics; others, the gentle flow of the forms; and still others strike a balance between these two kinds of union.

Matisse, in his drawing *Nude Study* (Figure 2.16), drives forms together with great intensity. Forms "grasp" and overlap each other almost aggressively. The upper part of each leg holds the lower part as if by pincers. At the neck and waist bold lines convey the weight and tension of overlapped forms strongly pressed together. How different is Ingres' interpretation of a standing female figure! In his study *Two Nudes* (Figure 2.17), Ingres's interpretation of the forms relies on precise delineation and subtle fusions of forms, rather than emphatic interlockings. In Raphael's drawing *Combat of*

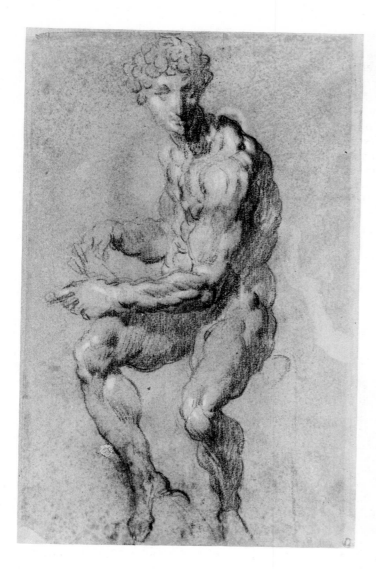

Figure 2.19
JACOPO TINTORETTO (1518–1594)
Study of a Model for the "Giuliano de' Medici"
of Michelangelo
Black and white chalk.
The Governing Body of Christ Church, Oxford.

a strong sense of aliveness through the energetic way these richly modelled forms interwork. Their almost serpentine ripple implies pulsating movement and great strength. It is worth noting that Tintoretto's drawing is an excellent example of structural and anatomical matters serving the factors of design and expression. Note the abstract and emotive energies of the forms and the sense of barely restrained action. Segantini's drawing *Male Nude Torso* (Figure 2.20) shows a less amplified interpretation of human forms as emerging from rounded rather than block-like solids. But there is an impressive clarity in the way these form-units interjoin. Note how insistently the lines ride upon the changing directions of the surface. They rise and fall with the terrain, explaining the

depth of every hollow, the height of every rise, and the degree of abruptness or flow in the union between the forms. A sculptor, using Segantini's drawing as a guide, could model these forms in clay and never be in doubt about the subject's structure.

Whether an artist stresses or subdues the joining of planes and forms, and whether he favors a block-like or egg-like schema, or, as in Rembrandt's drawing (Figure 2.10), a selective choosing between the two geometric mass concepts, he needs to apprehend the figure's subtle and complex forms as reducible to simpler masses that interjoin in various ways. Held in the mind's eye, unions such as those in Figure 2.24 help the artist to understand and control the forms he draws.

STRUCTURE AND VALUE

Most structurally explicit drawings rely on values to help clarify the figure's constructional nature, as can be seen by glancing at the drawings in this chapter. All forms are made visible by the presence of some illuminating source. Earlier, it was observed that when planes facing a light source are drawn as lighter in value than those turned away from the light, the substantiality of the form's structure is strengthened. But the structurally motivated artist is not primarily concerned with values for their ability to suggest illumination. Drawings that imitate the light and dark areas on a form—as photographs do—are merely recording the light's accidental behavior. Light is indifferent. It strikes any solid in its path, sometimes ex-

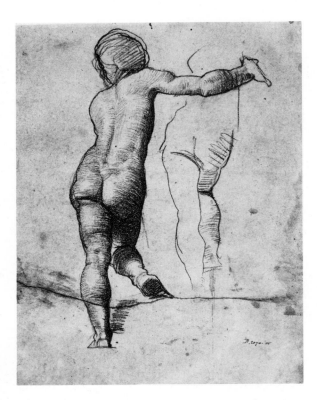

Figure 2.21
ALFRED STEVENS (1817–1875)
Two Studies of a Standing Figure, Back View
Red chalk. 18 3/8 x 6 1/4 in.
Victoria and Albert Museum, London.

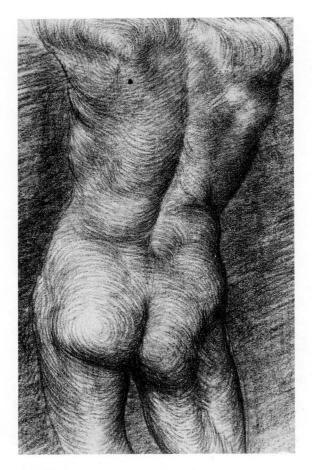

Figure 2.20
GIOVANNI SEGANTINI (1858–1899)
Male Nude Torso
Black chalk. 12 1/4 x 8 in.
Courtesy The Fogg Art Museum, Harvard University.
Bequest of Granville L. Winthrop.

plaining a form's structure, sometimes camouflaging or destroying it. Imagine a zebra standing before a fence made of diagonally crossed slats casting strong shadows on the animal. Merely copying the shadows would result in a richly patterned zebra whose forms would be lost in the visual confusion of stripes and cast shadows. Or, imagine a figure illuminated from several sources at once, as sometimes occurs when overhead lights are spaced across the entire ceiling, or when daylight comes in through windows from several directions. Such a figure will be brightly illuminated, but most of the forms will appear strangely flat, showing little useful value change. When artists do desire a sense of light-bathed forms, most will subordinate the sense of illumination to structural interests, as in Stevens's drawing *Two Studies of a Standing Figure, Back View* (Figure 2.21). Here, we can identify the direction of the light as coming from a point high on the left side. There is a sense of forms bathed by light, but the illuminating role of *value* is secondary to its volume-informing one. The figure's right leg *is* in shadow, but the value produced by the line groups that convey the leg's shadowed state is concerned first with modelling the form. The shadowed quality is merely the result of the heavier and more densely grouped, structure-seeking lines. Likewise, in Michelangelo's sheet of sketches, *Studies of a Madonna and Child* (Figure 2.22), values are used to explain the subtly differing directions of the planes that comprise the volumes. In drawings restricted to a sparse use of line to delineate edges, such precise differences in the tilt of planes are not possible. Although lines can efficiently describe a form's boundaries, values are generally necessary to describe its topography. Note that in both the Stevens and Michelangelo drawings, no "deserts" of empty, unexplained terrain exist.

Value, then, is able to convey the sense of light and to model form. It can also distinguish between the inherent values of a form. For example, values can show the dark tone of the hair against the lighter tone of a head or hat. The inherent lightness or darkness of a form, or any of its segments, apart from the effects of light upon it, is called its *local-tone*. When an artist intends to convey the local-tones of his subject matter he will usually simplify them to keep from weakening value's structural role. In Watteau's drawing *Study of a Young Negro* (Figure 2.23), the light tone of the headdress and the darker tone of the head are indicated by simple, flat values. Watteau unifies these areas by a band of dark tone that suggests the presence of light as it models the ovoid formed by the face, headdress, and hair. Note that in modelling these three

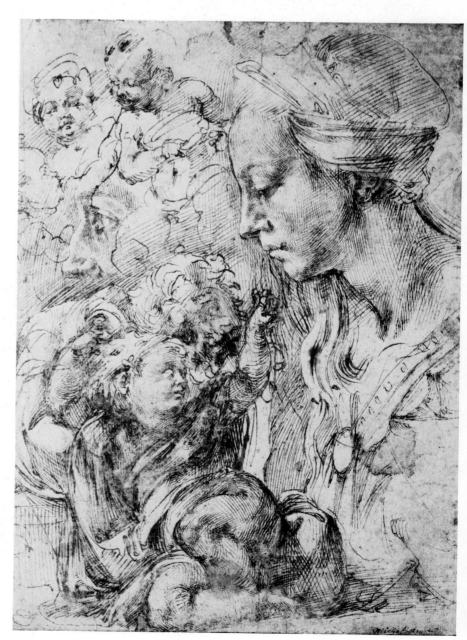

Figure 2.22
MICHELANGELO BUONARROTI (1475–1564)
Studies of a Madonna and Child
Pen and brown ink. 11 1/4 x 8 1/4 in.
Staatliche Museen Preussischer Kulturbesitz.
Kupferstichkabinett. West Berlin.

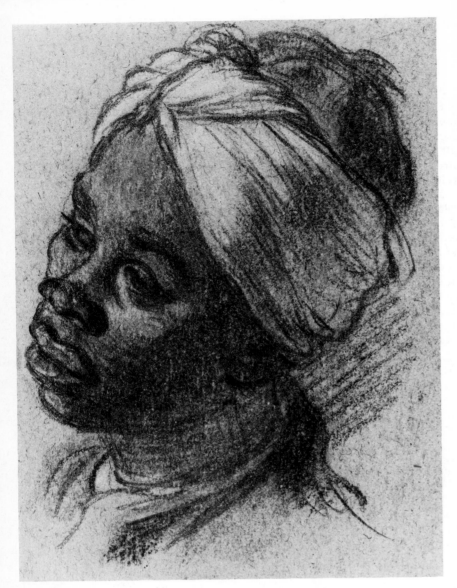

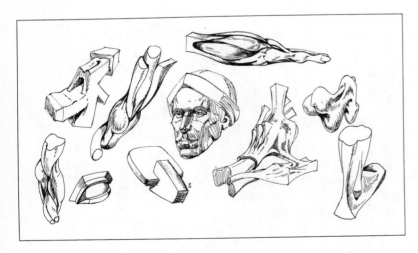

Figure 2.24

areas the artist emphasizes major and secondary planes. Note, too, how feelingly the value-producing line groups move upon the forms. Comparing Watteau's drawing to the similar view of the Madonna's head in Michelangelo's drawing, we see that Watteau's providing of information about the local-tones of the young black are in addition to, not in place of, structural clarity. In both drawings a major interest is the experiencing of the subject's important masses.

STRUCTURAL SUPPORTS AND SUSPENSIONS IN THE FIGURE

The skeleton provides a firm, armature-like system of support for the figure's more pliant muscular and fatty tissues. In Chapter Three we will examine the skeleton in some detail, but here we must add to our understanding

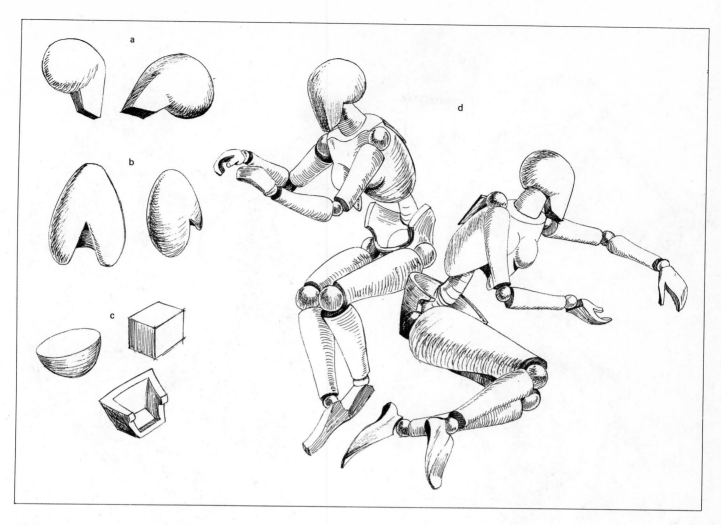

Figure 2.25

of the figure's structural nature a sensitivity to the supporting role of the skeleton beneath the "drapery" of muscle, fat, and skin. To sense those deep forms that hold, and to better understand the behavior of those more superficial forms that are held, we can temporarily envision the skeleton as reduced to a simple, manikin-like system of three large bony masses connected by spheres, cylinders, and wedges (Figures 2.24 and 2.25).

The three large masses of the skeleton are the skull, the rib cage, and the pelvis (Figure 2.25). Of the three, the skull is the most "visible," influencing the surface forms throughout the head. Reduced to its simplest geometric state, the skull can be represented by an ovoid upper segment which extends downward in front into a blocky lower segment (a). The rib cage is reducible to a large, egg-like form, small end up, with a "pie-slice" opening in its curved front plane that extends upward from the base of the egg to about its middle (b). Somewhat less visible in the figure than the skull, the rib cage is still a prominent mass, especially in the area of

the wedge-like opening. The pelvis is more deeply buried in the figure. A complex form, it can be reduced in several ways: into a half-sphere, a block, or a winged and slightly tapered, hollowed block (c). Note that the manikin-like figures (d) in our illustration show ball joints at the shoulder, elbow, knee, wrist, and ankle. These roughly correspond to the bony prominences found throughout the skeleton, occurring at the ends of the long, shaft-like bones of the limbs, or resulting from small, projecting bones, as at the knee. Most of these protuberances are visible to some degree in most poses, for example in de Gheyn's drawing *Studies of Four Women at Their Toilet* (Figure 2.26). Additionally, the ball joints in Figure 2.25d suggest the figure's mobility at these joints.

Compare the simplified skeleton in Figure 2.25d with the figure on the far left in de Gheyn's drawing. Imagining that skeletal armature inside of the figure in the drawing helps us sense how the muscular and fatty tissues are draped upon the skeleton; it also helps explain why the "container" of skin is stretched taut

49

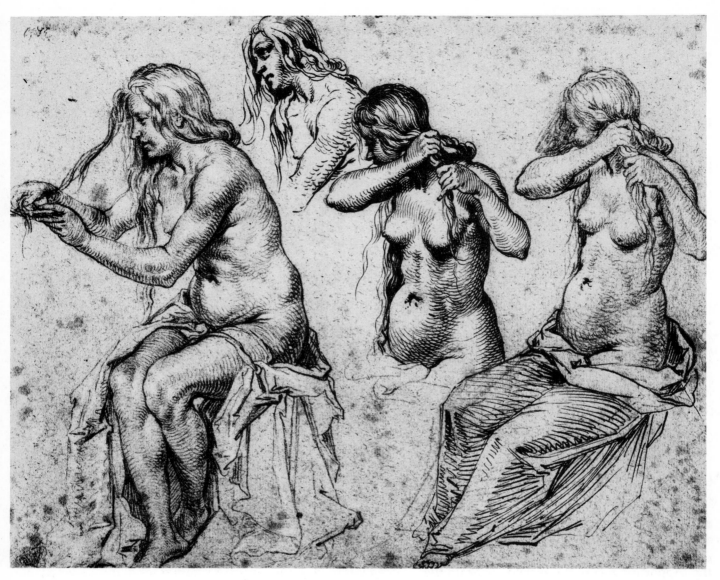

Figure 2.26
JACOB DE GHEYN II (1565–1629)
Studies of Four Women at Their Toilet
Pen and ink, some black chalk;
on gray paper. 26.1 x 33.6 cm.
Musées Royaux des Beaux Arts, Brussels.

in some places, as at the knees and hips, and why it is slack in other places, as in the chest and abdomen. Note how de Gheyn, in drawing the figure's fleshy forms, suggests the inner armature of the skeleton, how he integrates firm and supple passages everywhere, avoiding form-solutions that are wooden or rubbery. He does this not only at the joints, where the bones "come to the surface" but throughout the length of the limbs; and in the torso where, especially in the figure on the left, we sense the rib cage and pelvis through the heavily fleshed forms. Note, too, the clarity with which de Gheyn conveys abrupt and flowing unions between form-units.

Likewise, in Boucher's drawing *Seated Nude* (Figure 2.27), we sense the presence of an inner supporting system. Although this figure is rather heavily proportioned, even plump, the forms are not balloon-like or rubbery. As in de Gheyn's drawing, they show alternating firm and pliant passages that suggest the skeletal substructure. Comparing Boucher's drawing with its schematic counterpart in Figure 2.25d helps explain what holds and what is held.

Naturally, the skeleton's influence is more evident in lean figures, especially male ones. Géricault's study for one of the figures in his painting *The Raft of Medusa* (Figure 2.28) reveals a keen understanding of the skeleton's effect upon the figure's softer forms. Here, the rib cage and the outer "wings" of the pelvis are quite distinct. Throughout the figure the taut sheath of the skin hints at the forms below, suggesting the firm, inner structure pressing outward. Note that the head, only roughed in, is conceived as something like the schematic skull in Figure 2.25a. Although developed much further, the head in Guercino's drawing *St. Joseph* (Figure 2.29) is still modelled chiefly by large planes that do not surrender their dominance to the smaller details. In fact, notice that in all the structurally sensitive drawings we have been looking at in this chapter, the artist's

analysis of the subject's masses provides him with simple form concepts that guide his modelling the forms in values. As noted earlier, knowing a form's basic planar character provides a logical basis for establishing the light and dark tones upon it. Generally, when a form's surface changes direction, the values change. Both Géricault's specific depiction of small but pronounced surface changes and Boucher's modelling of large but subtly turning ones are enhanced by the artists' appreciation of the simple cubes, cylinders, ovoids, etc., underlying their subjects' forms. This appreciation, in harmony with an understanding of the skele-

Figure 2.27
FRANÇOIS BOUCHER (1703–1770)
Seated Nude
Red and white chalk on gray paper. 30 x 39.2 cm.
Rijksmuseum, Amsterdam.

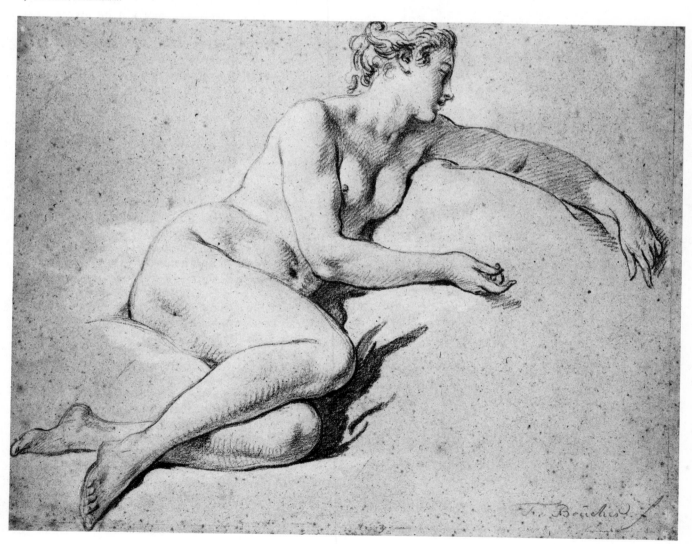

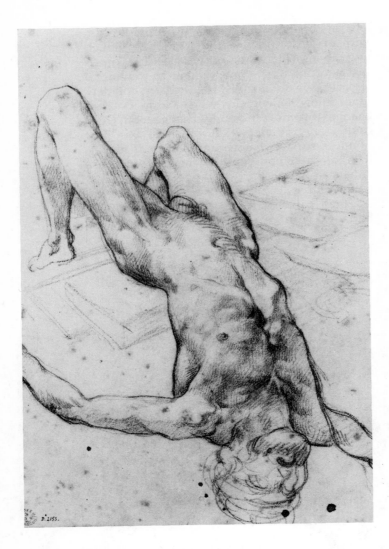

Figure 2.28
THÉODORE GÉRICAULT (1791–1824)
Study for one of the figures in ''The Raft of Medusa''
Charcoal on white paper. 28.9 x 20.5 cm.
Musée des Beaux Arts, Besançon.

here to comment briefly on some of its basic principals.

A fundamental concept of linear perspective holds that any view of any solid mass involves the foreshortening of some of its surfaces. For example, when we look directly at one plane of a cube, we must necessarily see the other two planes foreshortened. Sometimes we cannot see the foreshortened planes, for example when our line of sight is centered on the bottom plane of a cone or pyramid. More often, and especially in the forms of the human figure, any view of a form shows some of its planes turned away from our line of sight. Although the beginner may not be aware of it, any "easy" pose, such as a front view of a figure standing at attention, contains a great amount of foreshortening. Such a pose consists of a severely foreshortened view of the sides of the head, torso, and limbs. Depending on the eye level of the student in relation to the model, this pose will also show foreshortened views of the top or underside of various forms. For example, if the student is seated in front of the standing figure, he sees a foreshortened view of the *underside* of the model's nose and jaw, and a foreshortened view of the *top* planes of the model's feet, as in Figures 2.7 and 2.17.

The greater the degree of foreshortening, the greater the reduction—the shortening—of a plane's width. *All* planes except those at a right angle to and centered in the viewer's line of sight are seen as foreshortened, as Figure 2.30a shows. The more a plane is positioned in a line with the viewer's line of sight, the less he can see of its surface. When a plane is exactly in line with the viewer's line of sight only its near edge is visible, as in Figure 2.30b. Curved planes, by their nature, are always seen as foreshortened (Figure 2.30c).

Naturally, what is true for a single plane holds true for the flat and curved planes of any solid mass. The variously positioned forms of the figure in any pose are better understood by first determining their location in space in relation to your line of sight, and your *eye level*, that is, the height of your eyes from the ground plane upon which you are standing, seated, or even lying. For the artist the terms *eye level* and *horizon line* are synonymous. Our eye level de-

ton's influence in forming and affecting the simple, underlying solids, is vital to the creation of figure drawings that ring true. When artists are governed by these principles, their drawings—in line, value, or both—convey truths about the figure's structural nature rather than mere data about its surfaces.

STRUCTURAL ASPECTS OF FORESHORTENING

As with any form in nature, those of the figure are subject to the laws of perspective. Although an examination of perspective is not within the scope of this book* it is necessary

*For a fuller examination of linear and aerial perspective, see Nathan Goldstein, *The Art of Responsive Drawing* (Englewood Cliffs, N.J.: Prentice-Hall, Inc., 1973), chap. 5.

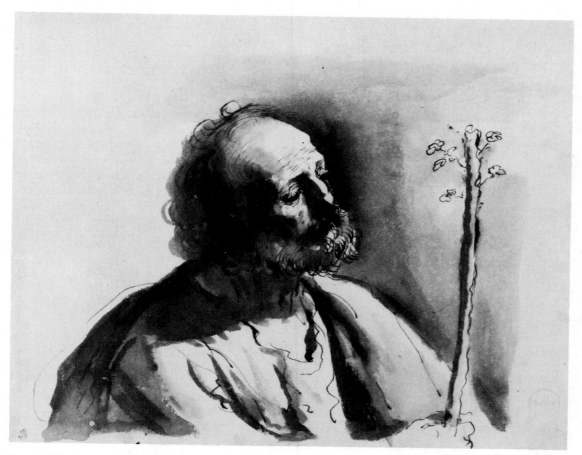

Figure 2.29
GIOVANNI FRANCESCO BARBIERI,
called GUERCINO (1591–1666)
St. Joseph
Pen and bistre ink. 16.8 x 20.7 cm.
The Art Museum, Princeton University.

Figure 2.30

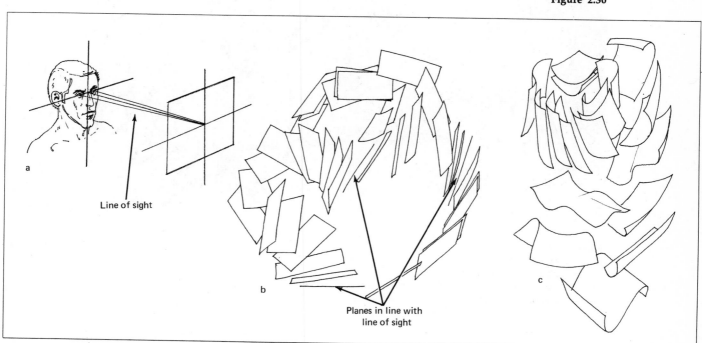

Line of sight

Planes in line with
line of sight

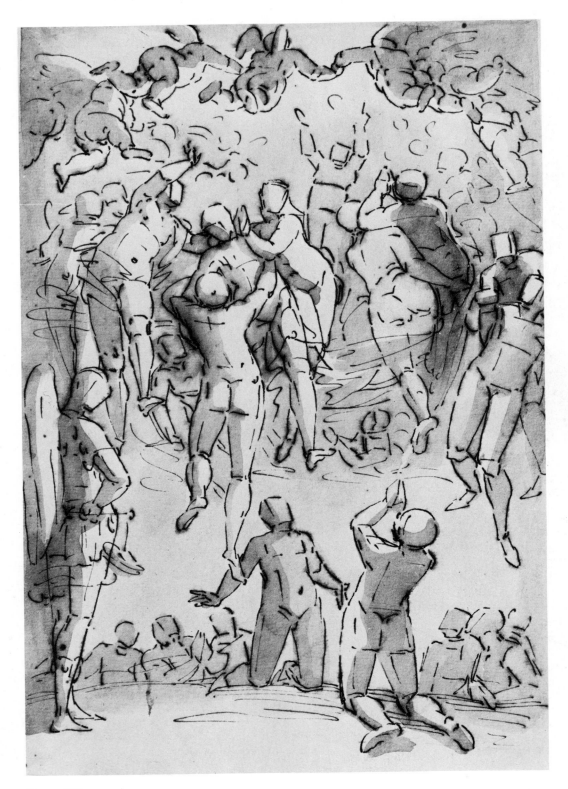

Figure 2.31
LUCA CAMBIASO (1527–1585)
Resurrection and Ascension
Pen, ink, and brown wash. 13 1/8 x 9 3/8 in.
Gabinetto Nazionale delle Stampe, Rome.

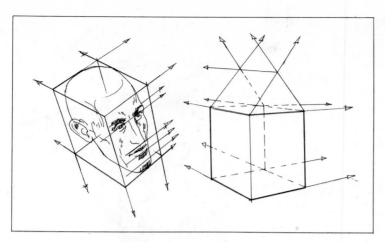

Figure 2.32

Figure 2.33
NATHAN GOLDSTEIN (1927–   )
Reclining Figure, Foreshortened View
Red chalk. 10 3/4 x 11 1/2 in.
Collection of the author.

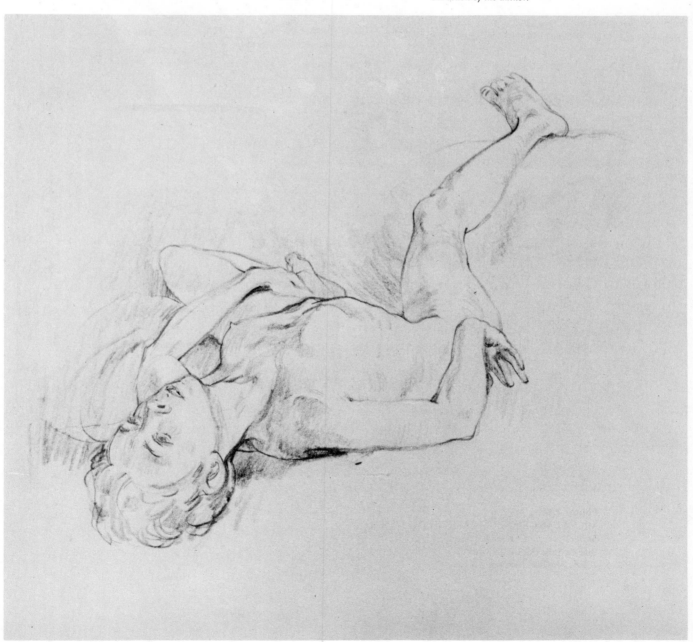

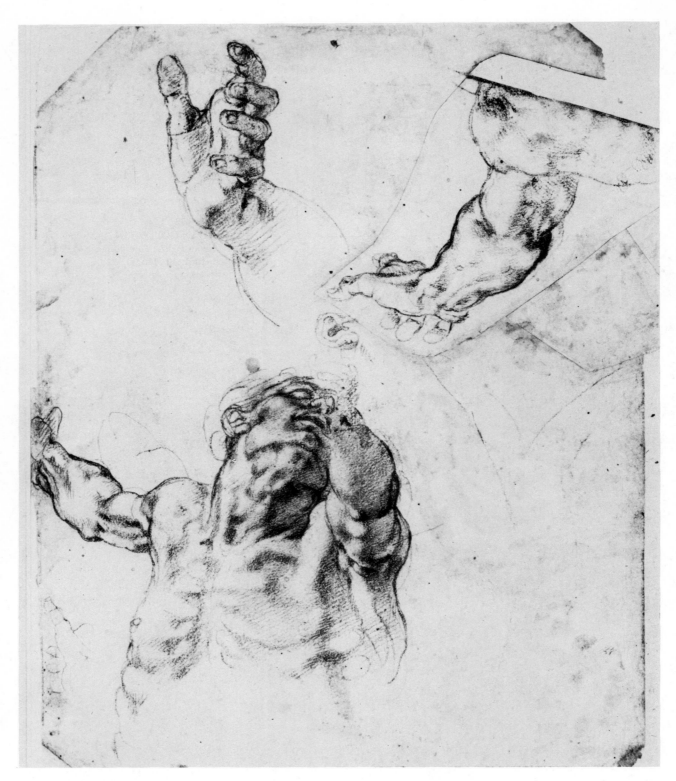

Figure 2.34
MICHELANGELO BUONARROTI (1475–1564)
Studies for the Crucified Haman
Black chalk. 33.3 x 22.7 cm.
Teylers Museum, Haarlem.

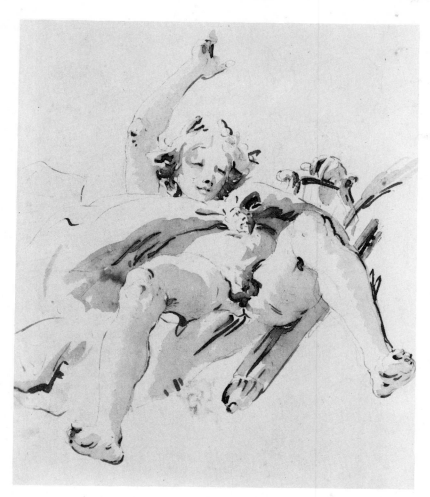

Figure 2.35
GIOVANNI BATTISTA TIEPOLO (1696–1770)
Apollo with Lyre and Quiver, His Arm Upraised
Pen and brown ink, brown wash over black chalk.
8 5/8 x 7 1/4 in.
The Pierpont Morgan Library, New York.

Figure 2.36
DOMENIC CRETARA (1946–   )
Sheet of Studies of the Female Figure
Red chalk on toned paper. 18 x 24 in.
Collection of the author.

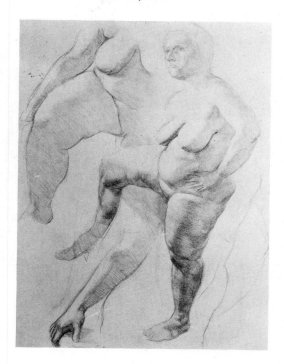

termines the high or low position of the horizon line in our field of vision. If we lie on the sand, looking at the sea, the horizon line is low; if we stand up, it is higher; and if we climb the lifeguard's tower, the horizon line is higher still. In Cambiaso's drawing *Resurrection and Ascension* (Figure 2.31), it is evident that the artist has envisioned a scene to be understood as occurring mainly above his (and consequently, our) eye level. Because the horizon line is low, we look down on only those few forms located below it, namely the feet and lower limbs of the three figures standing on the ground plane. All the other forms in the drawing, regardless of their tilt and degree of foreshortening, we see as positioned above our eye level. This is so even

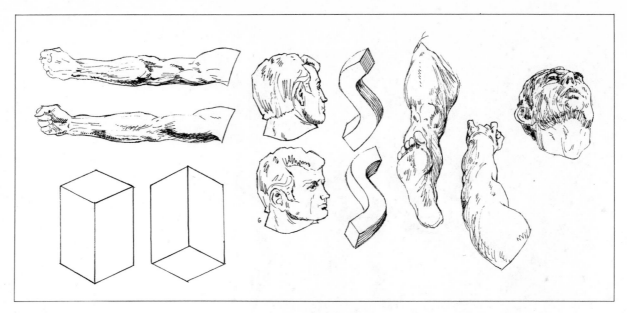

Figure 2.37

Figure 2.38
PETER PAUL RUBENS (1577–1640)
Bathsheba Receiving David's Letter
Pen and ink. 19.2 x 26.6 cm.
Staatliche Museen Preussischer Kulturbesitz.
Kupferstichkabinett. West Berlin.

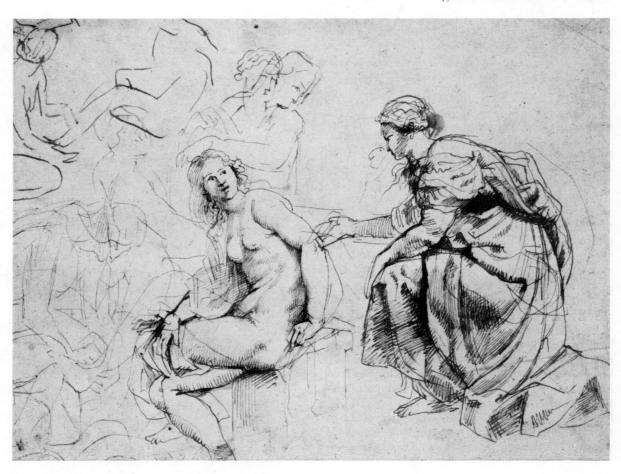

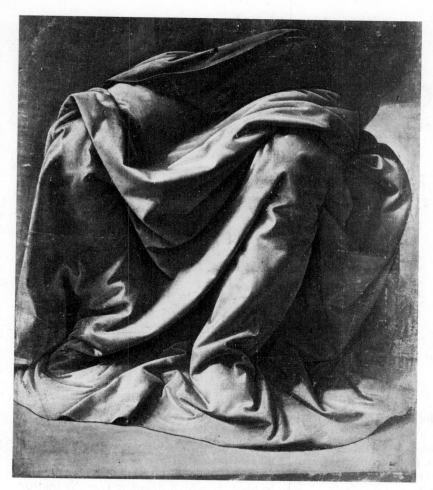

Figure 2.39
LEONARDO DA VINCI (1452–1519)
Study of Drapery
Brush, gray wash, heightened with white, on linen.
26.5 x 23.3 cm.
Cabinet des Dessins, Musée du Louvre, Paris.

though we do see the top planes of some of the forms, because we understand the overall location of the figures to be above our eye level.

We have all learned, or instinctively know, that horizontal lines which are actually parallel appear to incline toward each other, meeting at an imaginary point on the horizon line. We have all noted this apparent converging of lines when walking down a corridor or street. It is equally true that any group of parallel lines projecting back into space, that is, away from the viewer, at *any* angle, will appear to converge, as in Figure 2.32. Thus, the width of any form possessing parallel lines (edges), such as a block or cylinder, appears to diminish as it projects back toward the horizon line, or toward any imaginary point above or below it. Such forms appear to taper. Forms that *actually* taper, as many of the figure's forms do, will appear to do so to a greater degree than blocks or cylinders when projecting away from the viewer, as in Figure 2.33. Note that here the position of

the head and neck, the torso, and the upper and lower limbs are made easier to locate in relation to each other by the device of the near form always overlapping and "digging into" the form beyond it. The edges of the throat are overlapped and set into the torso, which in turn asserts its dominance over the upper right leg by a single line; the upper right leg does the same to the lower leg, which overlaps the foot. This dominance of the near over the far form holds true in the figure when the same forms are viewed from either end. In Michelangelo's drawing *Studies for the Crucified Haman* (Figure 2.34), a right arm projecting back and a left one projecting foward both show this principle at work. Comparing the two hands in the upper part of the drawing again shows how these overlaps and interlockings clarify the position of forms in relation to each other.

The ability to reduce the figure's forms to geometric masses (whether we begin by drawing them or only hold them in mind) is of par-

X X

Dealing in foreshortening,
The reduction of form to
geometric masses is important.

59

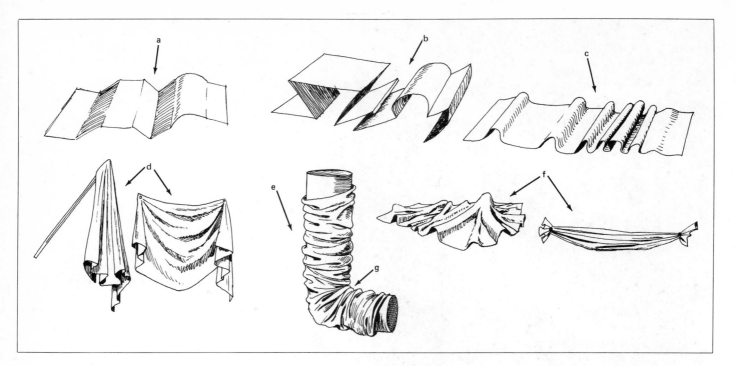

Figure 2.40

ticular importance in poses where the forms are drastically foreshortened. This ability is evident in Tiepolo's drawing *Apollo with Lyre and Quiver, His Arm Upraised* (Figure 2.35). But, as we have seen, foreshortening is an ever present phenomenon, even with forms only slightly above or below eye level. In Cretara's drawing, *Sheet of Studies of the Female Figure* (Figure 2.36), the forms are located both above and below the artist's eye level; and Cretara conveys this impression by his sensitive tapering of the forms and by the direction of the lines that model them. As these two drawings show, the figure's forms are more clearly positioned in space, and more convincingly drawn, when their geometric core is understood. Note that both drawings, although centuries apart, show a common understanding of the torso and limbs as essentially cylindrical, the head as ovate, and the feet as wedge-like. Additionally, both artists utilize a strong light source, both model the forms in three values, and both consistently stress the overlap of the far form by the near one.

For most beginners drawing any human form in severe foreshortening is difficult. Often the student begins to draw a foreshortened form as he actually sees it, but in the completed drawing the form looks as though viewed from overhead. What began as a foreshortened view of say, a leg, ends in a drawing that combines some of the student's observations with some of his *prior knowledge* about legs: that they are long forms, have certain familiar outlines, and contain some important characteristics such as the knee and the ankle. Yet the same student

can probably draw severely foreshortened blocks, cylinders, and cones, with some success. Indeed, if the students *and* the instructor of a beginning life-drawing class were each to draw a foreshortened cylinder, it would be difficult to identify which drawing was the instructor's. But, were the students and the instructor to draw a finger in the same position as the cylinder, the instructor's drawing would be immediately apparent. What has changed? Essentially, little. The finger can be understood as a modified cylinder, one with a number of abrupt and fluid planar changes, but still conforming to a tubular core. The instructor's drawing is the one most likely to have benefited from a grasp of the subject's *essential* mass, upon which the variations—the major and secondary planes—can be modelled, the resulting forms overlapped and interjoined, and a sense of the firm and supple characteristics of the finger conveyed. Each of these stages in the evolution of the form is assisted by the *nature* and *position in space* of its underlying, simple mass.

The instructor can call on another basic perceptual concept that serves structural interests. He knows that every volume has its definable limits—its outline, or *shape-state*. By noting the shape-state of a foreshortened volume he can more easily establish its position in space. The shape of a form defines the form's position in space and conveys important clues about its structure; it represents a form's totally foreshortened planes, which is what edges are largely comprised of. The beginner who means to draw the foreshortened leg but draws instead an overhead view has failed to observe the leg's shape-state. Forms in different positions may share a common shape, and the familiar forms of the figure may, in certain poses, offer very unfamiliar shapes (Figure 2.37). The ability to comprehend a form's shape as if it were a flat puzzle-piece is an essential perceptual skill.

STRUCTURAL ASPECTS OF THE DRAPED FIGURE AND ITS ENVIRONMENT

Most figure draughtsmen convey something of the action and structural character of the anatomical forms beneath the ''drapery'' of

Figure 2.41
REMBRANDT VAN RIJN (1606–1669)
St. Augustine in His Study
Quill and reed pens and ink. 18.3 x 15 cm.
Devonshire Collection, Chatsworth. Reproduced by permission of the Trustees of the Chatsworth Settlement.

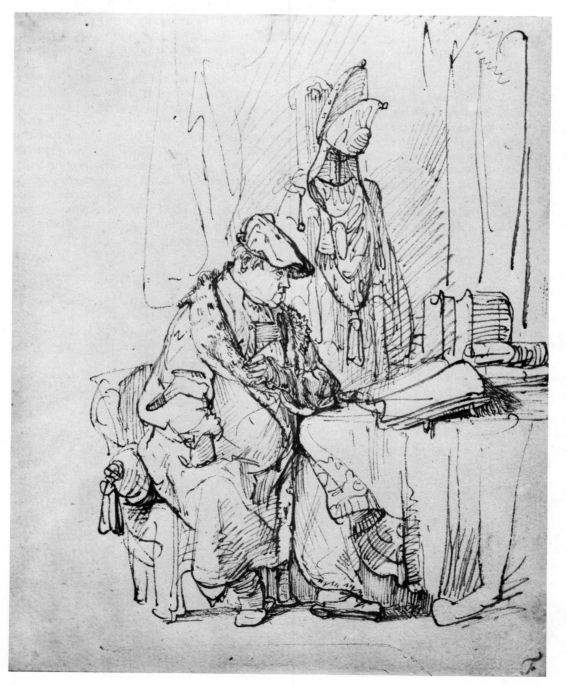

the skin—the tensions, weight, rhythms, and masses of the bones, muscles, and fatty tissues. In addition, their drawings suggest something of the general action and structural character of the figure beneath the drapery of clothed figures. In such drawings, the gestures and general structure of the limbs and torso are often clearly evident, even when the figure is voluminously draped, as in Rubens's drawing *Bathsheba Receiving David's Letter* (Figure 2.38). Here, there is little doubt about the position, weight, and robust character of the servant's forms. Not only does Rubens suggest the figure's action and structural essentials; in some areas, such as the servant's left upper arm and the left leg, he actually "draws through" the drapery to reveal the general contours of the forms beneath.

Clothing, then, can be thought of as a kind of loose, second skin. And, like skin, it requires firm structures to hold it up, yielding to the pull of gravity wherever it is free of support. Occasionally, drapery will be as taut as skin usually is. When this is the case, it will reveal almost as much about the forms it covers as the skin does. Even a loose garment will reveal something about the forms beneath: where forms interrupt the fall of a fold, or create folds where they press against the drapery, or where the drapery clings to the top surfaces of forms (Figure 2.39). In Rubens's drawing, the drapery

of the figure's left leg shows these conditions.

In drawing the draped figure the beginner should be as attentive to the ways in which drapery reveals the body's gesture and masses as he is to the ways in which the body's surfaces suggest deeper anatomical forms. This provides the student with a useful basis for selecting between the many folds and creases in the figure's drapery. He can, as Rubens does, emphasize those folds that reveal the figure's action and the general nature of its masses, and omit or subordinate those folds which obscure or confuse such actions and structural character. Note that Rubens explains the drapery's complex "topography" by the same means with which he models the servant's (and Bathsheba's) forms, namely, by reducing forms to their major and secondary planes, conveying the direction of those planes by line groups, and clarifying the way form-units interjoin.

Every figure-drawing teacher has seen student works in which an interest in structural analysis, design, perspective, and proportion diminished sharply when the student turned from drawing the figure's forms to drawing the drapery upon it. In such drawings there is usually an even greater deterioration of inquiry and association—of visual involvement—when the student goes on to draw the indoor or outdoor forms surrounding the figure. These drawings reveal the student's declining interest in

Figure 2.42
NICOLAS POUSSIN (1594–1665)
Bacchus and Ariadne
Pen, bistre ink washes, on pinkish paper.
15.6 x 25 cm.
Courtauld Institute of Art, London.

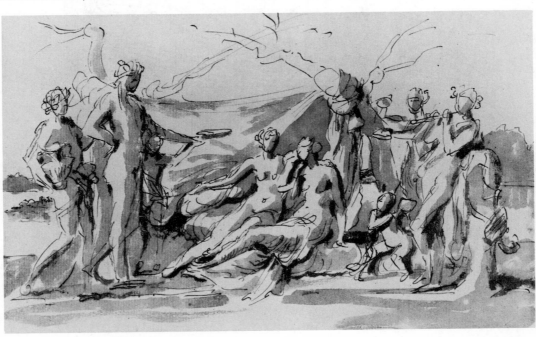

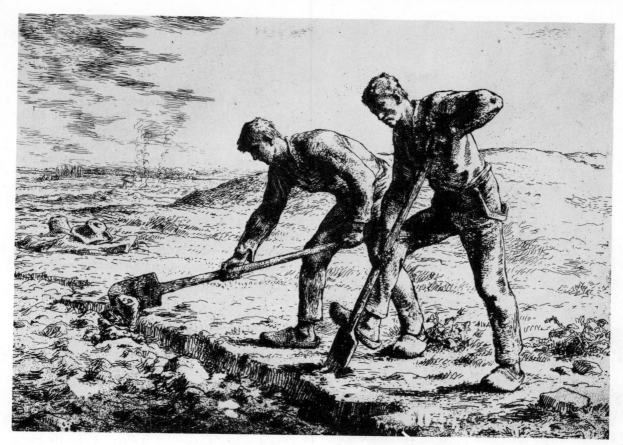

Figure 2.43
JEAN-FRANÇOIS MILLET (1814–1875)
The Diggers
Etching. 9 3/8 x 13 1/4 in.
S.P. Avery collection.
Prints Division, The New York Public Library.
Astor, Lenox and Tilden Foundations.

forms other than human ones. But it is fundamental to good figure drawing to recognize the structural and dynamic opportunities in drapery and in the masses and spaces that make up the figure's environment. Indeed, no important creative sensitivity to the figure's structural or dynamic character is possible without a comparable sensitivity to the structure and dynamics of all other forms in nature. Although we may prefer one kind of subject matter over another, until we can appreciate the visual-expressive potential of all kinds of subject matter we don't fully understand the possibilities of one in particular. Just as all forms can be reduced to simple geometric masses, so do they all suggest relational and expressive energies. Genuine perceptual sensitivity can respond to virtually any combination of man-made or natural forms. As John Steinbeck observed, "Love is a chain of love."

An analysis of the folds in any draped material shows that they conform to a few characteristic masses and movements (Figure 2.40). Usually, a fold can be reduced to three planes: an ascending plane, a flat or curved top plane, and a descending plane (a). Sometimes the as-

cending and descending planes are overlapped by the top plane, as in (b). Sometimes the "valleys" separating folds are broad and flat, sometimes they are narrow and concave, as in (c). When this is the case, the folds appear to roll in a wave-like manner. Unless interrupted by other forms, folds will radiate from a point at which a form interrupts its fall. When held at two points, both sets of radiating folds will dovetail as individual folds intercept each other (d). Tubular drapery, such as sleeves or pant legs, tends to fall in circular dovetail patterns, a series of zigzags, or in opposing V-shaped folds, as in (e). Occasionally, especially when the drapery is somewhat loose, Y-shaped folds occur. When stretched tight, valleys may disappear as folds push together, as in (f). When tubular drapery is bent, folds "rush" away from the point of tension (g). All other folds are variants of these types of folds, and *all* folds will conform in some degree to a wave-like rise, crest, and fall.

In master figure drawings the folds, whether of silk, wool, or skin, reveal the artist's understanding of their structure, weight, and gestural character. Although the figure is

63

This is well illustrated by Rembrandt's drawing *St. Augustine in His Study* (Figure 2.41). In addition to his remarkable grasp and control of the measurable matters of placement, scale, value, and texture, Rembrandt never fails to empathize with the structural character and plastic energy of his subjects. Examining the strong interplay of *all* the forms in this drawing, we can appreciate Kenneth Clark's observation that "here was one of the most sensitive and accurate observers of fact who has ever lived, and one who, as time went on, could immediately find a graphic equivalent for everything he saw."*

Figure 2.41 serves as a useful visual summary of the main points we have been discussing in this chapter. In this drawing we find an emphatic carving by major and secondary planes, the underlying geometric solids these planes create, a rich variety of interjoinings, the sense of firm and fluid segments of form, convincing foreshortening, and clues to the figure's forms revealed by the drapery. Note the heavy, almost water-soaked character of the drapery. And, as this drawing so clearly shows, the term *drapery* can be extended to include such diverse objects as hats, pillows, book pages, and, of course, skin. Rembrandt treats the vestments, tablecloth, chair, and robe with the same kind of inquiry and interpretation as he does the head and hands. Every form in this drawing is structurally lucid and all are depicted in a state of lively complemental interplay. For Rembrandt structural analysis is indeed a key to graphic invention.

Glancing at the drawings in this book, you notice that most of them depict little if any, of a subject's immediate surroundings. Sometimes a few lines or tones suffice to suggest some masses and a sense of space. But even in the most abbreviated of statements about a figure's environment, the quality of the artist's perception does not waver. Artistic freedom does not include the right to disregard a consistency of involvement and intent.

Again, this does not mean that each part of the drawing must be carried to the same degree of completion; drawings which do so are sometimes rather dull. It does mean that in drawing the figure's drapery and surroundings, a single kind and quality of interpretation should be discernable despite differences in the degree of emphasis.

Poussin's drawing *Bacchus and Ariadne*

*Kenneth Clark, *Landscape into Art* (New York: Transatlantic Arts Inc., 1961), pp. 30–31.

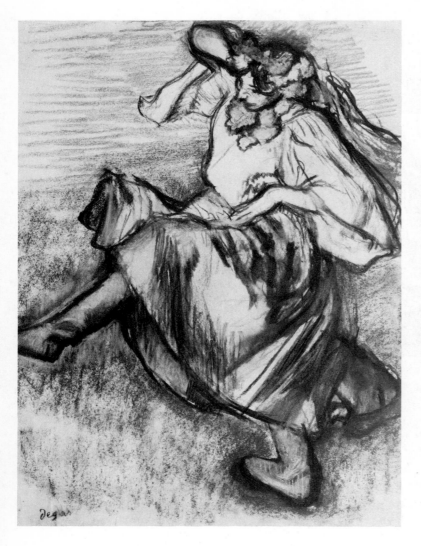

Figure 2.44
EDGAR DEGAS (1834–1917)
Russian Dancer
Pastel. 24 3/8 x 18 in.
The Metropolitan Museum of Art, New York.
Bequest of Mrs. H. O. Havemeyer, 1929.

often more fully drawn than some of the drapery and surrounding environment, in the best drawings nothing is drawn with indifference. Drawings that show a lessening of care to anything within their boundaries suffer a lessening of order and meaning. In the previous chapter it was noted that the best figure drawings hold to a point of view and to a consistent quality of involvement. Here it must be stressed that whatever the point of view, and even though some parts of a drawing are more fully developed than other parts, the consistency of the artist's inquiry and concern must extend to *everything* that constitutes his subject matter.

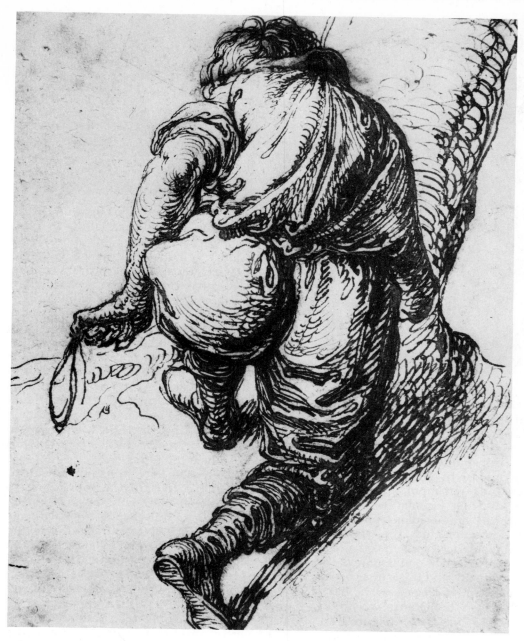

Figure 2.45
JACOB DE GHEYN II (1565–1629)
The Bird Catcher
Pen and brown ink on gray paper. 16.5 x 13 cm.
Museum Boymans-van Beuningen, Rotterdam.

(Figure 2.42) and Millet's etching *The Diggers* (Figure 2.43) show two very different but consistently held attitudes toward structure. Poussin's brief sketch probes the harmonious design possibilities of the subject's essential masses. Here, the structural factor serves a lyrical visual idea. But for Millet the weighty substantiality of the draped figures, their shovels, of the earth itself is a dominant theme. And the way both artists go about calling out these differing qualities is instructive. In Poussin's drawing, planes and masses are airy, open and flowing; in Millet's, they are firm, enclosed and

deliberate. Poussin's lines are animated, the tonal changes are gentle and in flux; Millet's lines are short jabs, the tones fixed and boldly contrasting.

Note how differently they treat the drapery. For Poussin the silky drapery serves as a means of connecting groups of figures; its graceful sweeps embrace the entire configuration in a decorative way. For Millet the drapery is coarse and volume-revealing; it tells about the forms it covers in an evocative way.

In drawing drapery artists often suggest the differences in the weight and texture of dif-

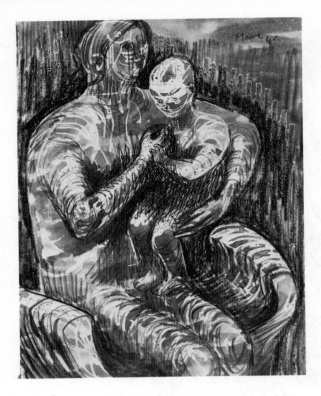

Figure 2.46
HENRY MOORE (1898–)
Study for sculpture "Madonna and Child"
Grease crayon, touches of pen, gray wash
background on white paper. 9 x 7 in.
Courtesy The Fogg Art Museum, Harvard University.
Gift of Meta and Paul J. Sachs.

ferent fabrics. Each material has its own structural character. Silk, cotton, wool, and other fabrics all fold in different ways. Each has its own "style" of accommodating itself to the forms it covers. Depending on the type of material, the snug or loose fit, and the figure's action, the drapery can be an important expressive tool. In Degas' drawing *Russian Dancer* (Figure 2.44), the dancer's animated movements are intensified, not obscured, by the drapery's powerful action. Note that Degas makes a relative distinction in the weight and texture of the blouse, the heavier skirt, and the leather boots. Observe also that hair, as Degas shows, has a drapery-like character. Sometimes, as in de Gheyn's drawing *The Bird Catcher* (Figure 2.45), the drapery carries virtually the entire responsibility for presenting the figure. Here, although only one arm is bare and the blouse and trousers fit loosely, we sense the body's forms and can tell that the figure is an adult, powerfully-built male.

Perhaps the most imposing truth about the figure is its vital substantiality—its presence as living form in space. This appreciation of the figure's spirit and substance has motivated the search for structural truths in realistic imagery, and has provided an avenue of approach for more subjective graphic inventions. An outstanding example is the *Study for Sculpture* by Henry Moore (Figure 2.46). If extracting the structural essentials from the live or imagined model is a kind of abstracting, so is our transposing of these essentials into lines and tones on a flat surface. Abstraction, it seems, is at the heart of any work of art. The best figure draughtsmen are the most adept at recognizing the simultaneity of their marks as referring to both physical facts and to the abstract activities that help enliven the forms.

We have seen how structural considerations, in addition to clarifying volumes, serve to stimulate the abstract activities that enliven the forms. Thus, in this chapter, we have come by way of the structural factor in figure drawing to one of the most important themes of Chapter One, namely, that the best figure drawings are not *re*-presentations, but *equivalent presentations*: graphic organisms that parallel living figures by coming alive in their own terms. An interest in the structural nature of one's subject is the perfect antidote to a fussy concern with detail. Figure drawings that are living graphic organisms emerge from felt perceptions of a subject's structural and dynamic truths, and not from a scrutiny of surfaces. As Henri Matisse put it, "Exactitude is not truth."

SUGGESTED EXERCISES

The following exercises can be done in any order and can be adhered to or adjusted to suit your own needs and curiosities. When an exercise calls for more than one drawing, try to vary the time you spend on each from a minimum of twenty minutes to a maximum of one hour. Use any medium and suitable surface, but avoid the harder graphite (lead) pencils, which promote timidity and tight handling. As you do these exercises, try several combinations of materials and vary the sizes of your drawings. However, avoid making very small-scale drawings. Little drawings tend toward cautious handling and are usually more difficult to control by virtue of their smallness. A minimum size of 10″ × 14″ and a maximum of 18″ × 24″ would be a useful range for these drawings.

1. Make three drawings of your hand. In the first, limit the drawing to simple geometric forms such as the block and cylinder. Show how these forms fit together in a simple, manikin-like manner. In the second drawing, analyze the forms of your hand for the major and secondary planes, relying mainly on line. Where it becomes necessary to use tonalities to clarify various overlappings, use line groups that "ride" upon the flat or curved planes in directions that convey the angle, the "tilt," of the planes. Emphasize the various interjoinings of forms. In the third exercise, draw your gloved (or mittened) hand, stressing the tensions in the fabric produced by the pose. Emphasize the larger forms and actions of your gloved hand. This should be the longest and most fully realized drawing of the three, but avoid fussy rendering of little surface details. Instead, tell more about the forms of the drapery and about the forms they cover. Imagine that a sculptor will use your drawing as a guide for a piece of sculpture. Ask yourself whether or not he could "read" the terrain in your drawing.

2. Rework or redraw several of your figure drawings to show a severe summarizing of the forms into simple geometric solids that are strongly interlocked and gracefully fused. Stress simple form-solutions and simple interjoinings. Emphasize flat and curved planes; at the edges, simple straight and curved lines. This emphasis on straights and curves promotes decision making based on your analysis of the essential nature of each form, plane, and edge. Such drawings are often admirably resolute; they show the strength and authority we associate with clear choices—even when they are wrong! Imagine a light source falling on the forms and simplify the drawing's tones to three values: the white of the page, a light gray, and a dark gray. These drawings need not be fully tonal; use tonalities where you feel they help explain volume and space.

3. Draw several imaginary figures in the manner of Luca Cambiaso (Figures 2.1, 2.5, 2.31). Your drawing should reflect Cambiaso's bold analysis of human forms, rather than his particular technique of drawing them.

4. Rework or redraw several of your life drawings in the manner of Tintoretto's drawing (Figure 2.19). Again, concentrate on the artist's method of analysis, not on his style of drawing.

5. Using Figure 2.25 as a guide or point of departure, devise your own manikin-like system of simple forms and redraw several of your life drawings using these forms to help re-shape and clarify the figure's essential masses. Continue with these drawings, working tonally, until their manikin-like forms become "absorbed" into the tones of the drawing. (Referring to the anatomical illustrations in Chapters Three and Four will help to develop a system of simple forms, and will help you carry these drawings further.)

6. Using the manikin system you have devised in Exercise 5, make several line drawings that show your "figures" in various severely foreshortened positions. Select one of these views and carry it further, using three values and absorbing the manikin forms into the developing figure-forms.

7. Again using your manikin forms developed in Exercise 5, draw several imaginary, simply draped figures. Assume the drapery to be made of a rather heavy material that will produce large but simple folds. You will find that drawing the folds of the drapery will lead you to rely more on values. It is difficult to convey the gradual inclination of a curved plane by a single line. Again, invent a light source, modelling with three values.

8. Using the Ingres drawing (Figure 2.17) as your subject, redraw it three times: first, as if you were high up and saw the figures far below you; second, as if you were lying on the ground just in front of the two figures; and third, as if you were standing in a position somewhat to one side of the figures, where one figure slightly overlaps the other. In all three drawings the forms can be reduced to more simple geometric solids.

9. Using Rembrandt's drawing *St. Augustine in His Study* (Figure 2.41) as a general guide, draw an observed view of a draped figure in an interior. Try to give the sense of firm and fluid masses that show strong rhythmic and tensional behavior. Give the sense of drapery's limp and clinging character to any materials or objects that permit such an interpretation. In so doing, do not lose sight of the need to grasp the essential structural character of all the forms.

10. Redraw Poussin's *Bacchus and Ariadne* (Figure 2.42) in the general manner of Millet's *The Diggers* (Figure 2.43); and redraw the Millet etching in the general manner of the Poussin drawing. You may not be able to "decipher" all of the planes and forms in the Poussin drawing, and should make any changes you wish.

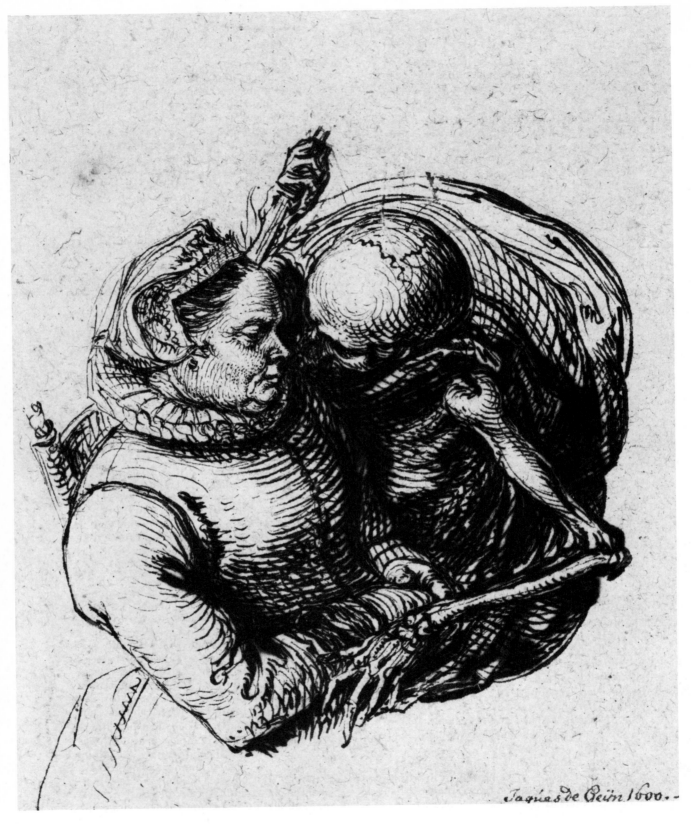

Figure 3.1
JACOB DE GHEYN II (1565–1629)
Allegory of Death
Pen and ink on gray paper. 16 x 13 cm.
Rijksmuseum, Amsterdam.

3

The Anatomical Factor

part one: the skeleton

SOME GENERAL OBSERVATIONS

Structural considerations uncover the essential nature of the figure's masses; anatomical factors explain the inner forms and forces that shape them. The ability to analyze the figure's structure is greatly affected by a knowledge of artistic anatomy, a far simpler study than medical anatomy. The student who disregards the study of anatomy restricts his drawing to a kind of rote recording of bumps and hollows he doesn't really understand. Without scientific information he lacks the means to select from or alter what he sees. He can neither experience nor endow his drawings with the creative freedom and authority that all good figure drawings possess.

No one can state just how much structural analysis is sufficient for good figure drawing, nor prescribe how large or small a part anatomical considerations should play. The structural and anatomical factors are interacting, and their role is determined by our perceptual, tempera-

mental, and aesthetic interests. But because both factors must participate in forming images that come alive, both must be well understood by the art student. It is no accident that the best exponents of figure drawing show a strong working knowledge of anatomy.

A complete exploration of anatomy is, of course, beyond the scope of this book. In this chapter and the next we will examine those anatomical facts of most importance to the artist. But we will do so in a rather unorthodox way. The approach to anatomical matters we take here is an attempt to bridge the often troublesome gaps between the clinically precise anatomy text, the living model, and the demands of creative figure drawing.

Too often the art student is unable to apply his knowledge of anatomy to the living individual before him. Most anatomical illustrations are dispassionate diagrams of the human mechanism. Their precision is needed to pinpoint articulations, insertions, and so on. Such illustrations are not intended to convey

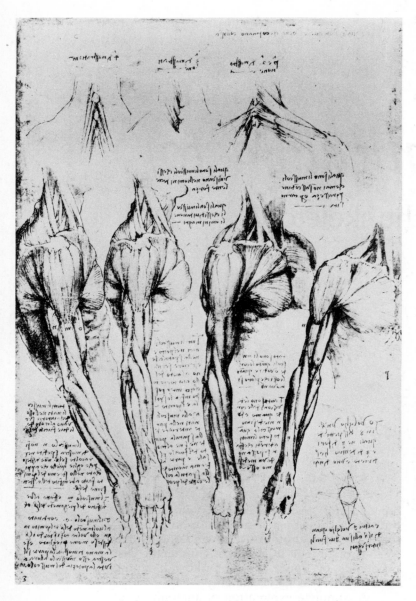

Figure 3.2
LEONARDO DA VINCI (1452–1519)
Myology of Shoulder Region
Black Chalk. 29 x 19 cm.
Windsor Castle, Royal Library.
By gracious permission of Her Majesty the Queen.

accurate and concise presentation of the figure's measurable and mechanical facts. Such texts at best are indispensable sources of much useful information, but they do not discuss the role this information may play in figure drawing. The student is still left wondering for what purposes and to what degree such knowledge is to be used.

May anatomical facts be intentionally ignored or altered? Should the student clarify or exaggerate bones or muscles that the figure only hints at? Will a concern with anatomical detail and accuracy intrude on the drawing's design and mood? How can anatomy play a part in the drawing's visual and expressive life—its dynamics? In not addressing these important questions the traditional anatomy book unintentionally presents a danger for the art student: it implies that anatomical clarity and accuracy are graphic goals. Although specific anatomical data is important, it is intimidating. Some students feel their creativity stifled by the demands that anatomical accuracy imposes. In studying from a text exclusively concerned with facts of a highly specific nature, the student often becomes self-conscious about making any changes. His initial, intuitive grasp of the figure's dynamics seem not to "fit" the facts, not to be a part of the figure at all. But, armed with an awareness of anatomy's possibilities as a source of creative invention, as a tool and servant of interpretive interests, the student can wisely pursue his study of this vital information.

Our purpose in this and the following chapter is twofold: to examine the more important aspects of the figure's skeletal and muscular systems, and to consider some ways in which a knowledge of anatomy can benefit our perceptual understanding of the figure and serve our creative intentions.

THE SKELETON

If the beginner in life drawing regards the skeleton at all, it is probably at those places in the figure where it presses against the surface, markedly affecting the terrain. Even then, these passages are only tolerated as complicating, lumpy interruptions of the otherwise smooth-flowing forms. They disconcert the student. He knows they represent parts of forms beneath the skin, but has no way of knowing their structure, function, scale, or, consequently, their representational importance or dynamic potential.

the living spirit of human form or to suggest anatomy's creative potential. There have been notable exceptions. Many of da Vinci's anatomical drawings suggest the figure's provocative dynamics. For example, in his muscle study, *Myology of the Shoulder Region* (Figure 3.2), we sense da Vinci's response to visual and expressive energies as well as to the anatomical aspects of human form. But most contemporary anatomy texts do not attempt more than an

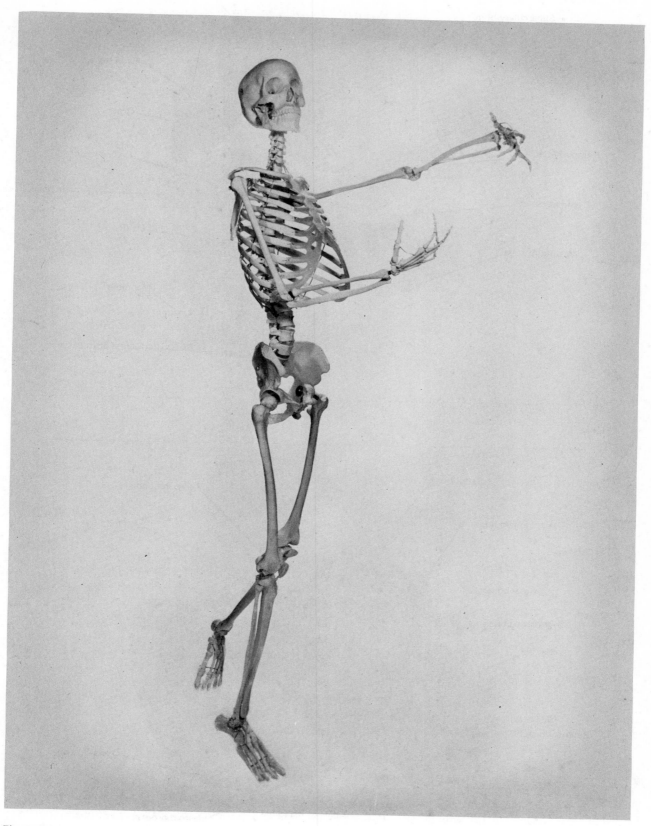

Figure 3.3

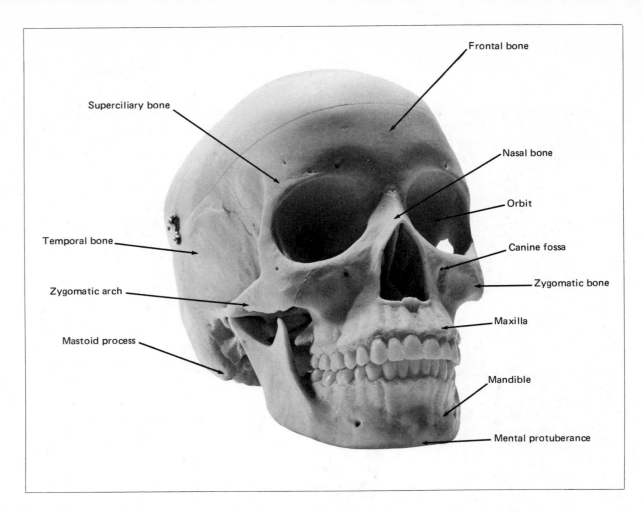

Frontal bone

Superciliary bone

Nasal bone

Orbit

Temporal bone

Canine fossa

Zygomatic arch

Zygomatic bone

Mastoid process

Maxilla

Mandible

Mental protuberance

Figure 3.4

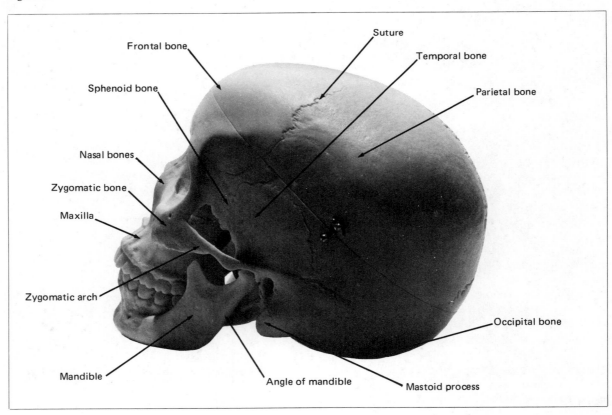

Frontal bone

Suture

Temporal bone

Sphenoid bone

Parietal bone

Nasal bones

Zygomatic bone

Maxilla

Zygomatic arch

Occipital bone

Mandible

Angle of mandible

Mastoid process

But the master figure draughtsman welcomes this evidence of the skeleton throughout the figure. He realizes the structural importance of the skeleton as both an armature and protective container for the figure's muscles and organs. Its armature-like nature aids his understanding of a figure's gesture as well as its proportions; its large, container-like forms help him establish the major masses of the torso and head. The skeleton's influence on the figure's forms helps the artist understand the pressures, weights, and tensions acting from below on the figure's container of skin. In some passages, such as the shoulders or hips, the planar character of various bones help the artist to better understand the interjoinings of various surface form-units. Additionally, the recurring presence of hard skeletal forms "at the surface" helps him explain the skeleton's role as a firm framework for the supple drapery of the figure's softer tissues.

THE SKULL

The skull consists of twenty-two bones (Figure 3.4). All but the jawbone, or *mandible*, are connected to each other by suture (dovetailed) joinings. For the artist the skull can be regarded as comprised of two major masses: the ovoid brain case, or *cranium*, consisting of eight bones, and the block-like formation constituted by the facial bones, numbering fourteen. Of the eight cranial bones, six are of structural importance: the *frontal*, the two *parietals*, the two *temporals*, and the *occipital*. The *sphenoid*, located mainly on the underside of the cranium, is of some interest only at the temples, where it appears to be an extension of the temporal bone. Of the fourteen facial bones, only the two *zygomatics*, the two *maxillae*, the two *nasal*, and the already mentioned *mandible* are of visual and structural importance.

Several planes and masses of particular importance in the front view are: the convex plane of the frontal bone (forehead); the small, inclined planes of the nasal bones, forming a short base for the projecting cartilage underlying the nose; the blocky masses of the zygomatic, or cheek bones, forming pronounced overhanging ledges; the curved and forward tilting plane of the maxilla, or upper jaw; and the squared-off "horseshoe" of the mandible. Also important are the ridges of the rather squarish eye sockets, which, in the living model, are in evidence both above and below the eye.

Other landmarks often visible in the fleshed forms are the *superciliary ridge*, a slight thickening in the outer, upper corner of the eye socket; that segment of the lower ridge alongside the nasal bone; and the *canine fossa*, a shallow depression below the eye socket.

From the side view the shallow indents of the temporal and sphenoid bones (temples), when overlaid by muscle, produce the rather flat planes of the side of the head. The contour of the cranium is accounted for by the frontal, parietal, and occipital bones. Below the temporal bone and joined with the outer ridge of the eye socket, a horizontal ridge of bone called the *zygomatic arch* connects the temporal to the zygomatic bone. In this view, too, the forward thrust of the maxilla and the angular nature of the mandible are substantial influences on the living forms. Note that the occipital bone extends backward somewhat, and that its *mastoid process* provides a small protuberance.

Understanding the skull's basic structure is essential in constructing the head in its various positions (Figure 3.5). Unlike the limbs or the rib cage and pelvis which are overlaid by substantial muscular and fatty tissues, the skull, even in heavily fleshed heads, exerts a strong influence on the surface forms (Figure 3.6). This is particularly true of the cranium's mass, whose egg-like form is always evident, whether the head is viewed from the front, side, or top. In Lillie's drawing, *Study of a Woman's Head* (Figure 3.7), the artist's appreciation of the skull's influence on the living forms is felt in the strong linear rhythms created by lines "chasing" each other along ridges and valleys, and in the rugged carving and interjoining of form-units. Note the subtle suggestion of the shape and downward tilt of the eye sockets, and of the underlying presence of the zygomatic, nasal, and maxilla bones. Note, too, the influence of the angular mandible on the drawing of the jaw. Here, the factors of structure and anatomy are strongly interrelated.

THE SPINAL COLUMN

The spinal column, comprised of twenty-four movable vertebrae and two immobile segments—the *sacrum* and *coccyx*—connects the three large, bony masses of the skeleton: the skull, rib cage, and pelvis. The vertebral column emerges from its base in the pelvis and, tapering as it rises, undergoes four curves along its route to the base of the skull. The four curves,

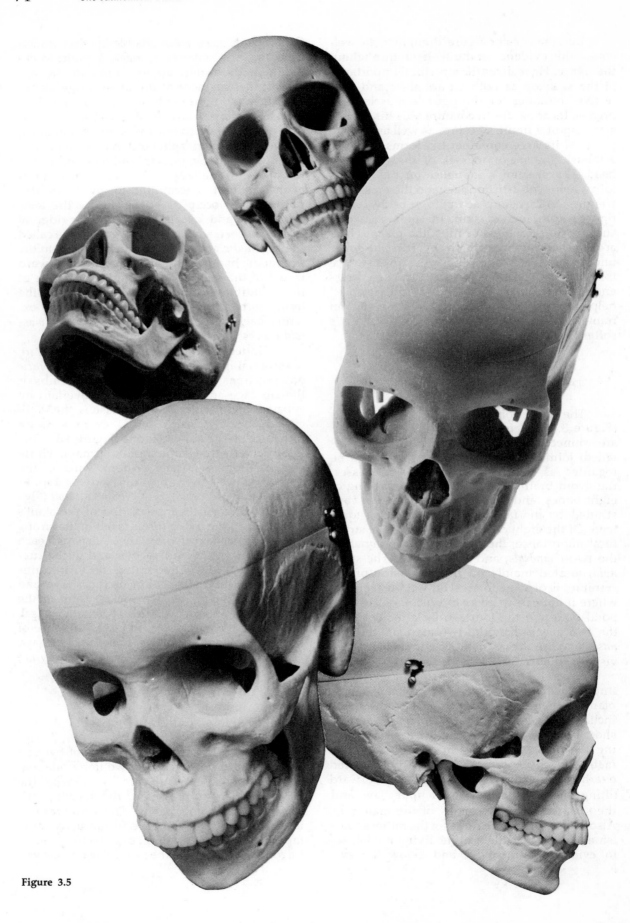

Figure 3.5

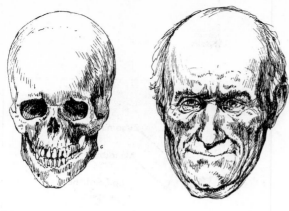

Figure 3.6

as can be seen in Figures 3.8, 3.9, and 3.10, are convex in the seven *cervical* vertebrae, concave in the twelve *thoracic* vertebrae, convex in the five *lumbar* vertebrae, and concave in the sacrum and coccyx.

Although the spine represents the central axis of the torso, and tall columns of deep muscle flank it on either side, making a deep, vertical valley all along the back, its presence at the surface is intermittent and not often pronounced. The central spurs of the spinal column (Figure 3.10) protrude mainly at the base of the neck, at the upper part of the thoracic region, and, when the back is bent, as in stooping, throughout the lumbar region. In most poses the *sacral*

triangle, a flattish, dimpled area marking the location of the sacrum is clearly evident.

Because the spinal column connects the skeleton's large masses, major pivotal or bending movements of this moderately flexible chain of vertebrae can occur only between these masses. Thus, the large bony masses are moved by the movements of the vertebrae between them. Movements of the head are initiated in the cervical vertebrae, and movements of the thorax and pelvis, in the lumbar vertebrae. The spine's construction, in addition to its rotating and bending actions between the large masses, also allows for a slight curving of the thoracic vertebrae in extreme bending of the rib cage to the side.

THE RIB CAGE

Like an egg small end up and somewhat wider in the front than in the side view, the thoracic cage is comprised of twelve pairs of ribs, the twelve thoracic vertebrae with which the ribs articulate, and the *sternum,* or breast bone (Figure 3.11). The ribs swing downward

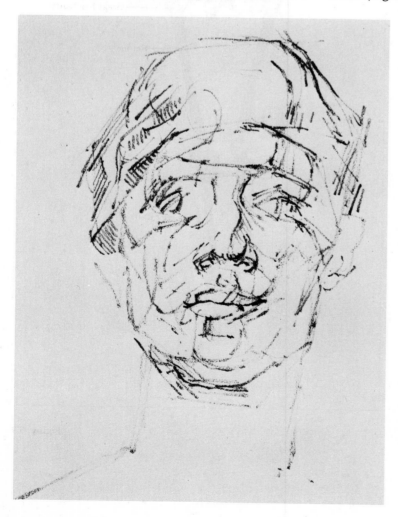

Figure 3.7
LLOYD LILLIE (1932–)
Study of a Woman's Head
Pencil. 9 x 12 in.
Courtesy of the artist.

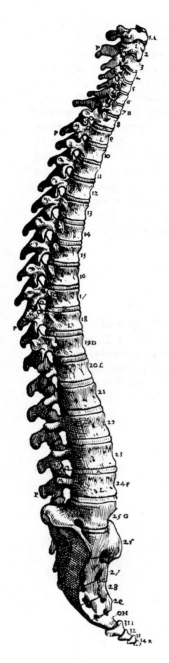

Figure 3.8
ANDREAS VESALIUS (1514–1564)
Plate 10 from *De humani corporis fabrica*, Book I
Engraving.
Courtesy of the New York Academy of Medicine.

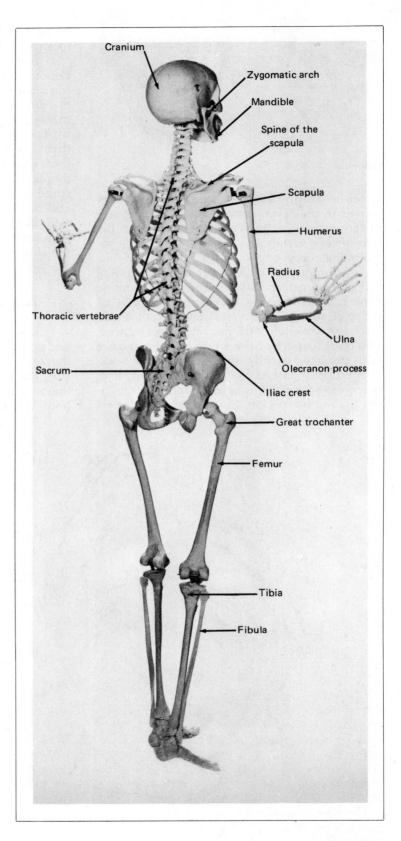

Figure 3.9

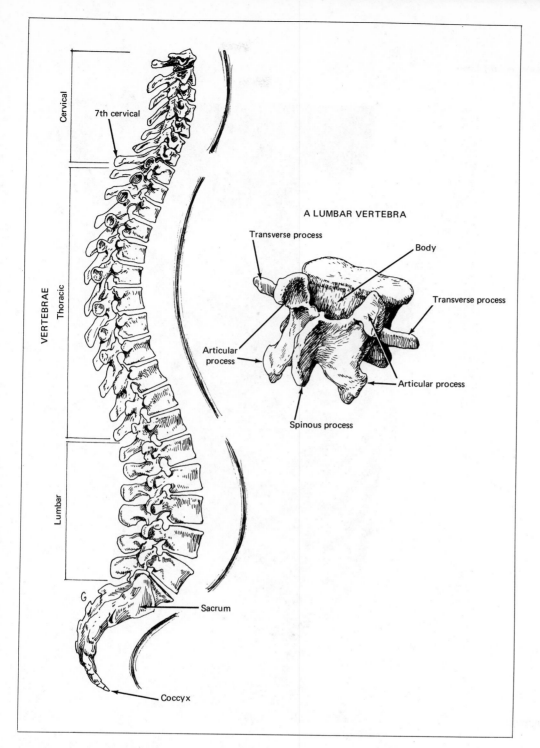

Figure 3.10

Cervical

7th cervical

VERTEBRAE

Thoracic

Lumbar

Sacrum

G

Coccyx

A LUMBAR VERTEBRA

Transverse process

Body

Transverse process

Articular process

Articular process

Spinous process

and out from either side of the vertebral column for a short distance, then turn sharply to curve toward the front, still turned downward. Their upward "homing in" on the sternum is completed by extensions of cartilage. The ribs themselves do not turn up toward the sternum. Counting downward, the eighth rib marks the widest point of the rib cage from the front view. Because in the back view the sharp forward turn of the ribs occurs at about the same point in each rib, there is a discernible change in the direction of the ribs along a slightly curved verti-

cal "line." These lines, marking the abutment of the planes formed by the ribs' sharp turn, are called the *angles of the ribs*. With the arms at rest, the inner edge of the scapula (shoulder blade) falls into a rough alignment with this angle (Figure 3.12). The resulting flattish construction of the back of the rib cage, still evident in the fleshed figure, is unique to man and accounts for his ability to lie "flat on his back."

The upper seven pairs of ribs, called *true ribs*, are directly attached to the sternum by individual straps of costal cartilage. Of the lower

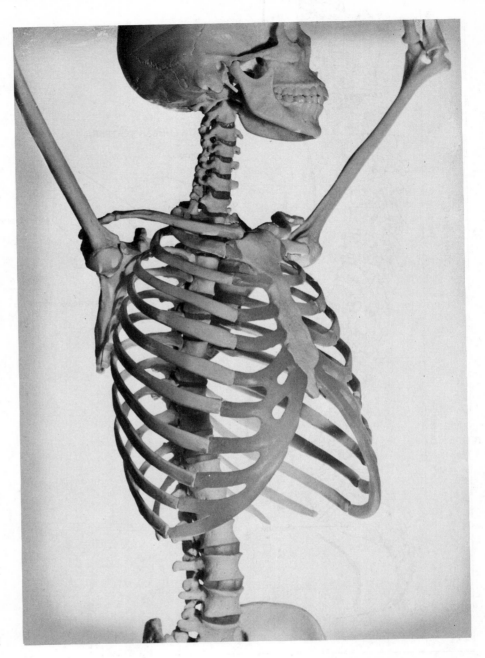

Figure 3.11

five pair, called *false ribs*, the cartilaginous straps of the eighth, ninth, and tenth ribs all join to form a common, thick band that connects to the lowest part of the sternum. The resulting thick rim of cartilage forms a V-shaped opening (wider in the male torso) in the lower half of the rib cage, called the *thoracic arch*, a frequently pronounced landmark in the fleshed figure. The last two pairs of ribs, called *floating ribs*, are smaller in length and terminate well within the body, making no sternal contact.

The dagger-shaped sternum, viewed from the side, tilts obliquely downward and forward from its highest point at the pit of the throat. It is about seven inches in length and is comprised of three fused segments. Each of the segments is tilted to a slightly different degree, turning more sharply downward in the lower two segments. The sternum is widest in the uppermost segment, the *manubrium*, notched on either side to receive the clavicles (collar bones), and notched at the top to form part of the familiar indentation of the pit of the throat (Figure 3.13). The *body*, or central segment of the sternum,

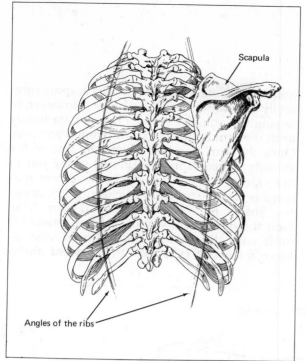

Scapula

Angles of the ribs

Figure 3.12

shaped, bony plate with a handle-like projection, its spine, near the top. Its medial (nearer to the figure's midline) edge is nearly vertical, its lateral (further from the midline) edge is markedly oblique, and its upper edge is nearly horizontal. Near the top, its projecting spine, beginning at the medial edge, rises above the horizontal upper edge and, at its extremity, turns sharply forward to meet the outer end of the clavicle. This outer end is called the acromion process. In meeting, the acromion process is located just a little beneath the outer tip

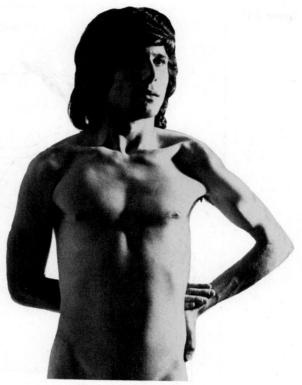

Figure 3.13

like the manubrium, is indented along both sides to receive the cartilage extensions of the ribs. In length, the body is almost twice that of the manubrium. The lowest and smallest segment of the sternum, the *xiphoid process*, is not often seen in the fleshed figure. Its tip marks the top of the rib cage's V-shaped, cartilage-rimmed hollow.

THE SHOULDER GIRDLE

From an overhead view the bones of the shoulder girdle look rather like a cupid's bow. The bow is formed by the S-shaped *clavicles* in front and the *spinal column* and *acromion process* of the *scapula* in back. The scapula is a trowel-

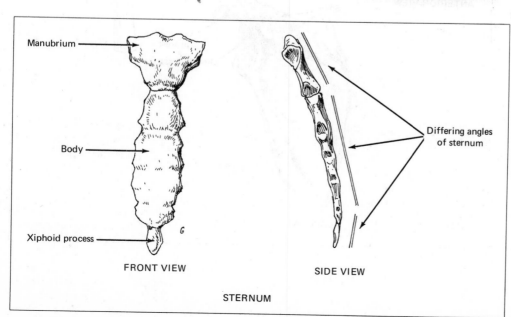

Manubrium

Body

Xiphoid process

Differing angles of sternum

FRONT VIEW SIDE VIEW

STERNUM

of the clavicle (Figure 3.14). The height of the scapulas (about 6½ to 7 inches) equals their distance apart at their pointed lower ends. At the outer, upper edge of the scapula, just below its junction with the clavicle, is the *glenoid fossa*, a rounded socket which receives the head of the *humerus*, the bone of the upper arm.

Because the scapulas are attached to the skeleton only at their junction with the clavicles, they give the shoulder girdle great freedom of movement, as when the shoulders lift up to "encase" the neck between them. Being slightly

hollowed on its inner surface, the scapula rides easily over the cone of the rib cage. However, in raising the arm, the scapula remains stationary until the arm approaches a horizontal position. Once the arm is raised above the line of the shoulders the scapula begins its swing out to the side of the rib cage. This movement outward is clearly shown in Michelangelo's drawing *Studies for the Libyan Sibyl* (Figure 3.15). Note the spine of the scapula turning forward to meet with the clavicle. On the right side, although the arm is raised, its backward move-

Figure 3.14

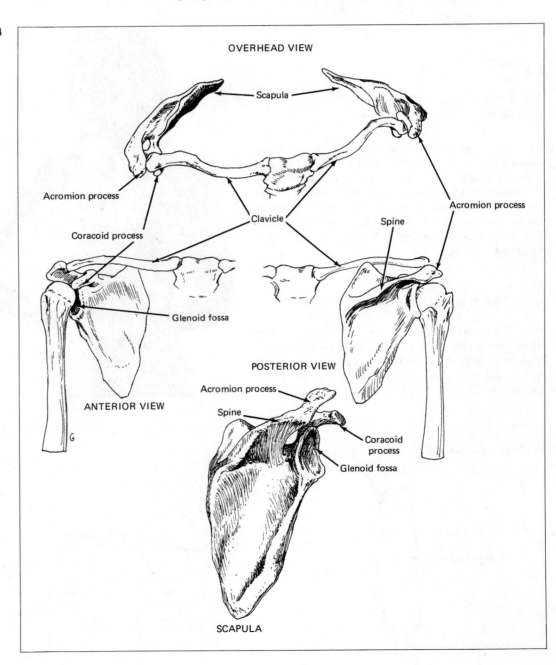

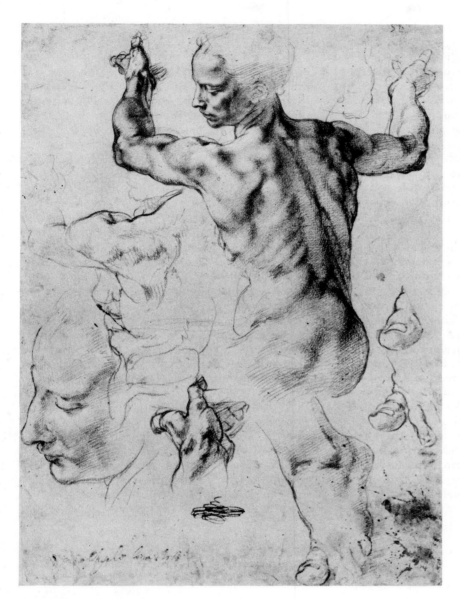

Figure 3.15
MICHELANGELO BUONARROTI (1475–1564)
Studies for "The Libyan Sibyl"
Red chalk. 11 3/8 x 8 3/8 in.
The Metropolitan Museum of Art, New York.
Purchase, 1924 Joseph Pulitzer Bequest.

ment brings the scapula nearer to the spine, causing deep muscles (the rhomboids) to bulge into the vertical folds seen on that side.

In this remarkable anatomical study, Michelangelo's knowledge of the interworking of bone and muscle are clearly expressed by his structural vocabulary, that is, by his ability to graphically communicate the volume of specific form-units and their interjoinings. Evident here, too, is a sensitive understanding of the design—the harmonies and contrasts—of human anatomy. Note, too, the expressive power of these heroic forms; an engaging contrast between the energy suggested in their athletic development and the delicate modelling by Michelangelo that "caresses" them into being. Here again is an example of the four factors brilliantly interworking.

THE PELVIS

The pelvis is the single bony mass of the lower trunk. It surfaces in only two places: at the base of the spine (the sacral triangle) and at the hips, where the *anterior superior iliac spines* are visible in the front and side views (Figure 3.16). These bony projections, especially visible in the female figure (Figure 3.17), are at the leading edge of the *iliac crests*, the thickened rims of the wing-like hip bones which, with the sacrum, form the basin-like container for the intestines and reproductive organs. In very lean figures certain poses reveal most of the iliac crests.

There are notable differences of proportion between the male and female pelvis. In the female the pelvis is wider, shallower, and less massive in bulk, the pubic arch more rounded and wider, the sacrum shorter and wider, and the pelvic cavity larger. The male pelvis is thicker and more angular overall, and, from the side view, appears to tilt forward to a lesser degree than the female pelvis does (Figure 3.18).

Although deeply embedded in the musculature and fatty tissues of the lower trunk, the pelvis exerts its blocky influence on the living forms. Kollwitz, in her drawing *Two Nudes* (Figure 3.19), makes use of the angular character of the pelvis to "shore up" her fluid handling of the figure's forms, and to bolster a design theme based on straight and curved lines. Note how often the skeleton "surfaces" in these brief sketches.

THE ARM

There are three major long bones in the arm. The longest and thickest is the *humerus*, the bone of the upper arm; in the lower arm, the *radius* and *ulna* are roughly parallel, with the ulna positioned slightly higher. In the fleshed figure the *medial* and *lateral epicondyles* of the humerus are generally visible, as are the protuberances at the extremities of both the radius and ulna (Figure 3.20).

A versatile joint at the elbow allows for bending and rotating actions by the lower arm. In bending, the ulna moves round the *trochlea*, a spool-like ending on the humerus. In rotating actions the rounded end of the radius revolves within the radial notch of the ulna and rotates upon the *capitum* of the humerus in a ball-and-socket manner (Figure 3.21). The opposite action occurs at the wrist, where the ulna is the bone that rotates and the radius engages in bending actions. When the palm of the hand is turned face up (supine), the radius and ulna are parallel; when the palm is turned face down (prone), the radius crosses over the ulna (Figure 3.21). At the wrist, the rounded head of the ulna (little finger side) is visible in the prone position; when the hand is supinated, it disappears. At the elbow, a posterior view of the extended arm shows the *olecranon process*, a blocky mass at the end of the ulna, to be in a rough horizontal alignment with the medial and lateral epicondyles of the humerus. When the arm is bent the three protuberances form a

Figure 3.16

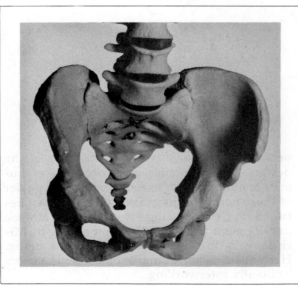
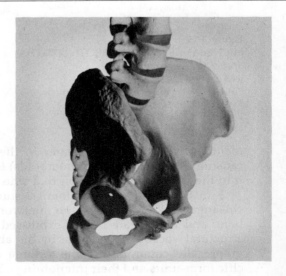

Figure 3.17

V-like arrangement, and the olecranon process becomes much more pronounced in form (Figure 3.22). At the shoulder, the head of the humerus often shows as an inner bulge in the mass of the deltoid muscle (Figure 3.23).

There are twenty-seven bones in the skeleton of the wrist and hand. In the wrist, eight *carpal* bones form a ball-like mound just below the heads of the ulna and radius. Embedded in the palm are the five *metacarpal* bones. The heads of these slender, curved bones (the knuckles) are visible when the hand forms a fist; when the fingers are extended, these protuberances all but disappear. There are fourteen *phalanges* (finger bones). Of the three bones in each finger, those nearest the wrist (the proximal phalanges) are longest; those next (the medial phalanges) are two-thirds the length of the proximal phalanges; and the bones of the fingertips (the distal phalanges) are two-thirds the length of the medial phalanges (Figure 3.24). The thumb is comprised of only two phalanges, the joint between them falling on a line with the metacarpal heads.

Most beginners draw the hands (and feet) too small. Actually, in length, the hand measures about four-fifths that of the head. Likewise, in width, the hand covers most of the face. When the fingers are extended and held together the outer edges of the index and ring fingers line up with the edges of the arm at the wrist (Figure 3.24).

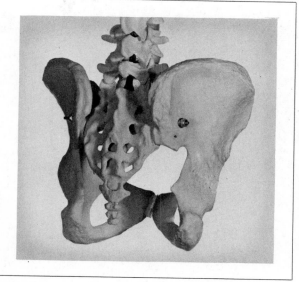

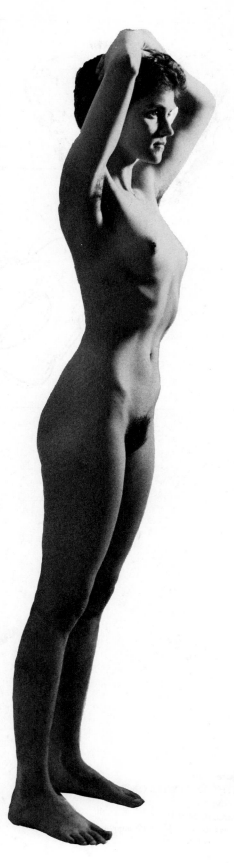

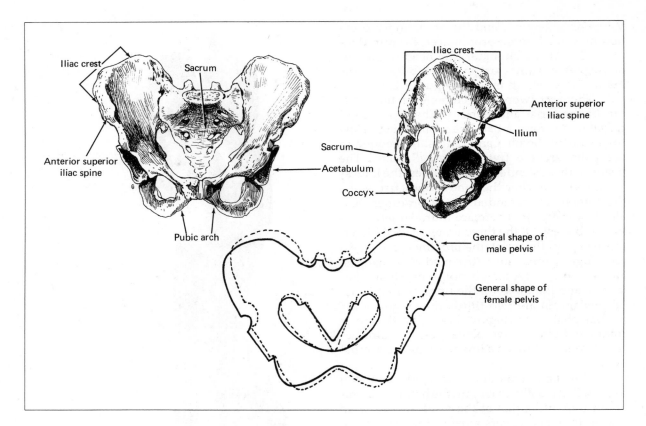

Figure 3.18

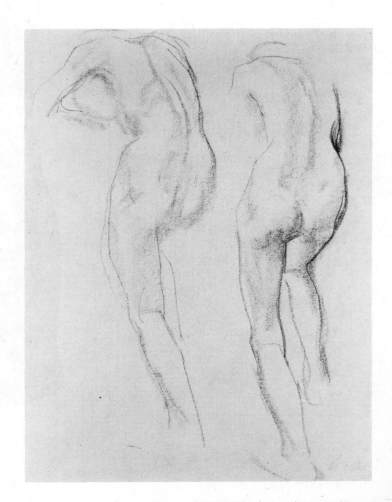

Figure 3.19
KÄTHE KOLLWITZ (1867–1945)
Two Nudes
Charcoal. 24 x 19 in.
National Gallery of Art, Washington, D.C.
Rosenwald Collection.

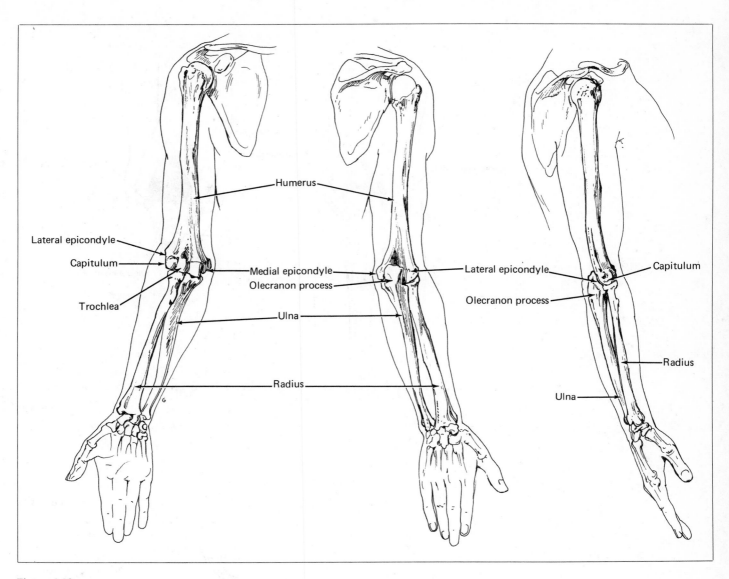

Humerus

Lateral epicondyle

Capitulum

Trochlea

Medial epicondyle
Olecranon process

Ulna

Radius

Lateral epicondyle

Olecranon process

Capitulum

Radius

Ulna

Figure 3.20

Figure 3.21

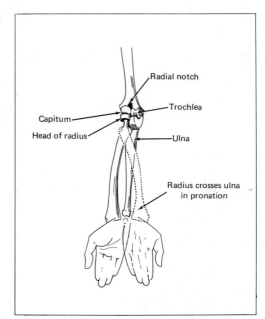

Radial notch

Capitum

Head of radius

Trochlea

Ulna

Radius crosses ulna
in pronation

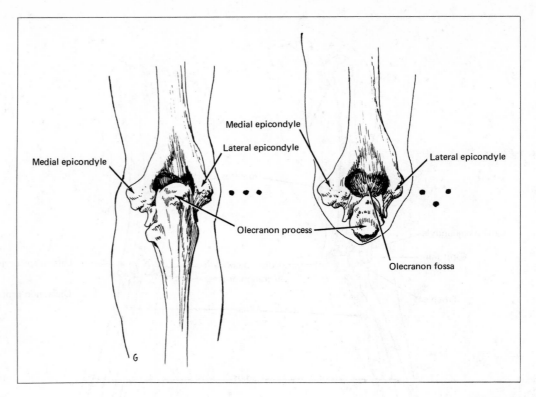

Medial epicondyle

Medial epicondyle

Lateral epicondyle

Lateral epicondyle

Olecranon process

Olecranon fossa

Figure 3.22

Figure 3.23

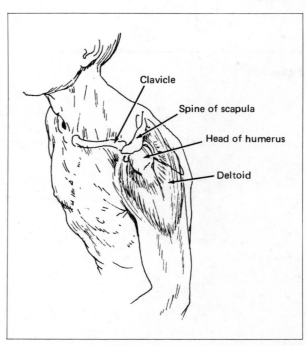

Clavicle

Spine of scapula

Head of humerus

Deltoid

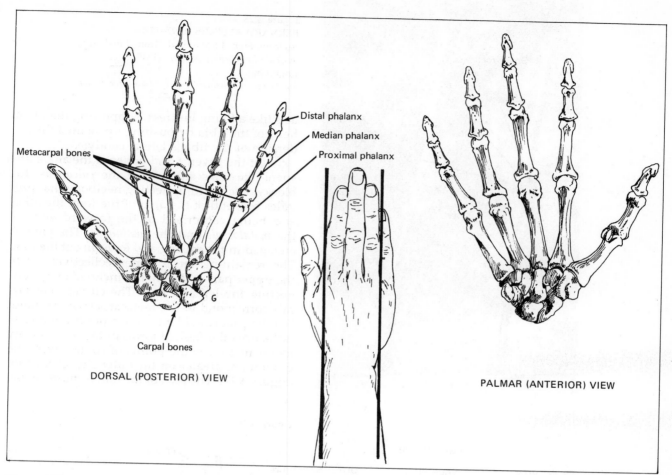

Metacarpal bones

Distal phalanx
Median phalanx
Proximal phalanx

Carpal bones

DORSAL (POSTERIOR) VIEW

PALMAR (ANTERIOR) VIEW

Figure 3.24

THE LEG

There are four bones in the leg and twenty-six in the foot. In the upper leg, the *femur*, the longest bone of the skeleton, provides the only bony joining between the torso and the lower limb. At the knee is the *patella* (kneecap), a roughly triangular, shield-like bone. In the lower leg are the *tibia* and *fibula*, in a fixed, parallel position (Figure 3.25).

The femur is visible in the area of the hip, where the *great trochanter*, a blocky outcrop of bone, shields the femur's slender neck and head; and also at the knee, where the medial and lateral epicondyles are visible in the fleshed figure. The femur's rounded head is received by the hollowed *acetabulum* of the pelvis in a ball-and-socket joint permitting a considerable freedom of movement of the upper leg. Seen from the front, the two femurs incline downward to meet at the knees; seen from the side,

the femur describes a subtle convex curve (Figure 3.26). At the broad, lower base of the femur the medial and lateral *condyles* articulate with the tibia. The femur's *patellar surface*, a smooth depression between the condyles, permits the patella to move in straightening the leg. The patella is always a pronounced landmark in the straightened leg, when the leg is bent, the patella "settles in" among the protuberances of the femur and tibia, becoming almost lost to view.

Only the tibia articulates with the lower end of the femur, its broad, flat head meeting with the femur's equally broad base. The tibia's shaft, triangular in cross section, produces a long medial plane and ridge at the surface, the familiar shinbone. One of the few places in the figure where the bone lies beneath the skin unprotected by muscular tissue, the shinbone is a prominent landmark in the lower leg. The fibula

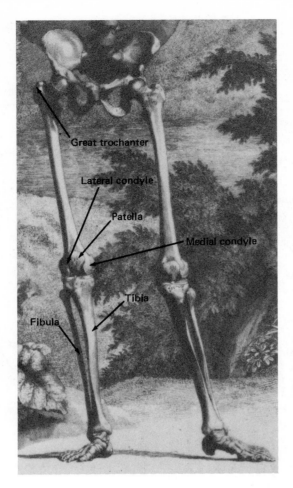

Figure 3.25
BERNARD ALBINUS (1697–1770)
Skeleton, Front View (detail), from *Tabula sceleti et
musculorum corporis humani* (1747).
Engraving.
The Francis A. Countway Library of Medicine, Boston.

acts like a flying buttress, supporting the broad
head of the tibia by pushing up against the underside of the tibia's lateral condyle.

Of the seven *tarsal* bones at the ankle, the
spool-like *talus* sits astride the *calcaneus*, the
blocky, backward projecting heelbone that provides one end of the arch of the foot, the other
end being comprised of the forward ends of
the *metatarsals* and the *phalanges*. The talus is
engaged in the raising and lowering of the foot.
The remaining tarsal bones collectively form
the upper part of the ankle's inclined ramp connecting the leg and foot. The curved metatarsals correspond to the metacarpals of the hand,
but their more evident curve more emphatically
influences the fleshed forms of the foot. As any
footprint shows, the points of contact with the
ground are greater on the outer side of the foot
(Figure 3.27). The arch of the foot is more visible

Figure 3.26

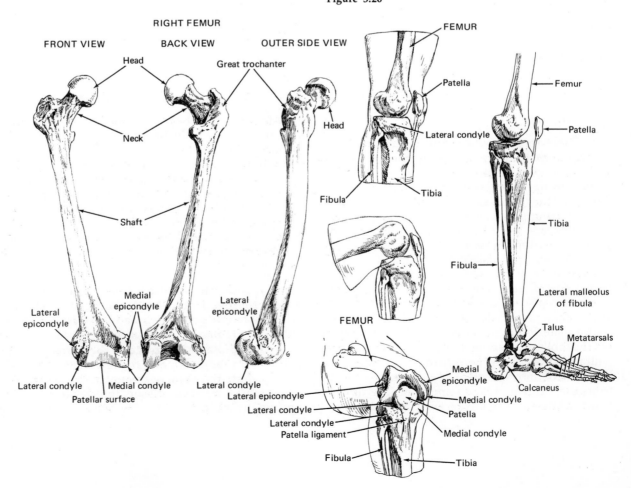

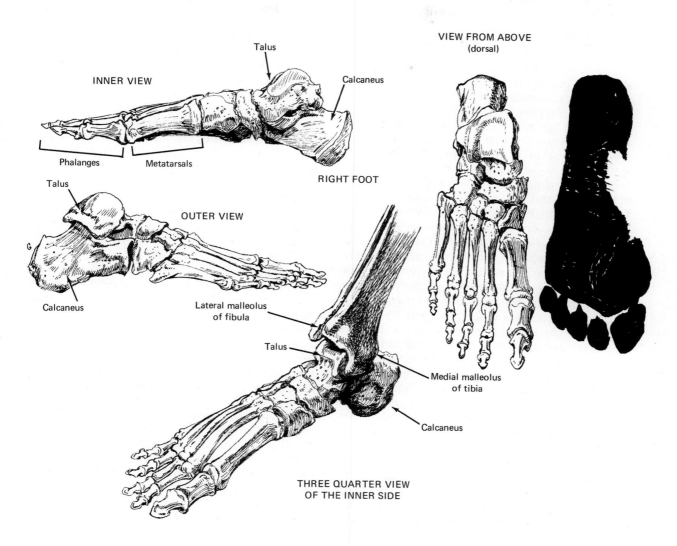

Talus

Calcaneus

INNER VIEW

Phalanges   Metatarsals

RIGHT FOOT

Talus

OUTER VIEW

Calcaneus

Lateral malleolus
of fibula

Talus

VIEW FROM ABOVE
(dorsal)

Medial malleolus
of tibia

Calcaneus

THREE QUARTER VIEW
OF THE INNER SIDE

Figure 3.27

Figure 3.28

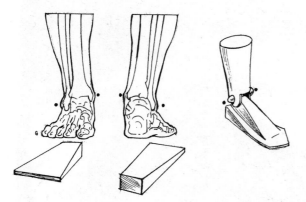

on the inner side view, the form of the foot rising almost vertically on that side, and its base
lifted from the ground between the metatarsals
and the calcaneus. A sizable protuberance produced by the *medial malleolus* of the tibia marks
the juncture of the tibia and the talus. On the
outer side the foot is flat upon the ground all
along the base, its form rising at a marked angle.
In the front view the protuberance of the *lateral
malleolus* of the fibula can be seen to be lower
than its counterpart on the inner side. The foot
is narrower and higher at the heel, wider and
lower at the toes, its essential mass being wedge-
like (Figure 3.28).

SKELETAL PROPORTIONS

No system of measurements can replace sensitive perceptual inquiry. Any system of skeletal measurements is of limited value since it refers to varying lengths of parts seen in the same plane, as when the figure is standing at attention. Knowing that the femur is twice the length of the skull is less helpful when the upper leg is seen in severe foreshortening; and the fact that the humerus is half again the length of the radius and ulna may confuse the beginner who observes the reverse to be the case (Figure 3.29). However, familiarity with certain relationships of scale and location *is* often useful in clarifying what is observed, and especially in guiding what is invented. In any pose, a prior knowledge of the skeleton's proportions can assist perception but should never dictate to it. For example, in drawing the figure in Figure 3.29, knowing that the foot is almost as long as the lower arm (from the elbow to the wrist), or that the length of the rib cage is half again that of the pelvis helps establish relationships where parts *are* more or less parallel to our line of sight. When parts are *foreshortened*, as the upper legs are here, knowing their length relative to other parts serves as a guide in modelling them so as to appear in proportion.

The measurements given below should be regarded as general, not precise. Several differing canons of proportion have been devised in the past. Some, like the heroic proportions of Michelangelo's *Adam* (see Figure 1.14) or those used by the Mannerists such as Pontormo to elongate the figure (Figure 3.30), were intentionally designed to endow the figure with superhuman qualities. Other canons, resulting in the more "plebian" proportions of the figures by Goya (see Figure 1.22) or Pascin (Figure 3.31) were necessary for their more realistic goals. The proportions offered here represent *average* calculations. But we should bear in mind that human adults may vary from less than five feet, to almost seven feet in height; they may be inherently stocky or lean, and may be powerfully or subtly muscled. More important, we should recognize that the artist, unlike the anthropologist, does better to support his perceptions with intuition than with calipers.

The traditional unit of measure in the skeleton is the skull. The average figure is about seven and one-half skull-lengths, rarely less than seven or more than eight. In both the male and female (Figure 3.32), measuring one skull-length down from the skull strikes a point at the tip of the xyphoid process in front and just above the lower end of the scapula in back. Measuring one more skull-length down strikes a point just below the highest point of the iliac crest in the male skeleton, and just at the highest point of the iliac crest in the female skeleton. Another skull-length down strikes a point about two inches below the great trochanter in both the male and female skeletons, and just at the carpal bones when the arm is held alongside the body. As Figure 3.32 shows, each of the remaining three and one-half skull-lengths falls

Figure 3.29

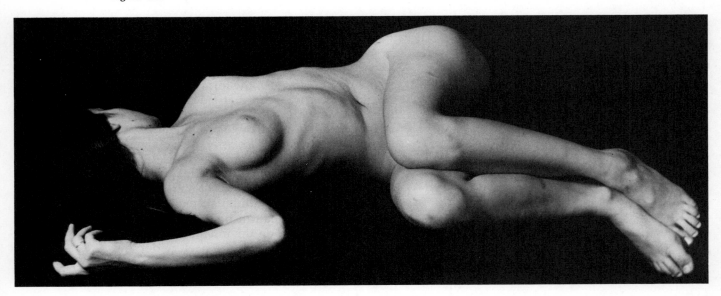

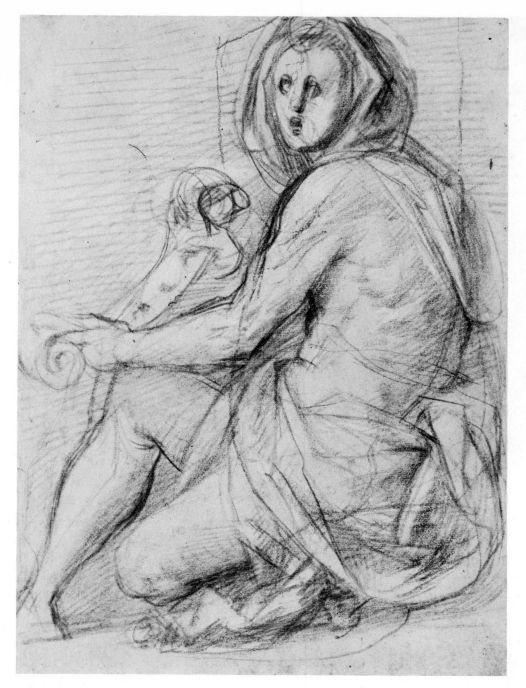

Figure 3.30
Copy after the *Sibyl* of
JACOPO DA PONTORMO (1494–1556)
Red crayon on buff paper. 11 1/4 x 8 1/8 in.
Courtesy The Fogg Art Museum, Harvard University.
Bequest of Charles A. Loeser.

between, rather than on, useful landmarks. However, this changes if we now begin to measure skull-lengths from the base of the foot upwards. The first length brings us to a point halfway to the knee, a second measure strikes the patella, a third evenly divides the femur, and a fourth strikes the top of the great trochanter.

It is useful to know which bones are roughly the same in length. As Figure 3.33 shows, the sternum, scapula, clavicle, pelvis, ulna, radius, and skeleton of the foot all measure just over or under one skull-length. The bones of the wrist and hand are about three-fourths of a skull-length, as is the sacrum and coccyx together. The rib cage, humerus, tibia, and fibula are likewise similar in length, about one and one-half skull-units.

Some additional proportions worth noting

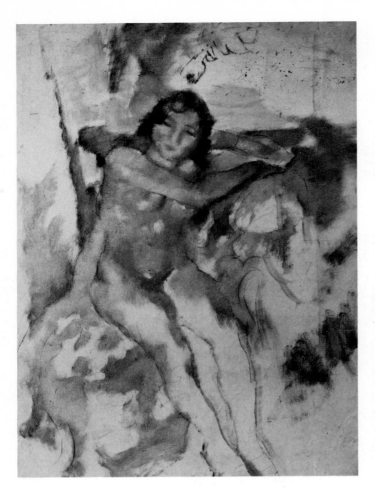

Figure 3.31
JULES PASCIN (1885–1930)
Marion (1929)
Charcoal and oil on canvas. 92 x 73 cm.
Musée des Beaux Arts, Grenoble.
Gift of Hermine David and Lucie Krohg, 1937.

are illustrated in Figure 3.34. It is one skull-length from the seventh cervical vertebra to the lower tip of the scapula, and one skull-length from that point to the iliac crest. Another length down strikes a point just below the great trochanter. The midpoint in the male skeleton is just at the pubic bone; in the female it is slightly above the pubic bone. Both feet placed together measure one skull-length when seen from the front view.

The three anatomical plates by the famous Renaissance anatomist Albinus (Figures 3.35, 3.36, 3.37) show in accurate detail the skeletal forms, proportions, and locations discussed in this chapter, and serve as a visual reference and summary.

Figure 3.32

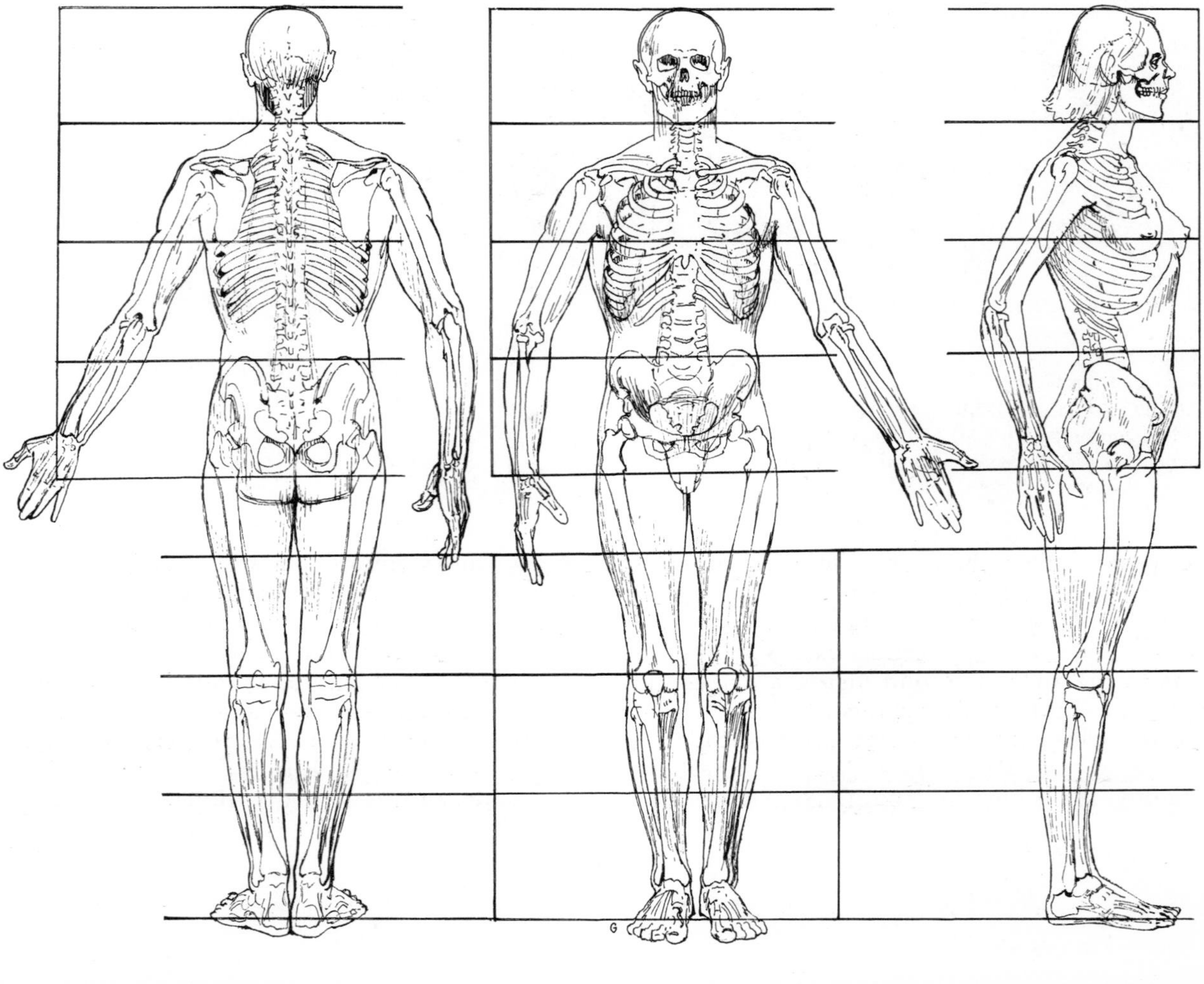

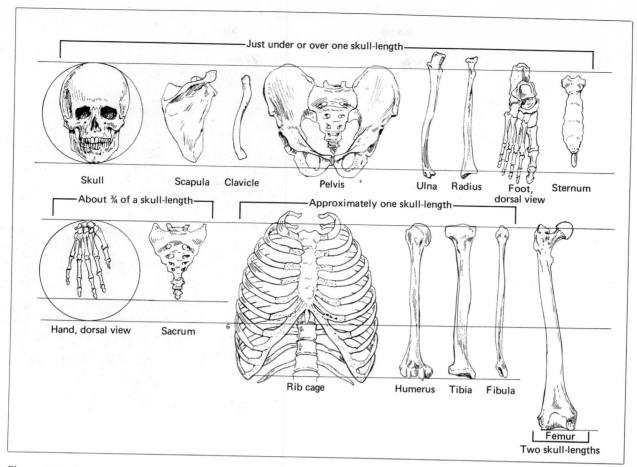

Skull   Scapula   Clavicle   Pelvis   Ulna   Radius   Foot, dorsal view   Sternum

Just under or over one skull-length

About ¾ of a skull-length

Approximately one skull-length

Hand, dorsal view   Sacrum   Rib cage   Humerus   Tibia   Fibula   Femur   Two skull-lengths

Figure 3.33

Figure 3.34

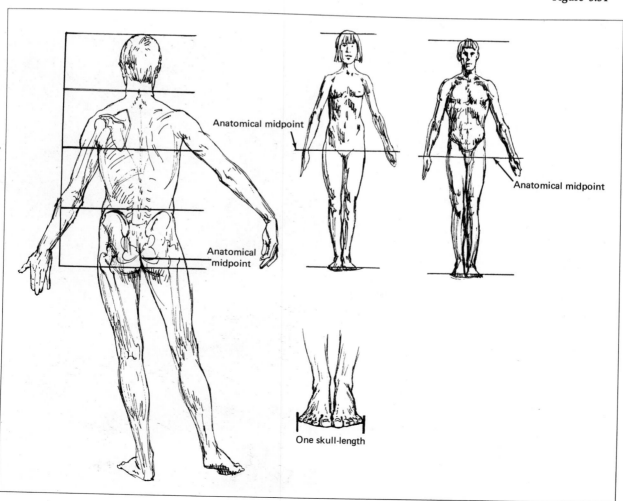

Anatomical midpoint

Anatomical midpoint

Anatomical midpoint

One skull-length

Figure 3.35
BERNARD ALBINUS (1697–1770)
Skeleton, Front View
Engraving.

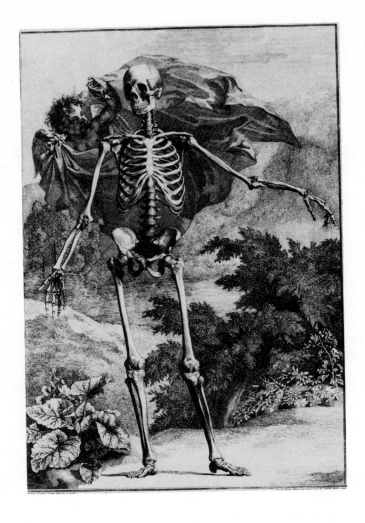

Figure 3.36
ALBINUS, *Skeleton, Side View*

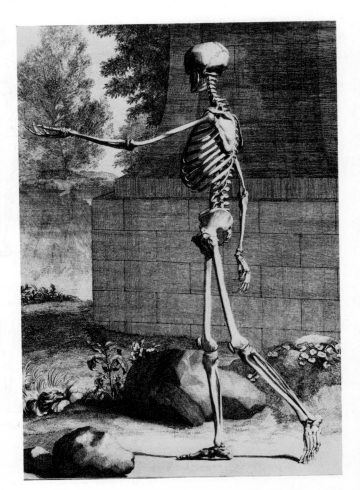

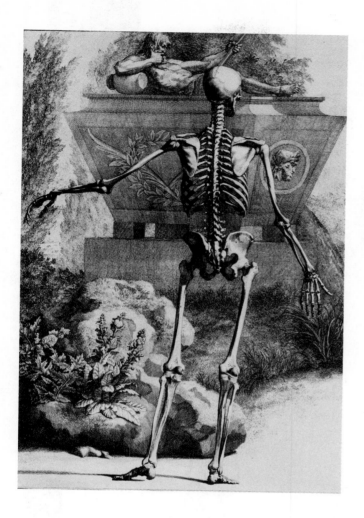

Figure 3.37
ALBINUS, *Skeleton, Back View*
Figures 3.35, 3.36, 3.37 are from *Tabula sceleti et musculorum corporis humani* by Bernard Albinus.
Reproduced by permission of The Francis A. Countway Library of Medicine, Boston.

Figure 3.38
DOMINIQUE INGRES (1780–1867)
Three Studies of a Male Nude
Pencil. 7 3/4 x 14 3/8 in.
The Metropolitan Museum of Art. Rogers Fund, 1919.

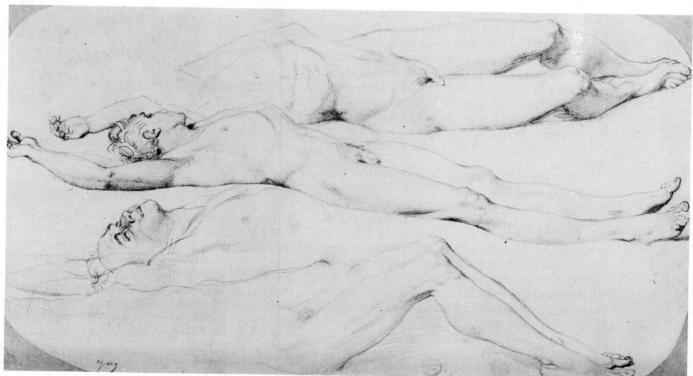

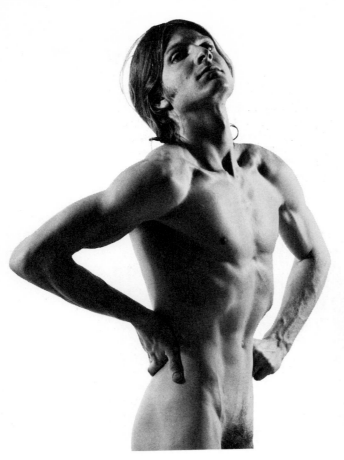

Figure 3.39

Figure 3.40

THE SKELETON
IN FIGURE DRAWING

A knowledge of the skeleton stimulates and guides good figure drawing. In Ingres's drawing *Three Studies of a Male Nude* (Figure 3.38), the elegant flow of the forms are enhanced by the artist's response to the skeleton's influence on the living forms. The protuberances at the joints serve to keep the forms from becoming too fluid and fast. Ingres uses them like commas, to provide pauses that establish a visual, measured pace. Note the skull's influence on the forms of the head, the clearly visible mass of the rib cage, and, at the hips, the tilt of the pelvis and the influence of the great trochanter. For Ingres, the skeleton serves to guide the drawing's design as well as the figure's structure.

It is important that we recognize the skeleton's potential for contributing to a drawing's visual-expressive character—to structural, plastic, and emotive matters. Indeed, in some poses, the skeletal frame is a very imposing aspect of what we see (Figure 3.39). The skeleton's presence is not necessarily more evident in the male figure. Recognizing the essential masses of the rib cage and pelvis in Figure 3.40 is fundamental to an understanding of this pose. In both of

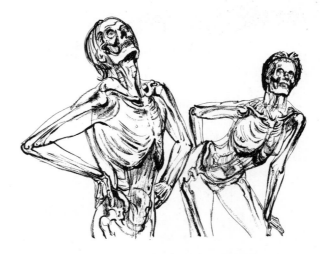

Figure 3.41

these poses the skeleton, in addition to forming structurally clear planes and form-units, produces strong energies—rhythms and tensions—that hold great potential for enlivening a drawing, as Figure 3.41 suggests. Then, too, we should take into account the expressive power—the physiological "drama"—of the skeleton pressing and pulling upon its encasing muscles, fat, and skin. That this anatomical "tug-of-war"

96

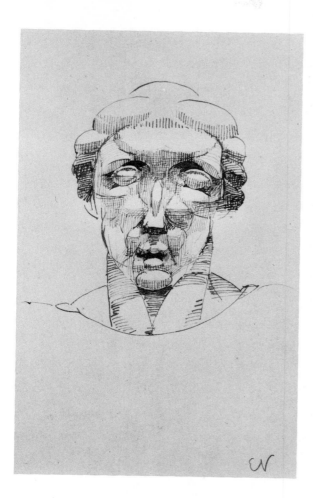

Figure 3.42
ELIE NADELMAN (1882–1947)
Head and Neck
Pen, black and brown inks on beige paper.
11.1/8 x 7 1/2 in.
The Metropolitan Museum of Art, New York.
Gift of Lincoln Kirstein, 1965.

can stimulate strong expressive qualities is especially evident in the drawings of Michelangelo (see Figures 1.14 and 3.15).

Nadelman's structurally insistent drawing, *Head and Neck* (Figure 3.42) is based on a sound knowledge of the forms of the skull. Hardly an accurate visual account of the skull's influence on the fleshed forms, the drawing does convey a strong architectural idea stimulated by the artist's intensifications of the skull's structural character. But the same skeletal structures can suggest entirely different interpretations.

Although structurally powerful, the main thrust of Rothbein's woodcut *Angel of Death* (Figure 3.43) is toward an enigmatic but moving expression. The artist's knowledge of the skull's forms enables her to alter and order them in a way that creates a provocative image, one that is both skeletal and fleshed, tangible and ethereal, foreboding and compassionate.

Even in drawings where the anatomical factor plays a minor visual role, the knowledgeable artist is able to integrate skeletal facts

Figure 3.43
RENEE ROTHBEIN (1924–   )
Angel of Death
Woodcut. 6 3/4 x 8 in.
Collection of the author.

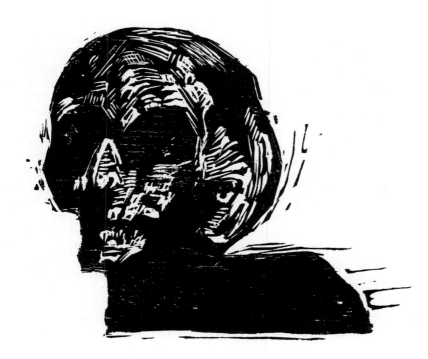

Figure 3.44
LEON GOLUB (1922–   )
Standing Figure, Back View
Pencil. 5 3/4 x 9 3/8 in.
Courtesy of the artist.

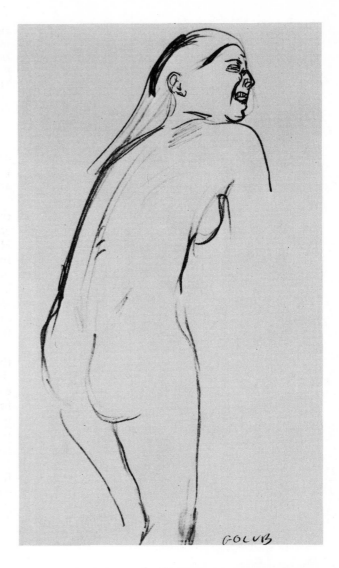

with creative needs. In Golub's drawing *Standing Figure, Back View* (Figure 3.44), the drawing of the spinal column and sacral triangle not only helps explain the form of the figure's back, but also intensifies the curved, forward "rush" of the torso, and contributes to the pattern and density of the drawing's linear design.

Although in most drawings the skeleton is suggested but not shown as such, Lebrun's drawing *Three-Penny Novel — Beggars into Dogs* (1961) (Figure 3.45) makes the skeleton itself a part of the subject (compare Figure 3.1). Here, drawn in swift, delicate lines, femurs, tibias, scapulas, and other indefinable bones add to the drawing's quiet terror.

In Picasso's etching *The Frugal Repast* (Figure 3.46), the skeleton's presence is felt throughout the drawing of both figures, and sometimes appears in surprising clarity, as at the shoulders, arms, and hands. Note the shallow depression of the temporal bones in both heads, the lateral end of the clavicle in the man's right shoulder, and the lateral epicondyle at the elbow. Note, too, the bones of the wrists and hands of both figures. But Picasso's interest in the skeleton is not clinical, and these anatomical niceties are not included merely for accuracy. Picasso's emphasis on the skeleton serves the interests of design and expression. As an agent of design it enriches edges and forms with engaging linear and planar activities, and, by Picasso's subtle distortions of skeletal facts, helps emphasize the squares and L-shapes formed by the torsos and arms. As an expressive agent the skeletal presence, by stressing the figures' lean but strong and graceful bodies, seems to evoke the durability of man in the face of his mortality.

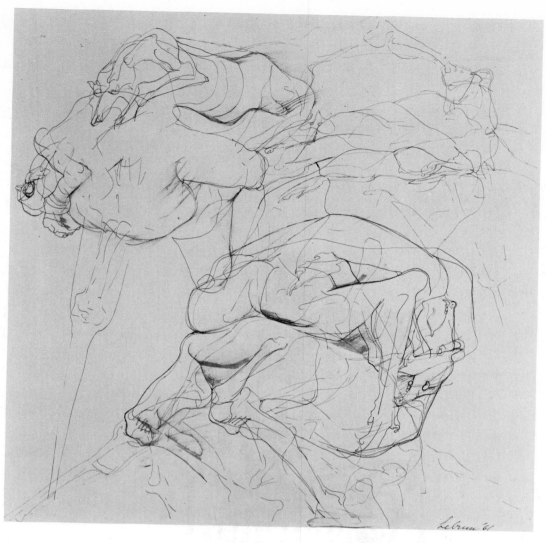

Figure 3.45
RICO LEBRUN (1900–1964)
Three-Penny Novel—Beggars into Dogs (1961)
Pen and ink. 37 1/4 x 29 7/8 in. ·
Worcester Art Museum, Worcester, Mass.
Anonymous gift in memory of Bertha James Rich.

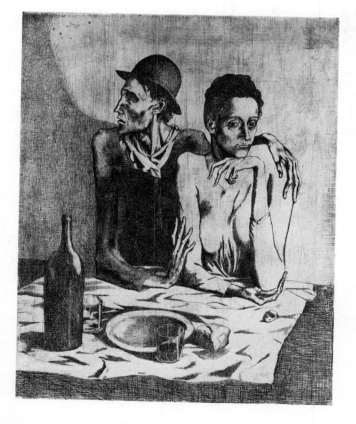

Figure 3.46
PABLO PICASSO (1881–1973)
The Frugal Repast
Etching. 46.3 x 37.7 cm.
National Gallery of Art, Washington, D. C.
Rosenwald Collection.

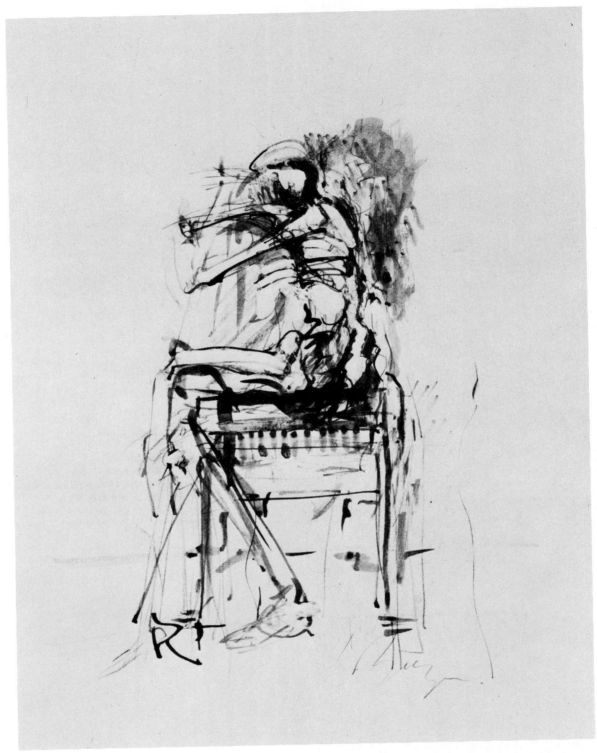

Figure 3.47
JOHN BAGERIS (1924–)
Seated Skeleton I
Sepia and black ink, some gouache. 10 x 13 in.
Collection of Mrs. Lucy Stone, Cambridge, Mass.

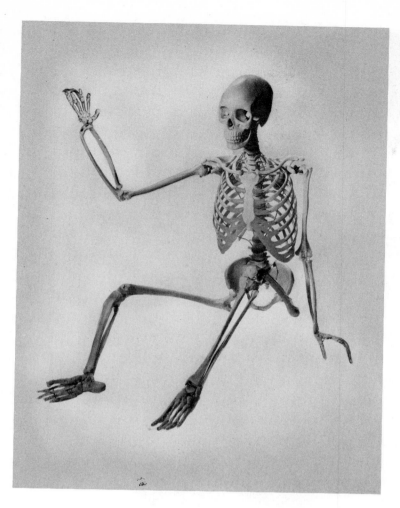

Figure 3.48

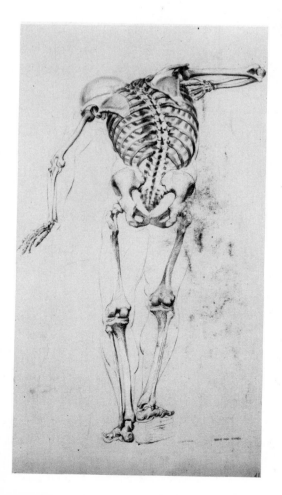

Figure 3.49
DANIEL HUNTINGTON (1816–1906)
Skeleton Study
Charcoal, crayon, and white chalk.
15 1/8 x 9 3/4 in.
The Brooklyn Museum.
Gift of the Roebling Society.

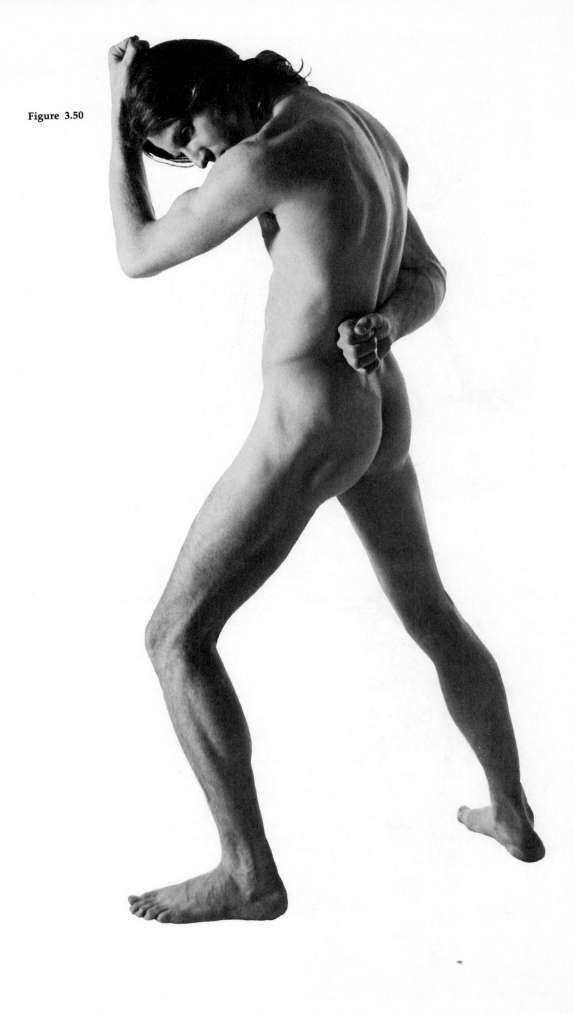

Figure 3.50

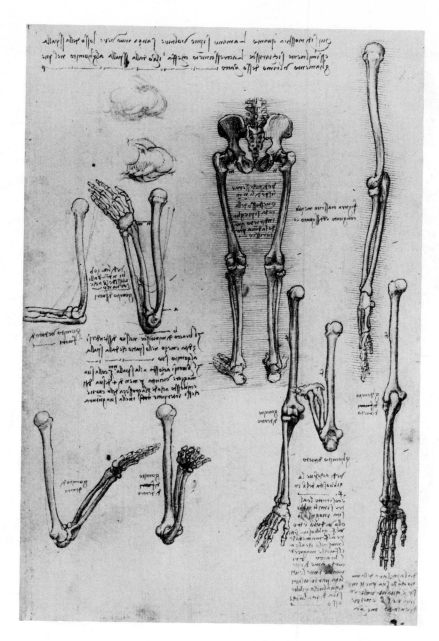

Figure 3.51
LEONARDO DA VINCI (1452–1519)
The Extremities
Pen and ink. 29 x 20 cm.
Windsor Castle, Royal Library.
By gracious permission of Her Majesty the Queen.

It seems fitting to end this brief review of some ways that the skeleton has bolstered and amplified the structures and meanings of figure drawings, or has served as the subject itself, with Bageris's drawing *Seated Skeleton I* (Figure 3.47). In an especially engaging interpretation of the skeleton, Bageris extracts powerful structural and dynamic meanings which, in drawings of the living forms, operate more subtly under the figure's fleshy "cloak." But, as this drawing amply demonstrates, a knowledge of the skeleton's masses can provide a rich source of intense dynamic energies. Although this drawing represents one artist's version of the skeleton's limitless potential for both suggesting and participating in structural and dynamic meanings, we can benefit from Bageris's "X-ray" glimpse of forces at work within the figure's armature. In drawing the figure, we need to penetrate the surfaces to experience the masses and actions that shape them from within. We may come away with a very different set of responses than the explosive ones in Bageris's drawing, but an empathic analysis of the forms and forces below the surface — and the anatomical knowledge that enables us to make such a penetration — is necessary if we are to avoid the trite and commonplace.

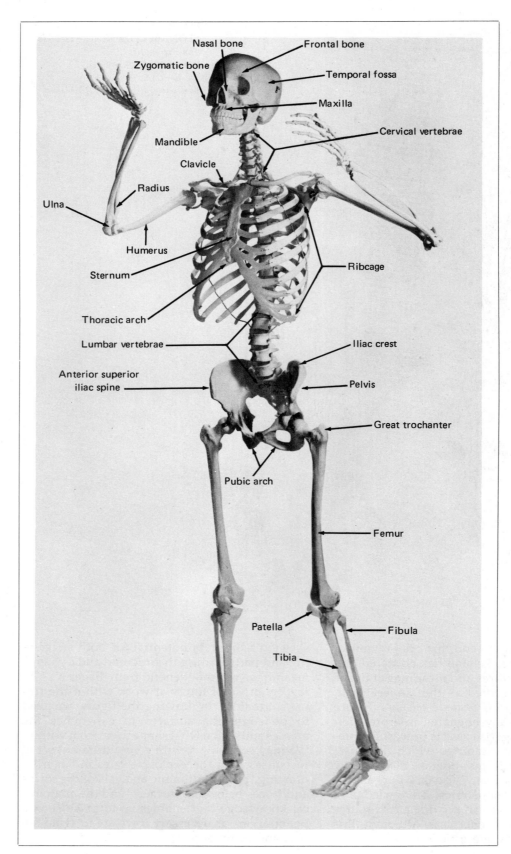

Figure 3.52

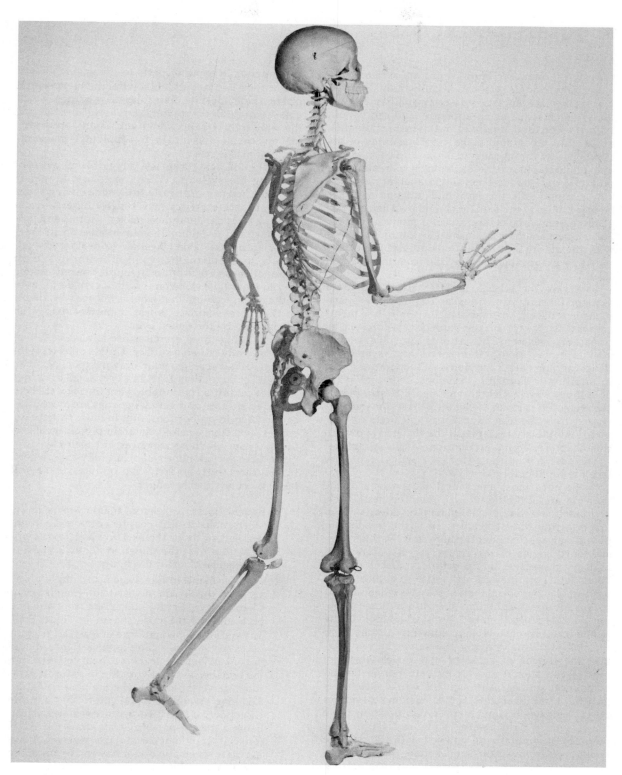

Figure 3.53

SUGGESTED EXERCISES

Clearly, the more we know about the skeleton, the more convincingly we can establish the figure's masses in space, suggest (as we saw in Chapter Two) the skeleton's role as an armature, and can benefit from its structural, emotive, and dynamic potential. To do this, we should make a serious study of the skeleton. Examining and making studies of plates and photographs of the skeleton is extremely important. And, because no single anatomy text can fully communicate the form and function of every bone (or muscle) the student should own at least two good anatomy books, and make a study of others. But the best anatomical illustrations cannot compare with the clarity and quality of understanding provided by examining and drawing from the skeleton itself.

Where the school or class cannot provide a skeleton for study, drawings can be made from specimens in museums of natural history or in local medical schools. Best of all, the student can purchase all or part of a skeleton. This is not as difficult or expensive as it may seem. Where necessary, several students can purchase a skeleton on a cooperative basis. In addition to authentic skeletons, there are available today very accurately detailed, life-size plastic skeletons, or parts of skeletons. These can be purchased from medical supply manufacturers or suppliers. All the photographs of the skeleton shown in this chapter were made from one of these replicas, in this case, a product of Medical Plastics Laboratory (see the bibliography).

Because most anatomical illustrations of the skeleton are of the traditional, standing front, back, and side view, one of the immediate advantages of drawing from the skeleton itself is the freedom to pose it in ways that permit you to study various foreshortened views of the bones, as in Figure 3.48. Equally important, the structural character of the bones and how they fit and relate to each other is more fully experienced than is possible when studied in illustrations and photographs. Huntington's drawing *Skeleton Study* (Figure 3.49) is an example of the richness of form available in drawing directly from the skeleton. This drawing also serves here to suggest the degree of accuracy and development of masses you should aim for in your more extended anatomical studies. Although the wired skeleton is limited in its movements, and some bones, in certain poses, will not occupy their correct position (note the skeleton's right patella in Figure 3.48), the importance of familiarizing yourself with the way the bones look from various angles more than compensates for these minor restrictions and inaccuracies.

Of less accuracy and detail are the inexpensive 12" to 15" plastic skeletons and life-size skulls available at most hobby and art stores. While not to be compared with the quality of the life-size replicas, these little skeletons are quite useful for studying the general relationships of scale and location, and are superior in some respects to the wooden manikins for use as "models." Likewise, the inexpensive, plastic skulls, despite their inferiority to those available from medical suppliers, are useful in studying the skull from various views and as an "armature" for muscle studies made by applying "muscles" made of plasticine.

The following exercises suggest some ways of studying the skeleton. Where necessary, they may be simplified to more nearly suit your drawing skills. Some of these exercises may suggest other ways of learning to understand the skeleton's forms and proportions, and to stimulate your interest in its creative possibilities. Don't hesitate to explore any approach to familiarizing yourself with this most important aspect of the human figure. The only wrong way to regard the skeleton is with a casual eye, born of the misconception that what is not actually visible on the figure's surface is less important than what can be seen by the naked eye.

In doing these exercises use any erasable medium and any suitable surface. Unless otherwise indicated, avoid making your drawings smaller than 10" × 14" or larger than 18" × 24". Very small drawings will not permit a comfortable handling of details in extended studies, and very large ones are more difficult to keep in proportion. And, in most of these exercises, objective accuracy is an important goal. Although none of these exercises are restricted to a given time period, none can be usefully experienced in less than thirty to forty-five minutes; some will take you considerably longer.

1. By referring to a skeleton, anatomy texts, or the illustrations in this chapter, draw a 12" high, detailed study of the skeleton as it would appear from the pose shown in Figure 3.50. Note the skeletal clues in the figure.

2. Using a manikin-like system of simple forms such as those you devised for exercise 5 in Chapter Two, lightly sketch one front and one back view of the pose shown in Figure 3.50. These drawings should be at least 12" high. If necessary, make a simple stick-figure model out of wire or pipe cleaners to help you establish the two views. Or, if working in a studio classroom, have the model take the pose in Figure 3.50 long enough to allow you to rough in the essentials of the two required views. Next, using a tracing-paper overlay, draw the skeleton as it would appear in the two views, allowing your schematic underdrawing to guide the degree of foreshortening of various bones, their scale, and their placement. Keep these skeleton drawings rather generalized and simplified. For example, the rib cage need not be drawn rib by rib, but should suggest the egg-like mass and something of the strap-like nature of some of the ribs.

3. Rework or redraw several of your figure drawings, thinning down the forms to exaggerate the skeleton's influence on the surface forms. The results should suggest emaciated figures.

4. Using the skeleton or any other visual reference material to assist you, draw either a ¾, an overhead, or a worm's-eye view of any of the Albinus skeletons (Figures 3.35, 3.36, 3.37).

5. Working from the skeleton itself or any of the illustrations in this chapter, draw any standing view of the skeleton as it would appear if wrapped in a thin, clinging material. Invent a drapery situation that shows the material stretched taut in some places and loosely draped in others. The entire skeleton need not be covered, and the material may wrap around some forms several times, thickening them.

6. Working from the skeleton itself, make the following series of carefully observed drawings:

   a. Several studies of different views of the skull.

   b. Several studies of different views of the shoulder girdle. Be sure to include a view that looks down upon the shoulder girdle. In the study of the back view, include the entire scapula.

   c. Several studies of the bones of the torso.

   d. Several studies of the bones of the arm and hand. In at least one of these drawings the lower arm and hand should be pronated (Figure 3.51).

   e. Several studies of the bones of the leg and foot, including the pelvis (Figure 3.51). In at least one drawing, show the leg bent at the knee.

7. Using Figures 3.52 and 3.53 as models, and any water-based medium in combination with your pencil or chalk, make a drawing of each pose in which you extract strong structural and dynamic ideas and energies, as Bageris has done in Figure 3.47 (see also his *Seated Skeleton* II, Figure 7.11). Don't hesitate to alter, omit, or add anything that would help make your drawings intensely personal responses to the subjects. Because these drawings should mirror *your* reactions to the two poses, the Bageris drawings should be regarded as examples of the creative freedom possible and not necessarily as goals.

8. Make a line drawing, in a broad and free manner, of four or five skeletons dancing, leaping, or floating around the page. Simplify the forms as much as you wish. Here, the point is to experience the gesture and design possibilities of the skeletal forms. Allow skeletons to overlap or to interpenetrate each other—as if the forms are transparent. Contours can be simplified into straight and curved segments or can exaggerate the ins and outs of a form's edge. Try to create interesting rhythms and shapes. Do so not by arbitrarily distorting the forms, but by permitting gesture and design responses to influence your general handling and style of drawing. These drawings may be more two- than three-dimensional.

9. Create a skeleton that is related to our human one but differs from it in proportion and, to some slight extent, in design. You can think of it as the skeleton of a pre-human "missing link" or as some human-like skeletal system of an inhabitant of another planet. Insist on making each bone so structurally clear, a sculptor could construct this skeleton by using your drawing as a guide.

10. Using the skeleton you invented in the previous exercise as a model, draw it again, this time in an action pose that produces some markedly foreshortened forms. Suggest what the figure might look like in the life-state by giving it a lean "cover" of skin. Without the musculature and fat to help support and shape this skin, it will of course behave much as clothing would, if draped upon a skeleton. Again, insist on volumetric clarity.

11. Draw a skeleton-like figure intended as an illustration for a magazine article on famine. Here, anatomical accuracy should be subordinated to an imaginative image that expresses the article's dire theme. Forms may be unfocused, fragmented, or distorted to the point of abstraction.

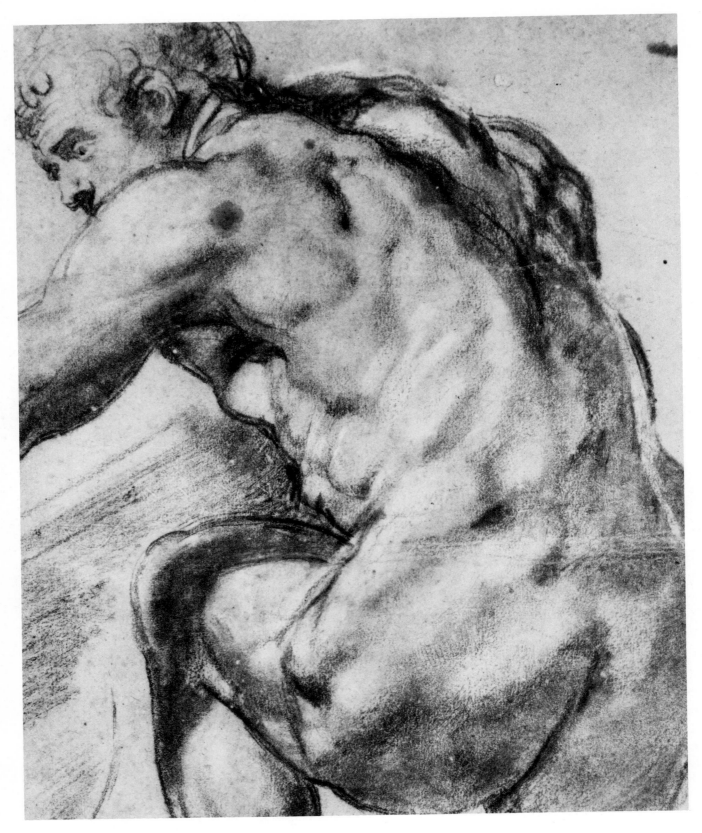

Figure 4.1
PETER PAUL RUBENS (1577–1640)
A Nude Man Kneeling (detail)
Black and white chalk.
Museum Boymans-van Beuningen, Rotterdam.

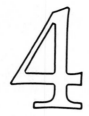

The Anatomical Factor

part two: the muscles

SOME GENERAL OBSERVATIONS

In this chapter we will examine three main themes concerning the muscles and the ways in which a grasp of major anatomical facts assists creative figure drawing. One theme examines the location and form of those muscles most influential in shaping the figure's living forms; a second theme considers their morphological role—how the muscles affect the body's surfaces; the third theme explores how the muscles may function as agents of structure, design, and expression. This last theme accompanies the first two, (a) to provide some immediate examples of how anatomy serves creative ends, and (b) to point out that the artist's obligation is not to anatomical accuracy, but to certain visually expressive truths.

In this condensed anatomical survey, visualizations carry the main burden of communication. Although important features concerning attachments and surface effects are described, the sense of the overall disposition

and character of the muscles is best studied through the anatomy illustrations and the reproduced drawings and sculptures.

One of the more distressing errors in the drawings of some beginners shows the head, neck, and limbs as only tenuously attached to the trunk. For example, the upper and lower parts of a limb are drawn as if each part ended before the next began. This tendency toward what may be called the "sausage-link syndrome" probably stems from the following assumptions by the student: Because the figure's forms are thinnest at the joints and appear most swelled between them, and because the segments must be free to bend, therefore each segment must be self-contained, its muscles terminating short of the joint. But, if this were true, the body would be immobilized. It is only by muscles crossing over joints to attach to bones on the other side, that mobility is possible. Muscles attach to bone or to other tissues by *tendons*, tough, nonelastic tissues located at the ends of the long muscles and at the edges of

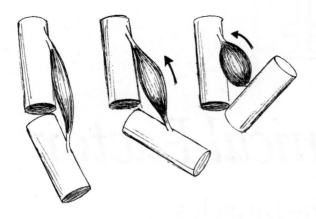

Figure 4.2

broad ones. Muscles function as levers in moving bones by acting across the joints, which in turn, act as points of support (Figure 4.1).

Although the figure's forms, mainly shaped by muscle, *do* taper at the joints, it is not the result of a bundle of muscles ending where another one begins, but of muscles thinning down to cords and sheets of tendon that often interlace with tendons of other muscles as they move across joints in both directions. Instead of sausage-link attachments, the head, neck, and limbs are deeply embedded in the torso by muscles and tendons woven far beyond the apparent end of any single part. Thus, throughout the body, most of the muscles appear braided in various ways.

Muscles work by contracting their fleshy fibers, or *bodies*. In contraction the muscle body is drawn together, growing shorter and thicker. To do this, one attachment of the ends of a muscle must be relatively fixed, the other, movable. A muscle's *origin* is the point of fixed attachment; its *insertion* is the movable point of attachment. In Figure 4.2 the muscle's upper attachment is the origin because it pulls the lower part toward the upper one. But Figure 4.2 omits an important characteristic of muscle movements. No muscle acts alone. Whenever a muscle or set of muscles contracts, other *opposing* muscles are activated to modify or regulate the action of the contracting ones (Figure 4.3).

This arrangement of muscles in opposition to each other is a dominant feature of the body, allowing not only for fine-tuned regulation of actions, but also for the return of parts after their movement. For example, in the lower arm the *flexor* muscles bring the fingers together in a fist, the *extensor* muscles extend the fingers, and the *supinator* muscles permit the hand to rotate. Additionally, these three muscle groups working in complicated harmony permit the many combinations of movements of the lower arm and hand.

MUSCLES OF THE HEAD

While the skull, as we saw in Chapter Three, is an ever-present influence on the sur-

Figure 4.3

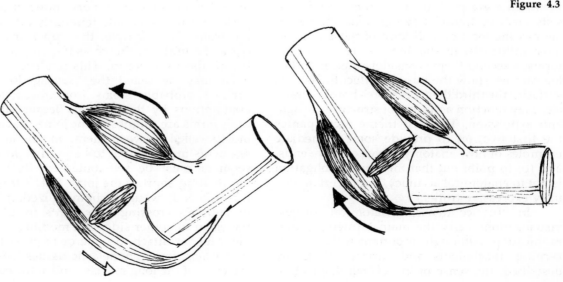

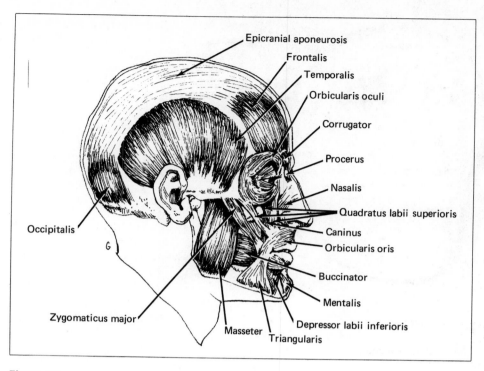

Figure 4.4

Figure 4.5

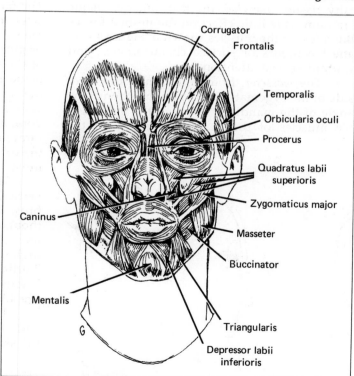

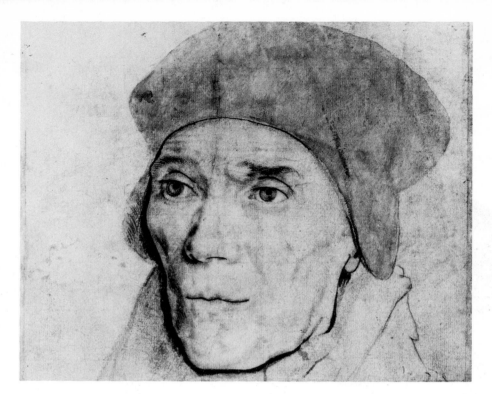

Figure 4.6
HANS HOLBEIN the Younger (1497–1543)
Cardinal John Fisher (detail)
Red and black chalk, brown ink washes, pen and
india ink on primed paper.
Windsor Castle, Royal Library.
By gracious permission of Her Majesty the Queen.

face forms of the head, the muscles of the head play a less important role. Most of the facial muscles are small, thin, or deeply embedded in fatty tissue; likewise, the thin muscles of the cranium have little effect on the fleshed forms. But a few of the muscles shown in Figure 4.4 do affect contours or surface characteristics, and warrant special attention.

The *masseter*, from its origin at the outer side of the zygomatic arch to its insertion at the angle of the mandible, is one of the most visible muscles of the head, accounting for the

obliquely turned bulge running from the corner of the jaw to the cheekbone. The lines of its body, if extended, would embrace the eye socket. The fan-shaped *temporalis*, along with the masseter, operates the closing and biting movements of the mandible. The temporal muscle originates and largely fills the recessed plateau of the temporal fossa, passing under the zygomatic arch to insert upon the coronoid process, the forward "prong" of the mandible. Far less visible than the powerful masseter, the temporal is nevertheless an influence on the surface form of the temple, producing a slight bulge in the otherwise recessed area of the temple (Figure 4.5).

The *frontalis*, a flat, broad muscle divided vertically, is of interest because it wrinkles the brow horizontally and lifts the eyebrows. Although its form contributes little to the contour of the forehead, its upper, curved origin, high on the frontal bone, will often show if the hairline is high enough. The frontalis muscle inserts into the skin of the brow and nose (Figure 4.5).

The *corrugator*, originating at the medial end of the superciliary arch and inserting into the skin of the eyebrows, is a small muscle that

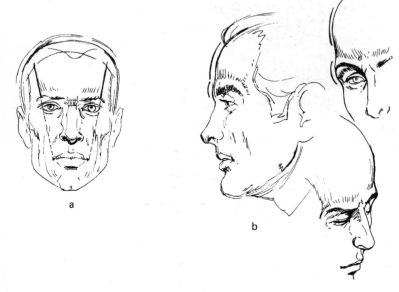

a

b

Figure 4.7

dramatically affects the surface of the forehead in frowning or when grief is expressed. It forces the vertical wrinkles of the brow and causes the eyebrows to "bunch up" near the nose (Figure 4.5).

Encircling the mouth is an elliptical muscle, the *orbicularis oris,* which has the unique distinction of having no bony points of attachment. Instead, it originates among some nine small muscles around the mouth, most of which seem "aimed" at the mouth, and inserts into the skin surrounding the lips. Contractions of this muscle produce the creases that radiate from the lips, most often seen in the elderly (Figure 4.5). The *orbicularis oculi* is also a circular muscle, encompassing the eye and operating the opening and closing of the eyelids. Here again, radiating creases, the familiar "crow's feet," testify to its encircling contractions (Figure 4.5).

Originating from the zygomatic arch and inserting at the corner of the mouth, the *zygomaticus major* provides an important oblique line of abutment between the planes of the side and front of the face, as can be seen in Holbein's drawing, *Cardinal John Fisher* (Figure 4.6). Note the effects of the frontalis and corrugator muscles, and Holbein's sensitivity to the bone and muscle throughout the head.

THE SURFACE FORMS OF THE HEAD

The forehead consists of the area represented by the frontal bone and closely corresponds to its form. In planar terms, the forehead can be divided into a broad center plane, sloping backward, and a smaller plane near each temple which abuts the center plane at a point about one-third in from the outer edge of the eyebrow. Both lines of abutment are tilted at an angle that, if extended, would cause them to meet at the mouth (Figure 4.7a). Often the rounded bulge of the frontal bone causes the central plane of the forehead to appear rounded to within an inch above the brows. Here the thickened ridge of bone above the eye sockets forms smaller bulges at the outer corner of the brow, and again near the nose (Figure 4.7b).

The eyeball is deeply set into the orbital cavity, the eyelids serving as upper and lower "awnings." The upper lid, the larger and more clearly defined of the two, is the more mobile. In shutting the eyes it is the upper lid that covers most of the visible eyeball. The eyelids closely follow the curve of the eyeball, the upper lid appearing to overlap the lower one at the outer corner of the eye. In the front view the crest of the curved lower margin of the upper

Figure 4.8

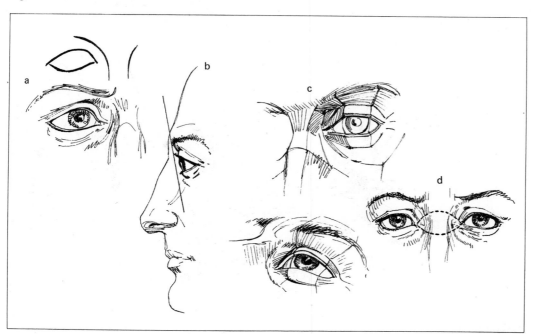

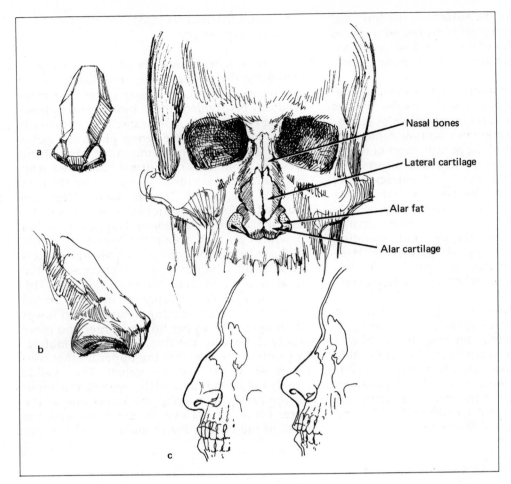

Nasal bones

Lateral cartilage

Alar fat

Alar cartilage

Figure 4.9

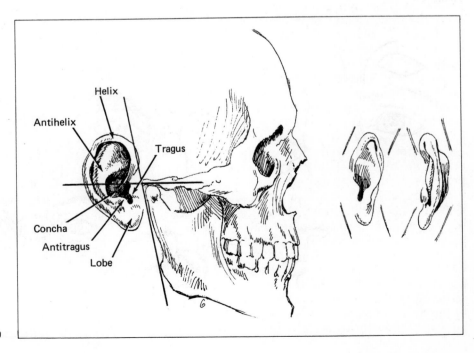

Helix

Antihelix

Tragus

Concha

Antitragus

Lobe

Figure 4.10

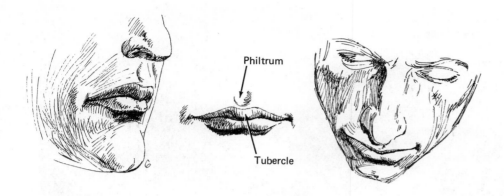

Philtrum

Tubercle

Figure 4.11

lid is near to the nose; in the lower lid the crest of the curve is away from the nose (Figure 4.8a). In the side view the eyelids align on an angle dropping backward (b). Like the forehead, the eyelids can be reduced to three planes each (c). Generally, in a front view the eyes are placed almost one eye-length apart (d).

The nose, wedge-like and inclined forward, can be reduced to four major planes: a central plane, often widening at the junction of the nasal bone and the *lateral cartilages*, and again, at the bulb of the nose; and two side planes, inclined obliquely downward from the central plane. The plane of the base of the nose, free of the plane of the face, may be horizontal or show a slight downward tilt, and is roughly triangular in shape. The nostrils are located nearer to the inclined edges of the triangle than to its midline (Figure 4.9a). The *septum*, the medial partition separating the nostrils, represents the lowest point of the nose in both the front and side views. The wings curving upward at an angle, in providing the beveled planes of the end of the nose, modify the plane of the base (Figure 4.9b). Both the bulb of the nose and the inner part of the nostrils may be either rounded or angular, reflecting the character of the cartilage underlying these forms. The nostril wings, however, are almost always rounded. Sometimes a central groove is visible at the tip of the nose, marking the junction of the two *alar cartilages* which shape the end of the nose and part of the nostril openings. In the side view, a change in profile is most likely at the junction of the nasal bone and lateral cartilage, and again, at the bulb of the nose (Figure 4.9c).

The ear (Figure 4.10) is located behind the upper angle of the mandible and is vertically centered on the zygomatic arch. In a side view of the fleshed figure the ear is roughly aligned between the eyebrow and the base of the nose.

Ovoid in shape, its major features are the *concha*, the hollow in the lower half of the ear; the *helix*, the rolled outer edge of the ear; the *antihelix*, the Y-shaped, inner curved form that is parallel with the helix near the bottom of the ear but turns away from it as the two forms rise; the *tragus* and *antitragus*, the two facing "bumps" near the bottom of the concha; and the *lobe*, which may vary from a barely perceptible form to a pronounced pendent. The shape of the ear varies greatly, but generally the helix emerges near the antitragus and above the earlobe. The helix describes a simple C-curve and turns sharply inward to the upper end of the concha, about halfway down the ear. Seen from a front view, the upper half of the ear is turned slightly downward toward the concha, the lower half, upward, and the antihelix obscures part of the helix.

The lips (Figure 4.11), centered horizontally on the midline of the head, occupy a position a little nearer to the nose than to the chin. Generally, the upper lip is slightly more forward than the lower, and is characterized by the *tubercle*, the swelled, central portion, and the two curled wings. Together, these three segments form a wide-spread M-shaped form. When closed, the lips are in contact at every point, making one lip appear thin where the other is thick. In the front view the upper lip appears to extend a bit more at the corners of the mouth than the lower lip does. When viewed from above, the overall curve of the lips upon the curved surface of the face becomes apparent. There are three areas which are not actually part of the lips but are important considerations in modelling them: the small, fleshy mounds near the corners of the mouth; the *philtrum*, or groove below the nose, whose oblique margins strike the two peaks of the upper lip; and the furrow under the lower lip.

Watteau, in his drawing *Two Studies of the*

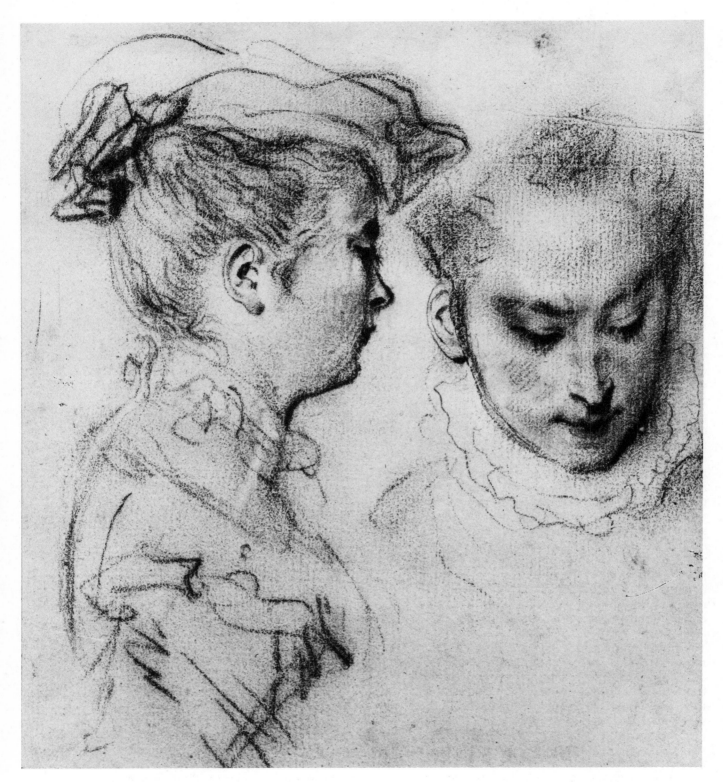

Figure 4.12
ANTOINE WATTEAU (1684–1721)
Two Studies of the Head of a Young Woman
Red and black chalk. 6 3/4 x 6 1/8 in.
Trustees of the British Museum, London.

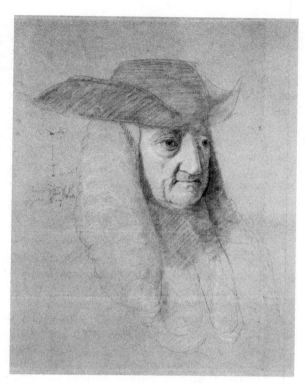

Figure 4.13
JOHN SINGLETON COPLEY (1738–1815)
Head of the Earl of Bathurst, Lord Chancellor
Black and white chalk. 26 x 19 1/2 in.
Courtesy Museum of Fine Arts, Boston.
The Karolik Collection.

Head of a Young Woman (Figure 4.12), is well aware of the terrain surrounding the lips and, indeed, is mindful of the surface anatomy of all the features discussed above *and of the areas separating them.*

When drawing the head, the beginner too often concentrates almost exclusively on the features just described, leaving the terrain between them unregarded. The results often show modelled features floating on a flat enclosure representing the shape, but not the structural nature of the head. A far better attitude toward the forms of the head is the recognition that *every part is a feature*, a unit of form that interjoins others, usually in a quite harmonious way. In most faces, as you can readily observe, the creases in the forehead "imitate" the eyebrows, the curved eyebrows "anticipate" the nose, the folds in the skin near the nostrils spread out to "measure" the mouth, the fleshy mounds at the corners of the mouth "parenthesize" it. This rhythmic play between form-units is a characteristic to be found throughout the figure.

Although the areas of the cheek, temple, and chin do not easily offer boundaries as clearly defined as in the forehead, it is important to appreciate the skull's influence in these areas. Because fatty deposits, sometimes considerable, are often the dominant factor in forming the terrain of the cheek and chin, the planes in these areas may vary widely. Nevertheless, in the cheek, the zygomatic bone and arch and even the canine fossa are often visible, even in heavily "padded" faces. And despite the familiar "double chin" and jowels in some corpulent figures, some traces of the mandible's angularities are never altogether obscured (Figure 4.13).

MUSCLES OF THE NECK

In the front view (Figures 4.14, 4.15) the contours of the neck are formed by the *sternomastoids*. Each originates at the sternum and inner end of the clavicle, sweeping gracefully upward to insert upon the mastoid process. Note the fullness of the longer *sternal* body compared to the strap-like *clavicular* branch. The sternomastoids oppose each other in turning the head left or right, but act in unison to lower and raise the head. Their tendonous attachments at the pit of the throat are almost always visible, even in necks otherwise devoid of muscular detail. The entire muscle becomes boldly evident when the head is turned far to one side and tilted downward (as will be seen in Figure 4.83).

Emerging from behind and about halfway down the length of the sternomastoid is the *trapezius*, providing an oblique line that ends near the outer tip of the clavicle. The trapezius is a muscle of the back, but in this view it offers the triangular wedge that fills in the area between the contour of the neck and the clavicles, to which it makes one of its several insertions.

Between the sternomastoids is a triangular area, its apex at the pit of the throat, its base abutting the base of the triangular underside of the chin. Most of the space between the sternomastoids is filled by the swallowing apparatus and by the larynx, whose lower part is formed by the ring-shaped *cricoid cartilage* (Figure 4.16). The U-shaped *hyoid bone* is located at the common baseline between the two triangular areas. Directly below it is the *thyroid cartilage*, its protrusion forming the familiar "Adam's apple."

In the side view (Figure 4.17) the contours of the neck are formed by the trapezius in back and by the larynx and tendon of the sternomas-

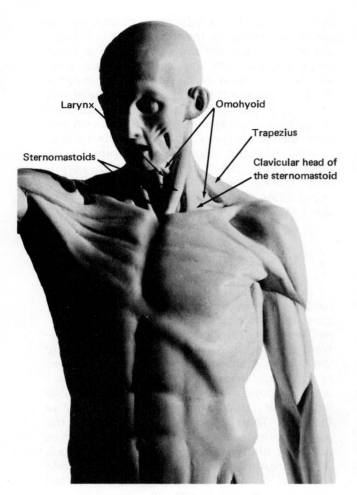

Larynx

Omohyoid

Trapezius

Clavicular head of
the sternomastoid

Sternomastoids

Figure 4.14

toid in front. The space between the trapezius and sternomastoid is filled by three muscles, somewhat recessed and thus not often visible. They are the *scalenus*, the *levator scapulae*, and the *splenius* (Figures 4.17, 4.18). Note that the scalenus is rather vertically placed, but the other two muscles are decidedly oblique. Emerging from under the forward edge of the sternomastoid are several muscles of only passing interest to the artist. The *omohyoid* is of importance as the only muscle to intrude on the triangular hollow between the trapezius and sternomastoid (Figures 4.14, 4.15), and for its occasional appearance behind the *sternohyoid*, itself visible when the chin is thrust forward, and, usually, in the elderly.

In the back view the contours of the neck are again formed by the sternomastoids, the lines of the trapezius cutting diagonally across them, making the neck appear shorter. In contrast to the pronounced surface activity often found in front and side views of the neck, the back view tends to be simpler, the form's cylindrical basis more insistent.

Here, it is important to remind ourselves that our examination of specific anatomical facts should mainly serve to broaden creative freedom, not to restrict it. At first glance, Michelangelo's drawing of the neck in the detail from *Studies for the Crucified Haman* (Figure 4.19) appears flawlessly accurate, but a closer examination shows that the artist has exaggerated

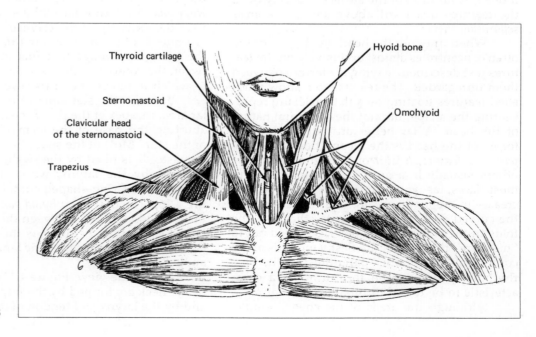

Thyroid cartilage

Hyoid bone

Sternomastoid

Clavicular head
of the sternomastoid

Omohyoid

Trapezius

Figure 4.15

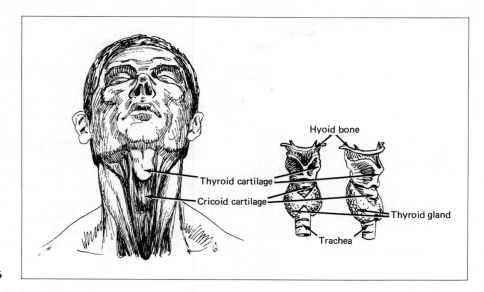

Figure 4.16

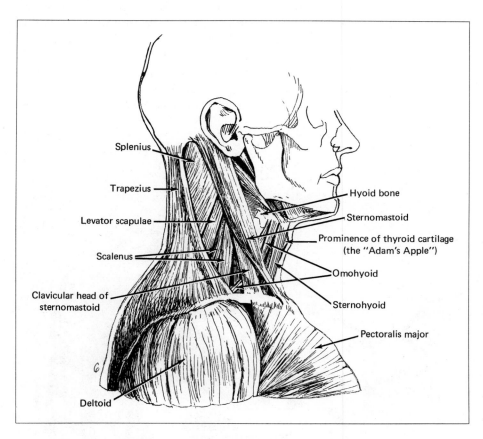

Figure 4.17

the scale of the sternomastoids and the forms of the larynx region. Indeed, such clarity of detail, more typical of the leaner, *ectomorphic* type, is an unlikely characteristic in a figure of such massive proportions. Michelangelo seems often to have given his figures the anatomical definition of lean, muscular types and the proportional heft of the athletic, *mesomorphic* type.

By contrast, Villon's etching *Head of a Young Girl* (Figure 4.20) seems to be less concerned with anatomical matters. Yet on inspection the forms, despite their cubist-like interpretation, are anatomically sophisticated. In both of these drawings a knowledge of anatomy serves as an agent for structural, plastic, and emotive interests of a unique kind.

119

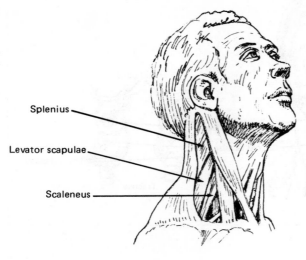

Splenius

Levator scapulae

Scaleneus

Figure 4.18

MUSCLES OF THE TORSO

In the front view (Figures 4.21, 4.22) the clavicles can be seen as firm bars of attachment for the muscles of the neck, shoulder, and chest, gracefully springing from them in all directions. The clavicle's upper surface receives the trapezius and sternomastoid muscles; its outer, lower surface holds the *deltoid*, the powerful encasing muscle of the shoulder; and, on the inner underside of the clavicle, the *pectoralis major*, the great muscle of the breast completes the clavicle's muscular encirclement. The pectoralis major, in addition to its origin on the underside of the clavicle, also emerges from the anterior (front) of the sternum, and from the costal cartilage below it. Thus, its origins roughly describe three sides of a square. Its insertion into the upper part of the humerus, instead of

Figure 4.19
MICHELANGELO BUONARROTI (1475–1564)
Studies for the Crucified Haman (detail)
Black chalk.
Teylers Museum, Haarlem.

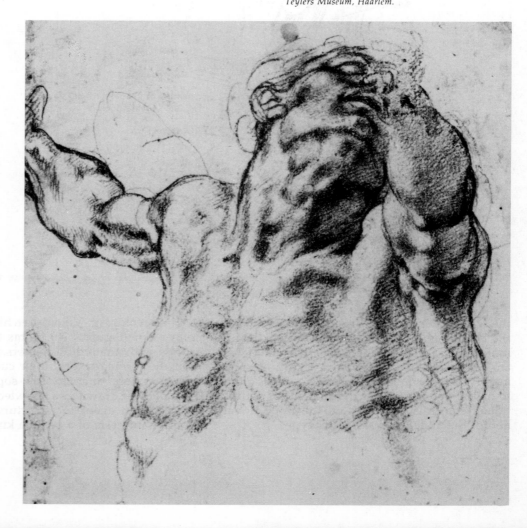

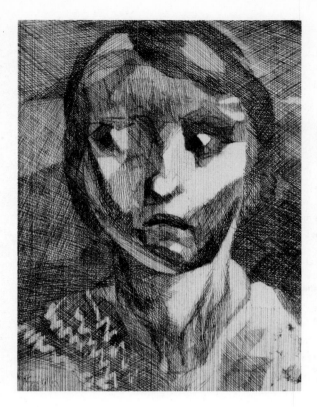

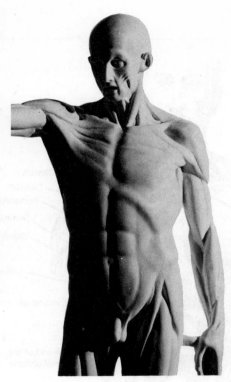

Figure 4.20
JACQUES VILLON (1875–1963)
Head of a Young Girl (2nd state, 1929)
Etching. 6 x 7 3/4 in.
Print Department, Boston Public Library.

Figure 4.21

providing the fourth side of the square, draws the upper and lower boundaries of the muscle together to a point at the armpit, creating the impression of a triangle, rather than a square. The muscle twists at its narrowest point, just before inserting on the arm. As a result, its lower fibers attach at a higher point on the humerus than the higher fibers, giving the muscle-bundles of the pectoralis major a handsome, radiating rhythm. These bundles of muscle fiber, also characteristic of the deltoid, give both of these prominent muscles a rich surface character (Figure 4.19). Note that one muscle-bundle of the pectoralis major, the one nearest the deltoid, is separated from the rest of the muscle by a narrow crevice. Note, too, how the pectoralis major slips under the deltoid on its way to insertion (Figures 4.21 and 4.22), and that the large crevice between these muscles grows wider near the clavicle. Like the pectoralis major, the deltoid, from its origin at the clavicle to its insertion almost halfway down the humerus, is somewhat fan-like in character. Together, these muscles create powerful forms of much grace and energy.

The mammary gland occupies the lower, outer corner of the pectoral muscle in both the male and female figure. In the male there is a general angularity to the entire muscle, the glandular and fatty tissues only subtly softening the area of the breast (Figure 4.23).

In the female the fuller breasts descend below the bottom margin of the pectoralis major. The form of the breast begins at the xiphoid process, but its influence can be seen as far up as the base of the manubrium. The breast is fullest at the lower, outer side. A common error in drawing these forms is placing them too high on the chest. Actually, there is as much height to the breast as to the pectoral region above it. An overhead view shows the breasts to be turned outward, the nipples located to the outside rather than centered on the forms (Figure 4.24). Thus, in the front view the nipples are decidedly to the outside of center. Only when one breast is in profile will the nipple on the opposite breast appear centrally positioned.

Below the pectoral muscle the torso's contour is taken up by the *latissimus dorsi*. Appearing at the armpit, it descends vertically, but because it thins as it descends and turns backward slightly at the end of its course, it is lost from sight a few inches above the waist. Actually a large muscle enveloping the back, in the front view only its thickened forward edge is visible. This muscle contributes to the V-shape of well-developed male torsos, especially when the arms are raised (Figure 4.25).

121

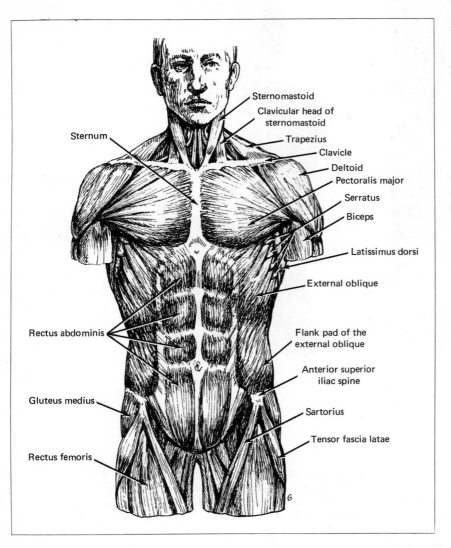

Figure 4.22

Sternomastoid

Clavicular head of
sternomastoid

Sternum

Trapezius

Clavicle

Deltoid

Pectoralis major

Serratus

Biceps

Latissimus dorsi

External oblique

Rectus abdominis

Flank pad of the
external oblique

Anterior superior
iliac spine

Gluteus medius

Sartorius

Tensor fascia latae

Rectus femoris

Figure 4.23
FEDERIGO BAROCCI (1526–1612)
Sketch for "The Entombment" in Santa Croce, Senigallia
Chalk on toned paper. 10 7/8 x 16 1/4 in.
The Art Museum, Princeton University.

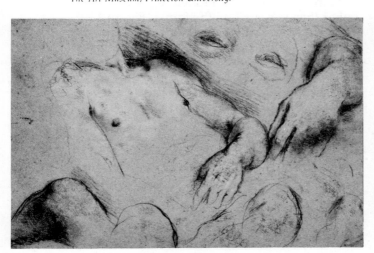

Figure 4.24
PHILIP PEARLSTEIN (1924–)
Two Nudes on an Old Indian Rug
Etching and aquatint. 23 3/4 x 29 5/8 in.
Courtesy Museum of Fine Arts, Boston.
Lee M. Friedman Fund.

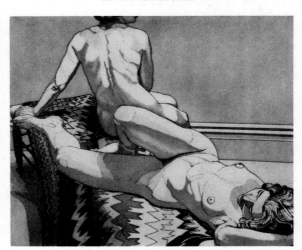

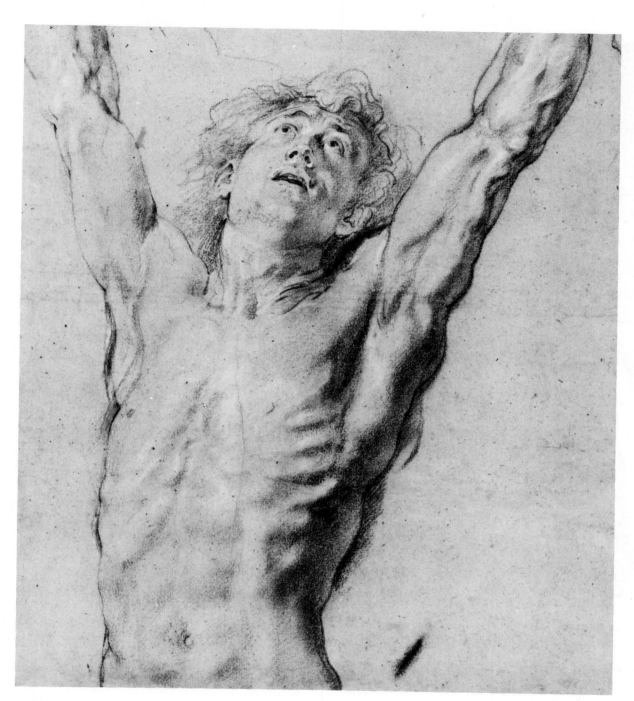

Figure 4.25
PETER PAUL RUBENS (1577–1640)
Study for the Figure of Christ on the Cross (detail)
Charcoal, heightened by white.
Trustees of the British Museum, London.

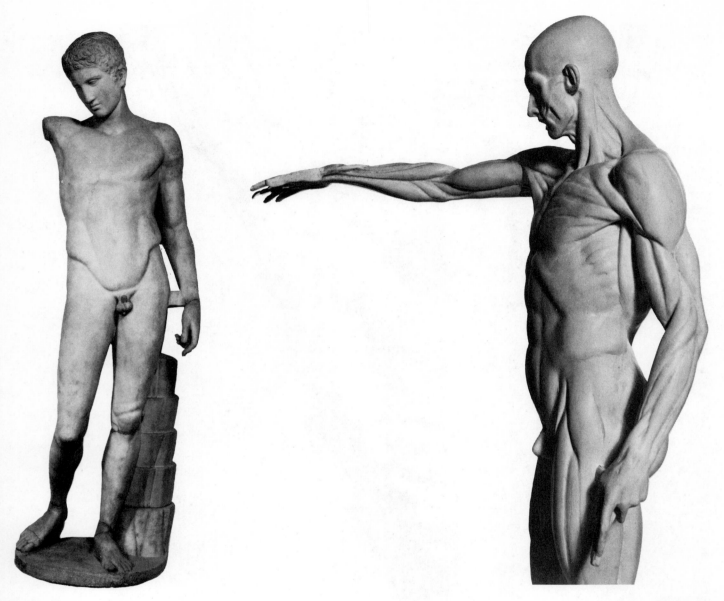

Figure 4.26
Classic Greek (450–440 B.C.)
Westmacott Athlete
Marble.
Trustees of the British Museum, London.

Figure 4.27

Slipping out from under the latissimus dorsi are four or five small, fleshy pads, or *digitations*, of the *serratus magnus*. This is a large but mainly deep muscle which originates on the lateral surface of the first eight or nine ribs, and inserts into the spinal border of the scapula by passing between it and the ribs. It operates the forward movement of the scapula. These fleshy pads are interlaced by thin digitations of the *external oblique*, a muscle that fills much of the area between the abdominal cavity and the latissimus dorsi. The external oblique continues the front-view contour of the torso, dropping backward from its high point near the thoracic arch until it reaches the waist, and turning somewhat outward below the waist. A thin muscle, the external oblique thickens markedly near its termination at the iliac crest. This thickened, fleshy mound at the root of the thigh, much favored by Greek and Roman sculptors, is called the *flank pad* of the external oblique (Figures 4.26, 4.27, and 4.28).

The *rectus abdominus* muscle fills the surface area of the abdominal cavity. It is divided vertically by tendon into two rows of four fleshy pads, themselves separated horizontally by tendon. The tendonous borders separating each horizontal pair of muscle pads become more chevron-like as they ascend. The lowest border, at the navel, is a true horizontal, but each succeeding border tends to peak more at the torso's midline. Note that the lowest group is twice the length of any of the rest. The abdominal group originates at the crest of the pubic bone and inserts among the cartilage straps of the fifth, sixth, and seventh ribs.

In the side view (Figures 4.27, 4.28), note the shape and scale of the chest mass in relation to the smaller, backward-tilting pelvic mass. In this view the trapezius, in its upper, vertical segment, roughly aligns with the forward edge of the latissimus dorsi. In its lower, forward-curving segment the trapezius glides into the forward edge of the deltoid, the two edges forming a lazy S-curve. There is a rough similarity in the shape, scale, and tilt of the pectoralis major and the flank pad of the external oblique. The latter's lower furrow appears to turn to meet the latissimus dorsi. Note the direction of the serratus digitations in relation to the angle of the interlacing fleshy ribbons of the external oblique, the ribbons aiming at the deltoid above and at the waist below. Notice also the undulating character of the torso's contour in front. This is formed at the top by the bold swell of the pectoralis major, followed by the thoracic arch, after which the subtle rise and fall of the muscle pads of the rectus abdominus provide the rest of the contour. Note that the backward-curving line of the lower abdomen appears to continue around the buttocks, the two edges suggesting a backward-tilting egg whose hidden upper margin would reach the waist.

In Figure 4.28 three scapular muscles are seen: the *infraspinatus*, in a line with the top of the deltoid; the *teres minor*, in the center; and the *teres major*, at the bottom of the group. Their common upward curve repeats the curve of the top margin of the deltoid. All three muscles originate on the scapula and insert into the greater tuberosity of the humerus, or high on its shaft. These muscles lengthen considerably when the arm is extended forward or raised high, even appearing in the front view. In Mi-

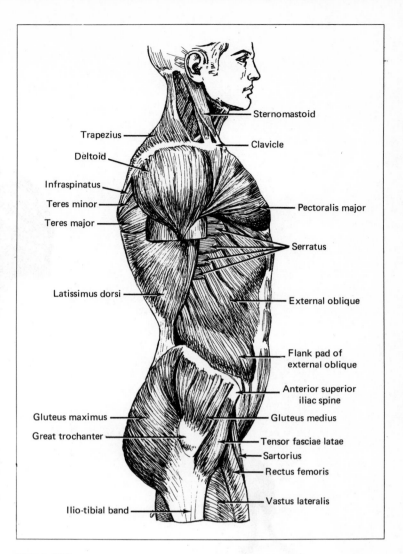

Figure 4.28

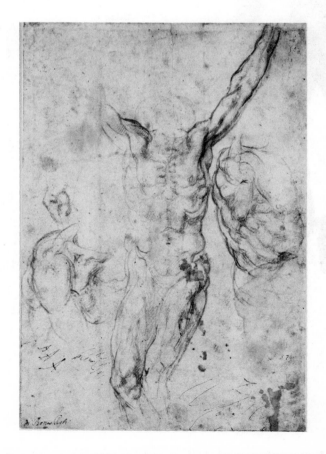

Figure 4.29
MICHELANGELO BUONARROTI (1475–1564)
Study for a Christ on the Cross
Black chalk. 12 1/2 x 8 3/4 in.
Teylers Museum, Haarlem.

Figure 4.30

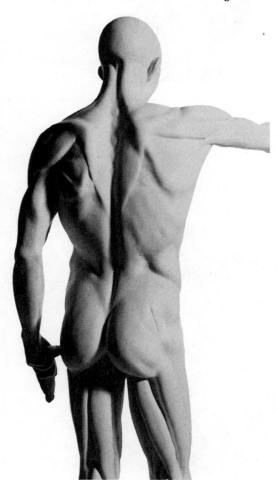

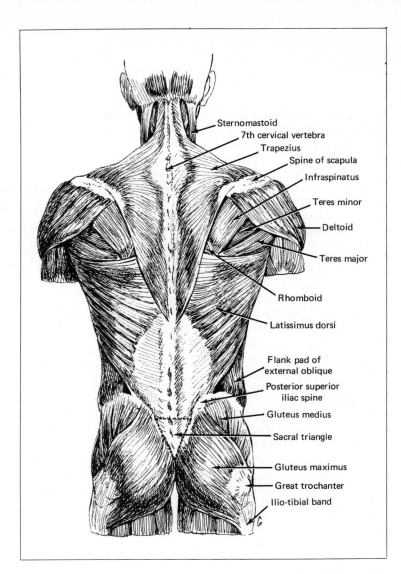

Sternomastoid
7th cervical vertebra
Trapezius
Spine of scapula
Infraspinatus
Teres minor
Deltoid
Teres major
Rhomboid
Latissimus dorsi
Flank pad of external oblique
Posterior superior iliac spine
Gluteus medius
Sacral triangle
Gluteus maximus
Great trochanter
Ilio-tibial band

Figure 4.31

chelangelo's drawing *Study for a Christ on the Cross* (Figure 4.29), the teres major is visible on the central figure's left side as a pronounced swelling behind the armpit that repeats the form of the deltoid. In this informing study, note the flank pads and the sternal attachments of the pectoral muscle on the central figure, and the latissimus dorsi and digitations of the serratus magnus and external oblique in the side view. As this drawing demonstrates, when the arms are raised, the clavicles are almost entirely hidden.

In the back view (Figures 4.30, 4.31) the trapezius appears as a four-pointed geometrical shape. The broadest and longest segment aims downward where it terminates at the last three thoracic vertebrae, the topmost segment appears truncated at the occipital bone, and the two side segments reach to the acromion processes of the scapulas. These scapular attachments and the clavicular attachments seen in the front view are the places of insertion of this large muscle.

The trapezius originates at the occipital bone and among all the spinous processes up to the last thoracic vertebrae.

An important characteristic of the trapezius affecting the surface of the fleshed figure is its several tendonous areas. The largest is a spearhead-shaped tendonous plateau that reaches to the occipital bone above and ends at the second or third thoracic vertebra. The seventh cervical vertebra, the last "outpost" of the skeleton of the neck, is located at the center of this flat patch of tendon. Two smaller but important tendonous areas related to the trapezius are at the spines of the scapulas. Because the fleshy portions of the trapezius are thicker than the tendonous parts, in some poses the "hills" of muscle in these three areas can be seen descending to the "valleys" of tendon. This is less evident at the shoulders, where the spines of the scapulas continue to protrude despite the trapezius's descent toward them, but the large tendonous diamond in the upper center of the back is usually easy to see (Figure 4.32).

Abutting the trapezius at the scapular spine is the deltoid, its lower margin cutting across the three scapular muscles as it leaves the torso to insert on the humerus. Note the enveloping nature of the latissimus dorsi, its upper edges curving upward as it goes to its insertion on the humerus. Below, the latissimus dorsi originates among thoracic and lumbar spinal processes, and from the iliac crest. Note the very large diamond shape formed by the oblique fleshy boundaries of the latissimus dorsi and by the gluteal muscles, whose curved, tendonous attachments to the iliac crests emphasize the presence of these bony masses. The flank pad of the external oblique is also visible in the back view.

Two areas in the back are affected by layers of deep muscle. The *rhomboid*, almost entirely hidden by the trapezius, extends from its origin on the spinal column—from the seventh cervical to the fourth or fifth thoracic vertebra—to its insertion on the inner border of the scapula. It operates the scapula's upward and backward movements. When contracted in pulling the scapula toward the center of the back, it forms quite pronounced vertical bulges that greatly affect the surface of the back. In well-muscled figures the influence of the rhomboid overtakes that of the trapezius even when such backward movements of the scapula are only slight. Note the vertical bulges on the right side of the figure's back in Rubens's drawing *A Nude Man Kneeling* (Figures 4.1, 4.33). The *erec-*

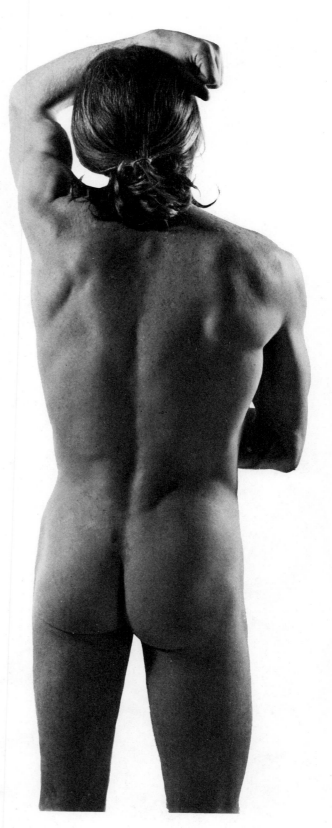

Figure 4.32

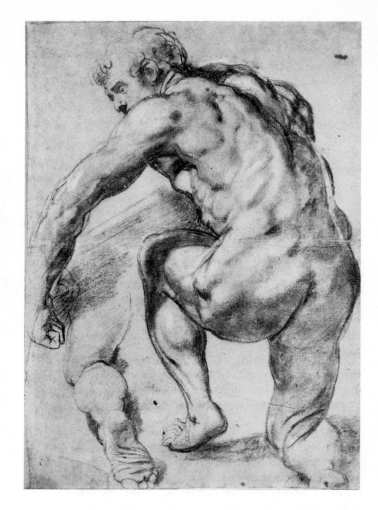

Figure 4.33
PETER PAUL RUBENS (1577–1640)
A Nude Man Kneeling
Black and white chalk. 52 × 39 cm.
Museum Boymans-van Beuningen, Rotterdam.

Figure 4.34
JACOPO DA PONTORMO (1494–1556)
Studies for the Pietà
Chalk. 18 × 24 cm.
Museum Boymans-van Beuningen, Rotterdam.

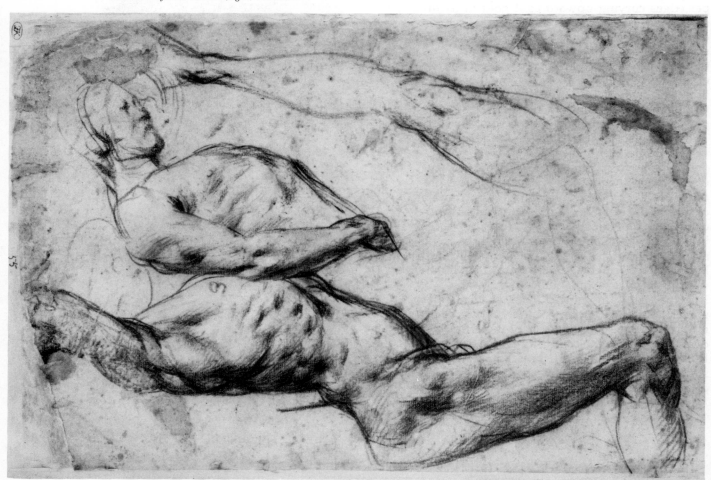

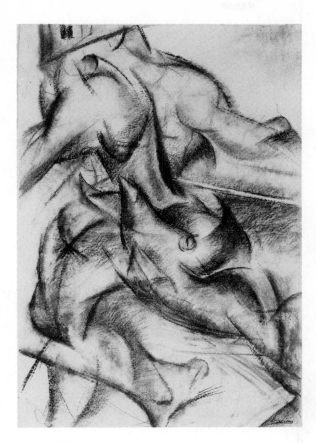

Figure 4.35
UMBERTO BOCCIONI (1882–1916)
Muscular Dynamism (1913)
Charcoal. 34 x 24 1/4 in.
Collection, The Museum of Modern Art, New York.

tor spinae, a group of muscles running on either side along the length of the spinal column, are also deep muscles that affect surface forms. In the fleshed figure, especially in the lower back, as can be seen in Figure 4.32, they suggest vertical columns flanking the long spinal valley of the back.

As we have observed, the anatomical forms of the torso are especially rich and rhythmic in change. Interweavings, eruptions, and abutments of masses play all around the torso, creating forms whose design suggests continuity from part to part. One dilemma of the student with a sound grasp of artistic anatomy is deciding how much of this rich visual activity to include in his drawings. The answer, of course, varies with the intent. In drawings made expressly for anatomical study, the more anatomical material we can explore, the better. But even here, care should be taken to see how the torso's anatomy strengthens and clarifies struc-

tural essentials, and what plastic and emotive sensations they may suggest. In Pontormo's preparatory sketch *Studies for the Pietà* (Figure 4.34), anatomical facts help explain the character of the torso's massive and rugged structure. But it is Pontormo's sensitivity to the design possibilities of the various digitations, the muscles at the shoulder, and directions of edges and shapes that creates dynamic activities throughout the drawing. In Chapter Five we will explore some ways in which anatomical formations stimulate dynamic actions such as these. But here, we should note that it is the artist's appreciation of the tensions and energies alive in the torso that guides his choices of what to stress and what to subdue, and thereby influences his handling of the drawing.

Whenever objective anatomical study is not a drawing's major purpose, its kind and degree of participation will be determined by visual-expressive interests. In Boccioni's drawing *Muscular Dynamism* (Figure 4.35), anatomy plays a large role, but not for purposes of study or even for structural clarity. As the title indicates, the drawing evinces the muscles' potential for exertion and action. Note the great amount of anatomical detail still discernible in evocation of the figure's muscular character: Deltoids, scapula, even a suggestion of the deep erector spinae tell us of the artist's understanding of anatomy.

Often, much of the torso's anatomy (as well as the rest of the figure) is obscured by considerable amounts of fatty tissue, a consideration to be dealt with later. But even when this is the case, artists with a sound knowledge of anatomy are able to draw figures whose underlying bone and muscle we "believe in"—that are alive both as figurative presentations and as graphic inventions. In Degas' drawing *Standing Nude Woman, Back View* (Figure 4.36), there is no doubt about the figure's skeletal and muscular presence, although very little anatomy is showing.

MUSCLES OF THE ARM

We have seen that the bones of the lower arm rotate to permit the hand to face up (supinate) or down (pronate), and that the radius and ulna are parallel in supination but crossed in pronation. This freedom to rotate creates a great number of possible contour arrangements of the arm. In fully rotating the hand, the thumb de-

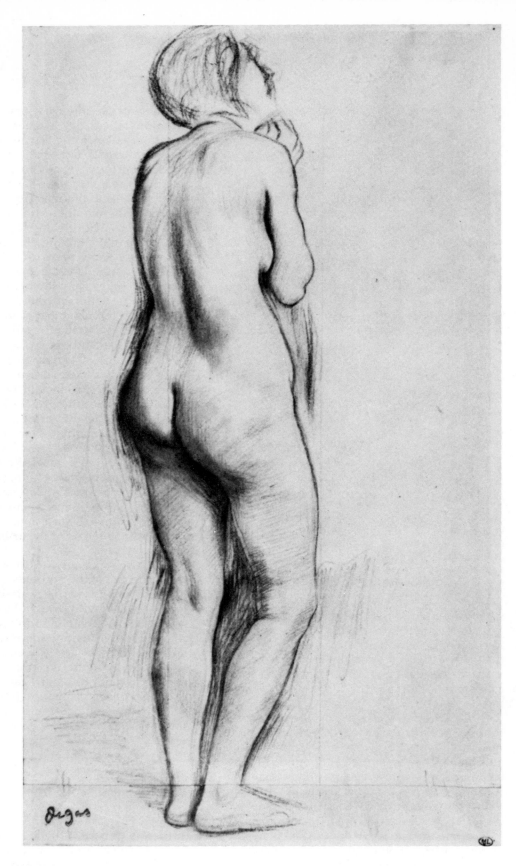

Figure 4.36
EDGAR DEGAS (1834–1917)
Standing Nude Woman, Back View
Black chalk on tan paper. 42.5 x 27.7 cm.
Cabinet des Dessins, Musée du Louvre, Paris.

scribes almost a full circle. Comparable changes in the location of the arm's muscles, and the form and contour changes that different views of the arm or various stages of rotation produce, require a more careful study of this limb. De Gheyn, in his drawing *Study of Arms* (Figure 4.37), examines just such changes. No doubt the changes due to this freedom of movement add to the apprehension some students feel in approaching the arm's muscle system. However, the anatomy of the arm is no more difficult than that of the torso. The upper arm is comprised of only a few muscles, and the lower arm's many muscles conveniently separate into three visual and functional groups, making it far easier to understand the structure and mechanics of the arm. In the hand, as in the head,

Figure 4.37
JACOB DE GHEYN II (1565–1629)
Study of Arms
Black chalk. 36 x 23.1 cm.
Rijksmuseum, Amsterdam.

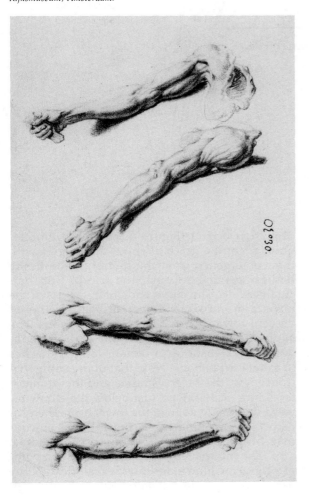

only a few muscles are of practical interest to the figure draughtsman.

As you can see in Figure 4.38a (and in all the illustrations of the supinated arm), when the arm is held with the palm face up, the short axes of the basic masses of the upper and lower arm are in opposition. Therefore, when the upper arm is seen to be wide, the lower arm is narrow, and vice versa. The upper arm, especially in well-developed figures, tends to be flatter on the sides than on the top and bottom. The lower arm is somewhat more rounded in the upper part; toward the wrist it develops a blocky character, broad, flat planes on top and bottom, narrow, flat planes on the sides. Whereas the upper arm can be reduced to a ball (deltoid) and a cylinder with flattened sides, the lower arm is egg-like above, tapering gradually to its blocky lower end. Although the hand can be aligned with the lower arm, when relaxed it turns naturally inward, toward the body.

Mechanically, the scapula and the scapular muscles participate in some operations of the arm and are part of it, but visually the arm, at least in the front view, begins with the deltoid. Notice in Figures 4.37 and 4.38 that the contour of the deltoid does not curve out farthest at the top, but lower down, nearer to its insertion point, just above the origin of the *brachialis*. The brachialis is overtaken in mass by the *biceps* and *triceps* to such a degree that in the supine front view the outer contour of the arm passes directly from the deltoid to the triceps, the single muscle of the back of the upper arm. But note that a small portion of the brachialis reappears at the inside lower end of the biceps. In the inner side view this small segment of the brachialis is of some importance, but in the front view the brachialis has scant influence on the surface forms of the living model.

In the supine front view, the biceps is centrally located on the upper arm, flanked on either side by the triceps. The biceps, as the term suggests, has two heads, originating at two places on the scapula: the short head, from the coracoid process; the long head, from the edge of the glenoid cavity. These heads unite under the deltoid and emerge in the familiar long and rather squarish muscle, which in contraction becomes more or less ovoid. The biceps inserts into the radius by a tendonous cord sometimes visible just above the bend of the arm, and by a thin tendonous sheath or *fascia*, along the upper inside of the lower arm. Here it acts as a kind of binder for the flexor muscles of the lower arm. The biceps partici-

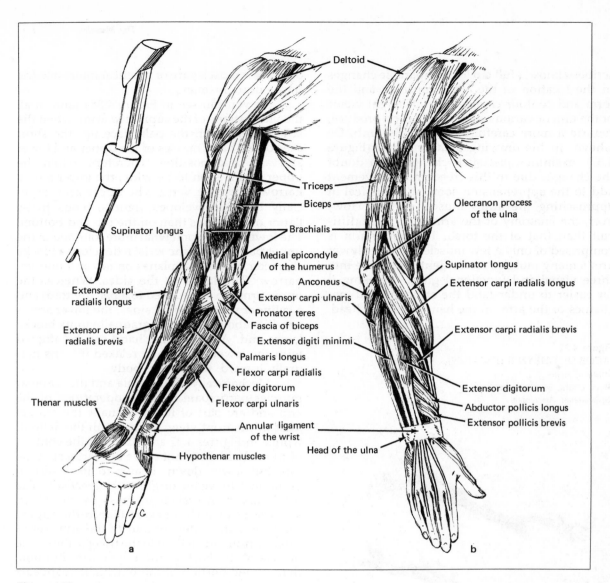

Figure 4.38

pates in supination; when we bend our arm and rotate our hand, the biceps will contract when the hand is supine and relax when it is prone.

The superficial muscles of the lower arm are basically either flexors, muscles that draw the fingers together into a fist, or extensors, muscles that extend the fingers. Additionally, some of these muscles work to supinate or pronate the lower arm and hand. There are two muscles, one a flexor and one an extensor, that are engaged in rotation. The *supinator longus* (also called the *brachioradialis*), and the *extensor carpi radialis longus* form a discernible mass that warrants our thinking of the lower arm as comprised of three muscle groups. When the arm is supinated the former continues the contour above the elbow, and the latter, below it. When

pronation occurs (Figure 4.38b) these muscles unite to form a graceful spiral that begins with their emergence from the humerus, the fleshy bodies seeming to push the triceps and brachialis aside. The curve ends halfway down the lower arm in two tendons that begin a straight descent toward their respective insertions. The supinator longus attaches to the end of the radius; the extensor carpi radialis longus attaches to a metacarpel bone. Note that in the supinated front view, the biceps's fascia and the pronator teres form a distinct X just below the elbow toward the inside edge of the lower arm. The pronator teres originates on the internal epicondyle of the humerus, inserting on the radius.

The internal epicondyle is a common point of origin for four more muscles, all flexors: the *flexor carpi radialis, palmaris longus, flexor digi-*

132

torum sublimis, and the *flexor carpi ulnaris*. The last-mentioned muscle provides the inner contour of the lower arm down to the wrist (Figure 4.38). The fleshy body of each of these four muscles tapers to a tendon at about the same point, about halfway down the forearm. In the living model these bodies are not seen separately but as a united form. In the supine position of the hand only two groups of muscles are of importance in substantially affecting surface form: the *thenar* muscles of the thumb, and the *hypothenar* muscles of the heel at the little finger side.

In the pronated front view, the triceps and the olecronon process of the ulna are prominent. Three small extensor muscles that share the diagonal position of the two large supinators are also quite visible: the *extensor carpi radialis brevis*, the *abductor pollicus longus*, and the *extensor pollicus brevis*. The latter two operate to extend the thumb.

The *extensor digitorum*, originating on the external epicondyle of the humerus, emerges from under the extensor carpi radialis longus, and runs vertically alongside the three smaller extensor muscles, sending one tendon to each of the four fingers. These are the familiar radiating cords on the back of the hand. Running between the *extensor carpi ulnaris* and the extensor digitorum, with which it shares its tendon, is the slender *extensor digiti minimi*, seldom seen on the surface. Beyond the extensor carpi ulnaris, near the elbow, the *anconeus*, which also originates on the external epicondyle, inserts nearby into the olecranon process and back end of the ulna. Despite its short "run" the anconeus creates a marked, triangular plane on the surface, and in the pronated arm appears as a focal point for the longer extensors (Figure 4.39).

Returning to the supine view, note that a subtle furrow extends from the bend in the arm to the thumb, separating the external group, the extensors, whose common point of origin is the external epicondyle of the humerus, from the internal group, the flexors, whose common point of origin is the internal epicondyle. An

Figure 4.39
UMBERTO BOCCIONI (1882–1916)
Study of a Man's Forearm (1907)
Pencil on buff paper. 8 1/4 x 11 5/8 in.
The Lydia and Harry Lewis Winston Collection.

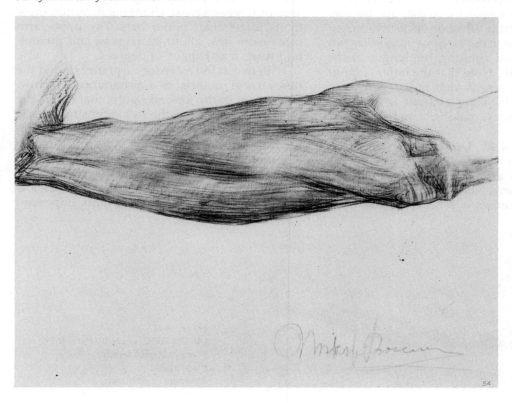

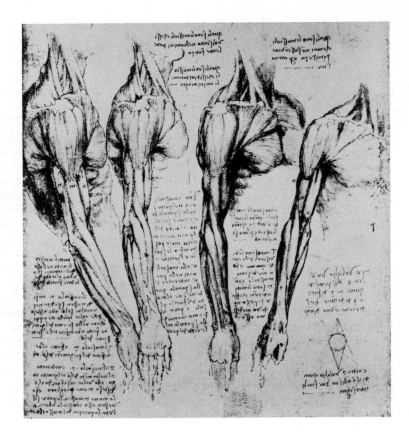

Figure 4.40
LEONARDO DA VINCI (1452–1519)
Myology of Shoulder Region
Black chalk. 29 x 20 cm.
Windsor Castle, Royal Library.
By gracious permission of Her Majesty the Queen.

exception in the external group is the supinator longus which is a flexor muscle and originates higher on the humerus. The extensor group appears higher on the forearm and more ruggedly shaped than the mass of the flexors. Between the two groups, just above the wrist, are two recessed flexors of little effect on surface form, except for the tendon of the *extensor pollicus longus,* visible as the cord running the length of the back of the thumb. Note that the outer contour of the supinated arm is rich in its changes of direction while the inner contour is relatively subdued in changes, making it reducible to a simple curve.

As Figures 4.40, 4.41 and 4.42 illustrate, the supinator group, gracefully bridging the upper and lower arm, is more in evidence in the outer side view. Note that this view of the supinated arm shows a reversal of the basic

masses of the arm, the upper arm being wider than the lower. Now, the outer contour is less active than the inner one, but in pronation both contours become equally active in changes. With the hand pronated 180 degrees, the forearm undergoes a twist, changing direction more in its lower than upper half. The upper arm turns even less, about 90 degress, and the deltoid turns least, about 40 degrees.

Between the extensor carpi ulnaris and the flexor carpi ulnaris is a pronounced furrow, easily seen in the fleshed figure, that marks the boundary separating the two opposing muscle groups and corresponds to the furrow seen in the front view. The ariconeus slips into this hollow to insert on the ulna.

From the outer side view the triceps, with its characteristic high fleshy mound and low tendonous plateau, becomes a more important

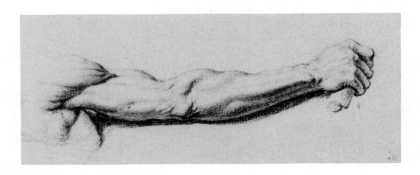

Figure 4.41
JACOB DE GHEYN II (1565–1629)
Study of Arms (detail)
Black chalk.
Rijksmuseum, Amsterdam.

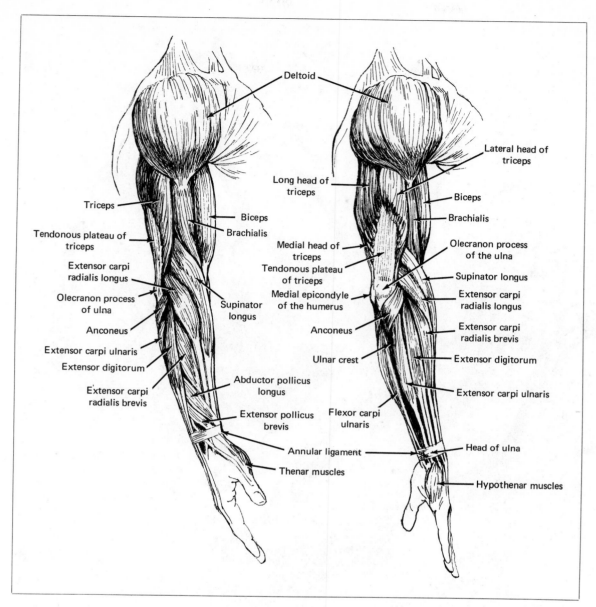

Figure 4.42

influence on the surface forms, especially in pronation. As the term indicates, the triceps is comprised of three heads. The inner head originates on the back and inner portion of the humerus; the middle head, below the glenoid cavity; and the outer head, below the tuberosity of the humerus. All three share a broad, tendonous sheath that inserts on the olecranon. In a well-developed arm it is easy to discern the inverted, V-shaped mound of the triceps muscle and the flat plane below it. The triceps extends the arm and is the antagonist to the biceps.

From behind (Figures 4.43, 4.44), the deltoid cuts across the triceps, turning out of sight before its insertion. The teres major and the latissimus dorsi aim for the armpit, meeting the

inner contour of the upper arm provided by the inner head of the triceps.

In the supine view the upper ends of the anconeus and the extensors carpi ulnaris, digitorum, and carpi radialis brevis all come together and sink beneath the extensor carpi radialis longus. Note the pronounced form of the internal epicondyle of the humerus.

In the pronated back view, the biceps and its fascia attachment are visible. Again, note the arm's greater degree of rotation below than above. Below the olecranon process, the anconeus begins the outer contour of the lower arm.

From the inner side view (Figure 4.45), the *coracobrachialis* can be seen between the biceps

135

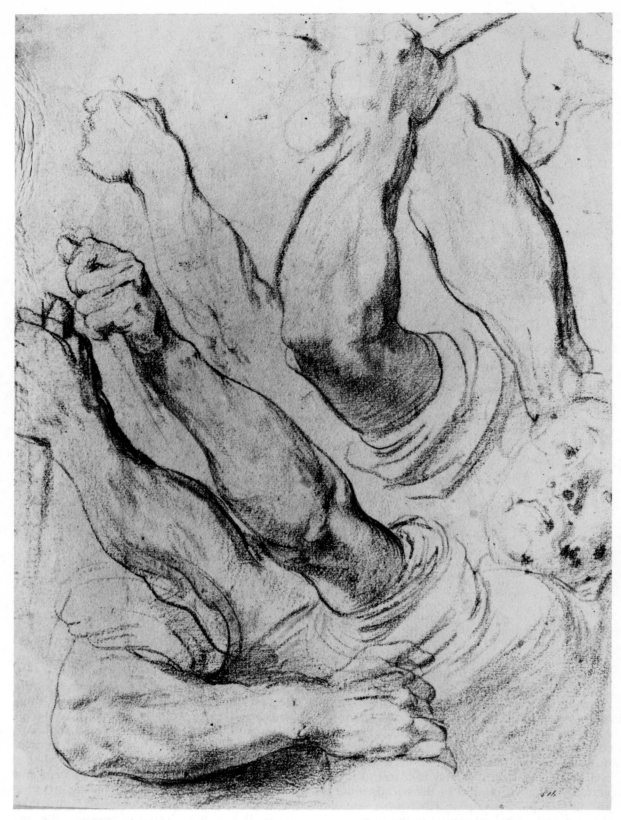

Figure 4.43
PETER PAUL RUBENS (1577–1640)
Studies of Arms and a Man's Face
Black chalk. 40.5 x 31 cm.
Victoria and Albert Museum, London.

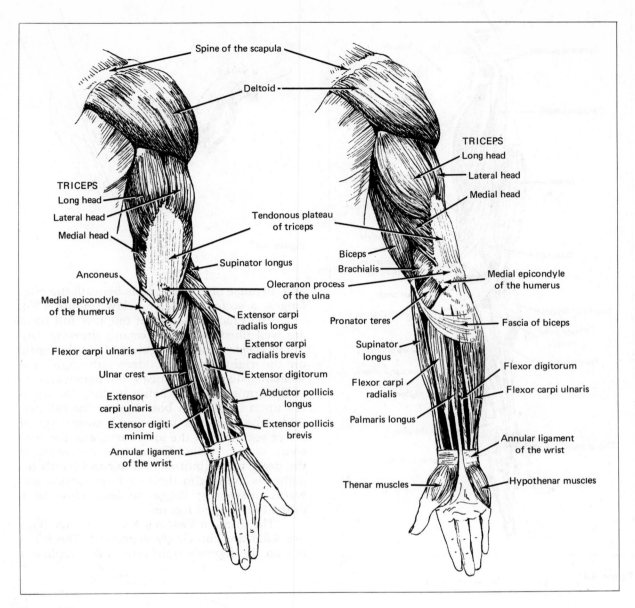

Figure 4.44

and triceps. Originating on the coracoid process of the scapula and inserting at about the middle of the shaft of the humerus, it becomes visible when the arm is extended or raised. When the arm is bent (Figure 4.46) the coracobrachialis and the brachialis, appearing below the biceps, form a curve that appears before and after the swelled center of the biceps.

The arrangement of the muscles in Figure 4.46 shows the long and medial heads of the triceps, the teres major, the biceps, the coracobrachialis, and the latissimus dorsi all interlaced at their entry into the armpit. The brachialis, aimed in the same direction, dies out before reaching the armpit.

In considering the structure of the hand,

we should take into account the bones of the wrist. Following the block-like character of the lower arm, the ball of the bones of the wrist give way to the "corrugated" plane of tendons on the back of the hand. This plane becomes a rather angular ramp when the hand is lower than the wrist, especially if the fingers are turned up (Figures 4.47a, 4.48). An overhead view of the hand (Figure 4.47b) shows the middle finger to be straightest, the others turning toward it. Note that the knuckles line up with the last joint on the thumb. The fingers tend toward rhythmic arrangements, even when at rest (Figures 4.48, 4.49). The top and side planes of the fingers are rather flat, giving the fingers a more angular and stepped appearance above,

137

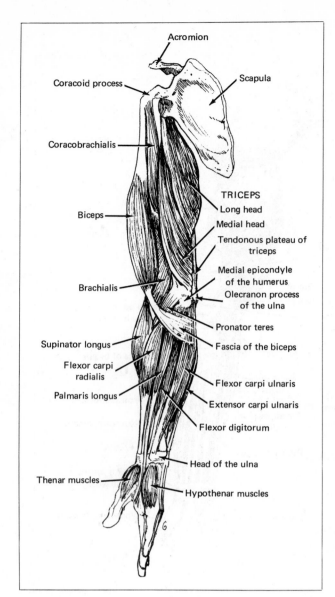

Figure 4.45

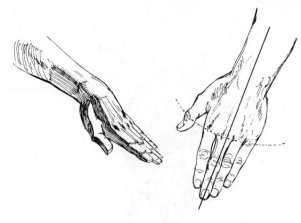

Figure 4.47

and, because of the fatty pads beneath the phalanges, a softer character below (Figure 4.50).

The graceful nature of the arm and hand are well illustrated in Flaxman's drawing *Two Young Women Sewing* (Figure 4.51). In the figure on the right the artist "draws through" the woman's sleeve to delineate the major aspects of the arm's form, the better to draw the drapery upon it. Note in both figures the full deltoids, the rounded upper and more angular lower segments of the lower arm, and the sure sense of their mass. The artist's awareness of the design possibilities of arms and hands together is evident in their rhythmic action upward, "answering" the gentle, descending curve of the two draped figures.

The arms in Pascin's *Reclining Nude* (Figure 4.52) are knowingly expressed. The bulging on the figure's right arm of the supinator

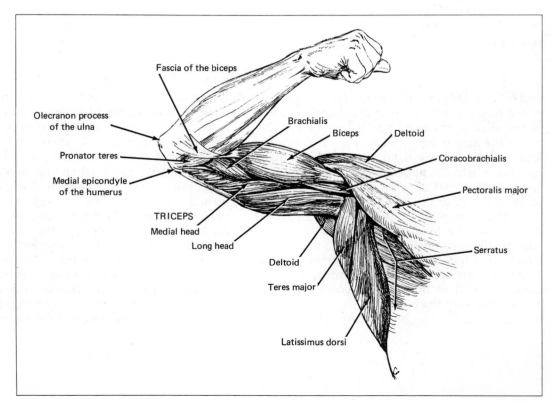

Figure 4.46

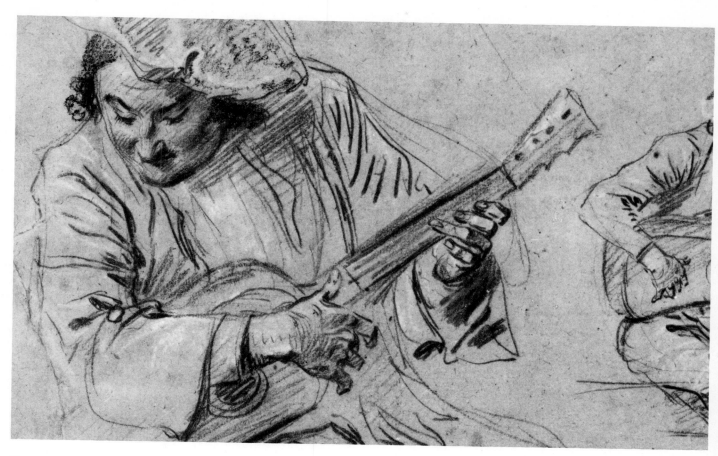

Figure 4.48
ANTOINE WATTEAU (1684–1721)
Two Studies of a Man Playing a Guitar (detail)
Red, white, and black chalk on tan paper.
Detail size 5 1/2 x 9 in.
Trustees of the British Museum, London.

and extensor muscles, the strong protrusion of the olecranon, and the interplay of muscles on the inner upper arm are not only the results of observation, but of sound anatomical understanding. Indeed, the slow, caressing line, emphasizing and simplifying as it moves, tells us of the artist's anatomical sophistication. Nowhere in this delicate, sensual drawing does the line fail to show Pascin's understanding of the structure; nowhere does it falter in conveying his interest in the arm's dynamic qualities.

Figure 4.49
HANS HOLBEIN the Younger (1497–1543)
Three Studies of Hands
Silverpoint, heightened with red chalk on gray paper. 6 1/4 x 4 5/8 in.
Cabinet des Dessins, Musée du Louvre, Paris.

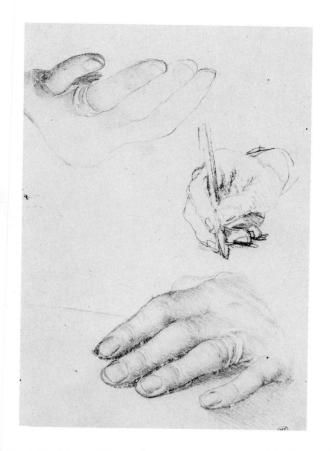

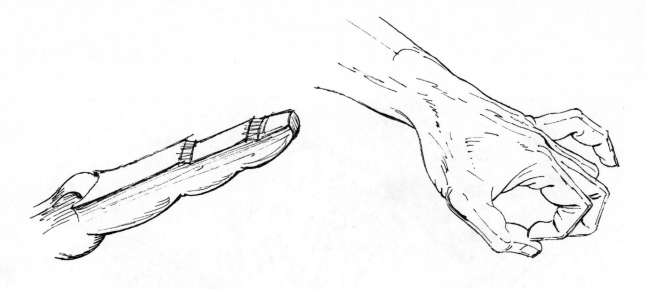

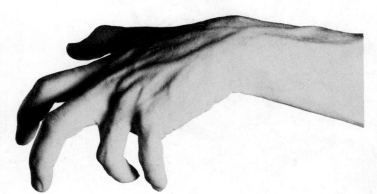

Figure 4.50

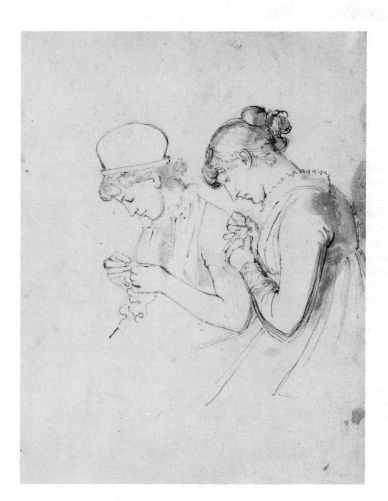

Figure 4.51
JOHN FLAXMAN (1755–1826)
Two Young Women Sewing
Pencil and pen wash. 7 x 9 in.
Courtesy Museum of Fine Arts, Boston.
Anonymous gift and William A. Sargent Fund.

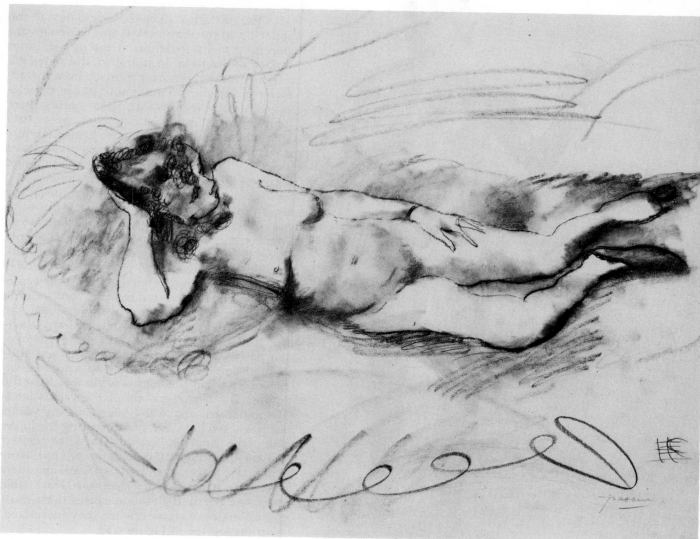

Figure 4.52
JULES PASCIN (1885–1930)
Reclining Nude (1928)
Charcoal. 19 7/8 x 25 1/2 in.
Collection, The Museum of Modern Art, New York.
Gift of Mr. and Mrs. Peter A. Rubel.

MUSCLES OF THE LEG

As we have seen, the pelvis provides the strong bony base that supports and permits movements of the upper body. Similarly, the bones and muscles of the lower extremities require the pelvis as a fixed base for attachments to enable the legs to move.

In the front view (Figures 4.53, 4.54) the *gluteus medius*, originating from the outer surfaces of the ilium and the iliac crest, begins the contour of the leg. The gluteus medius inserts upon the great trochanter of the femur, which, because of the bulk of the surrounding muscles, appears as a depression in the fleshed figure, rather than as a rise. This is an example of an occasional occurrence in the figure: what are prominent outcroppings of bone in the skeleton become the sites of depressions in the living model.

The oblique direction of the gluteus medius is duplicated by the *tensor fasciae latae*, arising from the anterior tip of the iliac crest and inserting into the *ilio-tibial band* at a point just

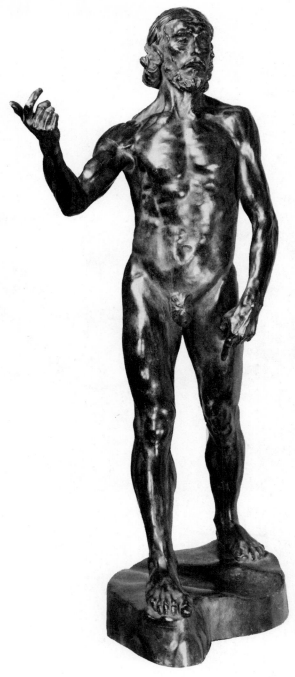

Figure 4.53
AUGUSTE RODIN (1840–1917)
St. John the Baptist (1878)
Bronze. Height 31 1/2 in.
Courtesy The Fogg Art Museum, Harvard University.
Bequest of Grenville L. Winthrop.

The sartorius likewise originates at the upper tip of the iliac crest. It spirals downward gracefully to its insertion at the upper, inner surface of the tibia. In doing so, it divides the centrally located extensor muscles from the *adductor* group on the inner side (those muscles which turn the leg inward). The sartorius, then, is an important muscular landmark, most easily seen when the leg and foot are turned slightly inward. Near the top the sartorius may appear cord-like; below, it creates a subtle depression between the extensor and adductor muscles.

Occupying the entire front of the upper leg, and thus providing its contour, is the *quadriceps femoris*, a muscle system important for its effect on the surface form. Actually, we see only three of the four muscles of this group, one being deeply embedded. They are the *rectus femoris*, originating on the iliac spine; the *vastus lateralis*, and the *vastus medialis*, both vastus muscles arising from nearby points near the top of the femur. All three muscles are extensors and share a common tendon that fits over the patella. Their individual masses are substantial and generally visible to some extent, especially when the leg bears the weight of the figure. The fleshy portion of the vastus lateralis ends well above the knee, but the vastus medialis, swelling out and obscuring the lower part of the sartorius, "crowds" the knee to insert low on the side of the common tendon. Note the *band of Richer*, a tendonous sheath obliquely stretching across this muscle group. Not visible itself, the restricting tendon causes these muscles to bulge out above it when they are relaxed, as in the left leg in Figure 4.55.

On the inner, upper leg, "isolated" by the sartorius, are the adductor muscles. Rarely seen individually in the living forms because of the fatty deposits in this region, the adductors influence the surface as a group, providing the armature for the rounded bulge high on the inner thigh (Figure 4.56). Of this group, the *gracilis*, emerging at the pubic bone and inserting high on the inner side of the tibia, is of importance in providing the inner contour of the thigh in the front view.

In the lower leg the muscles suggest two masses: those grouped from the outer edge to the tibia, and those of the calf. In front, the *tibialis anterior*, in its curving tilt, echoes the spiral of the sartorius. Positioned on the outer side of the shaft of the tibia, it is one of the more visible muscles in the lower leg, its long tendon inserting into the big toe, its fleshy upper half swelling when the foot is flexed (moved up-

below the great trochanter. The tensor fasciae latae is a small but substantial muscle often affecting the surface terrain. It forms, with the *sartorius*, an inverted V-shape. The resulting hollow at the point of their joining is also occasionally observed in the living model.

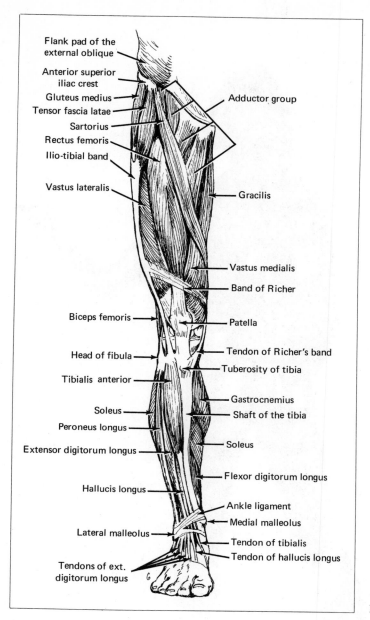

Flank pad of the external oblique
Anterior superior iliac crest
Gluteus medius
Tensor fascia latae
Sartorius
Rectus femoris
Ilio-tibial band
Vastus lateralis
Adductor group
Gracilis
Vastus medialis
Band of Richer
Biceps femoris
Patella
Head of fibula
Tendon of Richer's band
Tibialis anterior
Tuberosity of tibia
Soleus
Gastrocnemius
Peroneus longus
Shaft of the tibia
Extensor digitorum longus
Soleus
Flexor digitorum longus
Hallucis longus
Ankle ligament
Medial malleolus
Lateral malleolus
Tendon of tibialis
Tendon of hallucis longus
Tendons of ext. digitorum longus

Figure 4.54

ward). Between the tibialis anterior and the outer contour, provided by the *soleus*, a calf muscle, are the other three muscles of the outer front group. Often visible in various turning, extending, and flexing actions of the foot, they are: the *extensor digitorum longus*, the *peroneus longus*, and, emerging between the lower portions of these muscles, the *peroneus brevis*. The extensor digitorum longus originates high on the tibia and fibula, the other two, on the fibula only. All three muscles insert into the foot, the extensor digitorum longus, sending tendons to all but the big toe.

On the inner side of the tibia the medial head of the *gastrocnemius*, the large muscle of the calf, provides the highest segment of the contour of the inner lower leg. The soleus, appearing again on the inside, continues the contour, and the *flexor digitorum longus* completes it. This small muscle, emerging from under the soleus, inserts into the foot, its tendon joining those of two deep muscles to pass behind the tibia's medial malleolus. Note that the fleshy portions of the muscles of the lower leg, like those of the lower arm, taper as they descend, their tendons running down together until they radiate in the extremity. Note, also, that the medial malleolus is higher than the lateral malleolus.

The leg's deep "roots" become apparent

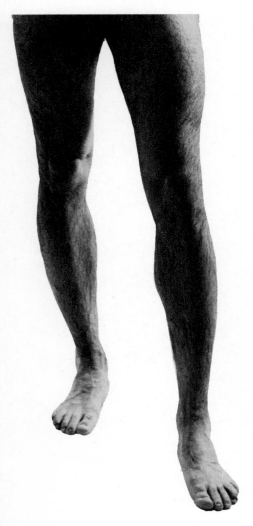

Figure 4.55

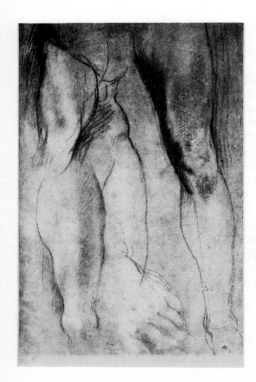

Figure 4.56
FEDERIGO BAROCCI (1526–1612)
Studies of Legs
Chalk. 41.7 x 27.3 cm.
The Art Museum, Princeton University.

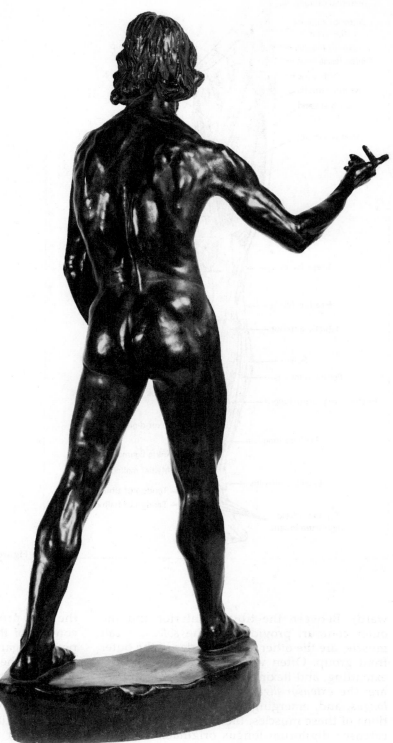

Figure 4.57
AUGUSTE RODIN (1840–1917)
St. John the Baptist (1878)
Bronze, Height 31 1/2 in.
Courtesy The Fogg Art Museum, Harvard University.
Bequest of Grenville L. Winthrop.

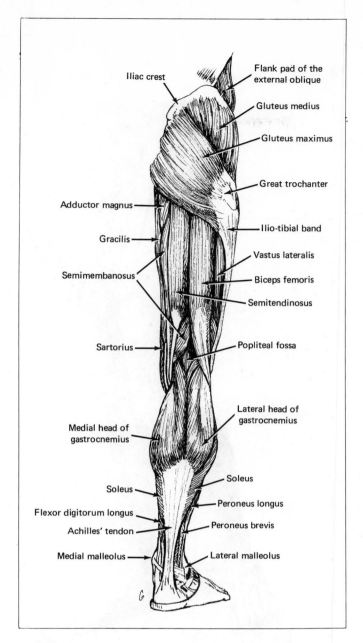

Figure 4.58

Iliac crest
Flank pad of the external oblique
Gluteus medius
Gluteus maximus
Great trochanter
Adductor magnus
Gracilis
Ilio-tibial band
Semimembanosus
Vastus lateralis
Biceps femoris
Semitendinosus
Sartorius
Popliteal fossa
Lateral head of gastrocnemius
Medial head of gastrocnemius
Soleus
Soleus
Peroneus longus
Flexor digitorum longus
Peroneus brevis
Achilles' tendon
Medial malleolus
Lateral malleolus

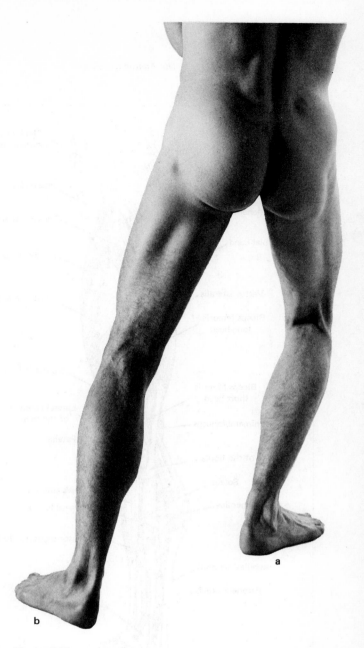

Figure 4.59

a

b

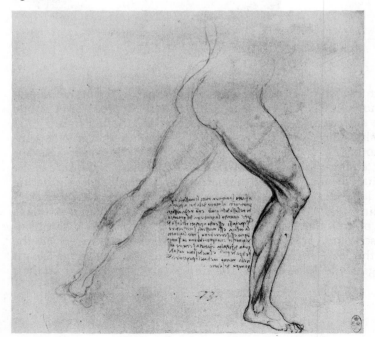

Figure 4.60
LEONARDO DA VINCI (1452–1519)
Myology of Lower Extremity
Black chalk, some pen and ink. 29 x 20 cm.
Windsor Castle, Royal Library.
By gracious permission of Her Majesty the Queen.

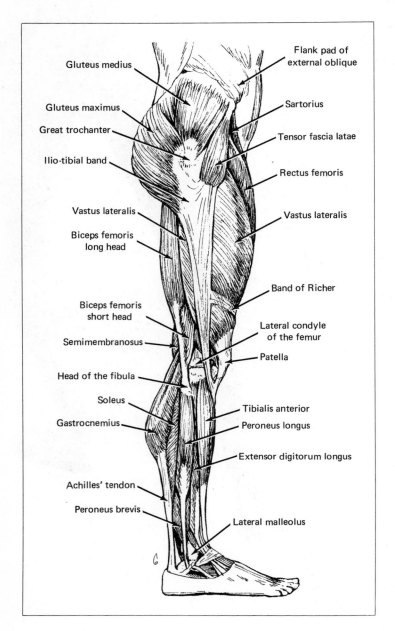

Figure 4.61

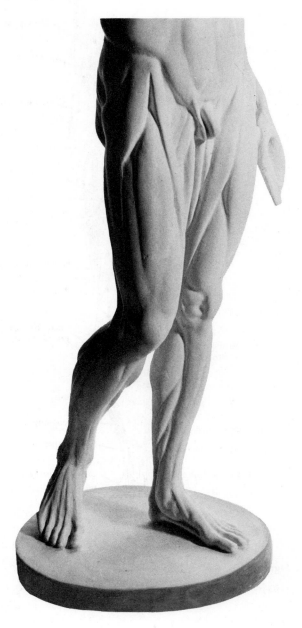

Figure 4.62

in the back view, embedding not much below the waist (Figures 4.57, 4.58). The attachment of the gluteus medius, high on the lateral surface of the ilium and iliac crest, marks the highest point of the leg's penetration into the trunk. The *gluteus maximus* reaches almost as high, emerging from the posterior surface of the ilium and from the sacrum and coccyx. It inserts just below the great trochanter and into the ilio-tibial band. Note the oblique angle of the top, bottom, and inner margins of the buttock muscle, but its vertical outer margin. Note, also, the lazy S-shaped depression along the outer edge of the

gluteal muscles, the great trochanter marking the center of the indented area. This subtle hollow is often seen in the fleshed figure.

The straight descent of the gracilis contrasts with the rich curve of the vastus lateralis overlaid by the ilio-tibial band at the side of the leg. The three hamstring muscles, all originating on the lower pelvis, function in pulling back or bending the leg. The gluteus maximus overlaps their common point of origin. Both the *semimembranosus* and *semitendinosus* insert on the inner surface of the tibia, but the *biceps femoris* inserts on the fibula. In thus parting from their parallel descent, to insert on opposite sides of the lower leg, they produce a pincer-like effect on it. Note that the semimembranosus appears again just above the back of the knee, and the *adductor magnus* fills the space alongside the gracilis, below the buttock muscle.

In the back view of the lower leg the gastrocnemius, originating at the inner and outer condyles of the femur, also parts at the back of the knee, resulting in a hollowed area, the *popliteal fossa*. This hollow shows only when the leg is bent, as in Figure 4.59a; when the leg is straight, the area appears somewhat convex, the result of fatty tissue in this location (Figure 4.59b). As this illustration shows, the hamstring muscles are almost never seen individually, but appear in the fleshed figure as a rounded mass. The two heads of the gastrocnemius constitute the major fleshy form of the back of the lower leg. The soleus, originating on both the tibia and fibula, runs down from under the bottom of the medial bulge of the gastrocnemius, and along the outer edge of its lateral bulge. As in the front view, the flexor digitorum longus emerges from under the soleus, continuing below the ankle where it turns forward and out of view. Note that the gastrocnemius and soleus join to the broad but tapering Achilles' tendon, which inserts on the calcaneus, the heel bone.

From the outer side view (Figures 4.60, 4.61) the gluteal muscles converge on the great trochanter. The ilio-tibial band, a long and tapering sheath of tendon attached to the outer condyle of the tibia, forks at the top to receive the fleshy fibers of the gluteus maximus and the tensor fasciae latae. The direction and cord-like character of the ilio-tibial band's lower portion parallels that of the lower end of the biceps femoris. Note that the biceps femoris appears in rough alignment with the peroneus longus. From this view the contour of the back of the upper leg begins with the gluteus maximus, continues with the long, simple curve of the biceps femoris, and is completed by the small but pronounced form of the semitendinosus. In the lower leg the gastrocnemius and the Achilles' heel provide the back contour.

In the outer side view, the rectus femoris above and the vastus lateralis near the knee account for the upper leg's front contour. In the lower leg, the tibialis anterior alone carries the contour to the ankle. At the knee, the forms of the patella and the head of the tibia influence the contour. Note that the sweeping curve of the front of the upper leg appears to continue through the gastrocnemius.

In this (as in any other) view of the leg,

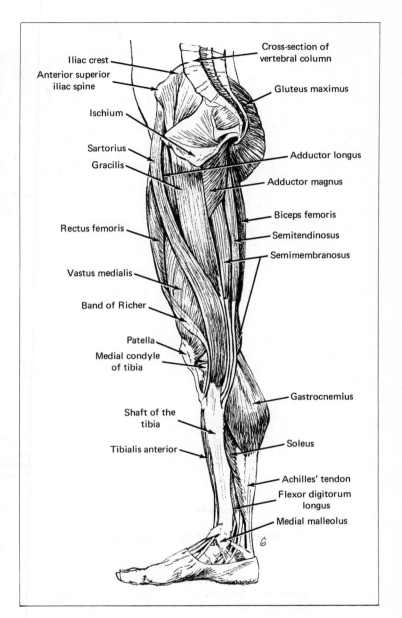

Figure 4.63

the muscles of the lower leg are more in evidence than those of the upper leg. The soleus is often discernible as separate from the gastrocnemius, and the two peroneal muscles are also often visible (Figure 4.60).

From the inner side view (Figures 4.62, 4.63) the sartorius, gracilis, and semitendinosus all converge on the tuberosity of the tibia. Note the broad expanse of the tibia visible in the lower leg. Note too, the similar angle of the upper part of the sartorius and the soleus. The fatty pad beneath the patella affects the surface form of the knee in this view, and the calcaneus,

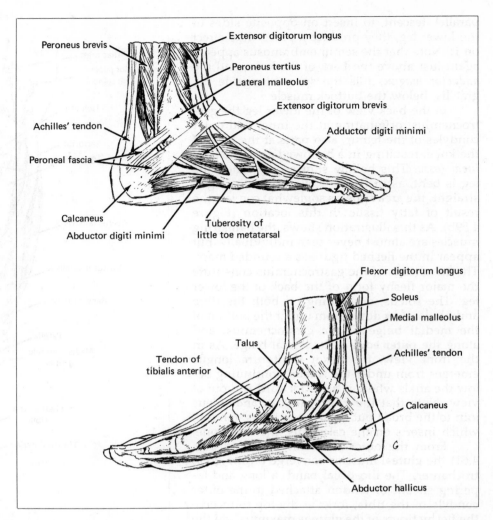

Peroneus brevis
Extensor digitorum longus
Peroneus tertius
Lateral malleolus
Extensor digitorum brevis
Achilles' tendon
Adductor digiti minimi
Peroneal fascia
Calcaneus
Abductor digiti minimi
Tuberosity of
little toe metatarsal

Flexor digitorum longus
Soleus
Medial malleolus
Talus
Achilles' tendon
Tendon of
tibialis anterior
Calcaneus
Abductor hallicus

Figure 4.64

thrusting backwards, affects the contour of the foot.

In the foot, as in the hand, muscles play a minor role. Here, the important surface characteristics are more the result of bone, tendon, and fat. On the outer (little toe) side the lateral malleolus of the fibula is a prominent landmark, the tendons of the peroneal muscles turning around from behind (Figure 4.64). Less evident, the small bump about midway between the heel and little toe represents the head of the fifth metatarsal; it also marks the insertion of the tendon of the peroneus brevis. The *extensor digitorum brevis*, positioned parallel with the long axis of the foot, appears as a subtle mound in front of the lateral malleolus.

On the inner side of the lower leg the medial malleolus, the tendons curving around it, the tendon of the tibialis anterior, and the pronounced masses of the heel and ball of the foot are characteristic features. From either side view the arched curve of the bones of the foot is an important trait, and from below, the consider-

able mass of the fatty pads behind the toes and at the heel, and the tendency of the toes to aim for the second, straightest toe should be noted (Figure 4.65).

Reduced to simple geometric masses (Figure 4.66) the arch bears a resemblance to the ramp of the hand. Note the "walkway" on the outside, and the straight drop on the inside of the foot.

The accompanying plates by the Renaissance anatomist Albinus (Figures 4.67 to 4.69) and the full anatomical figure after the original by Houdon (Figure 4.70) serve here as a visual summary of the material covered thus far. They provide the relationships of scale, location, and rhythm between parts of the figure, missing in the previous illustrations of those parts. Additionally, they serve to demonstrate that even an objective exposition of anatomical fact can have aesthetic worth, that we needn't regard the study of anatomy as an excursion which excludes art.

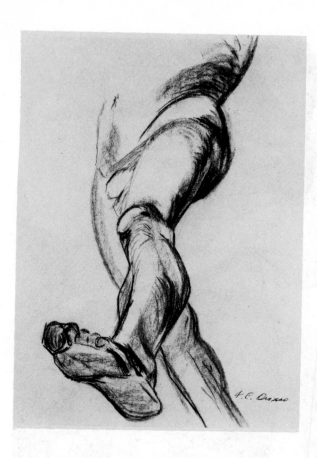

Figure 4.65
JOSÉ CLEMENTE OROZCO (1883–1949)
Legs (1938)
Charcoal on light gray paper. 25 7/8 x 19 5/8 in.
Collection, The Museum of Modern Art, New York.
Inter-American Fund.

Figure 4.66

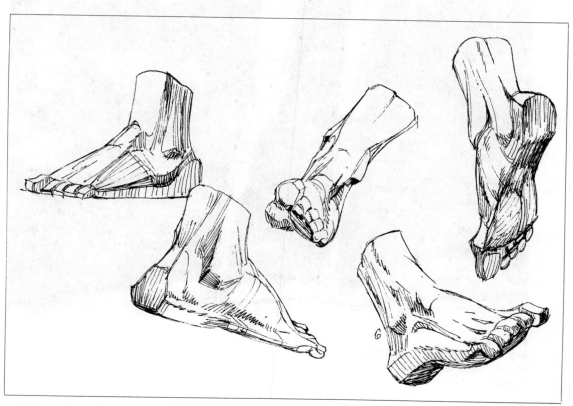

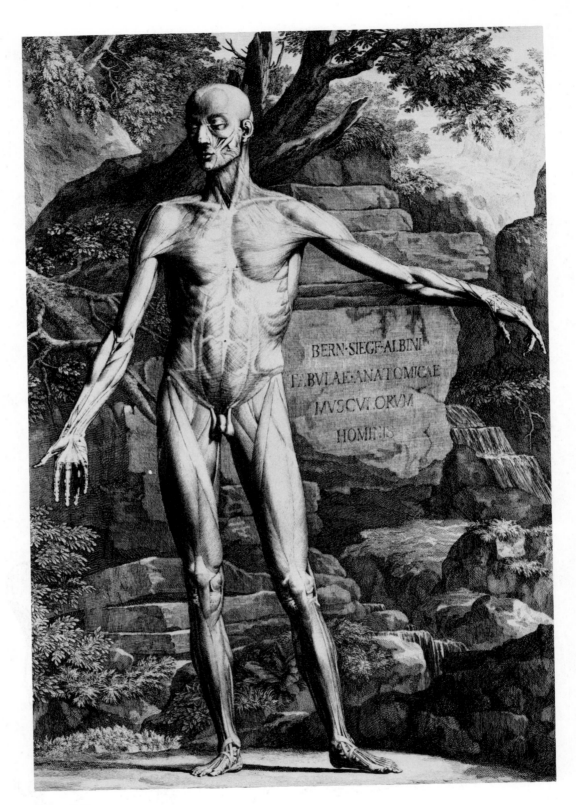

Figure 4.67
BERNARD ALBINUS (1697–1770)
Muscles, Front View
Engraving.

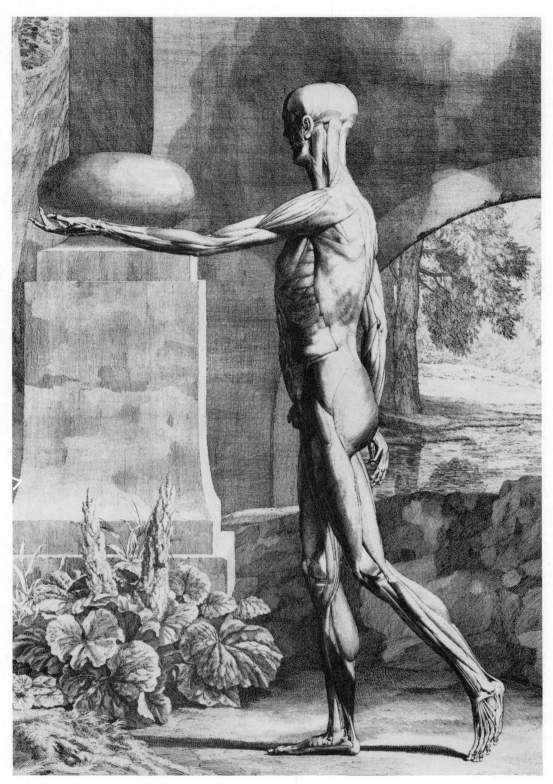

Figure 4.68
ALBINUS, *Muscles, Side View*

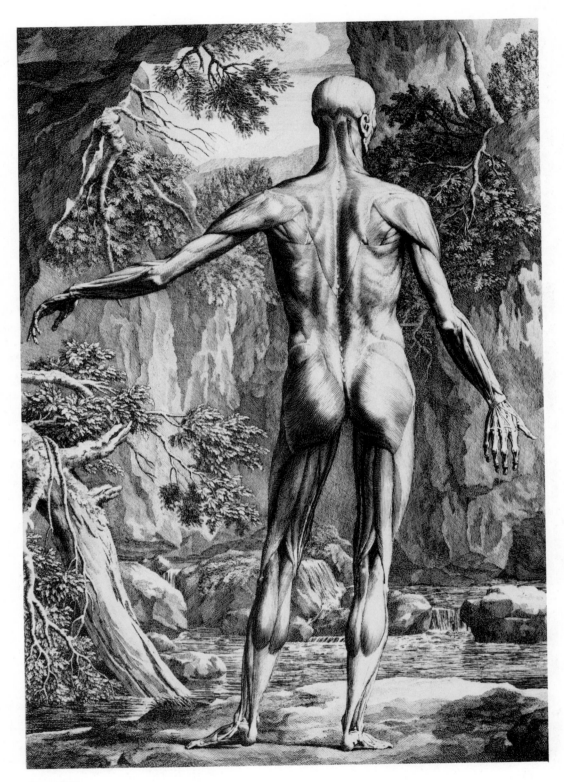

Figure 4.69
ALBINUS, *Muscles, Back View*

Figures 4.67, 4.68, 4.69 are from *Tabula sceleti et musculorum corporis humani* by Bernard Albinus.
Reproduced by permission of The Francis A. Countway Library of Medicine, Boston.

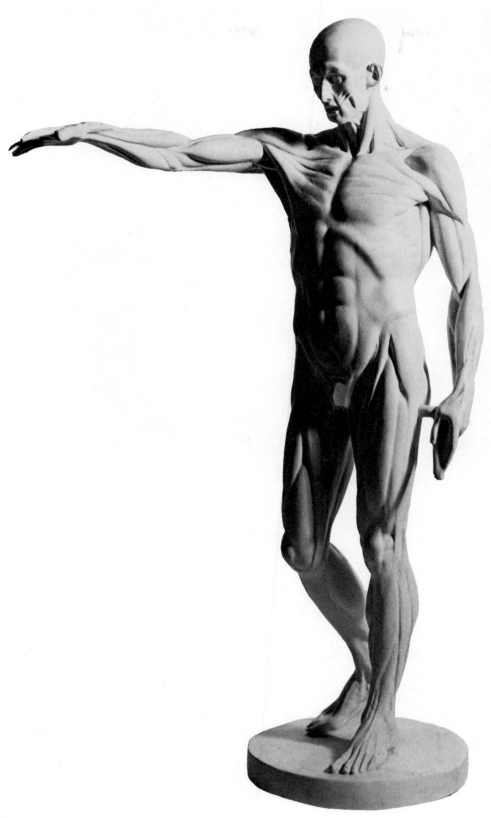

Figure 4.70

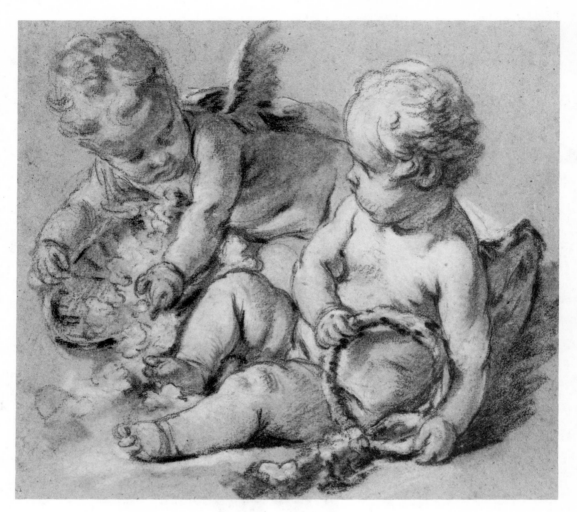

Figure 4.71
FRANÇOIS BOUCHER (1703–1770)
Cherubs
Black chalk, heightened with white
on light brown paper. 8 5/16 x 9 1/4 in.
The Metropolitan Museum of Art, New York.
Gift of Charles K. Lock, 1960.

SKIN AND FAT

In the living figure the skin and fatty tissue modify the musculature of even the thinnest person.* Although the skin represents a fairly even covering, it is slightly thicker in some locations, such as the palms of the hand, soles of the feet, and the upper part of the back. Additionally, its limited freedom of movement, the result of a loose attachment to the tissues beneath it, also varies somewhat. For example, the skin covering the top of the head, along the

anterior and posterior median lines of the torso, on the palms of the hands, on the feet, and even on the inner side of the lower parts of the extremities, is less mobile than the skin on the face, around the waist, and at the joints.

Superficial body fat is also unevenly distributed, and to a far greater extent than the skin. These differences in the thickness and flexibility of the body's covering, sometimes so pronounced as to create surface forms that are quite independent of the anatomical forms below, should alert us to the error of regarding skin and fat as uniformly softening the terrain of bones and muscles.

Generally, fatty deposits are heavier on

*Paul Richer, *Artistic Anatomy*, trans. R. B. Hale (Watson-Guptill Publications, 1971), pp. 78–81.

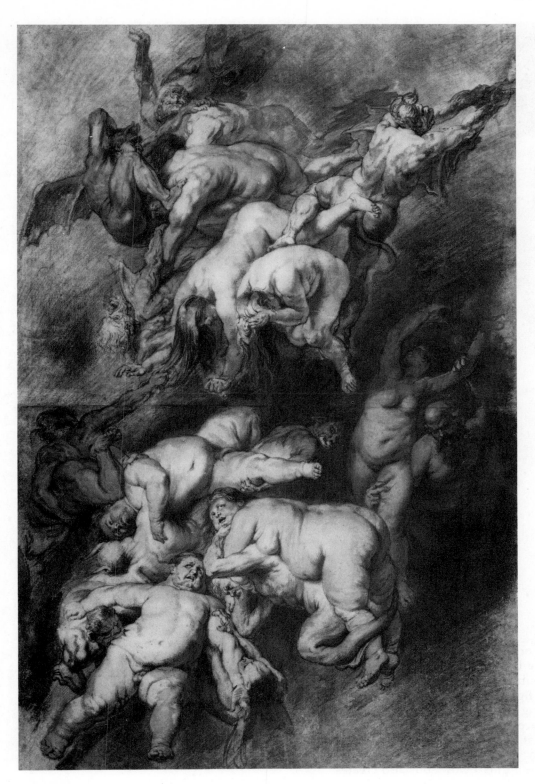

Figure 4.72
PETER PAUL RUBENS (1577–1640)
Fall of the Damned
Chalk. 29 1/2 x 20 in.
Trustees of the British Museum, London.

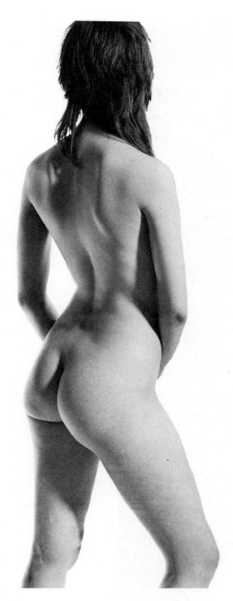

Figure 4.73

the torso than on the limbs, and heavier on the upper than the lower parts of the limbs. Normally, more abundant amounts of fat are present in the female figure, softening or leveling the valleys, padding or grading the hills, and providing the graceful surface undulations characteristic of that sex. In young children and in the excessively overweight, fatty tissue not only effaces the forms below, but also creates substantial forms of its own. These "rolls" of fat usually appear to encircle the forms they are on, as may be seen in the legs of the seated child in Boucher's drawing *Cherubs* (Figure 4.71), and in the obese figures in the lower part of

Rubens's drawing *Fall of the Damned* (Figure 4.72).

The amount of fat beneath the skin varies considerably. In areas such as the ears, the eyelids, and the nosebridge, there is no subcutaneous fat. Minimal amounts are present on the back of the hand, the foot, the sternum and clavicles, and at the wrists and ankles. Ample deposits are found on the torso, especially at the breasts, abdomen, and buttocks, and on the upper parts of the limbs. Although fatty deposits are far greater in the female breast, fat is present in the male breast also.

In the female, fat heavily invests the upper posterior part of the thighs. Above and behind the wings of the pelvis it fills in the depressions in the muscular terrain, accounting for the large, inclined plane that begins near the top of the buttocks and extends almost to the waist. In so doing, the fat obscures the hollow surrounding the great trochanter and the upper margins of the pelvis (Figure 4.73). No such plane exists in the male figure. Compare the squarish buttocks, the hollow at the great trochanter, the curving margins of the pelvis, and the columns of deep spinal muscles, which give this region a far different character in the male (see Figure 4.32).

Another drawing by Boucher, *Reclining Nude* (Figure 4.74), provides a good example of the modifying effects of fat. Here, despite the obscuring of the musculature, the stronger forms beneath still have an effect, however muffled, on the surface terrain. Thus, the figure's heavy forms are not arbitrary or without clues to the forms below. They subtly suggest the vastus muscles, the trapezius, the extensors and flexors of the arms, the tibia, and so on. A sound knowledge of anatomy enables an artist to know which bones and muscles will continue, though muted, to influence surface structure and which will be effaced by fat.

Gravity, too, plays a role in altering the position and shape of the figure's forms. In Boucher's drawing the weight of the abdomen causes it to overlap the upper leg. In Figure 4.72, gravity's effects on the breasts, abdomen, arms, and legs is emphatically stressed.

FURTHER OBSERVATIONS ON SURFACE FORMS

Let us now examine more specifically how bones and muscles influence the padded surfaces of the figure, and see how some artists

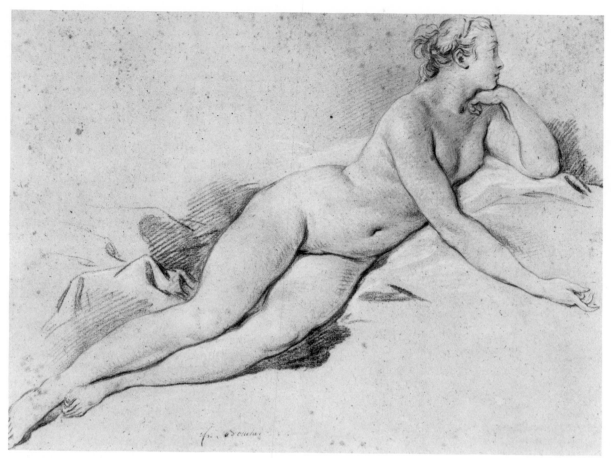

Figure 4.74
FRANÇOIS BOUCHER (1703–1770)
Reclining Nude
Sanguine chalk, heightened with white
on brown-gray paper. 12 7/16 x 16 3/8 in.
Courtesy The Fogg Art Museum, Harvard University.
Bequest of Meta and Paul J. Sachs.

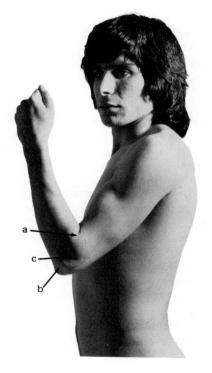

Figure 4.75

have utilized anatomical fact to enhance artistic
invention.

In Figure 4.75 small, dark planes suggest
the eye socket. Above, the ledge of the brow
protectively overhangs the eyes. Below the eyes
the dark, triangular plane, extending to the furrow at the nostrils, denotes the inner front plane
of the zygomatic bone and the canine fossa. The
planes surrounding the mouth, and those of the
chin clearly show the construction of the lower
part of the face. Note the depressions at the
corner of the lips.

The bulge surrounding the outer arm at
the elbow results from the bending of the supinator longus and extensor carpi radialis longus
(a). Below, the olecranon protrudes *after* the forward turning of the posterior contour of the

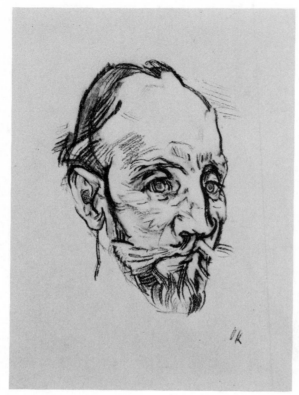

Figure 4.76
OSKAR KOKOSCHKA (1886–   )
Portrait of Josef Hauer (1914)
Black chalk. 41.1 x 30.9 cm.
Staatsgalerie Moderner Kunst, Munich.
Gift of Sofie and Emanuel Fohn.

upper arm (b). Between the bulge of the supinators and olecranon process the outer epicondyle of the humerus is visible (c).

Kokoschka, relying more on linear than tonal divisions between planes in his *Portrait of Josef Hauer* (Figure 4.76), indicates the above-mentioned construction of the eye and socket, the overhanging brow, and the division between the front and side planes of the face. For Kokoschka, these anatomical facts and those of the flattened plane at the temple, the wrinkles caused by the corrugator and frontalis muscles, the configurations of the ear and nose, the bony ridges above and below the eyes, and so on, do not represent obligations to objectivity, but opportunities for expressive design. In sensing the drawing's energy and strength we sense these qualities in the sitter. Note that the artist utilizes the design possibilities of the hair on the head and face to intensify the urgency of the rhythms that animate the portrait.

On the torso, the clavicles, sternum, and rib cage (especially the thoracic arch) are fre-

quently visible even in simple standing poses, as Figure 4.77 demonstrates. Often, as here, the hollows at the pit of the throat and at the xiphoid process (a,b) are deeply carved. In this view of the upraised arm the biceps and triceps seem to emerge from under the "cap" formed by the pectoralis major and the deltoid. Note the similarity between the angles of the thoracic arch (c) and the serratus muscles (d), and that both epicondyles of the humerus are visible (e).

In a well-developed male (Figures 4.77, 4.78), the pectoral muscles form a graceful, fleshy mantle over the rib cage, ending in a "cupid's bow" (Figure 4.78a) similar to the one formed by the clavicles (b). A third cupid's bow occurs at the torso's lower boundaries, formed by the flank pads of the external oblique and abdominal muscles (c). Some additional observations worth noting are: the torso's median furrow ending at the navel; the hollow marking the emergence of the sartorius and tensor fasciae latae muscles (d); the diamond shape formed by the clavicles and the sloping lines of the trapezius muscles (e); the hollows separating the deltoids from the pectoral muscles (f); the muscle pads of the abdominal muscles (g); the constricting of the leg muscles by the band of Richer (h); the gastrocnemius muscle visible on both sides of the lower left leg (i); and the wedge-like character of the feet.

Some of the above-mentioned landmarks and characteristics are seen in Michelangelo's *Study for the Nude Youth over the Prophet Daniel* (Figure 4.79). Of particular interest here is Michelangelo's exaggeration of the youth's chest. To do this, he subtly increased the width of the rib cage, making it necessary to increase the scale of the serratus, latissimus dorsi, and external oblique muscles, while slightly reducing the scale of the pelvic area. Michelangelo also stresses the massive upper body by selecting a pose that shows the widest dimension of the chest and a narrow view of the hips. Note the clarity of the peroneus longus (a) leading to the knee, itself so well explained by the heads of the fibula (b), tibia (c), and femur (d), and by the patella (e), and the patellar ligament (f).

Michelangelo is completely in control of the hierarchy of his forms—of small forms being subordinate to the bigger ones they collectively constitute. His involvement with anatomical and dynamic interests never supersedes his grasp of the essential structure of the figure's forms. The chest, despite all of the surface detail, is still seen firstly as massive, and blocklike; the limbs, as essentially cylindrical.

In Chapter Two we saw that small form-

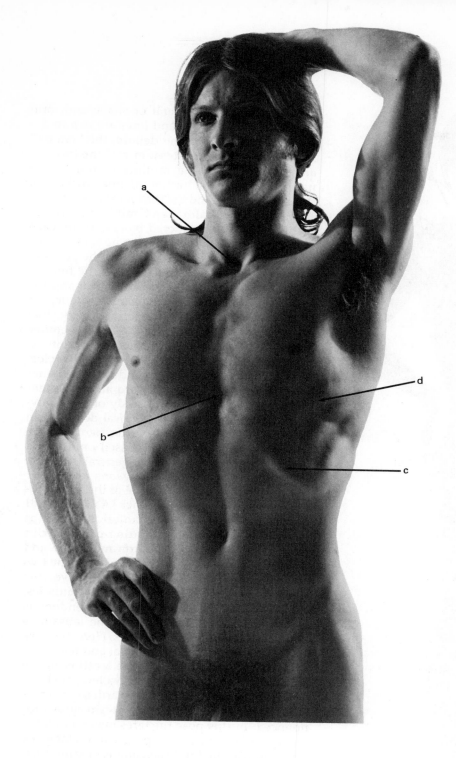

Figure 4.77

units can be seen as either emerging from simple structural masses, or as being reduced to such simple masses. Here we should understand these small form-units as being shaped by bone, muscle, and fat. Cambiaso poises his drawing *Hercules* (Figure 4.80) just at that intriguing point where we wonder if specific surface forms are being absorbed by larger geometric ones, or are emerging from them. Cambiaso's drawing provides an excellent example of the interworking of the structural and anatomical factors.

Examining Figure 4.80, it is instructive to see which anatomical landmarks and forms the artist selects as modifiers of the drawing's simpler masses. In the head the curved frontal bone and the zygomatic bone and arch are clearly indicated; in the neck the sternomastoids, the pit of the throat, the larynx, and the flow of the trapezius to the deltoid are suggested by a few, select "shorthand" marks that denote both the edges and structure of these forms. In the torso complex muscles such as the external oblique and pectoralis major are re-

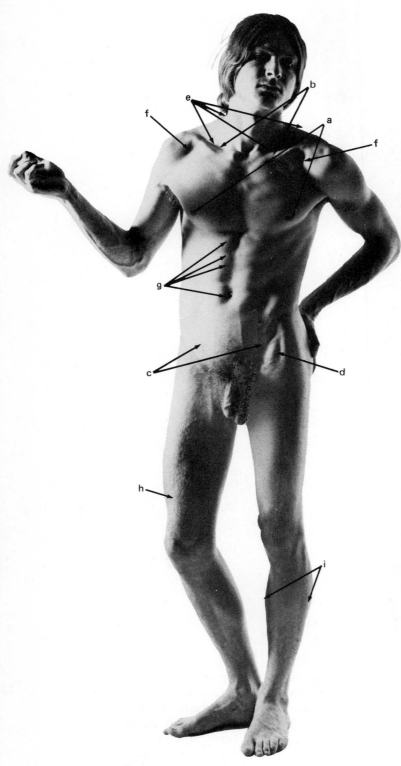

Figure 4.78

duced to the most general of shape and form clues. Yet, these shorthand lines are rich in detail. The hollow near the deltoid, the "lumpy" surface effects of the sternum and the thoracic arch, the nipples, the midline ending at the navel, and at least a hint of the interworking of the muscles at the side of the torso are all shown. And, in the limbs, although Cambiaso conceives them as essentially tapered blocks, again, each modifying mark *tells*. In the arm he suggests the swell of the deltoid and supinators, the bones of the lower arm at the wrist, and (in the figure's left arm) the tendons of the lower arm and the muscles at the base of the palm. In the leg he sorts out the tendon, muscle, and bone that construct the knee; he shows the gastrocnemius, soleus, tibia, peroneus longus, and hints at other muscles on the outer side of the lower leg. The construction of the feet indicate the bones of the ankle and the downward arc of the tendons to the toes. A careful study of this drawing reveals even more anatomical details than those just mentioned. Cambiaso's *Hercules* is an impressive feat of economy based on a sound grasp of the human figure's general structure and the specific anatomical reasons for it.

The scapula provides one of the most pronounced landmarks of the back. As Figure 4.81 shows, the scapula's mechanical function as part of the arm brings it gliding over the ribs toward the side when the arm moves up and forward. In this view we can make out the two tendonous plateaus of the back: above, the smaller one, between the trapezius muscles; below, the large diamond-shaped tendonous sheath, its margins defined by the latissimus dorsi muscles and the iliac crests. Here, because of the thick masses of the gluteal and flank pad muscles attaching to them, the location of the iliac crests is marked by curved valleys, not hills. With the rib cage bending forward, several ribs come to the surface, their downward curve pronounced. In this pose the teres major and latissimus dorsi form a sweeping curve along the torso, and, at the hips, the gluteus medius muscles overhang those of the buttocks.

In the legs the muscles of the posterior upper leg form a single muscular mass (Figure 4.81). On the outer side the form of the vastus lateralis is visible, strapped down by the ilio-tibial band. At the knee the tendonous cords of the ilio-tibial band and the biceps femoris are in sharp relief (a,b). On the inner side of the knee the tendon of the semitendinosus is visible (c). Note that in the lower legs the curve of the outer contour occurs higher than the curve

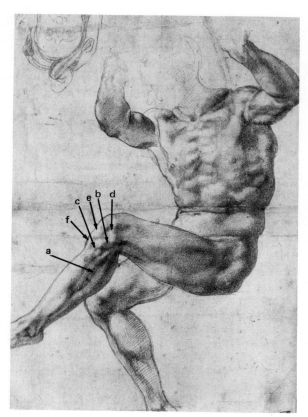

Figure 4.79
MICHELANGELO BUONARROTI (1465–1564)
*Study for the Nude Youth over the Prophet Daniel,
in the Sistine Chapel Ceiling Fresco*
Red chalk. 13 3/16 x 9 3/16 in.
*Courtesy The Cleveland Museum of Art.
Gift in memory of Henry G. Dalton by his nephews
George S. Kendrick and Harry D. Kendrick.*

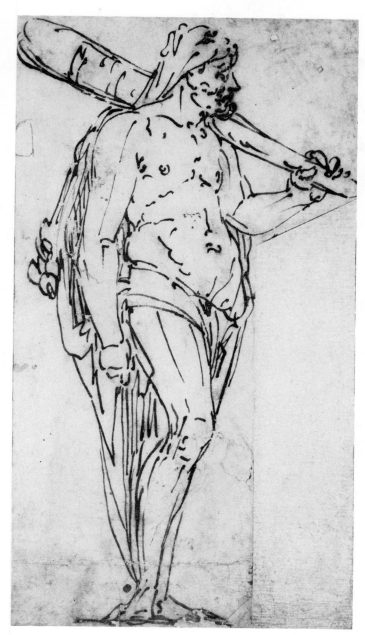

Figure 4.80
LUCA CAMBIASO (1527–1585)
Hercules
Pen and ink. 10 3/4 x 5 15/16 in.
*Courtesy The Fogg Art Museum, Harvard University.
Gift of Mrs. Herbert Straus.*

of the inner contour. In this pose the two heads of the gastrocnemius (d), the Achilles' tendon (e), and, on the figure's left foot, the tendon of the peroneus longus (f), are all noteworthy surface characteristics. The position of the right foot allows us to see that the foot is decidedly more narrow at the heel than at the toes. Notice that the shadow on the back stops just at the angle of the ribs, where they turn more sharply toward the front.

Michelangelo's brilliant study of the back (Figure 4.82) is a rugged landscape of muscle. But despite the gnarled and elaborate terrain, the forms never lose the continuity, the harmonious flow that human forms always possess. For example, the deep rhomboids overtaking the form of the trapezius, because of the left arm's position, create bulges that are in rhythmic accord with the surrounding hills and val-

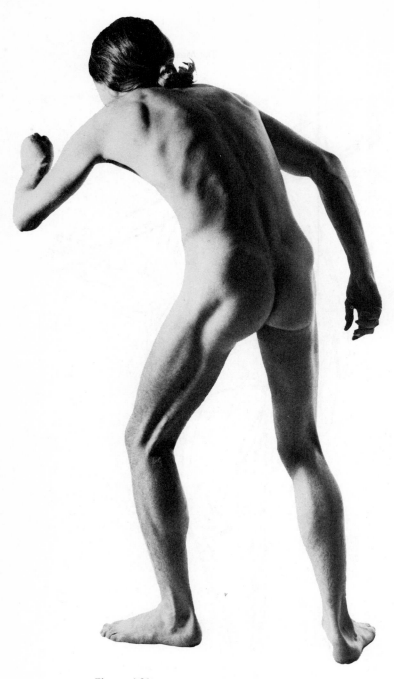

Figure 4.81

right when he advised: "He who finds it too much, let him shorten it; he who finds it too little, add to it; he for whom it suffices, let him praise the first builder of such a machine." But even if anatomical considerations are to play a minor role in your drawings, a working knowledge of the fundamental anatomical actualities must still precede their use if they are to have artistically useful meanings.

When the female torso of Figure 4.83 is compared with the male torso of Figure 4.77, various differences can be noted. There are obvious differences in proportion, such as the greater scale and heft of the rib cage, and the wider opening in the thoracic arch in the male; and the greater investment of fatty tissue in the breasts, the longer waist, and the wider pelvic area in the female. There are subtler differences in proportion too. In the female the neck appears longer, the muscles are somewhat smaller in girth, and the bones are more delicately fashioned, showing fewer abrupt eruptions at the surface. But these smoother, more rhythmic lines are due in great part to the leveling and grading effects of the female's more ample endowment of fat. Even so, the female figure discloses much of its bony and muscular systems, and these are, of course, the same in both sexes.

In Figure 4.83 the points of emergence and insertion of the sternomastoid, as well as its form, are very clear. With the arms upraised, the sternal attachments of the pectoral muscles become visible. In this position the clavicles rise sharply and become somewhat obscured by the overlapping deltoids and pectorals, and the latissimus dorsi (a) and teres major (b) come into view. The breasts, despite the uplifted arms, remain low on the chest. Note how the flank pad and the gluteus medius muscles provide the widening contours running from the waist, over the iliac crests, to the legs, and how the anterior iliac spines (c,d) project at points which, with the nipples, form the four points of an imaginary rectangle. The subtle mound below the navel is a characteristic of the abdomen in even the most slender female figure.

In Figure 4.84 the continuity of the scapular area with the arm is clear, as is the scale and fullness of the deltoid and the triangular arrangement of the bony projections at the elbow. Here the thickened rim of the thoracic arch provides the upper enclosing boundaries of the abdominal muscles which are lost below the waist in the rounded surface form of the abdomen. The graceful curve of the torso, continued by the backward tilt of the pelvis, is typical of

leys. Note the clarity of the seventh cervical vertebra (a), the lower margin of the trapezius (not often seen) (b), and the lower tendonous plateau (c).

In this drawing, accuracy sometimes gives way to creative intent and instinct. Perhaps it is Michelangelo's interest in the dramatic landscape of the back that accounts for the exaggerations and changes in the muscles of the upraised arm and in the lower back. After all, the freedom to interpret forms in any way that is visually logical and expressively accurate is a basic creative right. Da Vinci, who was fascinated by the study of anatomy, recognized this

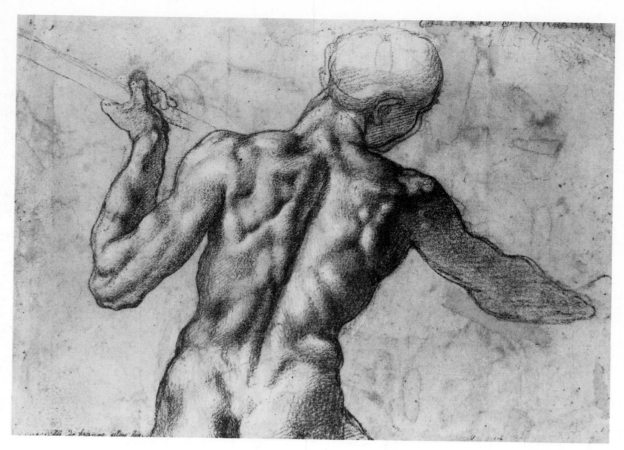

Figure 4.82
MICHELANGELO BUONARROTI (1475–1564)
Male Torso, Seen from the Back
Charcoal and lead white. 27.2 x 19.9 cm.
Albertina Museum, Vienna.

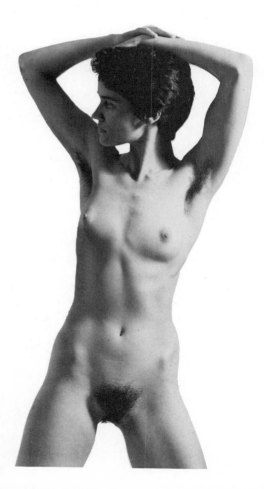

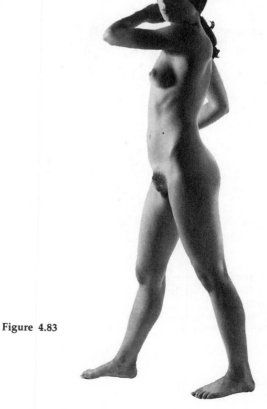

Figure 4.83

Figure 4.84

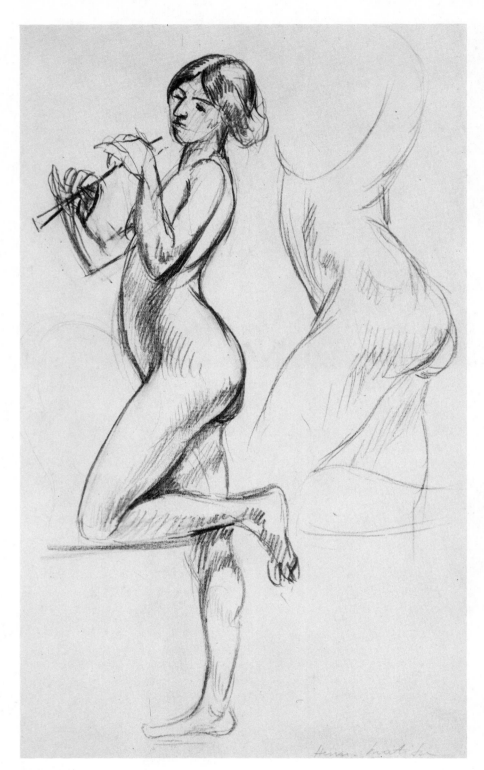

Figure 4.85
HENRI MATISSE (1869–1954)
Two Sketches of a Nude Girl Playing a Flute
Pencil. 13 3/4 x 8 1/2 in.
Courtesy The Fogg Art Museum, Harvard University.
Gift of Mr. and Mrs. Joseph Kerrigan.

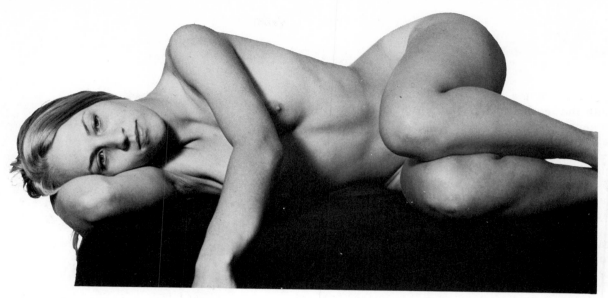

Figure 4.86

the female figure. A similar but more open curve characterizes the upper leg, its front contour turning sharply inward on approaching the knee to overhang the straighter lower leg, set a bit behind the upper one. Again, note the sharp relief of the anterior iliac spine. Usually, in the female the muscles of the legs are seen at the surface as collective, rounded masses. Only at the approaches to the knee and ankle do tendons break the smooth flow of the forms.

Matisse in his drawing *Two Sketches of a Nude Girl Playing a Flute* (Figure 4.85) calls out just those characteristics described above. The artist emphasizes the graceful arc of the torso, treats the legs as tapering cylinders (whose contours reveal Matisse's sure knowledge of anatomy), overhangs the upper leg, and suggests the more angular nature of the elbows. In the figure on the right, Matisse notes the gluteus medius and external oblique, and suggests the collective form of the muscles on the upper part of the uplifted leg, as well as the long, inclined contour running from the buttocks to the waist, a characteristic feature of the female's lower torso.

In the figure on the left Matisse extracts and intensifies these particular traits to support the drawing's theme of the female figure's potential for powerful visual rhythms. The more visual "obstacles" placed in the path of a straight or curved movement, the more time we need to make the visual trip. And here, the speed of the figure's forms is necessary to the drawing's vigorous dynamics. In the torso on the right Matisse does slow down—both the speed of the movements *and* of the lines—forsaking some of the figure's serpentine qualities in favor of its sculptural ones. Thus, the same artist, on the same page, adjusts anatomy's role to serve differing intentions.

In the torso sketch, Matisse employs an even-handed treatment of the figure's structure and dynamics, while in the full-figure sketch, he emphasizes movement rather than mass. This difference in stress points to the heart of the serious artist's constant concern to invent a personal "recipe" of response from these two basic ingredients of perception. As observed in Chapter One, these need not be mutually exclusive considerations. Here, the masses in the figure on the left seem to gain strength from the vigor of the actions they undergo; in the torso on the right the rhythms seem all the more impressive because they carry along so many factual aspects of the figure's structure and surface anatomy. Both figures in the drawing are structurally lucid and dynamically alive, but their recipes differ to a degree.

Some artists, such as Boucher (Figure 4.74) or Pascin (Figure 4.52), emphasize rhythmic movements; others, such as Cretara or Villon (see Figures 2.14, 2.15) stress the figure's architecture. But all artists utilize both of these interworking truths about the figure in whatever combination they find necessary.

Whether our drawings emphasize expressive design or structured masses is determined by our perceptual sophistication and our creative intent. Every view of the figure offers graphic ideas rich in both design and structure. In Figure 4.86 the bony armature persists through the layers of muscle and fat, affecting the surface forms, while these layers produce surface forms of their own. At the same time, supple undulations, shapes, and values set off strong patterns of harmonies and contrasts. These impressions of structure and design are continually interworking. For example, the median furrow, reinforced by the cartilage of the thoracic arch, is a structural fact; its visual "pull" with the tendon of the left sternomastoid, is a dynamic one. Similarly, the left upper arm and left upper leg are simultaneously understood as cylindrical volumes and as forms that move obliquely forward, "cancelling out" each other's direction. They create an hour-glass spatial cavity that echoes the hour-glass shape of the figure's torso.

In the back view shown in Figure 4.87, the earlier noted large plane of the female's lower torso is clearly evident. Note the gentle mound of the sacral triangle, the disappearance of the iliac crests beneath the fatty tissue at the hips, and the gluteus medius extending farther out at the side than the gluteus maximus. Note, further, that the lower tendonous plateau is more crowded by surface forms than it is in the male. In the extended arm the hollow on the outer side of the elbow is formed by the supinators' taking a different course from that of the extensors. Here, the relaxed hand is positioned below the long axis of the lower arm, and the differing positions of the arms show the range of the scapulas' movements on the back.

Lillie's interpretation of a similar back view pose (Figure 4.88) shows the surface anatomy discussed in the previous illustration transformed into engaging graphic ideas. Lillie, especially sensitive to the design possibilities of anatomy, exaggerates some forms, and seems to call to the surface some others that were probably only weakly discernible in the model. Here is a fusion of structural and dynamic discoveries, amplified by the artist's knowledge of anatomy and his instinct for dynamic order—an expression of certain truths about the nature of human form *and* spirit.

In the female, the greater distance between the rib cage and the pelvis accounts for the longer, more flexible waist area that keeps the upper torso from being pressed against the lower torso in a compacted, seated pose, such as shown in Figure 4.89. Here, the rib cage and pelvis approach a right angle arrangement, yet the upper torso appears free of compression against the forms below it. In the male, the larger rib cage and taller pelvis would bring these bony masses almost together, resulting in more compacted and altered surface forms. Note that there are two folds at the waist, the upper one representing the lower boundary of the rib cage; the lower fold, the upper boundary of the pelvis. In the male these folds are closer together.

In a standing pose the patella is quite visible (Figure 4.84), but in this seated pose it all but disappears between the broad heads of

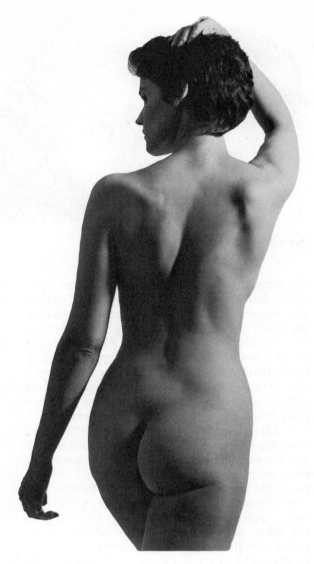

Figure 4.87

the femur and tibia. In the view of the upper leg in Figure 4.89 the gentle curve of the femur bone is reflected in the curve of the fleshed form. Here, the foreshortened view of the left upper arm clearly shows the rounded form of the upper part and the squarish form of the lower one. Note the ball-like mass of the bones of the wrist and the graceful rhythm of the hand.

Comparing Rembrandt's drawing of a heavy-set woman (Figure 4.90) with the woman in Figure 4.89, we notice the effects of substantial deposits of fat on surface forms. But, because fat is stored mainly on the lower torso and upper parts of the limbs, the skeleton and muscles still play an important role in shaping the surfaces of even obese figures, if only in the lower parts of the limbs and at the joints (Fig-

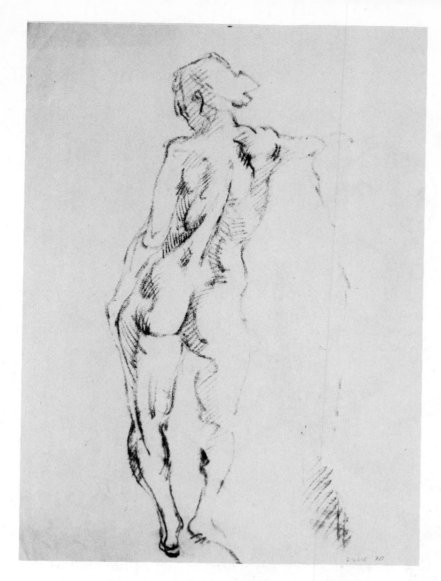

Figure 4.88
LLOYD LILLIE (1932–   )
Standing Figure, Back View
Black chalk. 12 x 17 1/2 in.
Courtesy of the artist.

Figure 4.89

ure 4.72). Moreover, bone and muscle continue
to influence, if only weakly, the *general* structural character of the rest of the forms, however
much overlaid by fat.

In Rembrandt's drawing, the shape of the
cranium, the angularity of the jaw, and the
bony passages and projections at the joints all
show the skeleton at the surface. And, except
for the abdomen, firm, inner masses and shafts
of support are sensed throughout the figure.
Rembrandt subtly suggests the rib cage, and
on the figure's left hip, the heavily overlaid
wing of the pelvis.

A major theme in this drawing appears to
be the figure's weighty substantiality. To convey this, Rembrandt simplifies the forms by
grouping many small planes into the major and
secondary ones they conform to. For example,
he interprets the legs as block-like and even
treats the knees as squared off. Likewise, the
lower torso hints at its spherical basis, the head
and upper torso suggest ovoids, and the neck

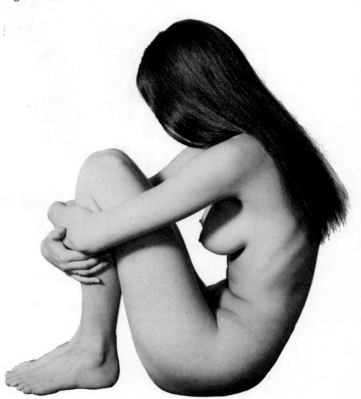

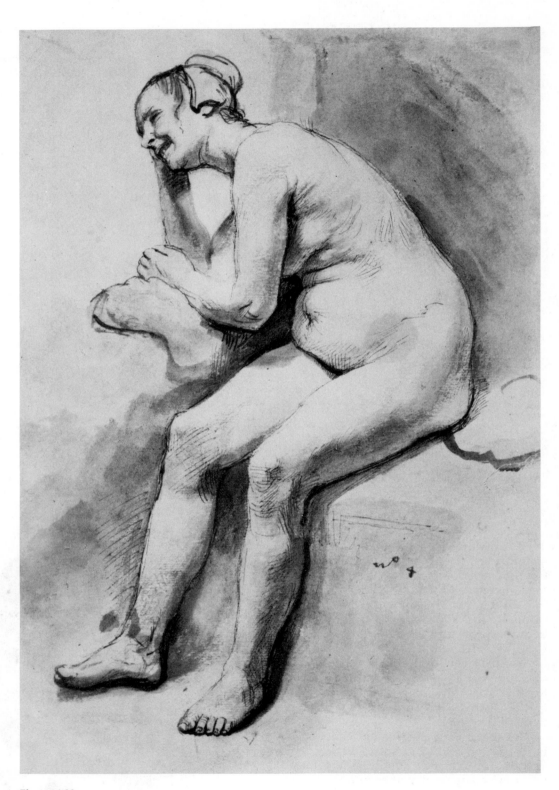

Figure 4.90
REMBRANDT VAN RIJN (1606–1669)
Seated Nude Woman
Pen and ink, some washes. 10 1/4 x 7 1/4 in.
Cabinet des Dessins, Musée du Louvre, Paris.

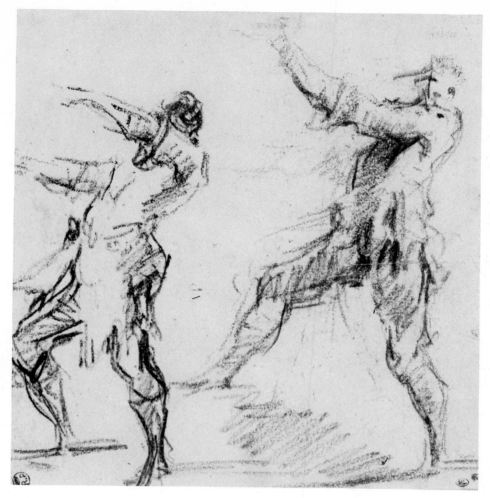

Figure 4.91
GIOVANNI BATTISTA PIRANESI (1720–1778)
Two Studies of a Man Standing,
His Arms Outstretched to the Left
Black and red chalk. 7 3/4 x 7 5/8 in.
Cabinet des Dessins, Musée du Louvre, Paris.

and upper limbs, cylinders. In discreetly hinting at the geometric essense of the forms, Rembrandt achieves a strong sense of solidity.

But nowhere is this move toward monumentality allowed to override important characteristics of surface anatomy that heighten the drawing's humanistic theme: a woman relaxed, lost in some pleasant reverie. Rembrandt always avoids dehumanizing solutions. Here, structural and anatomical factors interwork in a way that allows each to contribute to the sense of weighty human form. Rembrandt's grasp of *any* form's structural essentials helps him to convincingly and economically convey anatomical observations such as the complex structure of the knee, or the arrangement of the flexors and extensors of the arms. Conversely, his knowledge of anatomy assists his structural theme of summarizing the figure's forms. For example, the blocky plane in the left upper leg is only a modest exaggeration of the flattening

effect of the ilio-tibial band. And, in the lower leg, where many artists might use the pronounced line of the tibia's sharp edge to explain a change in planes, Rembrandt uses the tibialis as the dividing line between the front and side planes to continue the blocky L-shape of the entire leg. The tibia's influence on the surface of the lower leg is always visible, but Rembrandt wisely omits it here, gaining structural and visual unity.

Here, as in most of Rembrandt's figure drawings (and paintings), the formula is to resist simplifying structure when it would intrude on the humanistic aspects of his image, and to omit surface niceties when they would diminish its structural and dynamic clarity. Rembrandt recognizes that indiscriminate denotations of surface anatomy usually obscure a subject's important structural nature, and that drastic structural summaries may weaken its evocative, representational impact. Further, he

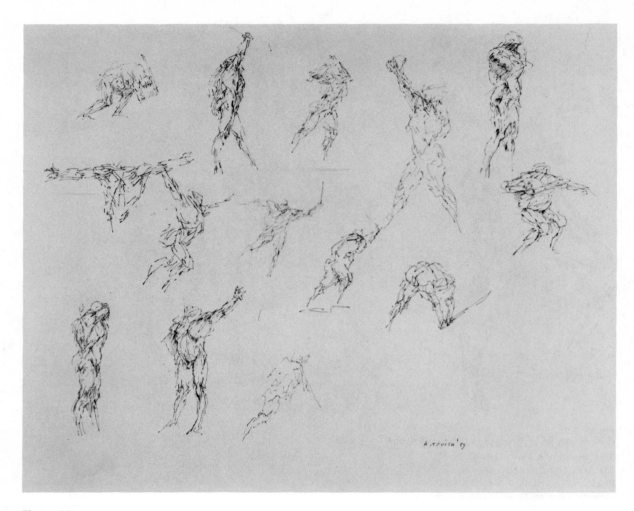

Figure 4.92
HAROLD TOVISH (1921–   )
Study for Man with Sword II
Pen and ink.
Worcester Art Museum, Massachusetts.

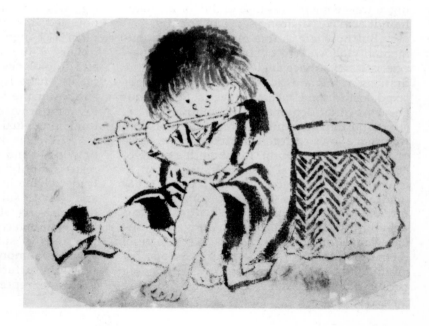

Figure 4.93
KATSUSHIKA HOKUSAI (1760–1849)
Boy with Flute
Ink and brush. 11.5 x 15.9 cm.
The Freer Gallery of Art, Washington, D. C.

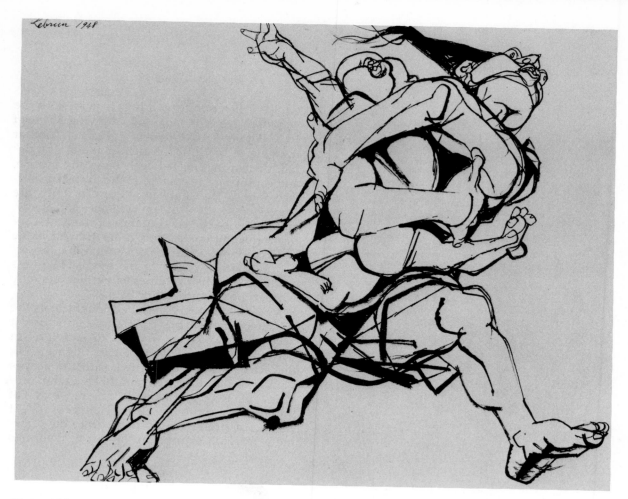

Figure 4.94
RICO LEBRUN (1900–1964)
Running Figure (1948)
Ink. 18 3/4 x 24 3/8 in.
Collection, Whitney Museum of American Art, New York.

knows that the figure's structure and anatomy must congenially interplay with its design and expression too, that the subject's substantiality of form and significance of spirit must be felt as well as seen.

A sound understanding of structure and anatomy is generally evident in master drawings of the draped figure. In Piranesi's studies of an action pose (Figure 4.91), the underdrawing of the nude figure helps him to establish the gesture and masses of the forms to be draped, and to drape these forms more convincingly. In the figure on the left the clothing, stretched taut upon the upper right leg, forms sharp folds that turn and radiate in a way that describes the form and action of the leg, and suggests that further raising of the leg must meet even more resistance from the restraining pant-leg. Despite the drapery, we know the tilt and mass of the upper torso and the differing tilt and mass of the hips. The arms and legs are still more fully revealed. In the legs Piranesi even suggests the upper leg's overlapping of the lower one at the

knee, and the contours of the tibialis and gastrocnemius muscles.

In Tovish's drawing *Study for Man with Sword II* (Figure 4.92), expressive design interests strongly modify structural and anatomical ones. In these first searching probes for forms to be finally realized as sculpture, the artist extracts gestures, energies, and relationships of the figure's parts in various positions, testing their emotive and dynamic possibilities. In exploring the substance and spirit of these figures, masses and meanings are interworking matters. This being so, the essential forms and dynamics of these quick sketches is usually clear. But, in passages of a few of these figures, certain inquiries into gesture, rhythm, or energy overtake structural and anatomical ones—and rightly so. If a hierarchy exists among the factors, clearly the search for a subject's visual and expressive meanings should precede the analysis of the masses that are to convey these meanings. For it is the subject's *total* visual-expressive condition that we first respond to,

171

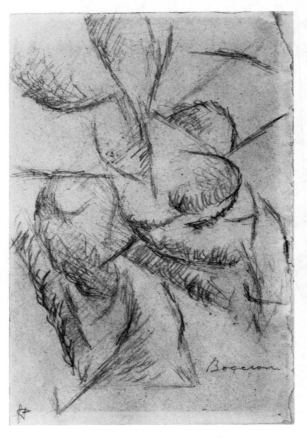

Figure 4.95
UMBERTO BOCCIONI (1882–1916)
Male Figure in Motion towards the Left (1913)
Pencil. 6 x 4 1/8 in.
The Lydia and Harry Lewis Winston Collection.

Figure 4.96
ARISTIDE MAILLOL (1861–1944)
Young Cyclist (1908)
Bronze. Height 38 in.
Courtesy The Fogg Art Museum, Harvard University.
Purchase, Friends of the Fogg and Alpheus Hyatt Fund.

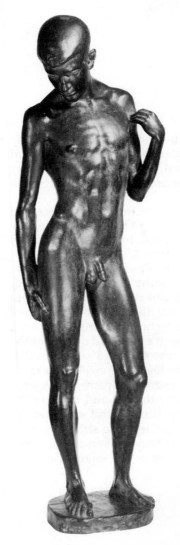

tainty of their understanding is evident in the way they use it. In Hokusai's drawing *Boy with Flute* (Figure 4.93) the seemingly casual contour drawing of the limbs is rich in anatomical detail, discriminating between bone and muscle, and capturing the essence of their effect on surface forms. The bony joints of the limbs are suggested by short lines at the knees and elbow, and we sense the continuance of the limbs beneath the drapery. Although the drawing of the head conforms more to convention than observation, the rest of the figure reveals Hokusai's ability to establish volumes and utilize anatomy with economy and authority.

While anatomy may be thought of as the substance that shapes the figure's structure, it need not always be wedded to structure. In Lebrun's drawing *Running Figure* (Figure 4.94), the artist is more concerned with the shapes than with the surface terrain that anatomy provides. By exaggerating the "ins and outs" of the figure's contours, Lebrun creates violent clashes of strong shapes that add to the drawing's forceful expression of terror. Lebrun's

that suggests its creative potential, and not the measurements, however important, of the subject's parts.

Tovish's knowledge of anatomy is apparent in the clarity of his "shorthand" graphic solutions to the anatomical complexities of torsos, arms, and legs. This is especially clear in the second figure of the top row, the first, second, and fifth figures of the middle row, and the first and second figures of the bottom row.

Even when great exponents of the figure do not emphasize anatomical matters, the cer-

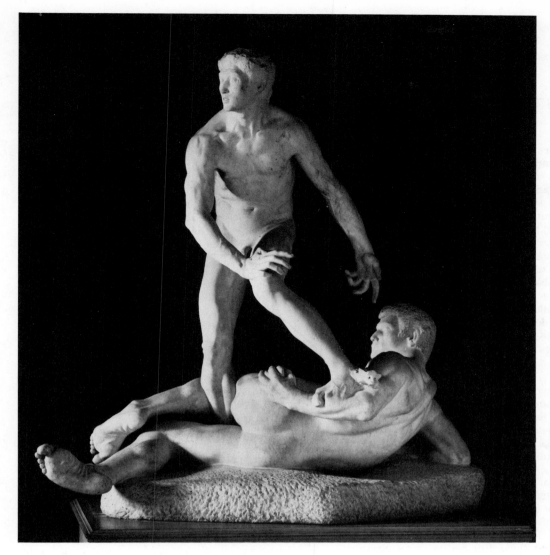

Figure 4.97
GEORGE GREY BARNARD (1863–1938)
Struggle of Two Natures in Man
Marble. Height 101 1/2 in.
The Metropolitan Museum of Art, New York.
Gift of Alfred Corning Clark, 1896.

mastery of anatomy enables him to create powerful interpretations of human forms, whatever their positions, as the inventive drawing of each of the arms and legs demonstrates.

While Lebrun distorts the figure's forms, he never ignores or violates fundamental anatomical facts. These distortions are not changes invoked without regard to the figure's essential form-character. On the contrary, they are intensifications of what bone and muscle really do to human surfaces. Even the strained-looking placement of the child's legs is only a slight exaggeration of an anatomically possible position. In studying anatomy it is good to hold in mind drawings such as these, to realize how important a knowledge of the figure's substructure is to the expansion of our options of response.

An example of just how far such knowledge may carry us into the realm of abstract and two-dimensional drawing solutions to the figure's limitless challenges is Boccioni's drawing *Male Figure in Motion towards the Left* (Figure 4.95). Here, despite the strong insistence on the two-dimensional activity of line, value, texture, and open-ended shapes, bone and muscle still stimulate dynamic activities, still help express human forms and movements.

In this chapter we have seen that the purpose of a knowledge of anatomy, whether we simplify, embellish, or objectively record the figure's forms, is to increase the relational and emotive force of our figure drawings. Anatomy's contribution to the factors of structure, design, and expression is the "ring of truth" without which figure drawings cannot come alive.

173

SUGGESTED EXERCISES

These exercises approach the study of anatomy taking into account its participation in creative figure drawing. You may expand on them in any way that will uncover additional facts about anatomy *and* its potential for stimulating graphic inventions. Although the anatomical illustrations in this book should suffice, these exercises may be done with the help of other anatomical texts (see Bibliography). As in Chapter Two, vary the scale and media of these exercises, but favor large rather than small drawings, and use erasable rather than permanent media. Unless otherwise indicated, work from the model. If none are available to you, work from the photographs provided here or in other books. Unless otherwise noted, there are no time limits on any of these drawings.

1. Draw two more-or-less simplified skulls: one front, one side view. Then place a sheet of tracing paper over these and draw the muscles of the head as they would appear in each view. Next place a sheet of tracing paper over the muscle drawings and draw schematic, planar versions of the two heads. Try to reduce the planes of these heads to the fewest necessary to convey the essential form-character of every segment of the heads, taking into account the forms of the muscles and the bones already drawn. These schematic heads should look somewhat like unfinished marble sculptures—strong planar decisions, but no fussy modelling. Lastly, reverse the planar drawing and, by vigorous rubbing with a spoon or any broad instrument, transfer the drawing to an illustration board or sheet of bristol or vellum paper and check for errors in proportion, location, etc. Using this transferred drawing as a guide, draw the surface forms of the two heads, making one female, the other male. These two heads should be more tonally developed than the others, the idea being to draw convincing, volume-informing representations of two heads.

   Of course, this process of developing a part of the figure from the bones up to the surface is an excellent way of studying every part of the figure, and is suggested for segments that you find especially difficult to understand.

2. Draw a three-quarter front view and a three-quarter back view of the flayed torso. Refer to the Houdon flayed figure (Figures 4.14, 4.27, 4.30, 4.70) but avoid choosing views that closely match these illustrations. Instead, select a view and pose that involves some small bend or twist in the torso. If your first attempt becomes overworked and confusing, make a second draft on a tracing paper overlay. In this way you can salvage those areas that are successful. If you wish, these two views may be begun by work-

ing from the model. Once the pose has been established, develop the muscular forms on the same sheet or on a tracing-paper overlay.

3. Using the flayed torso drawings of the previous exercise, place tracing paper over them and freely follow the undulating pathways of the contours and of edges of muscles. Allow your lines to move along the most rhythmic routes. Start by following the strongest movements, and later in the drawing shift to less evident or smaller curves and rhythms. Try not to lift your pencil or chalk at all. Instead, travel over earlier drawn lines to reach other areas, to strengthen the rhythmic energy of an area, or to leave off following edges to draw the muscle bundles of a part, or to describe the straight, curved, or radiating flow of muscle fibers. Try to keep the line moving, but should you stop, simply refrain from lifting your pencil until you begin again. This exercise intends to familiarize you with the graceful movements that course through the torso's musculature. There is no need to be concerned with structure or even unyielding accuracy. The more scribbled and "busy" these drawings are, the more rhythmic harmonies you have probably found.

4. From any standing pose of the male figure, reduce the surface forms to simple, planar masses that do not ignore or distort major anatomical facts. Next, from the same or a similar pose of the female figure, make another drawing in the same manner. Here, the results should show rather broadly "carved" figures, somewhat similar to Cambiaso's *Hercules* (Figure 4.80).

5. Working either from the model or, by using a mirror and your own free arm, draw the following:
   a. Any supinated view of the extended arm.
   b. Any pronated view of the extended arm.
   c. Any view of the arm in a bent position, with the hand either prone or supine. This drawing may show a quite foreshortened view.

   Next, on a tracing-paper overlay, draw the muscles as they would appear in these differing views. On another sheet of tracing paper make a study of the rhythms of the arm muscles, in the manner described in Exercise 3. Finally, returning to your original three views, rework or redraw them, suggesting lean, muscular arms that strongly suggest the bones at those places where they come to the surface. Here you should stress the clarity of the muscles as they might appear if the skin were translucent.

6. In the same manner described in the previous exercise, draw the following:

a. A front view of the legs, the weight on one leg, the other relaxed, but straight.

b. A side view of the legs, the weight on one leg, the other relaxed, but slightly bent.

c. A three-quarter back view of the legs, the weight on one leg, the other slightly raised by being placed on a small block or stool.

d. A front view of the legs as they would appear in a seated pose with the legs crossed.

7. Using your own hands and feet as models, draw as many life-size views of them as you can conveniently fit onto a sheet of paper about 20″ × 30″. Some of these drawings may go off the page; some may be partially hidden behind others. Use a mirror to increase the variety of poses and views. Here, begin each drawing with a light gray chalk, or any comparably light, colored chalk, using it to establish the general masses and proportions. Next, using a slightly darker tone of chalk, draw in a sparing and simplified way, the general masses of the bones and muscles of the hands and feet. Finally, using black chalk, allowing some erasures of the underdrawing wherever you wish to simplify or soften it, draw the surface forms as convincingly as you can, concentrating on the impression of solid, weighty volumes.

8. Using a light gray, or comparably light, colored chalk, draw one male and one female figure. These should be action poses. Make each figure about 30 inches tall, and suggest their muscles as strongly as might be the case if their skin were translucent. That is, draw these figures in a way that suggests the muscles below, but in a generalized, suggestive manner. Generalize small muscles and establish their collective mass instead. Here, too, favor emphasizing the rhythms and flow of the muscles. Next, lightly rub the drawings to further generalize and soften them, and continue the drawing with black chalk, establishing the surface forms, but allowing the under drawing to influence the amount of muscular detail to be shown. The completed drawings should be of rather lean but muscular figures, their skin only slightly translucent, permitting the forms and harmonies of the substructure to be strongly implied.

9. Using Figure 4.96 as your model, draw the figure from any other view. Imagine being able to step around to his left or right side to some extent. What would the forms look like from these views? It is best to develop these views by stages, working first with structural summaries on tracing paper overlays, until you work out the arrangement of the basic forms of these imagined views.

10. Using Figure 4.97 as your subject, make a free interpretation of these figures, allowing some modest exaggerations and distortions to express your impression of these two struggling figures. You can stress or subordinate volume;

you can, within reasonable limits, relocate parts of these figures, and even make anatomical matters play a minor role.

11. Using Figure 4.92 as an example, fill a page with small, action poses that show the interactions of structure, anatomy, and your feelings and ideas about the mood and energies of each pose. Although we have not yet discussed the factors of design and expression in depth, every pose suggests a mood, temperament, or emotive action; all possess harmonies and contrasts of direction, shape, value, and mass. Try to convey something about these visual and expressive states in each pose. Each of these drawings should be done in less than five or six minutes; even three minutes will allow for some comment on each of the four factors.

12. Make two or three copies of drawings by artists whose approach to figure drawing attracts your interest. Next, try to draw several figures in the manner of each of these artists. Study and copy their drawings in order to sense the artist's intentions and interests, but not to adopt their "handwriting." Select artists who draw very differently from each other. For example, Michelangelo, Degas, and Villon provide an informing collection of themes, attitudes, and approaches to the figure's anatomy.

13. Cover a small-size sculpture armature, manikin, plastic skeleton, or plastic skull with "muscles" you have shaped out of clay. If such supports are not available, make an armature out of simple wooden, metal, or cardboard forms, wrapping a thin-gauge wire around them to better hold the clay. If you make this a reclining figure the technical problems of a homemade armature are far easier to cope with.

14. Make a drawing of the model (or figure in a photograph) as he or she would look after gaining fifty pounds. Remember that fatty deposits vary throughout the figure.

15. Draw a flayed figure that represents your guess at what the "missing link" in human evolution looked like. Start by drawing a generalized skeleton that shows differences in proportion and structure. Then develop the forms as described in Exercise 8, taking into account the differences in the musculature that this skeleton requires.

16. Make a drawing of a draped male figure. Try to suggest as much as you can about the surface forms below. Make a similar drawing of a female figure. Think of the drapery as being wet, clinging to the forms in some places, its folds explaining the general masses in other places.

17. Rework or redraw some of your earlier life drawings, indicating important bony and muscular landmarks. In some of these drawings try to show the figures as emaciated, their bones and muscles strongly evident.

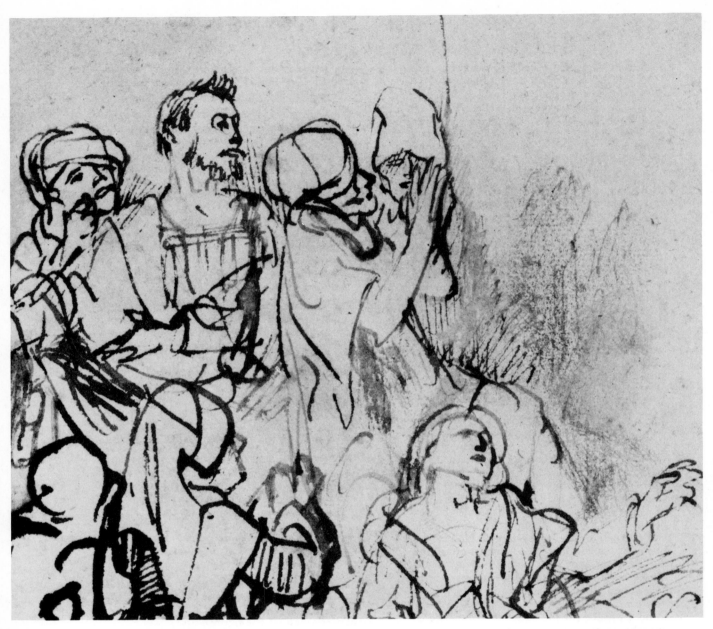

Figure 5.1
REMBRANDT VAN RIJN (1606–1669)
Study for the Group of the Sick
in "The Hundred Guilder Print" (detail)
Pen and ink.
Staatliche Museen Preussischer Kulturbesitz.
Kupferstichkabinett. West Berlin.

5

The Design Factor

the relational content
of figure drawing

SOME GENERAL OBSERVATIONS

In the three preceding chapters we concentrated on what can be thought of as the "semantics" of figure drawing—the structural and functional meanings of the figure's forms. In this chapter and the following we will examine the "syntax" of figure drawing—the ordering of the relational and emotive meanings of the figure's forms. Throughout our discussion we should bear in mind that separating design considerations from those of expression, insofar as it can be done at all, unnaturally divides interacting aspects of what we perceive as *one* phenomenon in a drawing. For example, the design "strategy" of Lillie's drawing *Running Figure* (Figure 5.2), is based on the rhythmic harmonies of an airy web of thick-thin and light-dark curvilinear lines. But the urgent speed of these lines, their furious calligraphy, and their allusions to supple, straining forms are powerfully expressive messages. All these lines are engaged in both "syntactical" functions simultaneously.

Although these two dynamic factors are interdependent, it is helpful to separate them for the time being, so that we may explore more fully the essential nature of each. However deeply interlaced they may be, each factor has its own discernible effects. Design affects our apprehension of a drawing's relational life and order—its plastic condition; expression affects our emotional response to both the psychological mood of the design *and* to the human theme or event depicted—its emotive condition. Design, then, is the visual condition of a drawing's abstract and representational occurrences, and expression is the emotive effects of these occurrences on the viewer. In this chapter we will concentrate on the visual, plastic phenomena at work in well-designed drawings.

Simply stated, a good design is one in which all the parts visually relate to form a balanced unity. But, don't we naturally associate the things we see? After all, isn't it almost impossible to keep from seeing that a finger belongs to the greater system of the hand, that a small fold in the brow is related to one in the

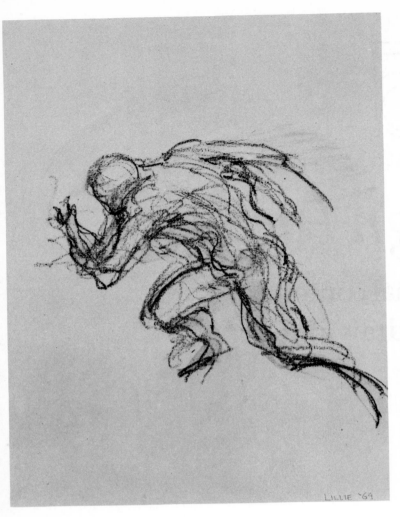

Figure 5.2
LLOYD LILLIE (1932–)
Running Figure
Pencil. 15 x 18 in.
Courtesy of the artist.

cheek, or that arms are shorter than legs? Of course we see these and countless other relationships, and when we draw, many of these relational bonds are denoted. But where we fail, all too often, is in denoting these relationships only in small clusters that do not *collectively* relate with each other. Thus, the finger may be seen as part of the hand, but its similarity or contrast with the fold in the brow or cheek may be missed; the arms and legs may be in proportion, but their collective shape or direction might not be related to other shapes and directions in the torso, or in some nearby object. In the best drawings, however, every line and value, every shape, or inference of movement is interrelated with others in some kind of visual activity that aims at a particular scheme of design throughout the drawing.

For example, in Rembrandt's *Study for the Group of the Sick in "The Hundred Guilder Print"* (Figures 5.1, 5.3) *all* the marks and the shapes and masses they suggest, every value, direc-

tion, and rhythm cooperate in building the drawing's dominant organizational idea: a large pyramidal configuration. A secondary design theme, the rich curvilinear rhythms that coil through the group of figures, animates and further unites the figures. Note that each of the figures, to varying degrees, suggests the triangular shape of the group; each carries the "seed" of the dominant design strategy.

A third system of circular shapes and forms provides still another visual theme that takes our eye into and around the group, giving us the sense of these figures as forms in space. Note how firmly Rembrandt builds this pyramid, the boldest lines and tones at its base. Note, too, that Rembrandt creates a path between the two kneeling figures in the foreground and the rest of the group. This path is soft and open, as if some force is about to enter the group. The figures look up expectantly.

Although sensitive to a figure's placement on the page, the design of many figure drawings does not reach out to engage the entire surface of the sheet. Usually it is concentrated in the figure itself. In Rembrandt's drawing, however, the shape surrounding the group actively contributes to the drawing's ordered, visual condition. The background's tones and the suggestion of a column help to establish the sense of space, its two triangular wings echo the pyramidal theme, and its scale is small enough to strengthen the group's masses and energies, but not to cramp them. Had the background area been larger, much of the drawing's energies and tensions would have been dissipated.

Villon's *Study for a Washerwoman* (Figure 5.4), is a good example of a design idea that is held to the figure itself. Again, a dominant design theme envelops the entire image. Here, a system of intersecting diagonals cascade down the figure. We feel these diagonal thrusts moving down for two reasons: first, the marks are vigorous and their value grows darker the lower they appear on the figure; second, as Denman Ross points out, our eyes tend to move in the direction of diminishing intervals,* and here, the crisscross of diagonals occurs more frequently in the drawing's lower section.

As these drawings show, in a good design all parts interrelate through various visual kinships and contrasts, every mark participating in the drawing's particular systems of ordered actions. And, as we saw in Rembrandt's drawing, there is usually more than one design system at work. Even Villon's brief sketch contains more than one theme. Consider the recurrent "beat" of three or four short lines that appear behind

*Denman Ross, *On Drawing and Painting* (Boston: Houghton Mifflin Company, 1940), pp. 75–79.

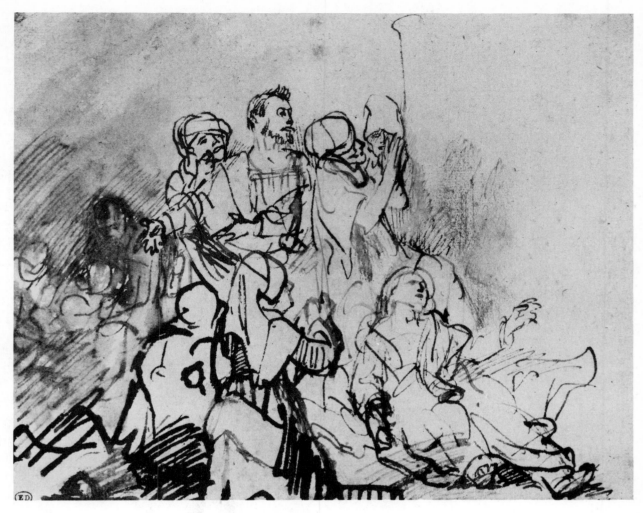

Figure 5.3
REMBRANDT VAN RIJN (1606–1669)
*Study for the Group of the Sick
in "The Hundred Guilder Print"*
Pen and ink. 11.7 x 11.4 cm.
Staatliche Museen Preussischer Kulturbesitz.
Kupferstichkabinett. West Berlin.

the figure's neck, at her right elbow, on the left shoulder, and in several places on the dress.

Further, a good design reveals an order of visual importance, a hierarchy of its design themes. Without such a hierarchy, Rembrandt's pyramid and Villon's cascading diagonals would be lost amid the confusion of competing systems; we would be unable to decide, or even to see, what visual-expressive meanings the artist intended. In Chapter One we saw that an important common denominator of the best figure drawings is the artist's insistence on stating a necessary point of view. But drawings made without regard for an ordering of their parts, or where a hierarchy of order systems is absent, do not convey a point of view, but only ambiguities and indecision. Such works do not make a total statement; they merely emit confusing utterances about their various parts.

Still another necessary condition for a good design is the balance of its parts on the page. Balance occurs when a drawing's measurable components of scale, shape, mass, value, position, etc., and its plastic forces—that is, its inferences of weight, movement, tension, and rhythm—achieve a distribution of parts and energies that convey a state of stability. This stability is based on visual activities that check and regulate each other—a system of compensations that suggest mutual restraint rather than immobility. In a balanced drawing we sense equilibrium in both the physical and visual weight of the forms *and* in the visual energies. Drawings without a balanced resolution of parts and energies cannot hold together. With weight and movement unchecked, forms and forces break loose; falling or floating parts and movements in conflict overwhelm any other aspects

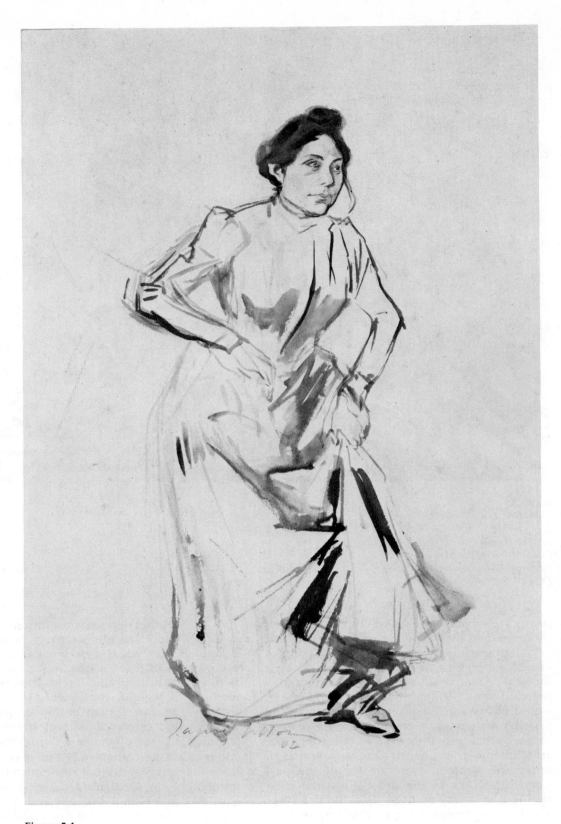

Figure 5.4
JACQUES VILLON (1875–1963)
Study for Washerwoman
Pencil and wash. 49.5 x 32.1 cm.
Courtesy Museum of Fine Arts, Boston.
Gift of Louis Carré.

of order in the drawing. In the confusion and disorder of imbalance, abstract and representational meanings are also lost, the chaos of conflicting and ambiguous visual clues making it impossible to sort these meanings out. In figure drawing the repose and tranquillity of a reclining figure can be shattered by a hovering dark tone, so placed as to appear about to fall; by unchecked diagonals that slide the figure down toward a corner of the page; or by any other element or energy that remains unstabilized in either its depictive or dynamic function. The balanced resolution of forms and forces is necessary, not only because we instinctively react with unease to a state of disequilibrium, but because the clarity of a drawing's total and unique content depends upon its balance.

Implicit in the foregoing is the need for a good design to be *unified*. In a well-ordered drawing the harmony and cohesion of the parts and energies, the artist's consistency of intent, and his manner of drawing—his style of handling—result in a unity of visual (and expressive) purpose. All good drawings appear to be "of a piece," having an ultimate oneness. Despite the often powerful visual "exchanges" between their contrasting parts, they convey a sense of necessity and belonging.

But the artist must be mindful of a danger inherent in the search for unity. In art the opposite of the chaos of visual "anarchy" is the boredom of visual rigidity and repression. When the desire to organize an image leads to its overstabilization, when it is too rigidly interlocked by similarities, the results—being obvious in their sameness—are dull. A chessboard is certainly a unified design, but it is a boring

one. In a good design unity is achieved by the "harnessing" of contrasts, by utilizing their contrapuntal behavior, as well as by the congenial merger of similarities. A good design always depends on variety, on the presence of stabilized differences, to keep from being overbearingly harmonized.

In drawing, then, to design is to clarify our meanings, to compose content in a visual syntax that communicates. And the requirements of a good design—the interplay, hierarchy, balance, and unity of a drawing's parts and dynamic energies—are met by our ability to perceive relationships. As Delacroix put it, "What does it mean to compose? It is the power to associate. . . ."

For the artist all things in nature have line, shape, scale, value, volume, color, texture, position, and direction *in relation to other things.* He knows that these measurable, physical properties have no visual meanings until they are related to other like or unlike properties. He knows, too, that these relationships needn't be recorded only as seen; that by selecting those which support his goals and subordinating all others, he can make visual associations that form a complete statement of his intent. Henry James once observed that "universally, relations stop nowhere, and the exquisite problem of the artist is eternally but to draw, by a geometry of his own, the circle within which they shall happily appear to do so." In a good design, then, the "circle," the field of energy within which relationships work, exhibits a sense of self-contained order, one in which we don't want to add or remove anything.

A sensitive design begins, as Delacroix's

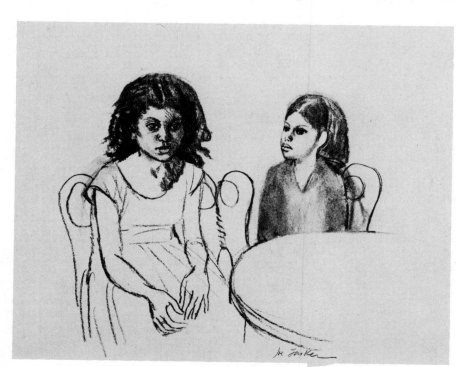

Figure 5.5
JOE LASKER (1919–   )
Two Girls
Black chalk. 22 x 28 in.
Courtesy of the artist.

observation suggests, with the ability to make estimates, comparisons, and judgments about the visual character—the similarities and differences—of a subject's physical and dynamic actualities. The artist translates these perceptions into visual terms by means of the visual elements—the six basic tools of graphic communication. (Color, an occasional participant in drawing, is omitted here because it is incidental to the essentials of this book.) Although a thorough exploration of the visual elements, more appropriate to a basic drawing book,* is not attempted here, it *is* necessary to examine these tools in more than a passing way to see some of their limitless relational possibilities.

THE VISUAL ELEMENTS

The six elements we will examine are *line, value, shape, volume, space,* and *texture*. Of these, line and value enjoy a special importance inasmuch as all the other elements are made manifest by one or the other, or by their combined use. Of these two elements, line is the more universally used, the more direct and sugges-

*See Nathan Goldstein, *The Art of Responsive Drawing* (Englewood Cliffs, N.J.: Prentice-Hall, Inc., 1973), chap. 8.

tive, the element most at the heart of the act of drawing. Even when the use of value equals or exceeds that of line in a drawing, many artists create those values by hatched lines that collectively produce the various tones we see. The function of space will receive further attention when we turn to examine the energies of the elements in action. Indeed, this elusive element, which gives visual meaning to the location of all the other elements, cannot be directly examined, for space has no meaning outside the context of the elements that interrupt it.

Line

As an element, *line* refers to more than drawn lines. Edges of shapes and forms, even when established by broad washes of ink or paint tones, function as lines of separation from adjacent shapes, forms, or spaces. The long axis of a shape or form is also "seen" as a line phenomenon. Not only is this true for the figure's more slender forms, but for all of its forms and form-units, large and small. An eyelid's curve is an essentially linear action. The long axis of the head may lie on a different "line" from that of the neck. Line runs through groups of shapes and forms that may differ in scale, value, texture, and substance; it may do so even when shapes and forms are separated from each other

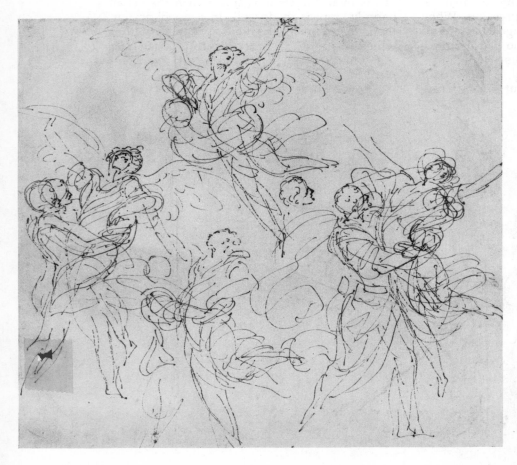

Figure 5.6
DONATO CRETI (1671–1749)
Studies for Jacob Wrestling with the Angel
Pen and brown ink. 21.6 x 24.3 cm.
The Art Museum, Princeton University.

Figure 5.7
WALT KUHN (1880–1949)
Seated Woman
Pen, brush and ink. 13 13/16 x 16 1/16 in.
The Metropolitan Museum of Art, New York.
Rogers Fund, 1955.

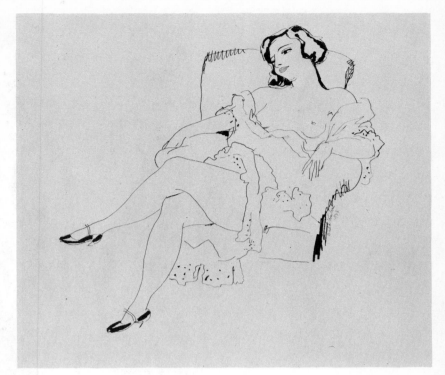

Figure 5.8
ROBERT ANDREW PARKER (1925–   )
Sheet of Studies of the Female Figure
Pen and ink. 17 x 21 in.
Courtesy of the artist.

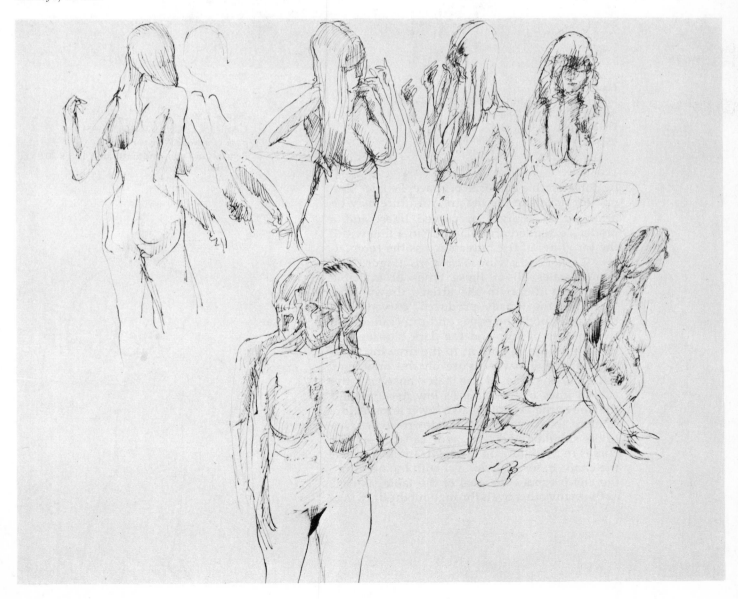

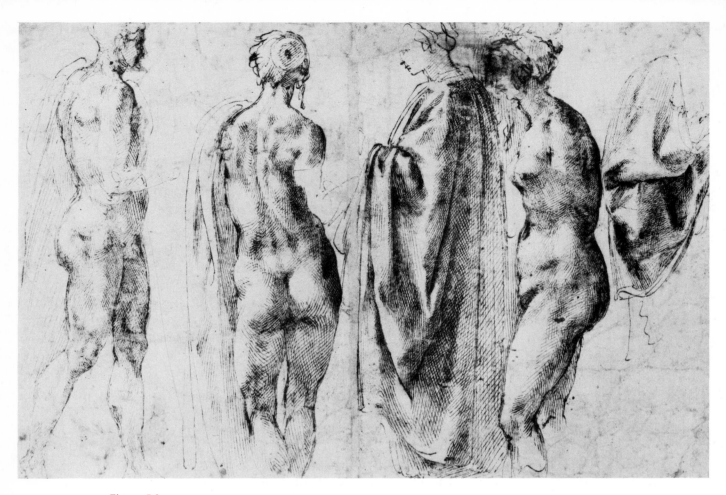

Figure 5.9
MICHELANGELO BUONARROTI (1475–1564)
Studies of Nude and Draped Figures
Pen and ink. 18 3/8 x 15 1/4 in.
Musée Condé, Chantilly. Photo Giraudon.

Figure 5.10
GASTON LACHAISE (1882–1935)
Back of a Nude Woman (1929)
Pencil, quill pen, and india ink. 45.5 x 30.9 cm.
The Brooklyn Museum.
Gift of Carl Zigrosser.

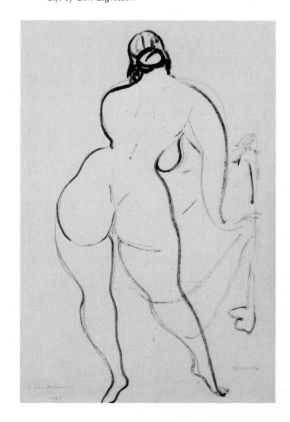

by considerable amounts of space. People "line up" for tickets to the theatre, furniture may be arranged in straight or curved lines, and a model's extended arm may be "in a line with" the top (line) of the bureau across the room.

Lasker's drawing *Two Girls* (Figure 5.5) demonstrates all of these types of invisible lines. In addition to the artist's drawn lines there are the tonally produced, curved lines describing both the edges and direction of the two masses of hair and the dark blouse. And these lines are important to the drawing's design strategy. In the figure on the drawing's left side, the line of the hair "answers" the curved lines of the blouse's low neckline and the line of the axes of the two lower arms. Additionally, the curve repeats the downward curves of the shoulder and skirt, and "calls" to similar curves in the figure on the right, and to those in the chair. In forming an oval with the neckline, the curve echoes the oval of the table, as well as the many other ovals throughout the drawing,

184

whether actually drawn or only implied. For example, in the figure on the left, we sense an oval "line" running through the arms and completed by the shape of the hair.

Lines do not exist in nature; they do not surround or run through forms and spaces. But lines convey descriptive, plastic, and expressive eloquence, which make them drawing's basic element for searching out a subject's gestural behavior, as shown in Creti's *Studies for Jacob Wrestling with the Angel* (Figure 5.6). Here, line is used to feel out the essential character of the action of the four groups of figures. In so doing, Creti extracts the linear design of these interacting figures to reveal that these images "wrestle" at the abstract, as well as the representational, level; these animated swirls of interlacing lines not only describe, they also enact these energetic activities.

Line is capable of suggesting differing functions, moods, and speeds. In contrast to Creti's lively calligraphy, the line in Kuhn's drawing *Seated Woman* (Figure 5.7) is, for the most part, slow, easy-going, and largely restricted to defining edges. Likewise, the unseen lines of rhythms and directions are also slow-paced. Instead of using lines to search out and act out strong rhythms and movements, Kuhn restrains their speed and assigns them the task of suggesting the figure's graceful, resting forms. But the artist's interest in using line to accent the subject's shape-state—the two-dimensional arrangement and nature of its forms—makes him hold back from suggesting heavy, limpid forms; the figure and the legless chair seem almost weightless. To "underline" the drawing's dominant line quality Kuhn alters the character of some of the lines of the chair, speeding them up in a series of bold scallops. He also reinforces his two-dimensional theme by a pattern of dots, and one of broad ink strokes. Both of these systems "rise" to the surface of the page, making the design function on the picture plane as well as in space. In doing so he calls our attention to the element of space as simultaneously existing in two-dimensional and three-dimensional terms—as interspace and field of space.

Notice that the artist's knowledge of structure and anatomy is evident in line's volume-informing delineations. Although an impression of weighty mass is intentionally subdued, the few lines used to define the figure tell a good deal about its essential structure and anatomy. Indeed, one of the more appealing qualities of this drawing is the large amount of abstract and representational content conveyed with such an economy of line. There are no unnecessary embellishments and no "unemployed" lines.

Parker's drawing, *Sheet of Studies of the Female Figure* (Figure 5.8), demonstrates an integration of several attitudes toward line. Hatched lines drawn in the direction of a plane's tilt in space serve structural purposes; other lines, especially those defining contours, take on a more animated, playful quality. Some lines, mainly in the drawing of the hair, suggest texture, and still others, running at right angles to the hatched lines of some shaded planes, serve as the long axis of various forms and establish a system of light and dark shapes. Parker successfully unites these differing interests in lines' structural, dynamic, and shape-making functions by intermingling the varying kinds of line throughout each figure.

As Parker's drawing suggests, drawn lines can take on different functions, often simultaneously, and can convey different emotive attitudes. All lines can be roughly sorted into several broad categories, but most lines *will* function in more than one way, or can alter their role and character along their course. A line begun as a gentle caress may end up as a vehement, gestural slash.

Structural lines, discussed in Chapter Two, *diagrammatic* lines—those loose, schematic lines that roughly indicate dimension, direction, shape and mass—and delineating, or *contour*, lines can impart a wide range of plastic and expressive qualities, although all are predominantly descriptive or investigatory in function. All three of these line functions are demonstrated in Michelangelo's *Studies of Nude and Draped Figures* (Figure 5.9). Diagrammatic lines, such as those in the right arm and drapery of the female figure (back view), underlie most of the structural lines that model the forms. Michelangelo doesn't employ a pronounced, independent contour line, but delineates forms by repeating, massing, or darkening structural lines as they approach edges.

Some lines, although they function in various descriptive ways, are often of an animated and curvasive, or *calligraphic*, nature. They call attention to their own abstract activity as well as to their representational roles and are often dynamically bold and emotive, as can be seen in Lachaise's drawing *Back of a Nude Woman* (Figure 5.10). But in figure drawing, as Lachaise's lines clearly indicate, the most expressive calligraphy has its depictive duties to perform, just as the most descriptively motivated lines have plastic and expressive obligations to the drawing's dynamic state.

A calligraphic attitude to line animates the forms in Rembrandt's drawing *Esau Selling His Birthright to Jacob* (Figure 5.11). Although we can discern diagrammatic, structural, and contour lines, all are activated by an energetic play of movements and rhythms between the often diagonally situated planes, forms, and tones that have calligraphic overtones. Many lines serve several needs at once. For example, the bold hatched lines of the tablecloth, while essentially diagrammatic and structural in function, are, in the context of the other lines of the drawing, strenuously calligraphic as

well. Rembrandt strengthens some contours, such as those defining the arms of the two figures, to gain both dynamic and representational clarity. The bridge formed by these arms spans the two halves of the drawing, a link that bolsters both the drawing's design and its dramatic impact. Note how structurally informing are the calligraphic lines of Esau's turban and boots. In this drawing, despite the rich variety of line—the range of value, width, texture, and length—all lines interrelate strongly. They call to each other by rhythms, directions, and textures, whose similarities offset their differences, together creating a cohesive order that is abstract as well as figurative.

Figure 5.11
REMBRANDT VAN RIJN (1606–1669)
Esau Selling His Birthright to Jacob
Reed and quill pen, and wash. 20 x 17.3 cm.
Trustees of the British Museum, London.

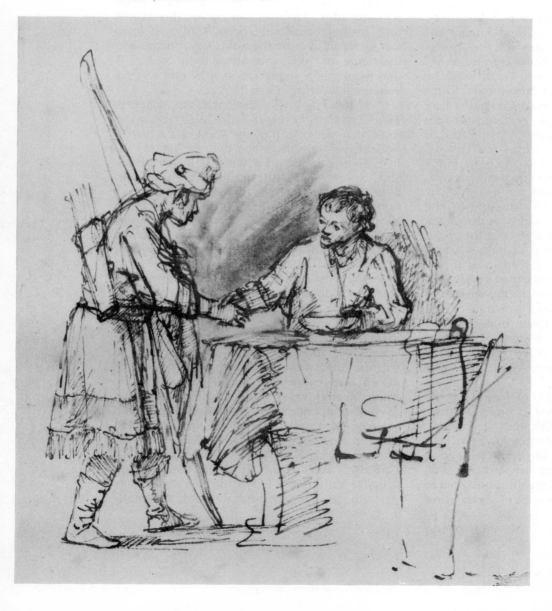

As Rembrandt's drawing demonstrates, descriptive lines can sometimes be so emotive, and expressive lines can be so descriptive that they cannot be defined as being predominantly one or the other. But as we see in the drawings of Lachaise, Michelangelo, and Kuhn, many artists prefer lines that plainly disclose a dominant attitude. In whatever way we would use line, a recognition of its ability to convey one or more of the several functions and characteristics discussed is important in learning to control this seemingly simple, but potent, element. When we consider the wide figurative and abstract range of drawn lines in conjunction with the "invisible" lines discussed earlier, we can readily appreciate why line is the key element in drawing.

Value

The second element, *value*, also offers a broad range of functions and relational possibilities. As we have seen, value is sometimes a byproduct of hatched lines and is often an important consideration in modifying the character of lines in drawings we would regard as purely linear. For example, while Figure 5.10 is clearly linear, the variations in the value of the lines play several important roles. Lachaise uses pure black to suggest weight, as in the shoulder and breast, and to suggest the dark tone of the hair. Gray lines, some of them very faint, permit him to indicate forms farther away, delicate drapery, and subtle anatomical notations.

Patches of tone, whether produced by hatched lines, washes, or broad chalk or graphite strokes, create shapes. These shapes, by their proximity to each other, can produce volumes; and, by the surface-state of the tones—the character of their application—various textures can be suggested. Such shapes of tone are often so fused, overlaid, or subtly graduated in value that their essential shape-state is obscured. But in Daumier's drawing *Head of a Woman* (Figure 5.12), the shapes of tone are distinct enough to serve as a useful example of their volume-creating ability. By grouping all of the many values of his subject into three tones—the white of the paper, a light gray, and a dark gray—Daumier also strengthens the sense of an ordered arrangement of values on the picture plane. These values, in addition to their descriptive function, enact a playful abstract idea of variously toned, curved shapes that seem to revolve on the page. Note the differing tones and textures, and the clarity of the planes that model the form of the

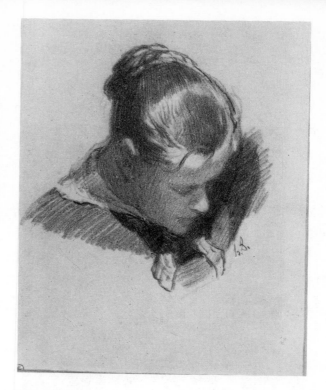

Figure 5.12
HONORÉ DAUMIER (1808–1879)
Head of a Woman
Black conté crayon. 15.2 x 18.7 cm.
Cabinet des Dessins, Musée du Louvre, Paris.

hair and the forehead, the most structurally developed passages in the drawing.

Value, then, exists in line, shape, mass, and texture. It is also an efficient and forceful means of representing both two- and three-dimensional space, as demonstrated in Degas' monotype *Woman Wiping Her Feet near a Bathtub* (Figure 5.13). A sense of atmosphere envelops the figure. This is suggested by gently modulated gray tones and by the contrasting "flash" of white at the upper left corner. This contrasting value holds its place in space because it suggests daylight streaming in through a far window, and because it is strongly overlapped by the bending figure. Two-dimensionally, the values, again limited to some three or four tones, are arranged into a design that consists of three interrelated tonal systems.

The first consists of the blocky shapes surrounding the figure, whose widely differing values serve to call attention to themselves as tones upon a flat surface. But they are related by a rough sameness in scale, by their encircling action, and by a subtle tendency to aim toward the center of the page—like dulled arrowheads. Some touch the figure, some are overlapped by it. A second tonal design forms a large, dark, inverted U-shape comprised of the figure's legs and buttocks, and repeated by a thinner, light gray shape fitted over the first, formed by

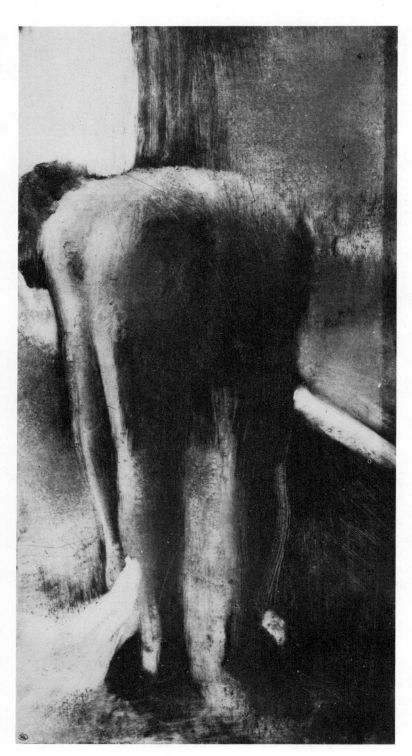

Figure 5.13
EDGAR DEGAS (1834–1917)
Woman Wiping Her Feet near a Bathtub
Monotype. 17 3/4 x 9 3/8 in.
Cabinet des Dessins, Musée du Louvre, Paris.

the woman's arm and back. At the open end of the dark shape are "flashes" of light tone at either ankle that associate with the longer, oblique light tones to either side of the legs and with the large, white shape at the upper left corner. A third tonal system forms an inverted Y-shape that reaches across the entire page, incorporating the oblique light tones of the towel and the bathtub rim as the "arms" of the inverted Y, its central stem being the vertical, dark, drapery-like shape that extends to the figure's back. These three tonal systems are interdependent and complementary. As we look at the drawing, first one, then another of these systems emerges, each graciously subsiding to allow the next its turn at our attention—yet all working together to form a unified, pulsating, tonal design.

In this Degas drawing we observe that values can make unlike things relate. Note that the white towel and the bathtub rim, though far apart, are visual "first cousins." Again, in Goldstein's *Crouching Figure* (Figure 5.14), the figure's right upper arm and leg and her chest are all affiliated by their common value. Value can also make like things contrast. In Figure 5.14 the shoulders and lower arms are almost symmetrical, but their contrasting values subdues their physical kinship. Likewise, the two legs differ in value, and while the raised leg is only subtly different from its tonal surroundings, the lower leg contrasts sharply with the values encircling it.

Value's ability to make dissimilar elements relate and similar ones contrast is an important compositional device. In Demuth's drawing *Clowns* (Figure 5.15), the dark legs of the lower figure are more easily associated with the dark tones above him than with the lightly toned legs of the standing figure. A similar visual bond is formed by the standing clown's head and the two pompons of his coat, while the relationship of the two heads is inhibited by their value contrast.

Picasso relies heavily on value to establish the design in his etching *The Painter and His Model* (Figure 5.16). Reading from left to right, simple vertical shapes of light and dark tones alternate until they come together and "fragment" in the drawing of the seated figure. Picasso intentionally makes the figure-ground relationship between the nude and her surroundings a complex and ambiguous one; it acts as an engaging visual counterpoint to the steady beat of the black and white vertical shapes that precede it.

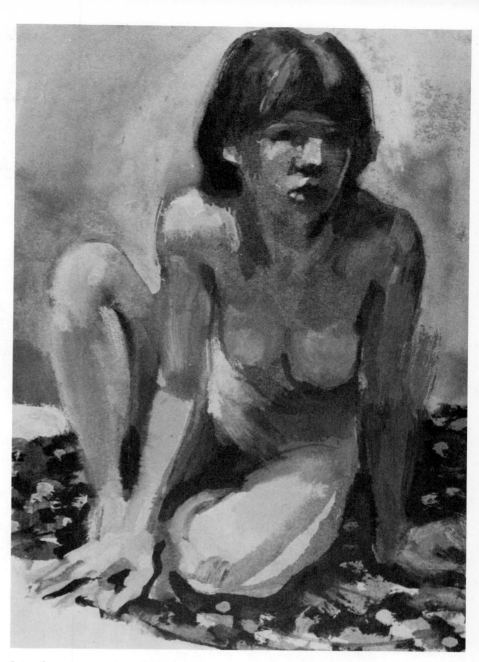

Figure 5.14
NATHAN GOLDSTEIN (1927–   )
Crouching Figure
Sepia ink and watercolor washes. 5 3/4 x 8 in.
Collection of the author.

Picasso uses the same value to relate the painter's upraised arm to the easel and to the diagonal edge of the background beyond the easel, and further relates arm and easel by aiming them at the upper center of the page. Note that the shape on the far left and that of the painter's figure are related by value and texture, but that both shapes are related to the background surrounding the painter only by texture. Picasso overcomes the tonal polarity among these shapes by relating them through texture. To associate opposing elements in some way, whether by a similarity in texture, shape, scale, direction, or position, is a sound practice of design. When elements bear no visual relationship to each other they remain disengaged from, and thus, harmful to, the drawing's order.

In addition to its potency as a relational force, value is an important structural tool (as we saw in Chapter Two), and is the necessary means of suggesting both the local tone and illumination of forms. As a structural tool, value is capable of carving the boldest masses or the gentlest nuances of terrain, as demonstrated by Tiepolo's drawing *The Death of Seneca* (Figure 5.17). Here, broad washes of tone, guided by the artist's sensitive structural and anatomical understanding, forcefully establish major masses, while smaller mounds and hollows are suggested by the undulating edges of these broad washes and by small, incisive daubs of tone.

The impression of an intense light bathing this scene is strengthened by the artist's consistency in darkening all planes turned away from the light source. Except for a few passages,

Figure 5.15
CHARLES DEMUTH (1883–1953)
Clowns
Watercolor and pencil. 7 1/2 x 11 in.
The Metropolitan Museum of Art, New York.
Bequest of Charles F. Iklé, 1963.

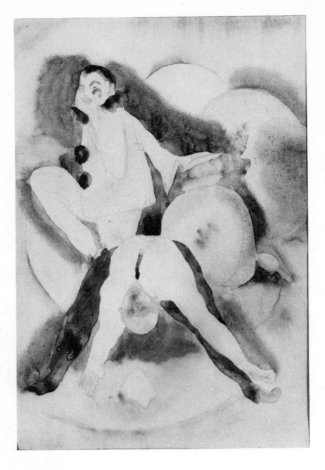

Figure 5.16
PABLO PICASSO (1881–1973)
The Painter and His Model
Etching and aquatint. 32.5 x 47.5 cm.
Courtesy Museum of Fine Arts, Boston.
Lee M. Friedman Fund.

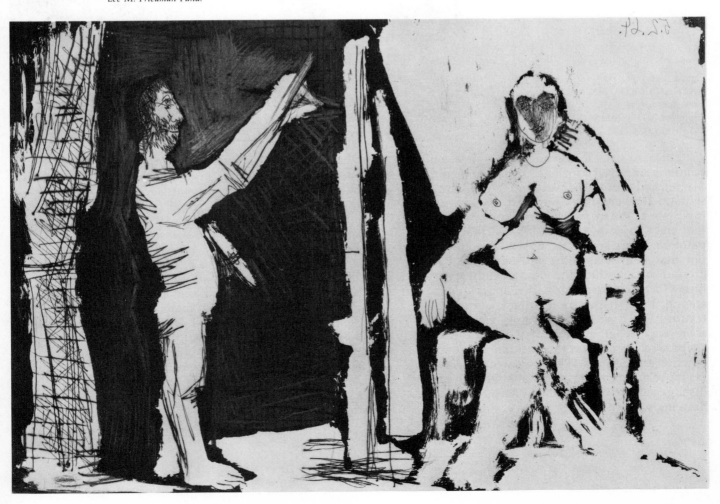

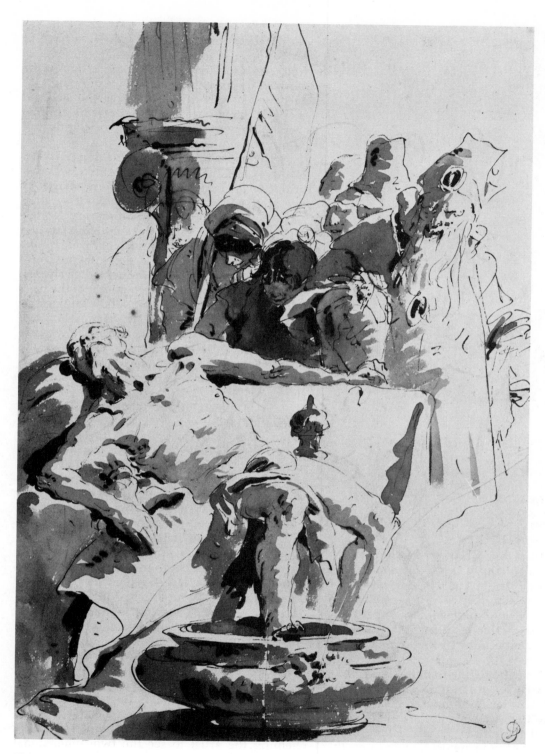

Figure 5.17
GIOVANNI BATTISTA TIEPOLO (1696–1770)
The Death of Seneca
Pen, brown ink, and wash. 34 x 24 cm.
Courtesy of the Art Institute of Chicago.
Joseph and Helen Regenstein Collection.

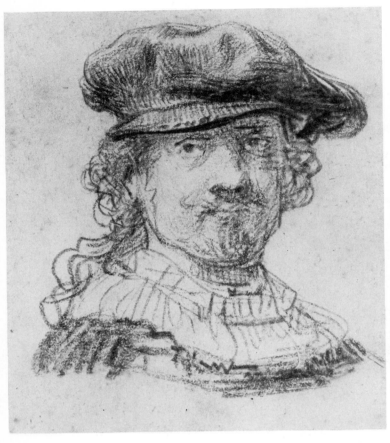

Figure 5.18
REMBRANDT VAN RIJN (1606–1669)
Self-Portrait
Red chalk. 5 1/8 x 4 11/16 in.
National Gallery of Art, Washington, D.C.
Rosenwald Collection.

such as the black mask or the dark-haired boy, Tiepolo doesn't identify the local tones of the figures and objects depicted; the impression of brilliant light would have been lessened had he done so. Strong light and the dark shadows it produces make local tones difficult to see.

But the gentle light in Rembrandt's *Self-Portrait* (Figure 5.18), permits both local tones and subtle tonal modelling to be easily seen. In this brief sketch, Rembrandt manages to utilize value's organizational, structural, and textural abilities, and to describe both the inherent tone of a part and the effects of light falling on it. Note the subtle movements that enliven the image. The beret, the collar, and the thin band of tone representing the jacket, in creating graceful undulations of these variously-toned shapes, move gently across the page, rippling "brackets" to frame the stilled head. Note, too, Rembrandt's economical and incisive tonal modelling, especially effective in the beret.

Shape

In examining line and value we have of course been discussing the other elements as well. After line and value, *shape* is one of the most omnipresent elements in drawing. Indeed, when we begin a drawing, the size and shape of the surface chosen represents our first shape judgment—and that choice will influence all our subsequent decisions.

The use of line for shape-making purposes is universal. Children and adults alike, whether primitive or civilized, naturally form images by denoting, and at the same time separating, their constituent parts by linear boundaries. A circle represents a head; ovals, the eyes and ears; and so on. What is generally unrecognized by the layman or beginner is that these shapes, once created, simultaneously produce other shapes, namely, the shapes of the remainder of the page and those which result from subdividing existing ones. The head's circular shape, when two ovals are placed within it, and two more are placed adjacently to either side, is dynamically affected by these oval shapes, just as it is affected by its relation to the enveloping shape of the page.

Such effects on the relational nature of a drawing's *figure and ground* state, that is, the shape-state of its parts and of the spaces between them, have important organizational meanings. To understand the overall shape organization of a drawing it is important to recognize these two distinct types of shape. *Figure* or positive shapes are those formed or enclosed by line or tone, and which represent either identifiable images or the presence of substance—of "somethingness." *Ground* or negative shapes denote the areas which separate or surround figure shapes. The ability to regard the visual properties of these two types of shape enables the artist to make better depictive and design judgments about *all* the shapes that subdivide his page.

As an aid in measurement, whether of the location, direction, scale, or contour of shapes, most artists find that reversing their figure-ground impressions helps them to see a subject's shape actualities more objectively. Similarly, reversing figure-ground impressions, by helping the artist to see the two-dimensional nature of his subject's parts and the spaces among them, enhances his appreciation of the dynamic possibilities inherent in their shape-states.

Responses influenced by this kind of "reverse seeing" are evident in Figures 5.13 and 5.14. In the Degas drawing, as we have seen,

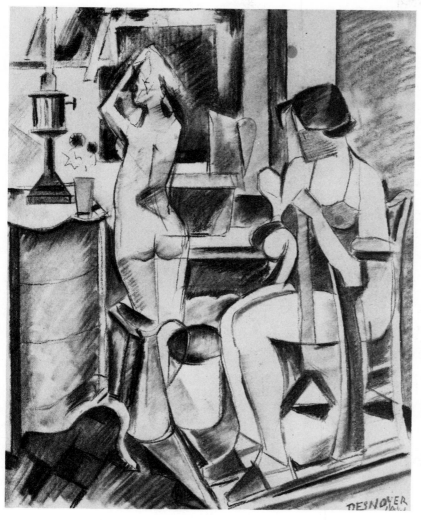

Figure 5.19
FRANÇOIS DESNOYER (1894–   )
Getting Dressed ("La Toilette"), 1941
Pencil and chalk. 6 3/4 x 8 1/4 in.
Musée National d'Art Moderne, Paris

intentional shape ambiguities endow most of the shapes with both positive and negative functions. In Figure 5.14 a light-toned wedge-shaped segment of the background takes on figural characteristics by actively forming the edges of the knee and shoulder. Again, at the ankle a dark oval shape, by appearing as an open space between the ankle, arm, and upper leg, seems to function as ground; but by actively inserting itself in that location it appears figural.

These drawings suggest some of the characteristics by which figure and ground are determined: small shapes and overlapping ones usually appear to be figural; large, or overlapped ones, ground. In virtually every instance, figure shapes are active—they assert themselves; ground shapes are passive—they accept those places on the page that figure shapes "permit." By reversing the characteristics of figure and ground shapes, the sense of three-dimensional space is lessened and the spatial relations of all the elements on the picture plane are increased.

Desnoyer's drawing *Getting Dressed* (Figure 5.19) demonstrates some other ways by which intentionally subduing figure-ground cues can heighten a drawing's two-dimensional impact. The artist makes the shape of the checkered floor less negative by giving it convex edges, a characteristic usually associated with figural parts. In some places, as in the bureau on the left, the shaded modelling suggests concave drawers, while the lines dividing the drawers show them to be convex. In other places, as in the light gray wedge-shape that touches the shoe of the seated figure, the artist avoids overlapping, thereby making it uncertain which

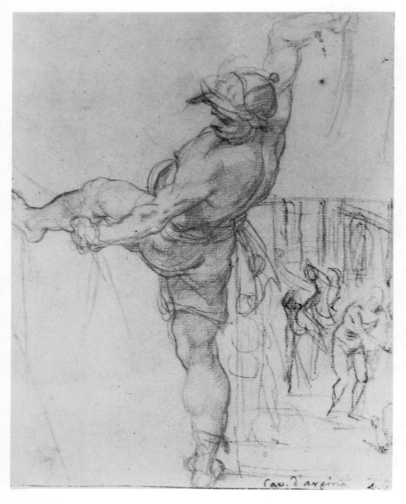

Figure 5.20
GUISEPPE CESARI, Cavaliere d'Arpino (1568–1640)
Studies for a Flagellation of Christ
Red and black chalk. 20.1 x 15.5 cm.
Cooper-Hewitt Museum of Decorative Arts and Design,
Smithsonian Institution, New York.

on sharply defined edges, work to amplify the drawing's two-dimensional design. Although the sense of masses in space is restrained to permit the shape-oriented design to assert itself, here, both considerations are compatibly integrated.

All shapes, of course, are produced by line or value, or by a combination of both. They can, as we have seen, stand for "thing," denote "empty" interspaces, or suggest both figure and ground at the same time. As Figure 5.16 shows, they can be textured, change value within their boundaries, or be "plain" and unvarying. Shapes can be geometric or organic in character; in complex forms they can show both traits. Shapes can be hard-edged, as we saw in Figure 5.19, but they can also be so unfocused as to appear cloud-like (Figure 5.27). Shapes can be closed or open. Closed shapes are those entirely encircled by line, comprised of tone, or by linear and tonal shapes arranged to form an enclosure. Open shapes are those showing breaks in the linear or tonal enclosure. For example, in Figure 5.16, the shapes denoting the seated woman and her immediate surroundings all show avenues of access to neighboring shapes.

Except for circles, squares, pentagons, and other shapes whose boundaries are more or less equidistant from their centers, all shapes suggest movement in the direction of their long axis. Even those few shapes that do not inherently imply movement will take on the directions and movements of the shapes they relate with.

As noted in Chapter Two, all masses have shape. Even the most complex pose imaginable, no matter how compacted and interlaced the forms may be, shows its particular shape when silhouetted. In figure drawing, a sensitivity to shape's informing presence is an important aid in making foreshortened forms more manageable. For Cesari to draw the foreshortened torso in his *Studies for a Flagellation of Christ* (Figure 5.20), he had to do more than piece together its form-units; he had to see (or envision) its general shape-state. Although his drawing does not dwell on "shapeness," underlying these forms are the artist's shape judgments. A confirmation of the search for shape early in the artist's drawing process can be seen in the unfinished sketch in the lower right. Here, Cesari relies on shapes to establish the basic design and disposition of the drawing's forms.

Many artists, recognizing shape as a potent agent of design, emphasize it in preparatory sketches for works in other media. Pous-

shape is nearer. Some parts are shown as transparent or interpenetrating, another effective way of lessening the impression of volumes in space. The artist permits some forms to remain unmodelled, sometimes neglecting even to explain their shape boundaries, or he aligns various edges to suggest that shapes in near and far positions in the room are on the same plane in space. This occurs with the line that marks the midline of the standing figure's legs, continues along the pitcher, and becomes the upper edge of the aforementioned wedge-shape—a shape, incidently, denoting a cast shadow, but reversed in value. All of these interruptions of figure-ground cues, and the artist's emphasis

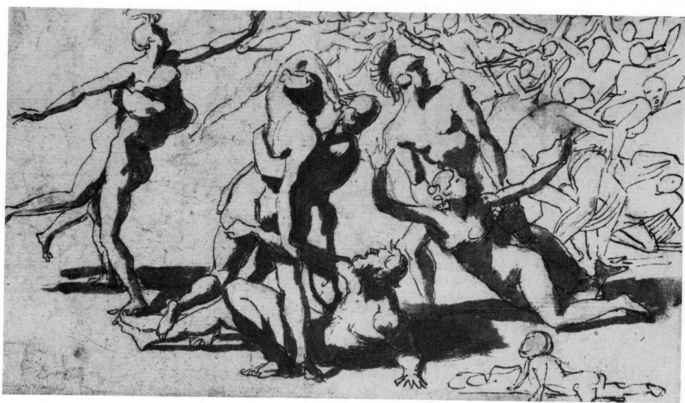

Figure 5.21
NICOLAS POUSSIN (1594–1665)
Drawing for the Rape of the Sabines
Pen and wash over black chalk. 11 x 8 cm.
Windsor Castle, Royal Library.
By gracious permission of Her Majesty the Queen.

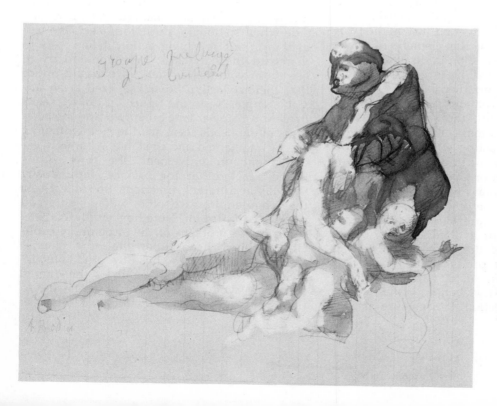

Figure 5.22
AUGUSTE RODIN (1840–1917)
Study for a Bas Relief
Pen, heightened with white on ruled paper.
5 1/2 x 7 9/16 in.
Courtesy The Fogg Art Museum, Harvard University.
Bequest of Grenville L. Winthrop.

sin's *Drawing for the Rape of the Sabines* (Figure 5.21), illustrates shape's importance in the artist's thinking in this preparatory sketch for a major painting. By imagining a strong light source, the artist creates a pattern of dark shapes that sometimes envelop more than one figure. Establishing these light and dark shapes, their inherently animated, often oblique and interdicting behavior, enables Poussin to examine and further plan the role of shape's plastic contribution of energy to the dramatic action scene he envisions for the painting. Again, in Rodin's *Study for a Bas Relief* (Figure 5.22), the design of his subject's shapes is clearly an important aspect of the artist's explorations.

The Poussin and Rodin drawings demonstrate, as our earlier examination of the structural factor disclosed, that a strong sense of shape can be highly compatible with boldly structured images. After all, planes, the basic building unit of masses, are shapes at various angles in space.

Volume

A drawing's shapes, then, like its lines and values (and textures, as we shall see) all function both two- and three-dimensionally. In doing so, they give two-dimensional design meanings to volumes in three-dimensional space. In Chapter Two we discussed volume as the goal of the structural factor, and examined the means by which its impression on a flat surface is achieved. Here we will consider the design functions of volume, noting in particular what effects a volume's scale, value, weight, and position in space (and in the pictorial field) have upon a drawing's design. And just as the two-dimensional aspects of the element of space were necessarily touched on in discussing line, shape, and value, so will its three-dimensional aspects emerge in examining volume.

In drawing, all volumes suggest two kinds of weight: real weight, the sense of gravitational pull on a solid mass; and visual weight, the sense of forces acting within and upon a mass for the purpose of stabilizing it or relating it to other forms or shapes in the pictorial field. A single diagonal line drawn on a blank page produces a sense of tension, imbalance, and a striving for a more stable position. Similarly the drawing of a tilted volume, by its position, shape, and the lines and tones that comprise it will also produce tension and imbalance that we feel as visual rather than actual weight. Unlike *physical* weight, visual weight can pull in any direction. For instance, in Fig-

ure 5.19, some of the forms, such as the standing figure and the bureau and lamp to the left, pull upward. Furthermore visual weight is felt to be as much a two-dimensional phenomenon as a three-dimensional one.

Visual weight (which will be more fully examined later, when its effect on all the elements can be discussed together) always influences our understanding of a volume's design function. Although it is a more evident force in drawings that suggest little physical weight (Figure 5.16), visual weight is an inherent property of even realistically conceived drawings.

For example, in *Three Studies of a Young Negro* (Figure 5.23), Watteau creates both a two- and three-dimensional balance by the location, movement, scale, and value of his subject's volumes. The three heads are arranged to form a triangle that exists both two- and three-dimensionally, as does the larger, curved, triangular "wedge," comprised of the figures' shoulders and torsos.

Two-dimensionally, the placement of the figures creates an inverted Y-shaped space between the heads, whose symmetry and centrality imparts a stable pivot point around which the configuration seems to rotate in a counterclockwise direction. Partly for representational reasons (the heads face counterclockwise), the direction of the rotating action is strongly influenced by the "swing" of the large wedge and by the rhythmic actions illustrated in Figure 5.24.

Three-dimensionally, Watteau's design strategy depends just as much on this enveloping, circular action. In the same way as a rotating disk will remain balanced but tilt to one side when stationary, these forms achieve balance by their revolving action. If we were to disregard their dynamic behavior and try to see these volumes as static, we would notice that their collective "disk" is fixed at an unstable angle. Now, the figure on the left leans precariously toward the other two, and the positions of the heads seem arbitrary — the drawing seems fragmented and unstable. Although less dependent on movement, the three heads "need" each other for balance. Individually they fall in different directions, but collectively they compensate each other's diagonality and achieve equilibrium. Note how subtly Watteau resolves the problem of the structurally explicit, "weighty" heads upon the more generalized and "fading" bodies. By gradually decreasing the clarity and value of the draped forms, he avoids disembodying the heads. At the same time, he takes advantage of the looser

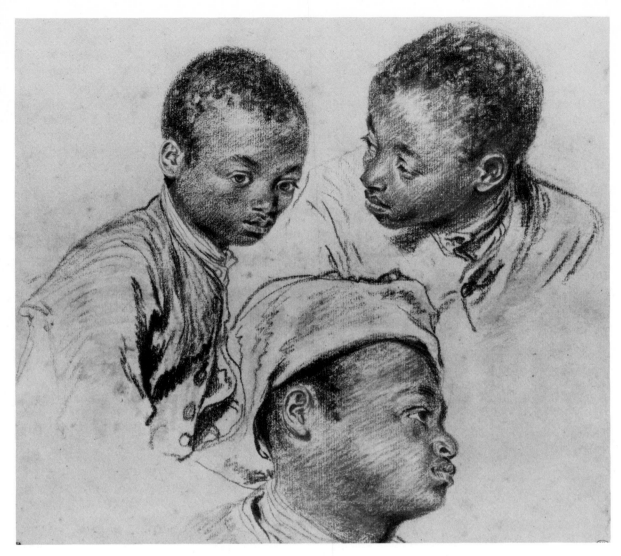

Figure 5.23
ANTOINE WATTEAU (1684–1721)
Three Studies of a Young Negro
Red, black, and white chalk, gray ink washes.
9 5/8 x 10 5/8 in.
Cabinet des Dessins, Musée du Louvre, Paris.

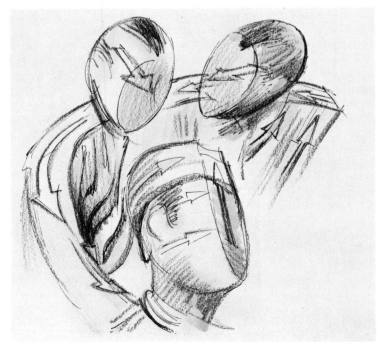

Figure 5.24

handling in the drapery to reinforce the overall rotation and to impart a sense of open space between the figures.

The sense of deep space, made more convincing by the "road" comprised of the shoulders, accommodates the three figures in a way that bolsters the drawing's two-dimensional space design. Seen this way, the large wedge stops just short of the drawing's left and right boundaries, avoiding the four isolated triangles of space that would otherwise have resulted.

As this analysis illustrates, masses, like all other elements, suggest movement. They do so by the physical and visual nature of their parts and functions, that is, by the nature of all their measurable qualities and dynamic activities. A volume's degree of action is largely determined by its depictive and visual weight— by its relational condition with other elements in the design, and by the artist's manner of expressing it. A form securely balanced and patiently rendered will appear less energetic than the same form aggressively drawn and tenuously balanced.

The volumes in Watteau's drawing move at a moderate pace, slowed somewhat by the overall gentle handling and by the thorough modelling of the heads that makes them at once independent from, and united with, the design. In contrast, the volumes of Rembrandt's drawing *Head of an Oriental with a Dead Bird of Paradise* (Figure 5.25) undulate and whirl with furious energy. The strong downward pull of the head's physical and visual weight is increased by the lively climbing action of the figure's scarf, which coils and "springs" upon the turban, adding its mass and weight to the head. Furthermore, by making the scarf intensely

Figure 5.25
REMBRANDT VAN RIJN (1606–1669)
Head of an Oriental with a Dead Bird of Paradise
Pen and bistre washes, some gouache. 11.7 x 11.4 cm.
Cabinet des Dessins, Musée du Louvre, Paris.

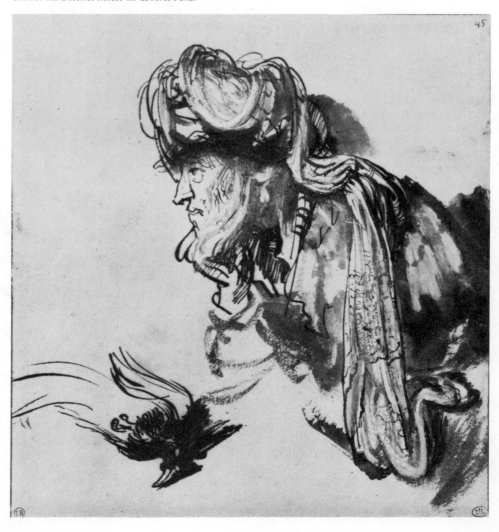

energetic, Rembrandt suggests that its "crescendo" of action in the turban—its wild swirls—cannot be contained there. So he provides an avenue of release through the head, beard, and arm by repeating the scarf's swirling actions in these forms.

Rembrandt's placement of the figure on the page also intends to heighten the downward pull upon the turbaned head, but for other reasons. The downward pull is necessary to establish balance in a configuration otherwise too tilted and located too far down in the lower right corner. And the means for this counterbalance, in addition to the scarf's contribution, are present in the downward aiming arrowhead-shape formed by the turban, the bearded head, and the hand. Also, Rembrandt emphasizes the physical weight of the scarf-laden turban by placing a deep shadow on its underside. To give the downward-moving thrust a visual "anchor" and goal, he places the dead bird enticingly close to the arm, thus extending the downward movement into it by providing a dynamic, if not an actual, connection. Whenever a small space separates any two or more parts, we "see" them as connected. This phenomenon is referred to as *closure*.

In Chapter Two we saw that drawing convincing volumes is a demanding perceptual skill, but in the hands of a knowledgeable draughtsman the impression of volume can survive strong attempts at its suppression. In Parker's drawing *Reclining Nude* (Figure 5.26), the volumes, almost overwhelmed by the artist's insistence on shape, still suggest broad structural and even anatomical facts. They do so because the blocky planes and simplified contours are neither arbitrary nor naive. They are intentional, sensitively diminished responses which amplify a particular design scheme that concentrates on shape. Parker's understanding of structure and anatomy make these few departures from shape count. Note in the limbs that the change in planes conforms to anatomical fact. The planes are simplified and they strive toward rectangularity, but they are not willful distortions. Likewise, especially in the legs, breasts, and head, the contours are greatly subdued in articulating form, but they are the result of knowing summaries, not caprice.

Because physical weight is an incidental quality here, Parker relies more on visual weight to establish balance. Although the hair, being more convincingly modelled than other parts, does suggest a degree of real weight, it is mainly the dark tone and bold shape of the hair that counterbalance the figure's location on the left side of the page.

Volumes, then, can vary greatly in the impression of solidity—from the sculptural clarity of forms by Michelangelo to the teasing ambiguity of those by Parker. They can also differ greatly in their degree of focus. Most figure drawings are more linear than tonal, and their forms tend more to be sharply delineated rather than blurred or vague. Some artists rely on volume's ability to be "lost and found" as a design device. In Moore's drawing *Women Winding Wool* (Figure 5.27), volumes vary widely in the clarity of their mass and edge, creating some passages of monumentality and some of mystery. By regulating clarity, Moore dramatically accentuates the subject's essential design: the action of the large, horizontal "figure eight" enveloping the two upper halves of the figures, and the pulsations of the light tones in the two lower halves.

Figure 5.26
ROBERT ANDREW PARKER (1925–   )
Reclining Nude
Ink and watercolor washes. 8 x 9 in.
Collection of Christopher Parker.

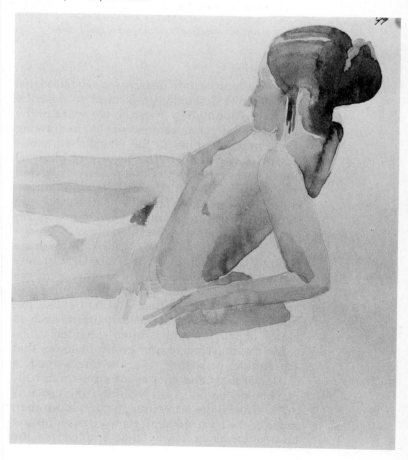

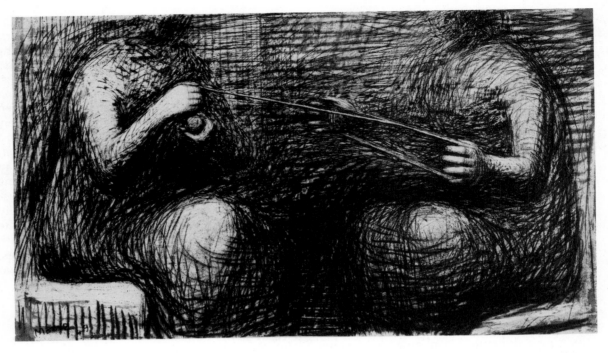

Figure 5.27
HENRY MOORE (1898–   )
Women Winding Wool (1949)
Crayon and watercolor. 13 3/4 x 25 in.
Collection, The Museum of Modern Art, New York.
Gift of Mr. and Mrs. John Poper in honor of Paul J. Sachs.

Texture

The term *texture* designates several visual phenomena. Generally, it is used to describe the tactile nature of a material; we speak of the texture of hair, skin, cement, or silk. In drawing the term also applies to the visual characteristics of drawn marks. The texture of charcoal lines differs greatly from that made by pen and ink. We can also distinguish textural differences between marks made with the same medium. The texture of the ink lines in Figures 5.6, 5.7, 5.8, and 5.9 — their density on the page and the nature of their calligraphy — differ strongly from each other. In a similar way, texture also refers to the density of other elements on the page. The shape-textures of Figures 5.19 and 5.21 are quite different. Texture also defines the visual repetitions of patterns such as plaids or stripes, and is often extended to include the massing of any group of forms that are similar in nature. Fingers intertwined, a cluster of folds and creases, or a pileup of ballplayers or boulders all exhibit different textures. The figure's textures include more than those of the hair and skin; some artists interpret human forms in a way that emphasizes the texture of their "hills" and "valleys," as Tintoretto does in his drawing, *Study for a Group of Samson and the Philistines* (Figure 5.28). In this drawing we can even discern textures within textures. For example, the recurrent, rhythmic beat of all the ovoid forms on the page creates one texture, while within the figure of Samson the ripple of the abdominal muscles, the thoracic arch, and other forms protruding on the torso create another more active texture of small, highlighted ovoids than is present in other parts of the figure.

Millet's etching *Man with a Wheelbarrow* (Figure 5.29), demonstrates several of these aspects of texture in drawing. Additionally, it shows how texture can serve to regulate the similarities of like and unlike things.

By describing the texture of the leaves, Millet unites all of the leaf-clusters, whatever their differences in value, shape, scale, and position. In using diagonal lines to suggest the texture of the contents of the barrow, he strengthens the contrast between the shaded portion of the hay and the shaded, wooden sides of the barrow. Those diagonal lines serve more than textural interests. By their tilt, they "reach" for

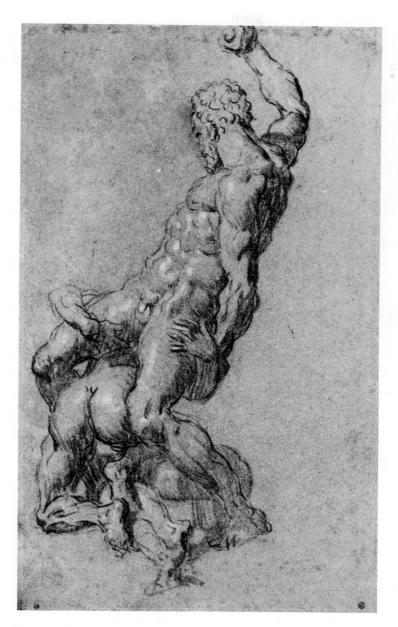

Figure 5.28
JACOPO TINTORETTO (1518–1594)
Study for a Group of Samson and the Philistines
Charcoal, heightened by white, on blue paper.
Musée Bonnat, Bayonne.

the point of the large, curving mass of leaves, creating a visual tension that carries their common arc through the figure. The direction also restrains the unity of the collective dark tone of the doorway and the loaded wheelbarrow, which would otherwise have been isolated in their overbearing similarity. Note that nowhere does a material's texture overtake its form. How often, in student drawings, is the form of the head lost in the concentration on the texture of the hair and skin! In such drawings, textures seem to rise to the surface of the page, conflicting with the sense of structural masses in space. That this need not occur is amply illustrated in van Dyck's drawing, *Head of an Apostle* (Figure 5.30).

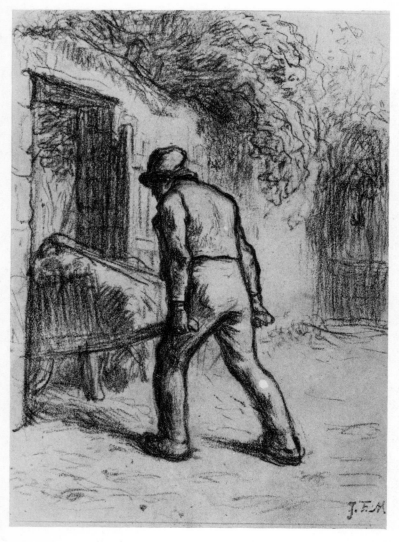

Figure 5.29
JEAN-FRANÇOIS MILLET (1814–1875)
Man with Wheelbarrow
Black conté crayon. 6 x 4 3/8 in.
Courtesy Museum of Fine Arts, Boston.
Gift of Martin Brimmer.

cerned with the virtuosity of their media than Manet, who delights in making the pen and brush produce a sparkling surface "fabric." Villon, in his etching *Kneeling Nude* (Figure 5.32), is even more unswerving in his concentration on the texture of the etched lines. He produces a system of mechanical, crosshatched shapes whose textures are as pronounced as their values. Villon's persistent texture suggests that the lines do not actively express forms, but rather that they obligingly halt to permit an edge or a value to occur. Here, the mechanical texture behaves mechanically. But, to avoid a too rigid result, Villon takes care to provide some line and texture variety. A secondary system of curvilinear lines creates gentle, even sensual, forms, and at the same time establishes a texture comprised of undulating shapes and edges.

In discussing the elements, we have already seen some of the visual energies at work: direction, tension, and weight are all powerful relational forces. Although we concentrated on the various manifestations of each element and on some of the ways it might relate to others in its class, we also observed some relational actions between different elements. To better understand how such energies issue from, and act on, elements, we now turn to examine the various ways in which elements form the visual bonds that consolidate a drawing's figurative and dynamic content.

THE ELEMENTS IN ACTION

In every drawing each of the six elements participates in several relationships at the same time. Indeed, lines and values being what the other elements are made of, always take an active part in the visual behavior of those elements. And because the behavior of the shapes, volumes, textures, and spaces they give rise to are engaged in visual activities with each other, a single line or tone may be shunted onto several tracks of visual association that will carry its kinships with other elements far across the pictorial field.

All visual relationships generate energies that suggest movement, or a striving for movement.* Some kinds of energy are discernible

But when a two-dimensional design is to be emphasized, it may be desirable to permit textures to come to the surface. Manet's drawing *Springtime* (Figure 5.31) communicates the airy, active feel of his subject by a profusion of differing textures. All alike in their energetic and lace-like nature, they unite in forming an almost page-filling design. Their unity is reinforced by the visual counterpoint of the drawing's few black and white shapes. Manet makes the forms of the figure and those of her surroundings less structurally insistent, and amplifies the textures, creating a design that functions well in either its two- or three-dimensional sense.

Manet's attitude toward the textural effects of his medium differs markedly from that of Millet or van Dyck. The latter are less con-

*Rudolf Arnheim, *Toward a Psychology of Art* (Berkeley and Los Angeles: University of California Press, 1972), pp. 75–89.

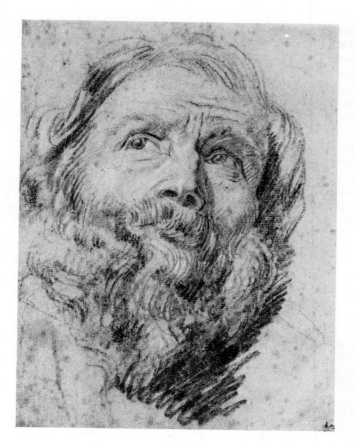

Figure 5.30
ANTHONY VAN DYCK (1559–1641)
Head of an Apostle
Black and white chalk. 10 1/2 x 8 1/16 in.
The Metropolitan Museum of Art, New York.
Gift of Mr. and Mrs. Janos Scholtz.

Figure 5.31
EDOUARD MANET (1832–1883)
Springtime
Pen, brush, and ink, on white, glazed paper.
12 15/16 x 8 3/8 in.
Courtesy The Fogg Art Museum, Harvard University.
Bequest of Grenville L. Winthrop.

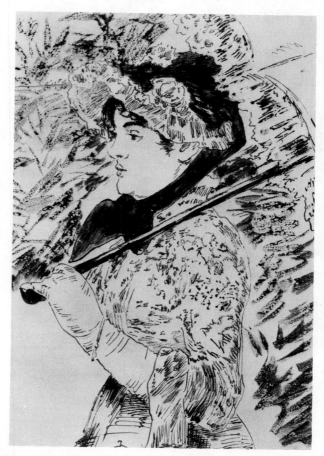

within a single element. For example, some lines, according to their handling and route, move quickly, as in Figures 5.6 and 5.10; others move slowly, as in Figures 5.7 and 5.8. The same is true for shape; the oval, for example, suggests leisurely movement; a narrow rectangle or triangle implies faster motion. And an even graduation of value seems to change faster and more gently than a modulation that occurs by abrupt differences of degree.

But other energies are generated only between elements: the visual impact and action of a large shape's size and movement depends for its meaning on its relation to the scale and behavior of other, smaller shapes, and even on its relation to the picture plane. An arm, a leg, a fold, and a tree trunk may all be related if the artist stresses the rhythm of their common S-shaped movement. Here, we should bear in mind that some or even all of the relational forces we will examine may simultaneously act upon some of the components of a drawing.

Relational energies can be grouped in several ways. This presentation is arranged to take into account the important influences that the representational actions of the figure and its surroundings have on a drawing's abstract order. Considering the simultaneity of the various energies interworking in most relationships—the relational "chords" that strike our senses—any attempt at classifying such interdependent qualities invariably fails to account for some phenomena too illusive and ineffable to be snared in print. All such classifications are really more convenient than defensible. They attempt to identify broad types of energy in order to heighten our awareness of the rich dynamic life possible in drawing. And, though some actions and energies elude any system of

Figure 5.32
JACQUES VILLON (1875–1963)
Kneeling Nude (1930)
Etching. 8 1/16 x 11 1/4 in.
Print Department, Boston Public Library.

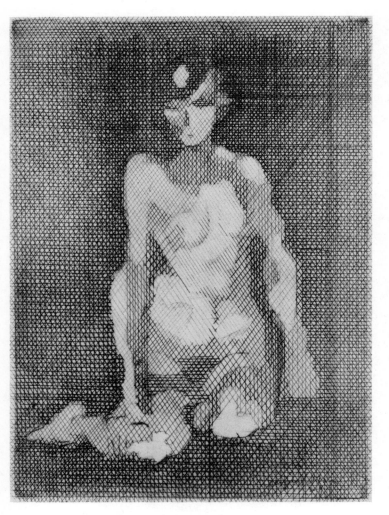

grouping, comprehending the nature of the many forces that *can* be described is the necessary route to apprehending those that cannot.

To understand the nature of these forces we must understand the term *movement* in its broader sense, as *any kind of action or change*. In addition to the obvious movements of direction, as when we draw a figure standing *up* with its arms hanging *down*, there are other motions that are not determined by the long axis of an element or of an identifiable form. We sense movement when groups of lines, shapes, or volumes relate by a gradual increase or decrease in their scale, value, texture, or spacing on the page.

The degree of energy of such movements is suggested by the gradient of change within or between the relating elements: by the collective shape and directional thrust of the group, by the force with which it ascends to domination in the design, by the number of visual "steps" involved in the change, and even by the vigor or delicacy of the artist's handling. For example, in Matisse's drawing *Dancer Resting in an Armchair* (Figure 5.33), a system of circles appears to radiate upward from the center of the page. Their similar shape and behavior and their gradually increasing scale and spread provide a strong common movement. A bold contrasting movement is seen in the downward rush of straight lines and shapes that gradually diverge from the center of the figure. We sense all these to be moving down, not up, because of (1) the visual need for "release" from the weight of the legs and lower torso, (2) the weight of the tilted rectangular shapes, and (3) not unimportantly, the suggestion of gravitational pull on the skirt-like folds. Note that Matisse unifies these totally opposing shapes and movements by making the collective behavior of their antagonistic thrusts form one irradiating burst of energy.

These two strong actions: the billowing up of circular elements and the rushing down of straight ones gain energy by the number of participants and the simplicity of their action. However, they are held in check by even stronger forces, namely, the bold, forward thrust of the figure and the curved movements of the arms and legs. By placing the figure on top of the system of overlapped shapes that surround it, Matisse creates a series of forward-moving shapes that "push" the figure toward us; and by their bold and simple contours, the limbs swing around in strong arcs.

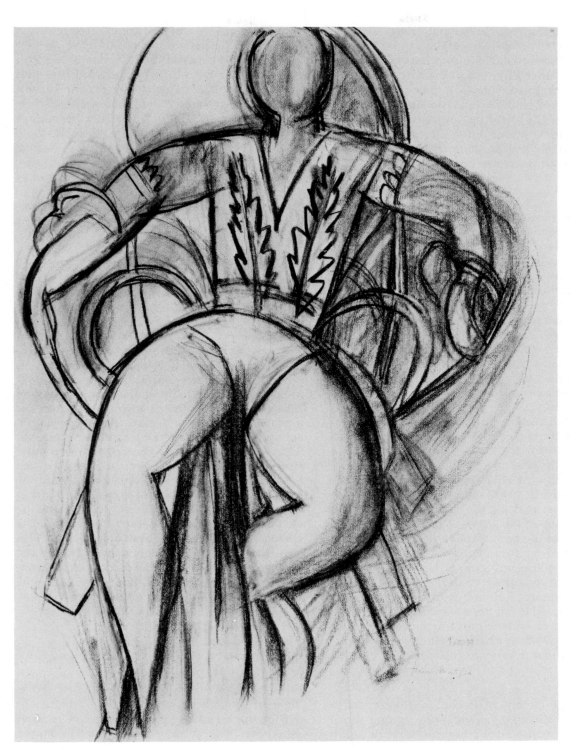

Figure 5.33
HENRI MATISSE (1869–1954)
Dancer Resting in an Armchair (1939)
Charcoal. 25 1/4 x 18 13/16 in.
National Gallery of Canada, Ottawa.
Copyright S.P.A.D.E.M.

Some kinds of relational energy, such as visual weight, physical weight, or tension, suggest that movement is either necessary or imminent, rather than occurring. Others, such as location or those concerning various types of similarity or contrast, will, depending on their context in the drawing, produce motion or a striving for motion. But the dynamics of *direction*, *rhythm*, and *handling*, are those most endowed with the sense of movement.

Direction

The discernible continuity of a single element or elements moving on straight or varied paths toward an intended point on or beyond the picture plane, or in a field of depth produces direction. Such movements often suggest visual or physical weight. The tapered and egg-like forms of a figure can move with vigorous speed toward a specific point (Figure 5.13). Long lines, shapes, and volumes, especially when their course follows simple straight or curved paths (Figure 5.33), make for stronger movement. Only shapes or volumes without a dominant axis are free of direction.

When changes in value or texture agree with the direction of a shape or a volume, the speed of those elements is increased. For example, in Figure 5.29, the downward-curving movement of the great mass of leaves above the wall gains energy by changes in the value's graduation and the texture's increased animation. Both changes occur along the same direction as that of the shape of the leaves. Again, in Figure 5.18, the force of the beret's movement to our right is heightened by the texture's loss of clarity and the value's lowered tone.

Thus, textures, values, and even interspaces (Figure 5.15) have directional movement. Blurred elements move faster than sharply focused ones, and the movement of any element can be slowed or checked altogether by other elements that overlap or intersect it.

Rhythm

Most clearly observed in the repeat of similarly directed movements among lines, shapes, or volumes, rhythm can be produced by a reoccurrence of similar characteristics of any kind among the elements. A certain "pace" in the grouping or density of the elements, a reoccurring texture or degree of tonal change, or a discernible pattern among like elements, all produce rhythm. It can be sensed among unlike elements when their sameness in direction or pattern is strong enough to withstand their contrasting identities and functions. For example, in Figure 5.15, round or half-round lines, shapes, and volumes, whether large or small, light or dark, near or far, all suggest rhythm by their curved basis. The more often a rhythm is reinforced, the stronger is its movement (see Figures 5.2, 5.25, 5.33, 5.40). Essentially directional, rhythms can suggest a sense of "beat," as does the reoccurrence in Figure 5.14 of a system of ovoids emerging from the figure's right knee, the shoulders, and the breasts. One aspect of this relational energy—the rhythmic accents in lines, as in Figures 5.2 and 5.4, or in shapes, as in Figures 5.15 and 5.16—overlaps the next category.

Handling, or Character

The stylistic or idiosyncratic accents and cadences of lines, tones, and shapes are a powerful source of moving energy. The artist's "handwriting"—the deliberate, playful, delicate, or vigorous nature of the elements—can make unlike elements relate, as in Figure 5.11, where diverse parts exhibit the unifying stamp of the artist's particular manner of presentation. Like things can be made to contrast when, for purposes of variety or design, the style is varied, as in the legs of Figure 5.14, or in the figures of 5.16. Partly a matter of the artist's neuromuscular coordination and partly the result of his temperamental and creative attitude toward the subject, the artist's handling creates a kind of visual meter that sets a certain speed among the elements and the forms they constitute. The character of the medium and tools always influence handling, and even perception. They not only limit the nature of the marks but, because of their various traits and limits, influence the kinds of observations the artist makes.

Location and Proximity

The relational energies of location and proximity are produced by the association of like or unlike elements according to their position on the picture plane or in a field of space. Elements equally distant from the horizontal or vertical center of the page may relate in their sameness of location. For example, in Figure 5.16, the dark and light halves of the background relate in part because they evenly surround the figures and roughly divide the page. Clusters of elements may relate by their density if surrounding elements differ markedly in scale, value, texture, or direction, as in Figure 5.17. Here, the entire group of shapes, forms, lines, etc., above the outstretched arm of Seneca, in

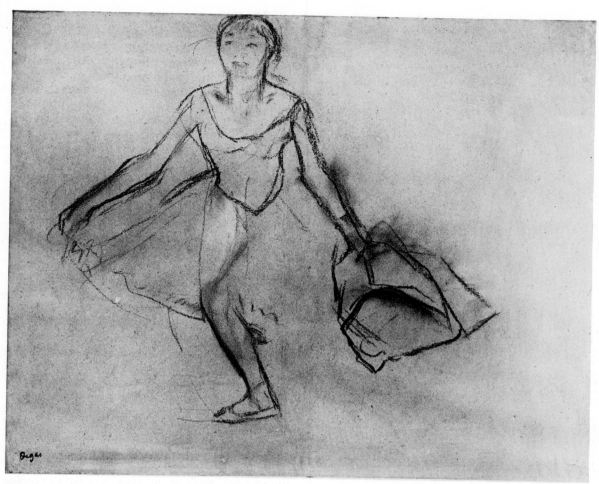

Figure 5.34
EDGAR DEGAS (1834–1917)
Sketch for a Ballet Dancer
Charcoal. 18 1/8 x 23 5/8 in.
Courtesy Museum of Fine Arts, Boston.
Gift of H. Walter Child.

addition to the many other relational activities within it, is related by the density of its components. Affinities based on location and proximity are strong visual forces. Symmetrically located parts form the strongest bonds.

Subdivision

In a related group of elements, subgroups may form because of similarities in shape, value, texture, or any other properties that distinguish them from the parent group. For example, in Figure 5.3, the darker lines in the lower left side of the page pull away from the lighter ones surrounding them; they still belong to the larger group of lines, but form a discernible subgroup. Again, in Figure 5.33, the large circle behind the figure and the circles below each arm, while

maintaining their visual union with all the other circular lines, shapes, and interspaces, form a subdivision. They do so by virtue of their more complete roundness, and because they are symmetrically arranged. Often, such subdivisions can gain enough independence to relate to elements quite far away. In Figure 5.4, the three or four darkest strokes on the dress call to the similarly dark ones of the hair.

All elements, as noted earlier, can form several links simultaneously. For example, in Figures 5.17 and 5.22, strong values create large, light and dark shapes—"super shapes"—from the many smaller shapes. These large shapes exist independently of any ties to one particular volume; they form their own abstract relationships. But the smaller shapes, although "re-

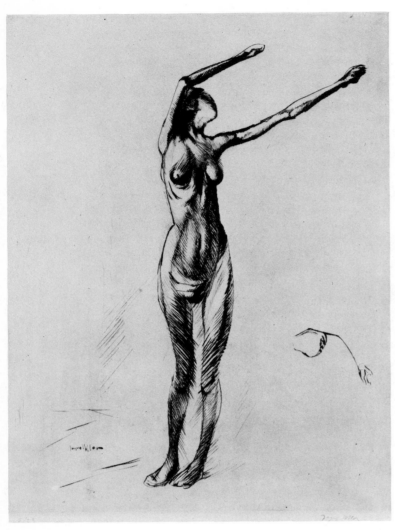

Figure 5.35
JACQUES VILLON (1875–1963)
Standing Nude, Arms Upraised
Drypoint. 54. 9 x 42.4 cm.
Courtesy Museum of Fine Arts, Boston.
Lee M. Friedman Fund.

cruited" into these super shapes, continue to function in forming volumes, disclosing directions, rhythms, and so on.

Elements, then, relate to each other in various combinations based on their similarities and contrasts with other elemental properties. The texture and value of lines, the shape and value of volumes, the texture and value of shapes, are all characteristics that determine how elements will associate with each other. Additionally, they will relate according to visual functions such as direction, rhythm, weight, or tension, and according to scale, handling, and proximity.

Visual Weight

As mentioned earlier, all elements possess visual weight in the picture plane. Thick lines and dark values weigh more than thin lines and light values, large shapes and interspaces weigh more than small ones, and pronounced textures are visually heavier than subtle ones. Although, as noted earlier, such weights can press in any direction, in many drawings visual weight, like physical weight, is resolved by being balanced seesaw fashion on either side of an imaginary fulcrum in the drawing's center (Figures 5.3, 5.5, 5.11, 5.13, 5.16).

Even Figure 5.12, which consists of a single, compact and centrally located configuration, shows its elements balanced around a central point. But here, additional visual weights keep the image from appearing to fall through space. The tone, shape, and location of the figure's right shoulder seem to push toward the left side of the page where they are (by the phenomenon of closure) visually anchored.

Directional energies are often the driving force behind visual weight. In Figure 5.12 the wedge comprised of the neck, neckerchief, and shoulder throw their weight to the side instead of downward. Similarly, the left shoulder and the dark cast shadow swing upward, their weight aimed for the upper right corner of the page. The shapes and tones of the hair provide a third group of elements whose visual weight goes toward the top of the page. These forces modify the physical weight and seem to keep the image secure in its location. Again, in Figure 5.10, the visual weight of the thick lines in the head makes for its stronger upward thrust.

Although directional forces usually accompany the actions of visual weight, the latter is present even when elements convey little or no direction. In Figure 5.16 the large, dark shape of the background has a strong sense of visual weight, but not of direction. More often, however, these two relational energies are seen working together, each intensifying the visual impact of the other. Whether we see a single element of a large segment of a drawing as *primarily* suggesting direction or visual weight largely depends on its context in the design.

Tension

A frequent characteristic of other energies such as direction, location, handling, and both visual and physical weight, tension, as used here, describes a sense of elements striving to meet or repel each other, or to change their shape or location. When two or more elements or parts of the same element are so arranged as to almost touch, we feel their striving to complete the union. Likewise, when elements or whole parts of a drawing are directed away from each other, we sense their desire to move farther apart. Arrangements in which the directional forces are ambiguous also produce a tension between the components—a sense of "stand-off" between conflicting energies. Thus, the two ends of a C-shape, if not too far apart, strive to complete the interrupted circle we feel the shape intends to be. Similarly, the five or six wedges of a star-shape strive to pull away from their common base, moving in the direction they point to. And lines formed into an H-arrangement suggest that whether we see the two vertical bars as attacking or retreating, the horizontal "bar" prevents their doing either, and creates a pulsating tension of forces pulling and pushing.

In our need to understand the visual condition of whatever we see, we sense tension in any arrangement that hints at its essential, simpler state. Just as our anxiety subsides when we see a parachutist touch down safely, so does our unease at viewing a drawing of a falling figure subside when we find a basis for its stability within the design. This stability neither completes nor neutralizes the act of falling. Indeed, it underscores the drama of the event by showing it against the "backdrop" of the drawing's total order. But it also prevents the act from causing the design itself to fall. When what fills our field of vision is itself in collapse, particular falling parts within it have little meaning. In Figure 5.21, the three groups of fighting figures in the foreground suggest a tenuous but balanced "tripod." The artist makes the action of each group more powerful by joining their visual forces, and, by showing their various falling states within the context of a stabilized design, gives them greater expressive impact. Here, strong tensions work to bring the groups together. Diagonal directions, in departing from the inherent stability of vertical and horizontal ones, produce tensions. In this drawing there is a high degree of motion and tension in the attraction and repulsion among the diagonally placed elements and in the groupings they make. Note the absence of a single vertical or horizontal movement among the figures, but an insistent horizontal "pedestal" of tone beneath them, helping to stabilize the design. In Figure 5.20 tension is experienced in the large figure's limbs. They strive (as do the arms of the star-shape) to pull away from each other, but are checked by their collective balance on the page,

and by the roughly equal tensions in all directions that cancel each other's thrusts. Ambiguous tensional forces are felt in Figure 5.27. The wedges formed by the bent arms, the directional thrust of the figures' weighty hips, and the downward slope of their laps all produce tensions that pull away from each other. At the same time, the link of the wool thread, the dark tone that envelops both figures, and the design's pronounced symmetry all produce tensions that make the two halves of the drawing come together. The result is a tension-filled confrontation—a balance based on mutual restraint.

The participants in a tensional conflict of any kind suggest a charged field of energy between them; they seem to be aware of each other. A single element may also contain tension within it, as in the C, H, and star-shapes, or as exists in any element that takes more than one direction. Volumes, especially those of the figure, suggest tension when inner parts press against their containers, as in Figure 5.28, or pull against each other, as in Figure 5.20; or when their structures show strong interjoinings and multiple directions. The artist's handling can increase or decrease the force of a tension by emphasizing its aggressive or gentle nature.

Figure 5.36
LENNART ANDERSON (1930–)
Variant on Ingres' Figure Odyssey
Pencil. 10 3/8 x 15 1/2 in.
The Graham Gallery, New York. Photo Geoffrey Clements.

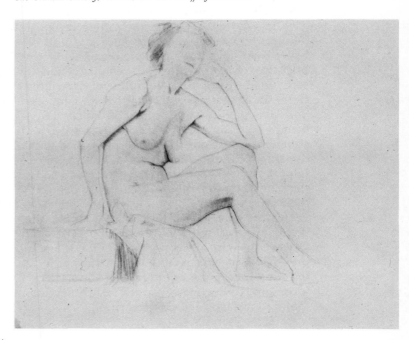

Figurative Influences

The physical requirements of representational forms in a given context act as a strong modifier of the relational bonds discussed above. For example, a drawing of a figure leaning against a fern will not appear balanced because of what we know about the structure and weight of both forms, though in formal visual terms such an image may be faultless. Replacing the fern with a cane will balance the figure in its representational sense, but may cause the design to collapse. To prevent this, the artist must compensate for the cane's weak, two-dimensional properties — its small visual impact — in the design. He may choose to increase its directional energy; he may join it in various strong rhythms or tensions; he may place larger objects around it; he may strengthen its contrasts of value or texture with other parts of the design; or he may combine several of these steps or turn to still others. For while the cane has the physical strength to support the figure, the artist must give it the visual strength to support the design.

As this example suggests, a drawing's two- and three-dimensional design must make visual sense at both the abstract and figurative levels. The more convincingly forms suggest recognizable objects, the more do their various identities, locations, and directions in space influence a drawing's balance. Representational forms, unless drawn with a regard for their two-dimensional condition, always weaken more than the design of the picture plane; they also diminish their own dynamic potential.

In Figure 5.11, a sensitive interplay exists between figurative and abstract needs, and between two- and three-dimensional ones. Rembrandt avoids splitting the design in half by softly fusing Esau's draped figure with the tablecloth, and by aligning the tablecloth's top and bottom edges with those of Esau's belt and coatfringe. This horizontal band creates a broad and subtle introduction—a visual "prelude"— to the dynamic action of the two arms. The dramatic import of the scene would have been far weaker if the link between the two figures had been only their clasped hands. Note how many lines and values are directed to those hands. Note, too, that Rembrandt relies more on visual rather than physical weight in his drawing of the table. Its presence is necessary to counter the weight of the standing figure, but to have made so large a form physically heavy would have weighted the drawing too much on the right.

Again, the design of Figure 5.17 discloses a knowing interplay of abstract and figurative order. Tiepolo's drawing, like Rembrandt's, relates two separate groupings of forms. A system of diagonal motions zig-zags through the figure of Seneca and the nearby group. Tiepolo places a drape's dark shadow in alignment with Seneca's left lower leg, and creates a large trapezoid out of his arms and the same dark shadow. Here, our appreciation of the weight and direction of Seneca's limp figure is essential to the drawing's design. Seneca's visual weight alone is too slight to provide the counterthrust necessary to balance the visual and physical weight of the nearby figures, as we see if we turn the drawing upside down. Tiepolo reinforces the dying figure's weight by introducing the drape on the left whose direction and modelling add visual weight toward the lower left corner of the page, but it is our sense of gravity's downward pull on the figure that completes the drawing's equilibrium. Note that Tiepolo emphasizes visual action to underscore physical inaction. The furled flag, the insistent swirls of the cornice, the drapery, and the pottery all serve to accentuate the stillness of death.

EXAMPLES OF RELATIONAL ACTIVITIES IN THE FIGURE

In examining the elements and energies of drawing we may seem to have drifted far from our earlier considerations of structure and anatomy. In fact, we have only been discussing another kind of structure and anatomy: that of the figure's dynamics. Like its physical counterpart, the dynamic "anatomy" of the figure is a given aspect of figure drawing and is present in any observed or invented pose. How these two anatomies will interwork is, of course, a matter of our perceptual understanding and our intent, but neither can be disregarded if our figure drawings are to have both dynamic and figurative life.

Although the relational activities in drawings that concentrate on the figure are active mainly within the boundaries of the image, such activities are still understood in relation to the page. Therefore, the location of a single figure on the page still requires sensitive compositional judgment.

The way Degas has placed the figure in his *Sketch for a Ballet Dancer* (Figure 5.34) reveals a fine balance of two- and three-dimensional considerations. Although we might question the visual necessity of the head touching the edge of the page, the integration of two- and three-dimensional weight throughout the drawing establishes a balance within the image and between the image and the page. Degas, anticipating the visual and physical weight of the large bouquet, places the figure well to the left of center. To have located the dancer farther to the right would have "tilted the scale" to the right side, and would have cramped the bouquet in the lower right corner of the page. To further lighten the load on the right side, Degas barely suggests the dancer's left leg, and simply omits the skirt covering it. Sensing the need for still more weight on the left side of the page, Degas strengthens the edges of the limbs and the costume on that side, giving them more visual weight. Even so, when we turn the drawing upside down, the bouquet retains its visual dominance. But, rightside up, our response to the figure's physical weight adds just enough force on the left to balance the drawing on the page. Of course, Degas could have easily balanced the bouquet by making the figure more structurally solid and thus, heavier, but that might have lessened the sense of the subject's graceful agility. Then, too, this is one of a number of quick, preparatory sketches. Partly notation, partly exploration, such drawings are complete when the simplest expressive order of a particular arrangement of forms yields promising ideas. Note some other forces working to convey the dancer's physical balance: a fan-like rhythm relates the arms, skirt, and bouquet in a way that poises the figure's right arm and the bouquet in a tension for balance. These energies, and the animated handling, make us experience the dancer adjusting to keep her balance.

In Villon's drypoint *Standing Nude, Arms Upraised* (Figure 5.35), an even stronger tension exists in the placement of the figure's arms. We sense their imminent movement downward, and even that they will swing back up on the other side of the page. Villon suggests this in several ways. First, the arms themselves carry a heavy burden of visual as well as physical weight. Notice that Villon models their form with solid black areas instead of the lighter crosshatching used throughout most of the rest of the figure. In the context of an otherwise near-symmetrical design, we feel diagonally placed forms of such weight to be striving for a location more consistent with the rest of the design. Secondly, what we know about human forms helps us recognize the arms are swinging, not reaching. A reaching action engages the

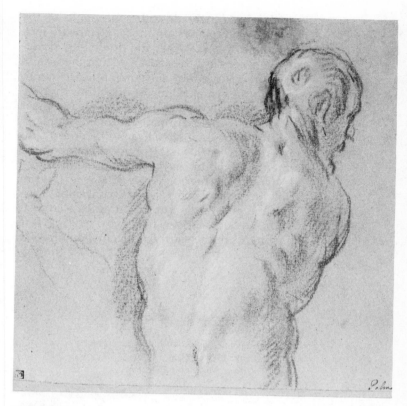

Figure 5.37
JACOPO PALMA, called GIOVANE PALMA (1544–1628)
Back View of a Nude Male Figure
Black chalk, heightened with white, on blue paper.
19.8 x 18.9 cm.
The Art Museum, Princeton University.

entire body, but here, the figure is almost "at attention" and turned *away* from the direction of the arms' motion. Without the assistance of the rest of the figure, such a movement is understood as a "frame" in a series of positions that make up the swinging motion. Thirdly, the figure's location in the center of the page, in making the counterswing possible, makes it more necessary. Lastly, Villon's modelling of the figure strongly hints at movement—teases us with diagonally drawn structural lines that suggest the back-and-forth swing. Even some lines on the left side of the page "beckon" the arms downward.

Villon's knowledge of anatomy provides him with a basis for establishing visual relationships that support his design theme without violating essential structural truths. For example, the direction of the lines modelling the legs, in their diagonal rush toward each other, not only reinforce the theme of motion, but also accurately describe the angle of the major curved planes of those forms. In fact, throughout the drawing, the modelling simultaneously conveys the artist's design theme and the figure's structural and anatomical generalities. Strong visual bonds of direction, rhythm, tension, and figurative behavior weave these forms into a single, animated human statement.

But appealing visual activity doesn't always require such visible evidence among the elements. Sometimes, as in Anderson's drawing *Variant on Ingres' Figure Odyssey* (Figure 5.36), forces work in a more concealed way. Here, the artist calls our attention to a circular motion enveloping the figure by making fine adjustments in the clarity and visual dominance of various forms. The shadow cast by the fig-

Figure 5.38
Persian Drawing, Safavid Period
(end of 16th Century)
Portrait of a Noble Lady with Elaborate Headgear
Brush and ink. 19.7 x 13 cm.
Cabinet des Dessins, Musée du Louvre, Paris.

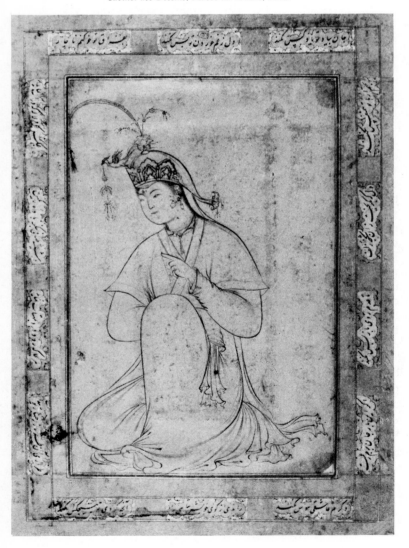

ure's right upper arm, the contour of the back, and the plane of the underside of the right upper leg, in being subtly darker than surrounding lines and tones, unite to form a half-circle. The V-shaped rhythm of the knees and the directions of the left upper leg and left forearm complete the circle. Anderson continues the rotating movement by aligning the thumb of the upraised arm with the edge of the trapezius muscle. Note that he subdues the impression of volume in the right lower arm and the lower legs; he even makes their shapes more open and draws them in a lighter line. Emphasizing these forms would have impeded the gentle rotating movement. A second design theme is based on a "family feeling" among the drawing's shapes. Anderson discreetly refines the contours to accentuate a system of S-curves, and "sharpens" the tips of shapes to emphasize their pointed endings. The resulting system of delicately fashioned "arrowheads" creates graceful darting motions between parts of the figure and the interspaces formed by the torso, arms, and legs. Note the reversed but similar shapes of the space enclosed by the arm, breast, abdomen, and leg, and the one bordered by the drape and legs. In the figure, sharp-pointed shapes, such as those of the right breast and left leg, relate with the surrounding interspaces, unifying and enlivening this seemingly straightforward drawing. Thus, the associations made by subgroups of line and shape, in transcending their depictive function, lend graceful plastic meanings to graceful representational ones.

Anderson is sensitive to the three-dimensional design of forms in a field of space. While he takes care to preserve the design of the picture plane, he also organizes the forms in space, varying the weight and focus of lines and values to call our attention to various points in space. For example, in subduing the clarity of the head, and in stressing the curve of the shoulder girdle, he gives the rotating action a three-dimensional basis as well as a two-dimensional one. And, in strengthening the values in places such as the armpits and waist, and in darkening the lines along certain segments of the contour, he not only heightens our understanding of the location of the forms in space, but also creates a spatial "beat" of such points of emphasis.

Here, as in all representational drawings, figurative energies influence abstract ones and vice versa. We tend to regard the drape as having less visual impact, not only because it is lightly indicated, but because in the context of the design it has little physical weight. Likewise, the rotating motion gains force where the torso adds its own weight to the action.

Just how influential the known properties of the figure can be is demonstrated in Palma's drawing *Back View of a Nude Male Figure* (Figure 5.37). Here, some of the answering thrust to the direction of the extended arm is effectively carried by the direction of the man's gaze to the right. Palma's drawing also demonstrates how useful a knowledge of anatomy is in providing and sustaining inventive responses to the figure's actions, responses that order and express as well as describe. Knowing the skeleton and muscles of the back enables Palma to accentuate those inner forms which enhance the force of the figure's twisting action. For example, to emphasize the torsion in the neck and head, Palma produces a system of reversed C-curves throughout the figure which, in contrasting with the turn of the head, amplify the force of its twist. Note that the artist stresses the curves of the scapula and the muscles on and around it to begin the arm's leftward movement well inside the torso. The wave-like undulations of the arm's contours suggest the leftward force of the "storm" gathered at the scapula, and, even beyond, in the curves of the ribs and contour of the right side.

In addition to the aforementioned gaze to the right, the only other major force that counterbalances the image's powerful leftward motion is the slight rightward arc of the torso itself. One enormous C-curve, its physical weight neutralizes the visual weight of the rest of the design. All the categories of relational energy are present even in this "simple" preparatory sketch. And, although the energies provided by direction, rhythm, visual weight, and figurative influences dominate, those of handling, location, subdivision, and tension play important supporting roles.

In the sixteenth century Persian drawing *Portrait of a Noble Lady with an Elaborate Headgear* (Figure 5.38), a different system of relational energies gives prominence to rhythms, handling, and location. Lines and shapes produce gracefully flowing rhythms whose elegance is reflected in the sure and fluid handling. Some lines, such as those of the shoulders, elbows, and knees, form a subgroup of large, simple curves; others relate by their smaller scale and by the action of the line clusters they are a part of, as do the lines of the radiating folds. The shapes achieve equilibrium by congenially answering each other's gentle movements. No-

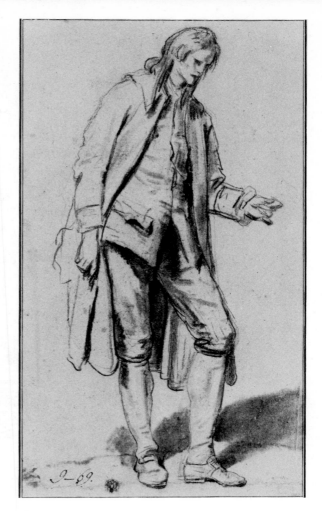

Figure 5.39
JEAN-BAPTISTE GREUZE (1725–1805)
A Young Man, Standing
Black, red chalk with gray and brown wash,
heightened with white. 50.7 x 29 cm.
Courtesy of the Art Institute of Chicago.

where do lines and shapes move unaware of the actions of their neighbors.

Three-dimensionally, too, there is a deliberate elegance among the volumes. Note the downward force of the two arms in contrast to the monumental rise of the figure's left leg; these moves and countermoves among the volumes occur leisurely, almost in slow-motion; they contrast with the faster movements in the drapery and headdress. By its location in the image, the figure's left arm takes on the necessary visual and physical weight to balance the drawing's heaviness on the left. It does so by gaining force from the downward flow of the headdress, and by overhanging the "empty" area of the lower right corner of the page.

Note how well these forms, despite the simplicity of their structure and the absence of tonal modelling, suggest convincing volumes. Such an economical statement of solid, graceful masses conveys the artist's sound grasp of

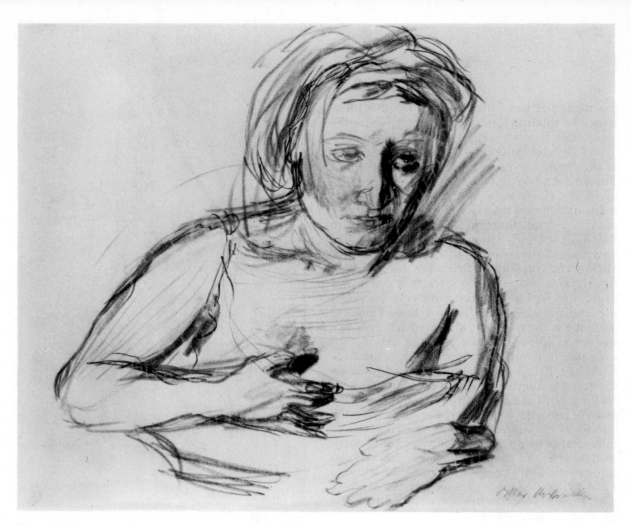

Figure 5.40
OSKAR KOKOSCHKA (1886–   )
Bust of a Girl
Red crayon. 17 3/4 x 21 7/8 in.
Courtesy of the Art Institute of Chicago.
Gift of Tiffany and Margaret Blake.

structural and anatomical essentials, as well as a penetrating sensitivity to dynamic order. Although these forms are insistently stylized — as much the result of convention as of personal response — they reveal a conviction and eloquence that no convention of figure drawing can provide (or suppress).

Greuze's drawing *A Young Man Standing* (Figure 5.39), differs in many ways from the previous drawing, but in both works forms are simplified, enhancing the sense of motion. Although the Persian artist employs a fixed system of curvilinear form-solutions and Greuze summarizes forms according to their inherent geometric nature (an attitude that anticipates Cézanne's approach to form), both artists make us conscious of the directed motion of the shapes and volumes, and of the lines and tones that produce them. For, at the heart of any form is its particular orientation in space. The more we strip away its surface embellishments, the

more we reveal its directional nature. In doing so, subdivisions of lines, shapes, values, and masses emerge, grouped according to direction and scale. Here, as in Figure 5.38, we can discern such groups of related elements. Note, for example, that the shapes of the neck, collar, cuffs, hands, and shoes are all related by their scale; and that lines denoting edges of forms and shadows relate by the common wedgelike shapes they produce.

For some artists, the abstract visual forces must take on the fury of a storm. For them, creating a figure's living presence has little to do with surface niceties or refined adjustments of proportion or even of relational nuances. They are concerned with establishing vigorous energies that become the visual equivalents of those which animate the living figure. But their drawings, while more intuitional than deliberate, are never unreasoned or arbitrary. There is, in fact, as compelling a necessity in the ordering of the marks as there is in the most classically-arranged image. Naturally enough, their drawings tend to utilize strong directional and handling energies.

This is clearly the case in Kokoschka's drawing *Bust of a Girl* (Figure 5.40). Unlike the drawings already examined in this section, where to varying degrees forms suggest energies, here we feel that energies "consent" to imply forms—that is, the real subject matter is the *behavior* of visual forces suggested by the model, and not the physical behavior or character of the model. Although the best components of figure drawing always contend with the factors of structure, anatomy, design, and expression, each artist evolves a personal formulation of these interacting considerations. Kokoschka's solution places structure and anatomy in subordinate roles, making them the servants of design and expression. He does this not out of indifference to the figure's static, measurable aspects, but because his main interest is in evoking its dynamic ones.

Here, urgently racing lines and values seem only partially concerned with depictive tasks. In sweeping across forms, in leaping from one edge to another, they reveal how forcefully Kokoschka responds to the subject's clues for such actions. In addition to the almost frenzied pace of the handling, the artist makes effective use of various other devices that speed up visual motion.

He avoids sharply focused shapes and forms, simplifies their contours, omits surface details, and gives the entire configuration a tension-producing tilt. Only in the head, the focal point of many of the drawing's moving forces, do these devices abate somewhat, permitting a more structured treatment. Strong rhythmic actions heightened by blurred edges and the furious drawing of the hair, of the various tones, and of the folds in the dress further add to the expression of energy.

Although we can hardly select two artists more opposite in temperament for comparison, note that Kokoschka, like the anonymous Persian artist, uses the device of the overhanging arm to balance the figure on the page. Had Kokoschka drawn the figure's left arm and hand with the clarity and visual weight of the right, the image would have remained too heavy on the right side. Because the elements are all strongly engaged in motion, we sense tensions throughout the drawing. Each line and value strives for change or continuance, each form only tenuously occupies its space on the

page; the woman's hair and hands never really settle into any one position. Yet Kokoschka gives us a stabilized design. Despite the drawing's violent calligraphy and action, no directional thrust remains unchecked. In fact, the image suggests an arrangement approaching symmetry. There is a near-symmetry of plastic forces as well. Circular motions predominate, but are regulated or checked by various diagonal movements. Only the overall tilt to the right side threatens to unbalance the image, and this, as noted above, is answered by the overhanging arm's wedge-like thrust to the left; a giant tension, it summarizes all the drawing's smaller ones.

In Tchelitchew's stormy drawing *Self-Portrait* (Figure 5.41), everything suggests motion, even values. There is movement in the forceful undulations of the light tone of the hair, and in its darkening as it turns downward to define the side of the head. Similar movements animate the drawing's smaller values. The artist inten-

Figure 5.41
PAVEL TCHELITCHEW (1898–1957)
Self-Portrait
Sepia, wash and brush. 11 3/4 x 7 1/2 in.
The Metropolitan Museum of Art, New York.
Gift of Mr. and Mrs. R. Kirk Askew, Jr., 1968.

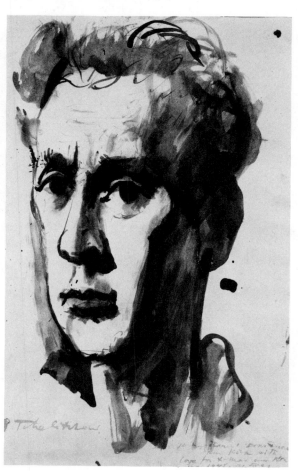

sifies the energies that strong directions and rugged handling generate by making the image fill the page. There is a tensional ''strain'' on the boundaries of the page by the strong force of vertical movements. The same drawing in a larger pictorial field would lose some of its visual and expressive impact.

ANATOMY AS AN AGENT OF DESIGN

In Chapters Three and Four some references were made to the role that anatomical considerations may play in stimulating dynamic activities. Here, we will examine several drawings to see how relational forces may be generated by a figure's surface anatomy.

Cézanne, in his drawing *Rowing Man* (Figure 5.42), establishes a rhythm comprised of long, diagonal hills and valleys that accentuate the figure's straining, forward thrust. Especially clear in the center figure, the rhythm is formed by the teres major, the external oblique, the pectorals, the thoracic arch, and the midline furrow of the rectus abdominus muscles. Cézanne's lively handling, the undulating lines, and the angle of these swelling forms (which is even more extreme than the angle of the torso) all combine to produce a strong sense of physical and visual action. To achieve this rhythm Cézanne not only stresses the volume and rhythmic action of these surface forms, but also subdues or omits others.

By contrast, in Michelangelo's *Studies for ''The Punishment of Aman'' for the Sistine Chapel*

Figure 5.42
PAUL CÉZANNE (1839–1906)
Rowing Man
Pencil. 22.7 x 29.9 cm.
Museum Boymans-van Beuningen, Rotterdam.

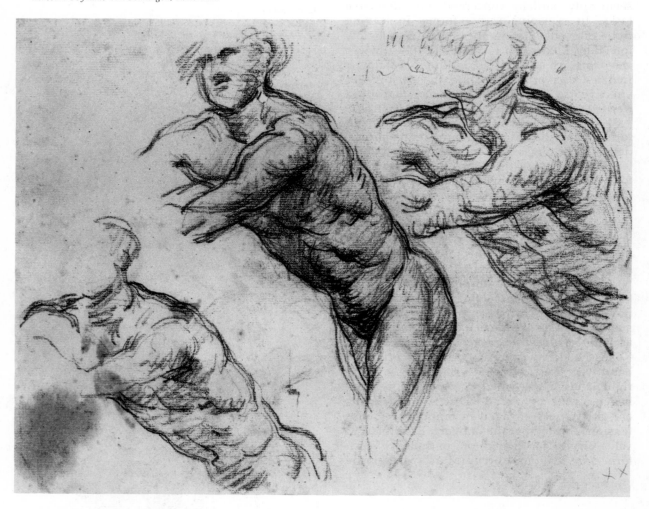

(Figure 5.43), we find every surface change that bone, cartilage, and muscle can provide, with some forms additionally exaggerated or invented. In the torso Michelangelo enlarges or exaggerates the clarity of the flank pads and surrounding forms, the serratus muscles, the thoracic arch, the ribs, and the muscle-bundles of the pectoralis major. In the legs he elaborates on the form of the rectus femoris, even suggesting different constructions for this muscle in each leg; in the left leg he shows the adductor group with the clarity it would have only in the flayed figure.

By these anatomical changes Michelangelo creates a different kind of rhythm from the fast-moving one in Cézanne. We sense a pulsating beat, both visual and physical—a constant rise and fall of ovoid forms. Instead of enhancing directional movement, this rhythm slows down the figure's vertical thrust. This occurs because the human eye hunts for and "feeds on" change of any kind. The eye is a rover, constantly searching for visual problems to solve. Simple structures, rhythms, and textures are quickly understood and as quickly dismissed. But when the eye encounters complexities it slows down to explore and experience them. We might be quickly bored by the easy structure and pattern of a new picket fence, but would dwell on an old, battered, and irregular one, finding it more visually engaging. So does the figure of Aman make us pause to follow the always interesting changes in the rippling surfaces and contours.

The contrast between the fast movement of the figure and the "braking" action of its surface activity creates tension throughout the image; the forms do not so much seem to move as to strive for movement. This tension is in harmony with the contrast between the bold pressure and straining of inner forms against each other and upon the figure's surface, and the delicacy of the handling. Note that Michelangelo unifies the figure by making some of the smaller form-units echo much larger forms. For example, the complex form of the figure's right knee, in addition to relating with other form-units in the torso, also repeats something of the contours that describe the limbs and torso.

That the same anatomical forms can initiate and serve an endless variety of relational activities is seen in Boccioni's drawing *Reclining Male Nude* (Figure 5.44). He utilizes the torso's anatomy for visual functions as different from those of Figures 5.42 and 5.43 as the Cézanne and the Michelangelo differ from each

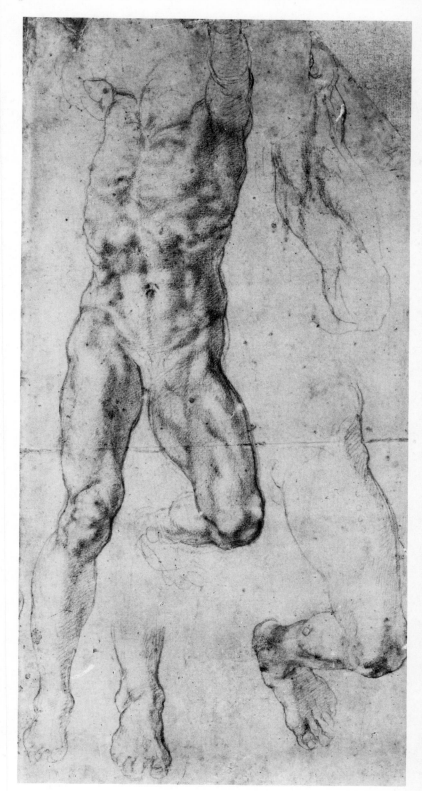

Figure 5.43
MICHELANGELO BUONARROTI (1475–1564)
Studies for "The Punishment of Aman"
for the Sistine Chapel
Chalk. 16 x 8 1/4 in.
Trustees of the British Museum.

217

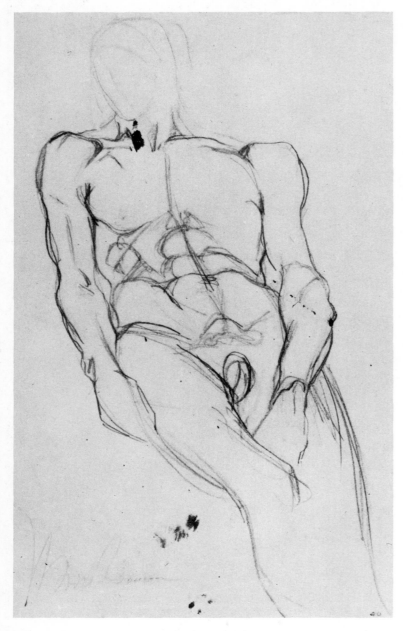

Figure 5.44
UMBERTO BOCCIONI (1882–1916)
Reclining Male Nude (ca. 1909)
Pencil. 11 7/8 x 7 1/2 in.
The Lydia and Harry Lewis Winston Collection.

weight of the muscles themselves. These contending knots of shape slow down the flow of the figure's shape and relate with other large and small shapes in the image. The artist, in simplifying these shapes, stresses straight and curved lines that reinforce the drawing's two-dimensional design as well as its rigid and supple form-traits. Thus, Boccioni, in responding to the figure's anatomical *and* plastic condition, gains insights that enhance both the figurative and dynamic force of the drawing. A subject's form always contains the seeds of its dynamic solution.

Boucher suggests the vitality and power of the sea god in his drawing *Triton* (Figure 5.45) by a large diamond-shape comprised of the figure's arms, and by a system of diagonals and wedges—shapes and directions well suited to evince energy and motion. Bold rhythms emerge from the repetition of these angular shapes and interdicting thrusts, urged on by Boucher's aggressive handling. But it is Boucher's sound grasp of structure and anatomy that provides tangible justifications for many of these powerful abstract actions. Throughout the figure, bones and muscles and the form-units they make furnish the artist with plenty of visual "ammunition" for these dynamic exchanges. For example, in the left arm, the wedge-like shape of the deltoid digs hard into the biceps and triceps below, while they counter with a pincer-like swing under the deltoid and, at their opposite end, mount their own assault upon the supinators at the elbow.

Again, among the forms of the chest and back, muscles overlap and interlace aggressively, and, in the arrangement of the hands, the block-like fingers provide a variation of the explosive force of the hair. Here, as in Kokoschka's similarly energetic drawing (Figure 5.40), Boucher stabilizes the visual energies among the parts, and in the figure's overall surge to the left, by using an essentially symmetrical design, and by investing great visual and physical weight in an overhanging arm. Here, too, a rotating action envelops the forms. This action, along with Boucher's use of swelling curves, keeps the design's angularities from making the drawing too brittle or harsh.

Surface anatomy, even if only of the most general kind, can continue to guide associational bonds, as Hiroshige's drawing *Two Women Playing* (Figure 5.46) indicates. The contours of the robes that describe the backs of the two women, in addition to providing visual "parentheses" that unite these figures, take

other. Boccioni subordinates the sense of volume, to concentrate instead on the shapes of the torso's surface forms. A pattern of shapes formed by groups of large and small muscles engage in movements against each other, creating two-dimensional tensions that parallel those produced by the pressure, strain, and

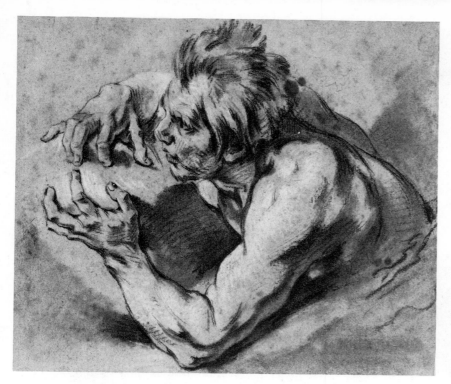

some of their graceful flow from the nature of the forms they cover. These contours, especially the one on the left, supply us with a surprising amount of information about the figure's anatomy. In that contour we can locate the beginning of the gluteal muscles, sense the absence of any obstruction to the robe's fall until the gastrocnemius muscle, and follow the edge of the lower leg to the ankle. Additionally, it describes the oblique and tapering nature of the supporting right leg. Hiroshige's sensitive summary of the figures' larger masses enables him to more effectively convey their congenial arrangement in the spatial field.

THE FIGURE AND THE ENVIRONMENT

In the best drawings of the figure in an environment, the figure is always an integrated component of the rest of the drawing. Whether it dominates the design or represents only a small part of it, the figure, at least in its formal, visual sense, relates with other parts of the drawing and is part of a consistent visual syntax. It can be thought of as part of a large still life, interior, or landscape design. To do so is not to disregard the figure's singular nature and importance; on the contrary, by integrating the figure and its surroundings to create a greater unity, we enlist the environment's differing character as a visual "foil" against which the figure's unique qualities and meanings can have greater visual and expressive impact.

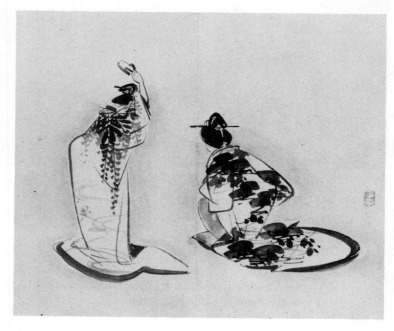

Treating the figure in a distinctly "special" way only isolates it from its surroundings, destroys the drawing's unity, and obscures the very meanings that the special attention endeavors to stress. Too often, beginners who include the model's surroundings lavish attention on the figure at the expense of its environ-

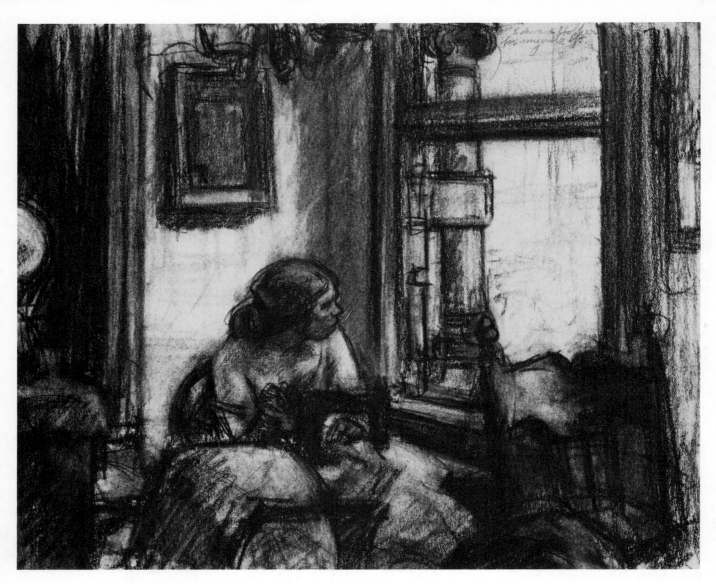

Figure 5.47
EDWARD HOPPER (1882–1967)
Drawing for Etching ''East Side Interior''
Conté and charcoal. 8 15/16 x 11 1/2 in.
Collection, Whitney Museum of American Art, New York.
Bequest of Josephine N. Hopper.

ment, unaware that the figure's representational and dynamic meanings depend on a visually logical and consistent integration of the *entire* subject. As we have seen, the figure can come alive with little or no surrounding support, but when other forms are part of the design, they must relate with the figure's forms.

Hopper, in his preparatory *Drawing for Etching ''East Side Interior''* (Figure 5.47), builds a classical design of vertical and horizontal units. Shapes and values, lines and volumes, all conform to a checkerboard alignment in which the seated figure participates. She does not, at first glance, attract our attention. That is commanded by the strong, bright shape of the window, made even more visually compelling by its dark frame and by its alignment with the

chair below it, adding to the window's vertical motion. To the left, the dark picture on the wall echoes the window's shape, while throughout the drawing, other vertical directions and light-toned shapes relate with the window, further strengthening its visual impact. The window attracts these shapes and directions; even the sewing machine strives to move to the right.

Only a few areas that contrast with the drawing's hard geometry seem to resist the window's magnetism. The globe on the far left, the curved chair, the woman's head, and a few dark shapes in the lower left corner emerge as a secondary system of organic shapes and forms that begin to command attention. Once this system is recognized, we also sense that the figure's central location, added to the curvilinear units encircling it, give the figure a unique visual power. Additionally, her sharp glance toward the window, and the slight, leftward tilt of the torso, in revealing both physical and visual resistance to the window's attracting force, heighten her importance in the design. Hopper, by firmly integrating the figure in the design, establishes a visual unity that can bear the gradually accumulating attention and importance that her location, form-character and human gesture command. To have given her more prominence in scale, value, or in "finish" might have destroyed the drawing's unity and the visual activities that support the artist's *human statement*. For, our appreciation of her precious aliveness, of the sudden gesture that suggests an unseen interruption, depends

heavily on the abstract and representational context in which we find her.

In a similar vein, the seated figure in Rembrandt's drawing *The Artist's Studio* (Figure 5.48), is *found* to be unique and important, rather than announced as such. She occupies an even smaller portion of the design than does the figure in Hopper's drawing and, in strictly visual terms, seems even more relentlessly regarded as an object. Far from stressing the figure's visual impact, Rembrandt almost camouflages her forms. He does this by matching the light tone of her torso with that of the nearby wall, and the darker tone of her skirt with the shadowed areas surrounding it. Additionally, he makes the forms surrounding the figure more structurally assertive, draws them in a

Figure 5.48
REMBRANDT VAN RIJN (1606–1669)
The Artist's Studio
Pen and ink with wash, touched with body color.
20.5 x 19 cm.
Ashmolean Museum, Oxford.

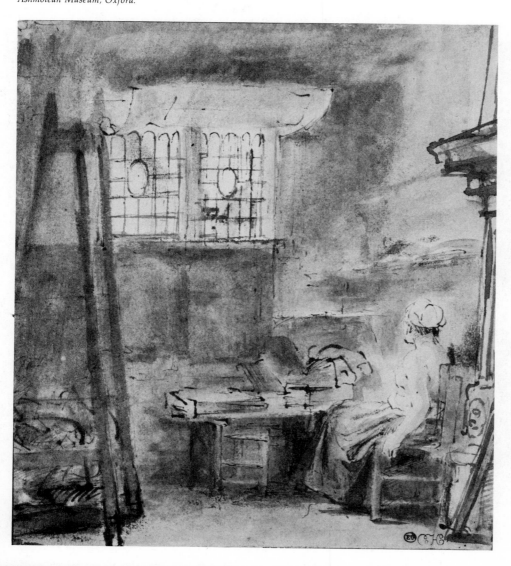

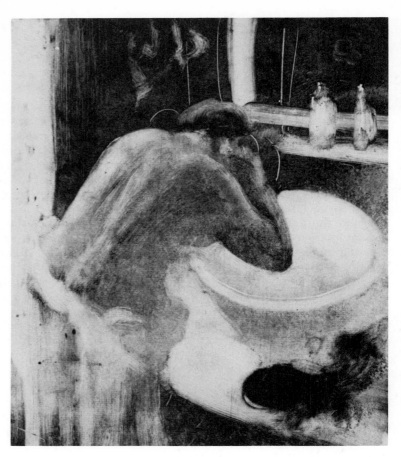

Figure 5.49
EDGAR DEGAS (1834–1917)
The Wash Basin
Monotype, black ink. 12 5/16 x 10 3/4 in. (plate)
Sterling and Francine Clark Art Institute.
Williamstown, Massachusetts.

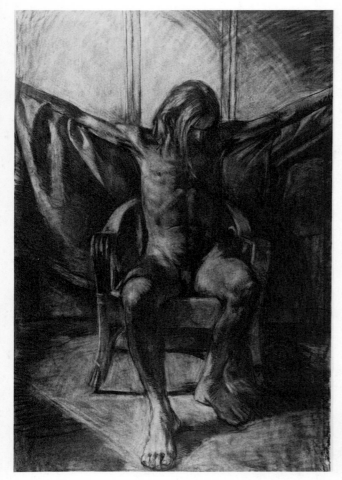

Figure 5.50
DOMENIC CRETARA (1946–)
Seated Male Figure, Arms Outstretched
Raw umber chalk. 69 x 46 in.
Courtesy of the artist.

more rugged manner than he does the figure, and further restrains her visual impact by having the chair overlap her back, while minimizing the effects of overlappings by the figure's forms on her surroundings. The overall effect makes the figure something of a visual "rest area" between the more vigorously handled segments on either side. As in Figure 5.47, Rembrandt's design strategy is also based on a pattern of vertical and horizontal lines and shapes. Here, an overall light tone muffles the beat of rectangular shapes that appear throughout the drawing; even the woman's torso and the direction of her bent legs suggest conformity to this grill-like pattern.

But, although completely integrated in the design, she is not a minor component in its order. In fact, despite her small scale and "quiet" visual behavior, she is the keystone of the design. Rembrandt reveals her dynamic role as subtly as he describes her figurative one.

The long diagonals of the easel at the far left, by contrasting with the drawing's system of vertical and horizontal movements, create the need for some answering diagonal. This is provided by the figure's lower arm and leg, and by the long lines of the fireplace behind her. By making the seated figure take part in both the "grill" movements and the diagonal ones, Rembrandt gives her location and form a strong sense of necessity. Another diagonal links the windows to the figure. This results from the alignment of the circle in the window on the right, the staggered corners of the two dark shapes on the wall, and the woman's head. Rembrandt further strengthens the figure's relational play with the windows by giving them a common value and vertical-horizontal orientation on the page. And, in reserving the drawing's strongest value contrast for the figure and the nearby dark tone below the table, Rembrandt furnishes still another means of *indirectly* calling attention to the seated figure. In creating this gentle interior scene, Rembrandt does more than describe the small, light-bathed figure resting in a corner of the large studio. By abstractly conveying the importance of this small and subtle segment of the design, he deepens our comprehension of her human significance in a large, inanimate setting.

When the figure *is* dominant in the design, its stronger dynamic condition must be regulated by equally strong relational bonds with the environment. In Degas' monotype *The Wash Basin* (Figure 5.49), the leaning figure is kept from upsetting the balance of the design by counterthrusts to its strong diagonal location. These answering diagonals are comprised of the white shelf, the overall shape of the basin and tabletop, the top edge of the figure's robe, and the black shapes of the mirror and the one below the tabletop. Additionally, long black and white vertical shapes and the folds of the woman's drapery also help to modify the figure's tilt.

In Cretara's *Seated Male Figure, Arms Outstretched* (Figure 5.50), the figure's dominant scale and location is further amplified by its symmetry, but is integrated by the similarity of the figure's values to all those below the top edge of the drapery. By matching the figure's values so closely to these dark tones, the contrast between the drawing's lower three-fourths and its lighter upper fourth makes a visual impact as strong as the figure's contrast with the environment. Note that the figure's slight rightward location, and the head's glance to the lower right corner are balanced on the left by the intensity of the large dark shape of the arm and drape, and the large light shape of the wall. The artist also diminishes the weight on the right side by placing the man's left leg back and by adding a dark wedge at the lower left corner to counter the lighter wedge on the right.

The observant reader may already have noted that in earlier discussions of balance, as here, the problem often comes down to the impression of elements seeming to weigh more to the right of center than comparable elements to the left of center. That we do judge parts to have more weight on the right can be easily proven if we examine Cretara's drawing (or any of the others in this book) by holding it up to a mirror. While the reasons for this phenomenon are obscure, the phenomenon is nevertheless a universal, given condition of perception which we must take into account in establishing a balanced resolution of forces.*

The beginning art student, struggling to make his figure drawings come alive, may sense some of the figure's underlying structure; he certainly realizes the need to support his growing understanding by the study of anatomy; and he has always known, even as a child, that the human figure can convey a limitless range of expressive meanings. Yet most beginners have

*Another strange phenomenon is that we evaluate a part located high on the picture plane as weighing more than if it were located lower. For a useful discussion of the phenomenon of visual weight, see Rudolf Arnheim, *Art and Visual Perception* (Berkeley and Los Angeles: University of California Press, 1969), chap. 1.

never seriously considered the importance of examining the abstract forces released by the elements which, in paralleling the order, vitality, and motion of living organisms, "fertilize" the image and give it life. Developing an aware-

ness of the dynamic cues in the subject and of the means of translating them into ordered, graphic terms is essential to creating figure drawings that enact and evoke as well as define.

SUGGESTED EXERCISES

Unless otherwise indicated, the following exercises are not restricted to any particular media or sizes and have no time limits. But because they vary widely in purpose, give some thought to selecting a medium and size suitable to the nature of each exercise. In each, establish a design strategy based on visual ideas that originate in the subject, that is, let the pose suggest the placement of the image on the page and the major visual activities of the figure's forms. Once

you have formed an attitude about the character of the subject's visual condition, stick to it. Our first impressions are usually guided by our temperamental interests, the ones most likely to produce original results. They are usually the right ones to base our interpretation on. In each exercise, whatever the particular goals, remember that you are always trying for a balanced resolution of the elements and energies.

Figure 5.51
ANDREAS VESALIUS (1514–1564)
Plate 25 from *De humani corporis fabrica*, Book II
Engraving.
Courtesy of the New York Academy of Medicine.

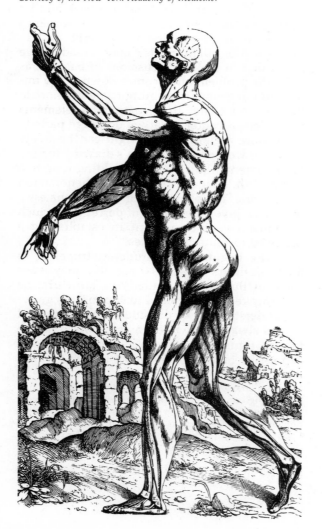

1. Working from a model, make the following drawings *of the same pose:*
   a. A gestural line drawing, somewhat in the calligraphic and rhythmic nature of Figures 5.2, 5.3, and 5.6. Emphasize strong directions and a sense of animation.
   b. A deliberate, continuous line drawing, somewhat in the manner of the contour line used in Figure 5.7. Your design should rely on shapes rather than on a profusion of lines, and should stress the subject's two-dimensional aspects.
   c. A structural, volume-informing line drawing which may include a moderate amount of line-formed values. Intentionally emphasize physical weight in establishing balance.
2. Working from a model, and using an erasable medium such as stick charcoal or soft graphite, restrict your drawing to values only. These values may be formed by groups of lines, but avoid explaining edges or folds by lines only. Here, include the model's immediate surroundings. If you wish, apply a moderately dark tone to your paper before you begin to draw, and use an eraser as well as your charcoal or graphite to establish the tonalities. Now your goal is to suggest movement within values, and through their shape and handling. This drawing need not include the entire figure, and should not exceed forty minutes. In general, promote a bold, aggressive handling.
3. Working from a model, make the following drawings *of the same pose:*
   a. Using Figures 5.15 and 5.16 as rough guides, draw the model in a manner that intentionally makes for figure-ground ambiguity.

b. Using Figure 5.17 as a rough guide, draw the model in a manner that makes for strong light and dark tones. Be sparing in your use of line; try instead to make values establish the forms. For this drawing you may wish to use artificial light to produce strong value contrasts.

4. Working from a model, make the following drawings *of the same pose:*

   a. A drawing that subdues the sense of volume and relies mainly on visual weight for balance.

   b. A drawing that emphasizes a strong sense of volume and relies mainly on physical weight for balance.

5. Working from the draped model in an environment, and using Figure 5.31 as a rough guide, make a pen, brush, and ink drawing that relies heavily on texture as a major means of organizing the design.

6. Using Figure 5.51 as your model, make a free adaptation of these forms as they might look in the living model. Although your drawing will not show the figure in the flayed state, emphasize the textural character of the muscles, as in Figure 5.28.

7. Using Figure 5.52 as your model, make the following two drawings:

   a. With Figure 5.33 as a rough guide, and by inventing any environment necessary, interpret Figure 5.52 for its possibilities.

   b. With Figure 5.40 as a rough guide, and by inventing any environment necessary, use pen, brush, and ink to establish a drawing that conveys a powerful sense of motion.

8. Using Figure 5.19 as a rough guide, *invent* a pose that suggests the figure's imminent movement. Do this through the pose, the modelling, and the handling.

9. Using Figure 5.19 as a rough guide, *invent* a two-figure composition in an interior or exterior setting that emphasizes shape, texture, and value.

10. Make the following two self-portraits:

   a. With chalk or graphite on a sheet no larger than 9" x 12", and using Figure 5.30 as a rough guide, make a drawing that fills the page. Here, the structural lines that model the forms should also function to balance the design on the page.

   b. Using Figure 4.20 (Villon's *Head of a Young Girl*) as a rough guide, and working actual size, make a "drawing" using small cut and torn shapes of white, gray, and black paper. Don't use more than three degrees of gray for this collage, and think of it as a kind of mosaic process. Try to convey a sense of volume, shape, and value order.

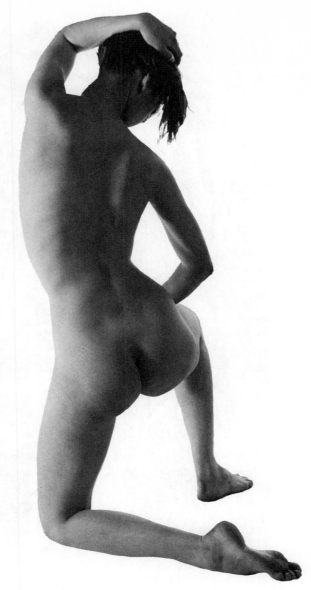

Figure 5.52

11. Rework or redraw two or three of the exercises done for Chapter Four, freely interpreting the forms to emphasize strong rhythms among the muscles.

12. Working from the model arranged in an environment, make the following three drawings:

   a. A drawing in which the figure is almost camouflaged by value, shape, and placement among the surrounding objects, as in Figures 5.47 and 5.48.

   b. A drawing in which the figure is dominant, but strongly integrated in the image, as in Figures 5.49 and 5.50.

   c. A drawing that may stress or subdue the importance of the figure in the design, but which is strongly animated, relying on strong actions and directions, as in Figures 5.40 and 5.45.

225

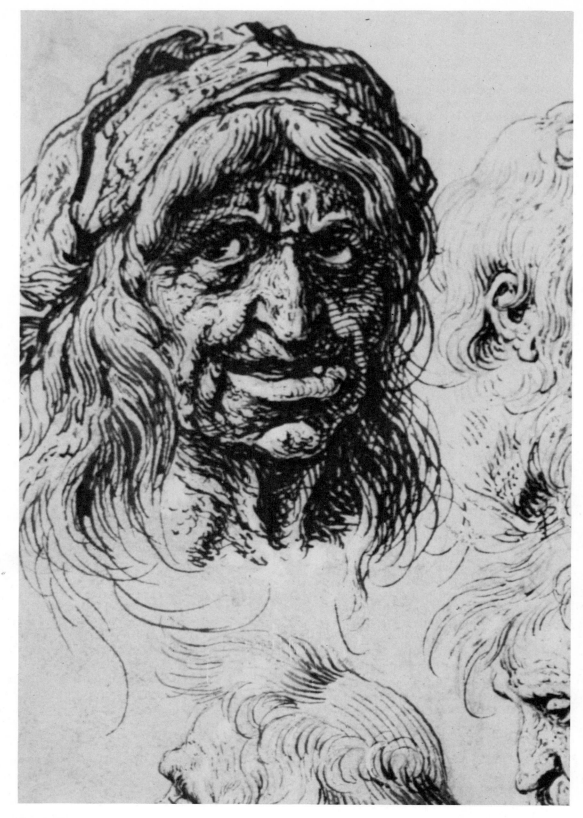

Figure 6.1
JACOB DE GHEYN II (1565–1629)
Study of Four Heads (detail)
Pen and ink over charcoal, white chalk highlights.
Teylers Museum, Haarlem.

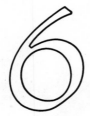

The Expressive Factor

the emotive content
of figure drawing

In Chapter Five it was observed that design and expression are really aspects of the same phenomenon: the dynamics of the elements that form the drawing. That these factors are deeply interwoven is evident in the expressive nature of the very terms that describe most of the relational categories. Direction, rhythm, handling, weight, and tension suggest types and degrees of moving and pulsating energies, and of strivings for change among the parts of a drawing. In responding to these visual activities we do more than recognize their presence — we *experience* their differing kinds of behavior. We cannot help but empathize with these abstract and representational thrusts, stresses, weights, and tensions, for their expression is inherent in the character of the marks that shape the drawing's parts and in the design of the parts themselves.

The design reflects more than the artist's conscious plan. He relies on intuitions and feelings as much as on intellect to order his responses to the subject's unique human and visual condition. If the design is the mind's strategy, that strategy is influenced by feelings that the mind initiates, and by emotive qualities in the subject and in the emerging drawing. The energies within and among the elements do more than function in their visual, or formal and depictive roles. They allude to psychological and spiritual states we can apprehend, and that enable a drawing to express, instead of only describe, human and visual events and attitudes. Delicacy, daring, sorrow, sensuality, are expressions we can sense pervading the best figure drawings. The lines and tones that express playfulness are not the lines and tones of pathos, and the energies of anger are unlike those of love. It is through these emotive marks and forces that figure drawings take on universal importance. Such qualities raise a drawing out of its time and culture and make the image a symbol that holds meanings for any society, at any time.

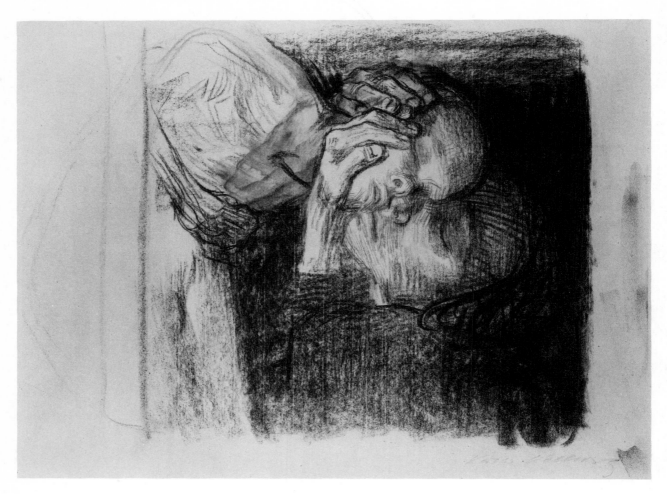

Figure 6.2
KÄTHE KOLLWITZ (1867–1945)
Mother and Child
Charcoal. 18 7/8 x 24 3/4 in.
National Gallery of Art, Washington, D. C.
Rosenwald Collection.

We can all apprehend Rembrandt's love (Figure 5.3), Kokoschka's excitement (Figure 5.40), Picasso's humor (Figure 5.16), Hopper's melancholy (Figure 5.47), and De Kooning's rage (Figure 1.31). And we experience sensitive emotive meanings in drawings that seem to focus more on visual issues, that seem less expressively motivated. Cambiaso's enthusiasm for structure (Figure 2.31), Desnoyer's thoughtful explorations of two- and three-dimensional space (Figure 5.19), Manet's spirited play with texture (Figure 5.31), and Moore's engrossment with monumental form (Figure 5.27) are all discernible expressions, each conveyed by elements and actions that imply these attitudes.

Expression, then, should be understood as issuing from more than the emotional or psy-chological state of the figure's representational situation; it is a quality inherent in the drawing's dynamics too. Both meanings of the term are important in figure drawing and must complement each other. In drawings where they conflict we sense an aimlessness of purpose, a confusing ambiguity of expressive cues. A drawing of a fist can express power, threat, avarice, confidence, or fear. Without some emotive clues beyond the depiction, the fist is only described; it can be identified, but not experienced.

If drawings are to convey some emotive temperament the artist must first discern it in what he observes or envisions. As the poet Horace observed, "If you wish me to weep, first you must grieve." But, in contemplating the expression of his model the artist searches for more than outward physical manifestations of a mood or event. He also searches for the figure's essential plastic and structural characteristics, not as ends in themselves, but because they reveal those dynamic properties by which the artist can evoke the figure's expression in ways that mere description cannot. For the crux of a figure's expressive content is conveyed by the overall condition of its forms.

This is why so many artists begin their drawings by establishing the figure's gesture. By temporarily disregarding the figure's smaller surface-effects and details, and by seeing its arrangement of forms as *one* subject and not a collection of separate parts, the artist perceives the figure's essential masses, plastic activities, *and* mood.

The best figure drawings begin with a grasp of generalities that excite the artist's interests and end with those necessary specifics demanded by his original excitation. It is the artist's adherence to his original theme that tells him when the drawing is complete—when he has conveyed his interpretation of the subject's important physical and dynamic conditions. And this must be done by deduction, not induction. To reverse this process and draw each segment sequentially does not allow for perceptions that uncover the general structural and dynamic conditions of the figure as a whole —perceptions essential to its figurative as well as evocative state.

Among the most common results of such a piecemeal approach are unintentional distortions in proportions and in the location of parts, and the loss of the relational activities necessary to a drawing's balance and unity. To begin with details is to end with a disorganized collection of them, for details greedily devour essentials and strongly resist an ordering of the figure's forms. Bypassing a felt analysis of the figure's dynamic and structural "armature" invites results that appear frozen on the page; no unified energies or expressions emerge.

But, if expression is largely conveyed by the character and mood of the drawing's abstract and structural condition, it is also, and importantly, a product of the subject's recognizable state. Facial expressions, physical actions, the event in which the figure takes part, that is, the "story-telling" aspects of the subject matter, strongly affect the drawing's expression. But, as noted earlier, these two sources of expression must be mutually supportive. A precise and delicate rendering of a figure drowning would suggest a conflict between form and figurative content. People don't shout their whispers or scream quietly.

A compatible rapport between these two aspects of expression is demonstrated in the detail from de Gheyn's drawing, *Study of Four Heads* (Figure 6.1). The artist does more than skillfully denote the physical expression of an old woman's grimace. Her fearful disquiet is carried in the rapid lines of the hair and in the gnarled and nervous lines of the face, in the abrupt changes of harsh values, and in the tortuous shapes and forms of the head and bonnet. The intensity of her gaze is heightened by the circular movements around the eyes and throughout the head. By rhythmically repeating lines in the hair, bonnet, face, and neck, de Gheyn endows the image with a nervous vibrancy. Visual tensions abound in this nearly symmetrical image, reinforcing the anatomical ones in the strained features. The unusual contrast of the fixed gaze and the animated movements and handling adds to her expression of anxious displeasure.

Kollwitz's *Mother and Child* (Figure 6.2) is a moving evocation of love and death. The hands that embrace the child's head hug with a tender intensity born in the abstract nature of ruggedly carved arcs enveloping gently rounded forms. The intimacy between the mother and child is revealed in the subtle fusion of their faces, and in the tender sensuality of the modelling that continues across them. Kollwitz bathes the forms in tones; only the child's cheek and the mother's hand are in light. The drawing's strong horizontal and vertical directions are contrasted only by the diagonal movements of the ghost-like arms that grip the child. Note how visual and physical weight carry on the same struggle that the figurative image depicts.

As the de Gheyn and Kollwitz drawings make clear, drawings made with a desire to realize an observed or envisioned expressive state must call on those dynamic forces that can evoke that state. Without some empathic involvement we lack a basis for selecting and ordering those dynamic and figurative clues essential to expression. Drawings developed without some expressive goal, whether that expression is to be found only in the character of the drawing's relational life or in the interplay between the expressive forces in the subject and in the elements, are like rudderless boats; they develop in no certain direction, but drift according to the winds of chance.

What we have stated should not be understood as a license for unfocused self-expression. Creative expression communicates the artist's apprehension of the subject's visual and spiritual condition. We learn about the artist's ability to feel and intuit by how effectively he conveys *the figure's* expressive meanings, not merely his own. Using the figure only as a springboard for an emotional high dive makes the drawing's real subject the artist, not the model. A conscious concern with self-expression too often deteriorates into an essentially nonvisual emotional binge—in subjective vagaries—that does not reveal responses to certain truths or potentialities in the subject's abstract and human condition. However, highly subjective interpretations that extract essential dynamic and psychological qualities in the figure or situation can be most eloquent (Figure 1.31, 6.13).

Expressive power is revealed not only by the figure's structural nature, as can be seen by comparing Picasso's simplified and granite-like figures (Figure 2.7) with the animated and supple figure by Tintoretto (Figure 2.19), but also by the means used to model the forms. De Gheyn's spirited calligraphy and Kollwitz's gentler strokes disclose something of the drawing's psychological tone. Even in drawings of figures that do not express a strong human emotion such as anxiety, grief, joy, and so on, the artist's interpretation and handling of the forms will convey a particular expressive attitude. The model's nonchalant pose in John's drawing *Nude Study* (Figure 6.3) could as easily have suggested melancholy, monumentality, or furious motion. Imagine what Michelangelo, Degas, Kollwitz, or Kokoschka might have done with this pose and these forms. John's responses lead him to the harmonious cadence of the curvilinear edges and volumes; he extracts their easygoing, rhythmic lilt. Hair and limbs, lines and tones, all move along in playful accord, all support the artist's interpretation of the figure as embued with graceful form and motion. But

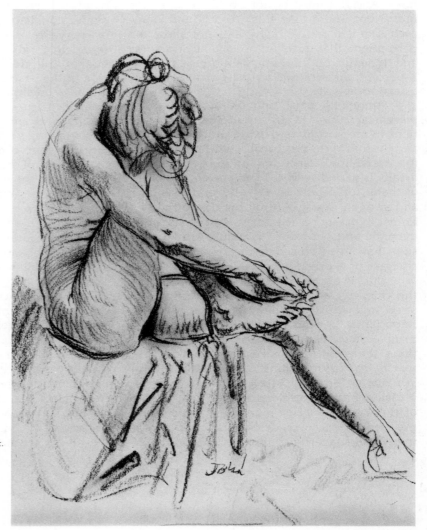

Figure 6.3
AUGUSTUS JOHN (1879–1961)
Nude Study
Red chalk. 9 x 11 5/8 in.
*The Metropolitan Museum of Art, New York.
Rogers Fund, 1908.*

the visual and expressive potentialities of most poses are great enough to support a wide range of interpretations. Michelangelo would probably have found monumentality here; Degas, a unique blend of sensuality and classicism; Kollwitz, a poignant sentiment; and Kokoschka, vehement energies.

Imposing physical weight can be a strong agent of expression, as in Figures 4.72, 4.74, 4.90, or as it is in Ingres' preparatory sketch, *Study for the Portrait of Louis-François Bertin* (Figure 6.4). Ingres bolsters the figure's implacable and assertive stance by selecting a pose that stresses both the sitter's considerable bulk and

Figure 6.4
DOMINIQUE INGRES (1780–1867)
Study for the Portrait of Louis-François Bertin
Chalk and pencil on pieced papier. 13 3/4 x 13 1/2 in.
The Metropolitan Museum of Art, New York.
Bequest of Grace Rainey Rogers, 1943.

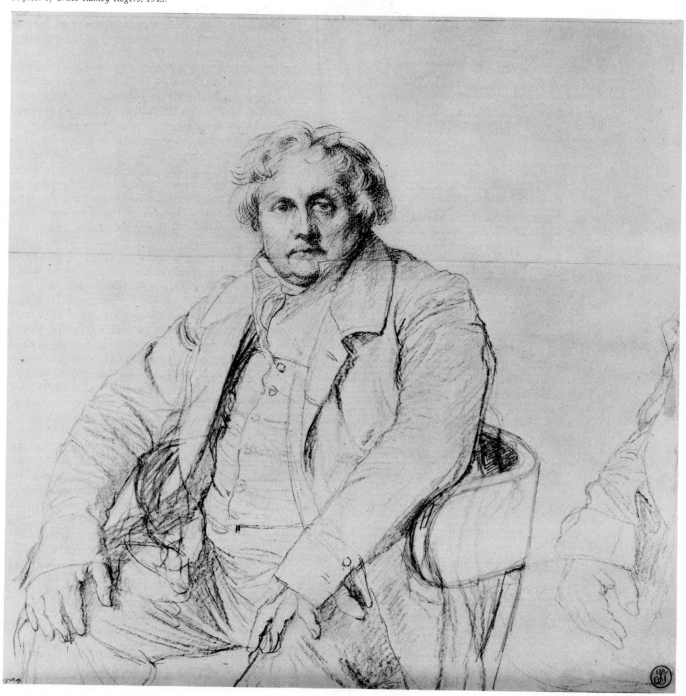

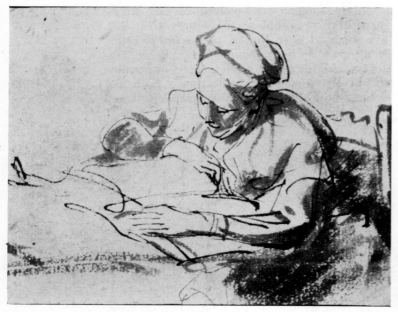

Figure 6.5
REMBRANDT VAN RIJN (1606–1669)
Woman Reading
Pen and brown ink, brown wash. 2 5/8 x 3 7/16 in.
The Metropolitan Museum of Art, New York
Rogers Fund, 1926.

a stable arrangement of his forms. There is strength and resolution in the large U-shaped curve of the two arms, reinforced by the similar-curving chair-back and the figure's legs. These grand curves, by the large spaces and forms they envelop, also suggest bigness, substantiality, and stability. These abstract expressions of staunchness and solidity amplify the sitter's determined stance and gaze. Too often, the beginner relies on the model's facial expression to impart the drawing's mood, but as Ingres demonstrates, the mood is best conveyed through the entire image. Note that Ingres, in drawing the small active forms of the tumbled hair and claw-like fingers, adds subtle psychological insights and visual counterpoints that further emphasize the figure's imposing bulk.

THE INHERENT EXPRESSION OF THE ELEMENTS

We have said that in addition to the emotive content of the subject's figurative situation there is the emotive character of the drawing's elements. Such characteristics evince recollec-

tions and insights about movements and energies that we feel as expressions of various kinds. In Chapter Five we discussed the inherent visual nature of the elements, and saw how each mark either adds to or detracts from a drawing's balance and unity. We were interested in the differing functions and energies of the elements for order-forming purposes. We saw how an indifference to the relational life of the elements, in failing to clarify both a drawing's abstract and figurative conditions, seriously alters and weakens its meanings. Now it only remains to point out that these differing visual activities also carry emotive content which, if overlooked, also diminish meaning.

Every mark is felt as well as seen by the viewer. A vigorously drawn arc representing a downturned mouth, lips pressed tightly together, contains the force of the mouth's frowning gestural expression to a far greater degree than the same arc hesitantly drawn. Additionally, the bold arc, in relating with the inherent traits of other lines and tones, becomes part of a larger system of expressing elements that further support the emotive force of the frown. But if the arc is to express discontent, the artist must, as Horace noted, first experience that discontent—it must be part of his perception. The most careful description of the figure's forms cannot communicate what felt lines and tones can evoke.

In neglecting to support what he sees with what he feels, the beginner's lines and tones continue to express; they convey his indifference or inhibition in the presence of the figure's dynamic expression. Such drawings may be accurate inventories of forms, but the forms fail to come alive for they lack an expressive incentive. Lebrun had this failure to feel in mind when he observed that all too often "in teaching, we neglect to sponsor passion as a discipline. The only discipline we teach is that of the deadly diagram supposedly to be fertilized later by personal experience. Later is too late."*

Each of the elements can enact a broad range of expressive actions. Lines, tones, shapes, and so on can suggest fast or slow movements; they can seem playful, threatening, nervous, lazy; they can relate gently, or aggressively; and they can relate with others to form reassuring or uneasy states of balance in a drawing. Even the elements we use to make a diagram or a doodle suggest their inherent and

Rico Lebrun Drawings (Berkeley and Los Angeles: University of California Press, 1961), p. 25.

distinctly different expressive personalities. Just how great a range of expression the elements can convey is demonstrated by the drawings throughout this book, each reflecting the artist's excitement, curiosity, and identity with the emotive nature of his subject *and* of the emerging drawing. In Figure 1.18 the sensually rhythmic lines, the rugged shapes and forms, and the vigorously-stated values and textures all amplify Rubens' expressive message. A more mechanically oriented use of elements would have violated the artist's intent. But Villon's interpretation of a figure (Figure 5.35) depends on just such an orientation; using the elements more vigorously would have hampered *his* intent. And Kuhn's interest in an easygoing image (Figure 5.7) could not have been served by the types of expression in the elements in either Rubens' or Villon's drawings.

By calling on powerfully active elements Rembrandt enlivens what might otherwise have been a rather ordinary domestic scene (Figure 6.5). Rembrandt suggests the woman's excited engrossment in the book by his fast-moving calligraphic lines, nervously active shapes and forms, and vigorously-handled tonalities. These furiously active elements abstractly fuse the figure and the book (probably the Bible), their bold motion suggesting an intensity and illumination that elevates the simple act of reading to an engaging expression of dedication and wonder that has universal meaning.

When de Gheyn changes his expressive goal, his use of the elements change also. In Figure 6.6 the expressive behavior of the elements in the three views of an old man's head are more rhythmic, gentler, and the illumination less harsh; the tonal changes are more gradual; the shapes "friendlier" and less gnarled than those of the woman's head.

Hence, in using the inherent emotive character of the elements to reinforce their figurative themes, the best artists make the elements perform as metaphors. Sometimes the event represented is enigmatic and can only be understood by experiencing the behavior of the elements. The faint, quavering lines in Daumier's drawing *The Imaginary Invalid* (Figure 6.7) stand for the tremulous unease of the pa-

tient and of the two strange attendants. Symmetrical and delicate at first glance, the drawing's agitated lines and the single shock of dark tone surrounding the patient's head begin to alert us to the scene's quiet nightmare, which grows in terror while we watch.

By way of an interesting contrast to Daumier's deceptively light and gentle handling, Aronson's drawing *Rabbi III* (Figure 6.8), dark and seemingly brooding, is a statement of tranquil introspection, and the dominant behavior of the elements support that theme. The stable monumentality of the shapes and forms, the unchanging tone of the background, the gentle transitions of tone in the head, the figure's centrality, and its union of physical and visual weight all attest to an enduring serenity. Only the sudden bursts of black strokes, harshly carving planes and hollows, intrude like blows while they strengthen the forms.

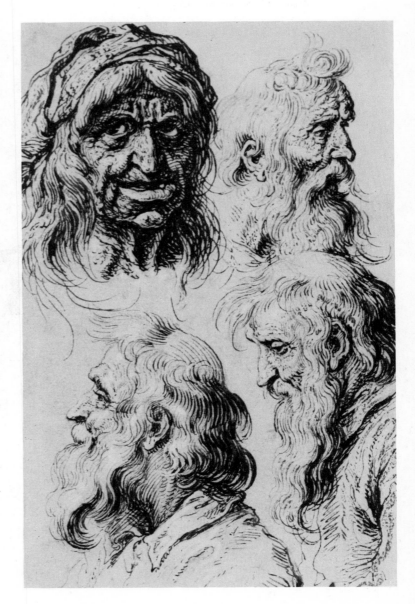

Figure 6.6
JACOB DE GHEYN II (1565–1629)
Study of Four Heads
Pen and ink over charcoal, white chalk highlights.
14.8 x 9.6 cm.
Teylers Museum, Haarlem.

The dynamic power of the elements in Kuhn's drawing *Study for "Roberto"* (Figure 6.9) abstractly augment the power described in the hefty forms of the resting acrobat. Similar to Aronson's drawing in its stability and inferences of perseverance, Kuhn suggests a sense of raw strength and confidence by the rugged nature of the elements. There is nothing facile about the man or the handling; both are bold, straightforward expressions of inherent vigor.

What can happen when we disregard the figure's suggestions for dynamic activities that make the act of figure drawing an exciting encounter with life, and not a dutiful interrogation of a subject, is indicated in Figure 6.10. While the artist is skillful in measuring and in analyzing a part's essential mass (although the forms of the legs and the general area of the shoulders seem uncertain), there is little relevance between the nature of the forms or the pose and the nature of the elements. Nowhere do the lines that model the forms suggest an awareness of the rhythmic arrangement of those forms. The figure's shapes and edges seem spiritless; they seem not to have been regarded as sources for evoking something of the figure's

Figure 6.7
HONORÉ DAUMIER (1810–1879)
The Imaginary Invalid
Pen and black and gray ink, and gray wash
over black chalk. 12 8/16 x 13 7/8 in.
Yale University Art Gallery, New Haven.
Bequest of Edith Malvina K. Wetmore.

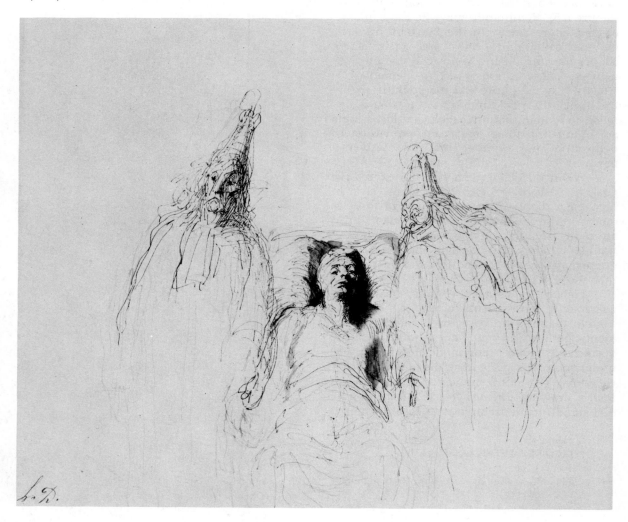

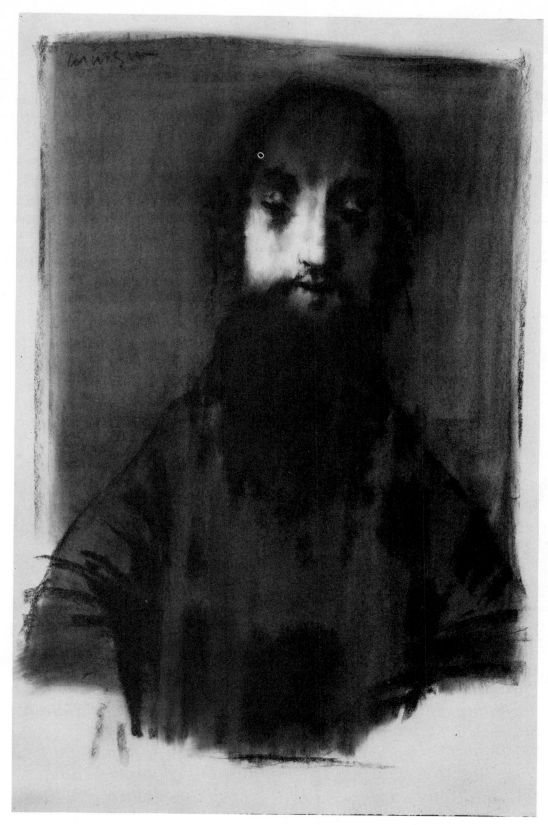

Figure 6.8
DAVID ARONSON (1923–   )
Rabbi III
Brown pastel. 40 x 26 in.
Courtesy Museum of Fine Arts, Boston.
Gift of Arthur E. Vershbow, Benjamin A. Trustman,
Samuel Glazer and Dr. Earl Stone.

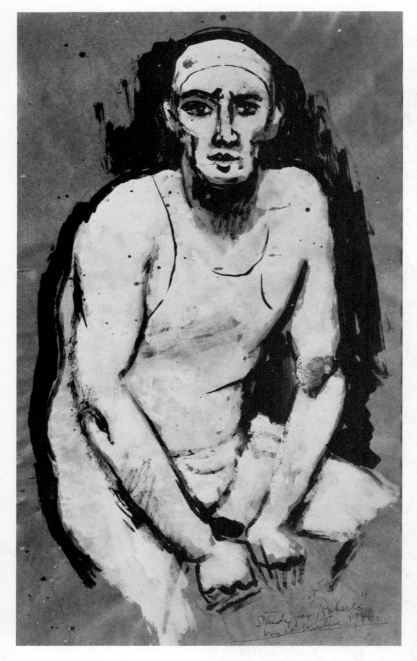

Even the artist's preoccupation with a mechanical style of crosshatching is nowhere made visually . or expressively *necessary*. Instead, the lines appear to be only the product of a manner, a method; they have a sameness throughout which causes them to be seen as a texture that rises to the surface, weakening the forms they are meant to model.

As noted earlier, in avoiding an encounter with a subject's plastic and emotive qualities, we reveal a timidity to encounter these vital sensibilities in ourselves, and our drawings will disclose this fact. This is not to suggest that figure drawings must be stridently dynamic.

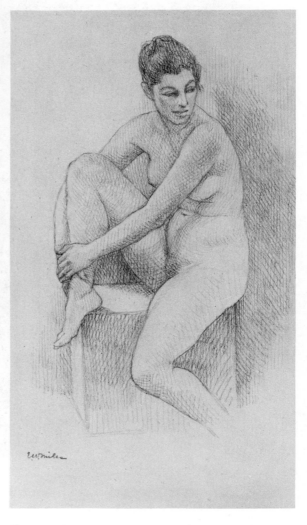

Figure 6.9
WALT KUHN (1880–1949)
Study for ''Roberto''
Brush and india ink, heightened with white.
8 1/4 x 13 7/8 in.
Courtesy Museum of Fine Arts, Boston.
Charles Henry Hayden Fund.

rhythms and energies. As a result, the forms themselves do not convince. Hands that do not grip at the abstract, feeling level do not do so at the representational level. In the absence of an empathic involvement, the sternomastoid doesn't strain in its action, the lower right leg doesn't press against the upper leg, and the figure itself fails to sit upon the block.

Figure 6.10
EMILY WINTHROP MILES (1893–1962)
Seated Nude
Pencil. 14 1/2 x 11 3/4 in.
The Metropolitan Museum of Art, New York.
Gift of Mrs. Darwin Morse, 1965.

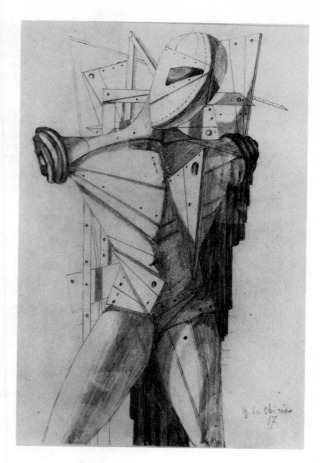

We have seen excellent examples of drawings in which the dynamics are subtle and delicate (Figures 1.15, 5.36). But delicacy is not timidity. It is a special kind of caring about nuance and inflection, a style of expression, and as such, an affirmation of intent. Timidity is only a style of evasion.

DISTORTION

Since figure drawings are the results of analysis, selection, emphasis, and intent, strictly speaking they are distortions of human forms. They all carry the stamp of our aesthetic persuasion, imagination, and idiosyncrasies. But sometimes an artist's interpretation demands changes that drastically alter human proportions, forms, or textures. In the best figure drawings these more obvious changes are never the product of impulsive fancy or private symbolism; rather they are attempts at philosophical assertions that cannot be expressed in the more straightforward figurative modes. Often such drawings use the figure metaphorically. De Chirico, in his drawing *The Condottiere* (Figure 6.11), creates an image that may be a man becoming a still life or a still life becoming a man. Either way, the drawing offers intriguing considerations. Of particular interest here is the artist's insistence on a considerable amount of specific anatomical fact. Note the highly altered but still discernible clavicles, pectorals, abdominal muscles, and flank pads. In the figure's left leg there are even suggestions of the adductor group and of the rectus femoris and vastus muscles.

The term *still life* takes on a horror meaning in Peterdi's engraving *Still Life in Germany* (Figure 6.12). In drawing these brutalized and withered extremities, the artist's emphasis on their intricate system of muscles, tendons, and

Figure 6.12
GABOR PETERDI (1915–   )
Still Life in Germany (1946)
Engraving. 12 x 8 7/8 in. (plate)
The Brooklyn Museum.
Gift of Gabor Peterdi.

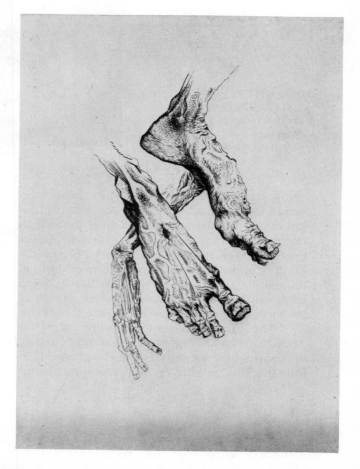

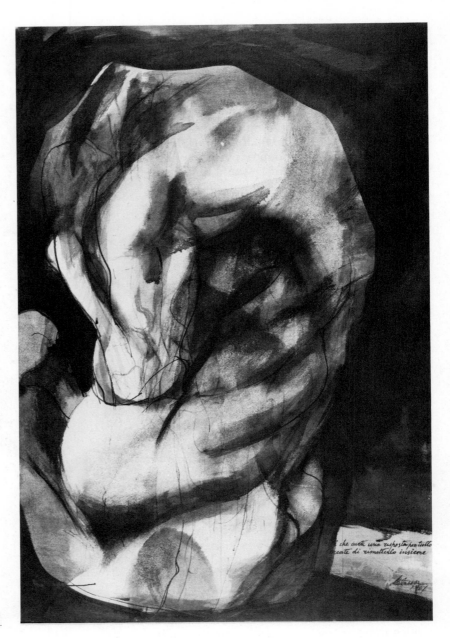

Figure 6.13
RICO LEBRUN (1900–1964)
Lone Great Mutilated Figure
Ink on paper. 39 11/16 x 28 in.
Worcester Art Museum, Worcester, Mass.

veins suggests his disgust with those who would destroy such magnificence. Peterdi distorts these broken forms to magnify the suffering and evil that are his theme, but he draws the forms with the care and patience of a medical illustrator. This deliberate precision of line, the emphasis on texture, the relentlessly sharp focus, all beckon us to consider the causes of such vile cruelty with the same patient concern.

The forms in Lebrun's drawing *Lone Great Mutilated Figure* (Figure 6.13), though largely unidentifiable, not only evoke the character of human forms but convey a sense of anguish and tragedy in their struggling interactions, and because of their rough-hewn structure and the harsh light that strikes them. Note how the background's brooding tone, the cast shadows, the medium's texture, and the forceful handling all intensify the expressive mood. Comparing Lebrun's drawing with Figure 6.10 reveals how steadfastly the sense of aliveness may evade forms that denote facts, and how intensely it can pervade forms that evoke feelings.

In Tchelitchew's *Study for "The Crystal Grotto"* (Figure 6.14), the forms of the skull undergo a metamorphosis that suggests land-

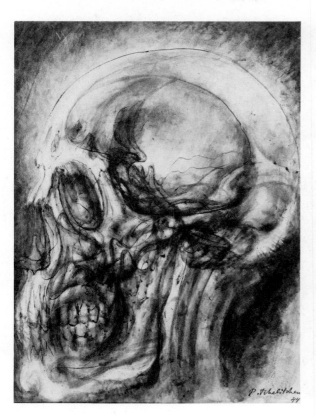

Figure 6.14
PAVEL TCHELITCHEW (1898–1957)
Study for "The Crystal Grotto"
Ink wash. 14 x 11 in.
Collection, The Museum of Modern Art, New York.
Gift of Mr. and Mrs. Sam A. Lewisohn.

Figure 6.15
ABRAHAM WALKOWITZ (1880–1965)
From Life to Life, No. 1
Pencil. 12 9/16 x 8 1/2 in.
The Metropolitan Museum of Art, New York.
Alfred Stieglitz Collection, 1949.

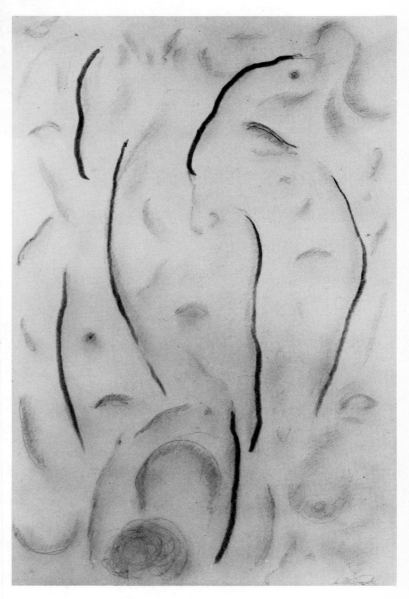

scape and cave formations. The "double-exposure" effect, especially evident in the facial bones, creates a strong vibrating motion, strengthening the sense of a change of subject matter. But even such a subjective interpretation of the cranial forms reveals the artist's authoritative understanding of anatomy.

Walkowitz, in his drawing *From Life to Life, No. 1* (Figure 6.15), fuses figures in a way that hints at cloud-like formations while at the same time stressing the two-dimensional pattern of the elements. Either reading of the image evinces the sensual pliancy and rhythms of human form. Note the delicate nature and handling of the lines and tones, and the resulting delicate movements.

THE EXPRESSIVE ROLE OF THE MEDIUM

The intrinsic character and range of the materials used in drawing have a decided influence on a drawing's emotive nature. By their range of textural effects, their erasable or permanent nature, and their adaptability to different uses, they always affect the artist's handling and even the kinds of judgments he will

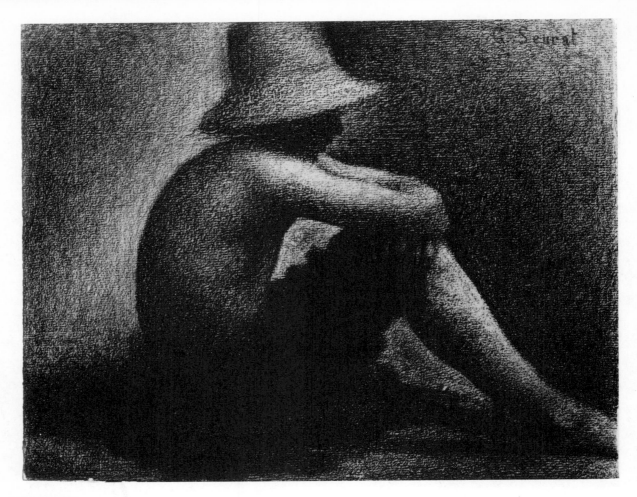

Figure 6.16
GEORGES SEURAT (1859–1891)
Seated Boy with Straw Hat
Black conté crayon. 9 1/2 x 12 3/8 in.
Yale University Art Gallery, New Haven.

Figure 6.17
MICHELANGELO BUONARROTI (1475–1564)
Study of Adam for "The Creation of Adam" in the Sistine Chapel (detail)
Chalk on tan paper.
Trustees of the British Museum, London.

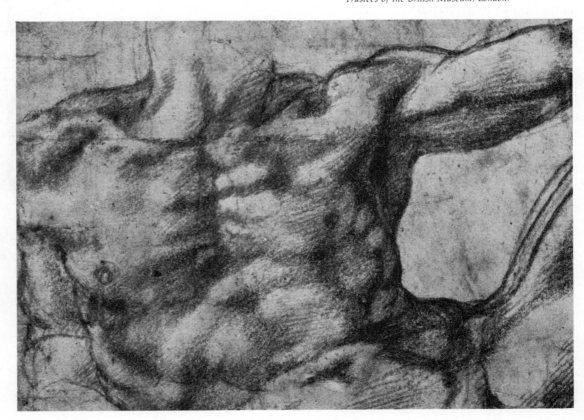

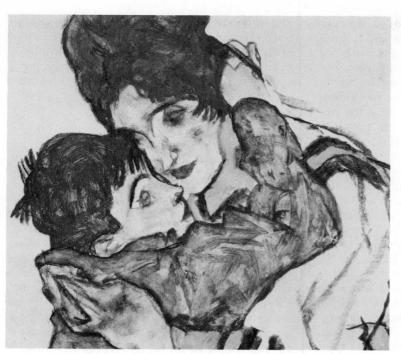

Figure 6.18
EGON SCHIELE (1890–1918)
Mother and Child (detail)
Black crayon, watercolor, gouache.
Courtesy Museum of Fine Arts, Boston.
Edwin E. Jack Fund.

Figure 6.19
ANDREA DEL SARTO (1486–1530)
Red Chalk Studies
Red chalk. 7 x 10 1/2 in.
Trustees of the British Museum, London.

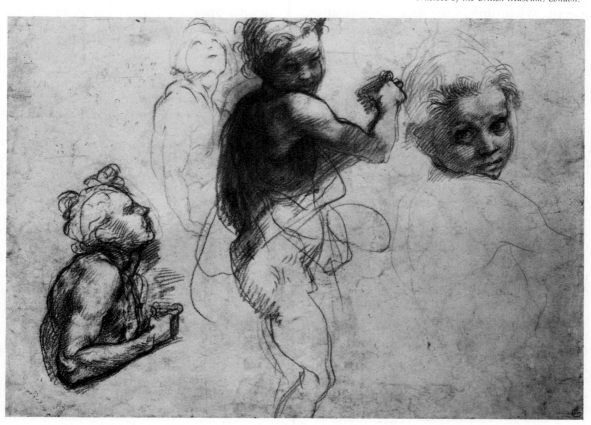

make. Because the reed pen cannot easily suggest the gradual tonal changes that are natural to the sable brush, an artist working with the pen will avoid such graduations of tone, but may heavily rely on them when using the brush.

The effect of different media is evident when we compare Degas' treatment of the figure using chalks (Figure 1.29) with a similar figure done in an ink monotype (Figure 5.49). Degas takes advantage of chalk's dry, abrasive character to create masses and light effects with blunt strokes and subtle blending; using inks, which in the monotype technique can be removed as easily as applied, he models the forms by broad swipes of a brush or cloth, stressing their shapes and directional "speed," rather than their structure (as in Figure 1.29).

Had Tchelitchew used a soft, graphite pencil and Wolkowitz, a brush and ink, each would have been restricted by their medium from making many of the linear and tonal judgments we see in their drawings. But each would no doubt have gone on to utilize what their medium *could* produce. Their meanings might have been as successfully conveyed, but not often by the same graphic maneuvers.

The mood of some drawings seems to depend heavily on the particular medium employed. When this is the case, considerations concerning its use rate close in importance to the factors of structure, anatomy, design, and expression. The stately solemnity of Seurat's conté crayon drawing *Seated Boy With Straw Hat* (Figure 6.16) owes something to the medium's compatibility with the artist's interest in monumental forms. Seurat, in selecting a paper with a pronounced grain, and by using the side of a stick of conté crayon, utilizes the textural properties of both to create the gentle play of broad tones that convey their quiet grandeur.

It would be extremely difficult to attain these results with a sharpened, harder chalk on a less grainy paper. But such materials are exactly suited to Michelangelo's fascination with the "drama" inherent in the powerful tensions and pressures among the bones and muscles pressing against the figure's surfaces (Figure 6.17). And Schiele's need for a more sensual and spontaneous expression of rhythmic shapes, lines, and tones leads him to a use of mixed media: black crayon, watercolor, and gouache (Figure 6.18).

All good drawings exhibit a congenial rapport between meanings and media, but an overdependence on the powers of a medium to convey our intent may cause the medium to dictate the results instead of enhancing them. Such drawings often provide a showy display of facility that makes the drawing's dominant expression an exhibition of cleverness, not a statement of felt responses based on something observed or imagined.

EXAMPLES OF EXPRESSION IN FIGURE DRAWING

Here we will examine further ways in which the expressive meanings of a drawing's figurative state are advanced and reinforced by the expressive character of its abstract behavior. Although the range of possibilities of the elements and energies to reinforce figurative meanings is limitless, these few examples may serve to suggest something of the inventive freedom possible, and to encourage us to trust our intuitive responses more. Our reactions to a subject's essential character and situation, in the first few moments of our seeing or imagining it, usually carry the key to how we should proceed to draw. It is the editing and censoring of our initial impression that makes us lose sight of our original motivation for having begun the drawing. This occurs when structural, tonal, textural, or other demands divert us from the drawing's overall theme and purpose, or when our second thoughts force us to resist, even to withdraw, our personal responses in favor of a more realistically "correct" image.

The surprised expression in the faces of the two front-view heads in del Sarto's drawing *Red Chalk Studies* (Figure 6.19) is imparted by more than the raised eyebrows. The lines in the forehead and those defining the hairline also spring up, making the lines function structurally and expressively at the same time. Note how the artist, in those lines that rough in the three figures on the right, searches for the gesture and the general shapes and masses of his subjects. These first few lines already show as much concern with the dynamic as with the measurable aspects of the figures. They underlie the more developed parts of the figures, and help the artist to give those parts their animated force.

The emotive power of Lebrun's drawing *Figure in a Dust Storm* (Figure 6.20) benefits from the rhythmic lines, the vague and "lost" edges, the delicate and light-toned values that model the forms, and the substantiality of the forms above and below the fast-moving tone

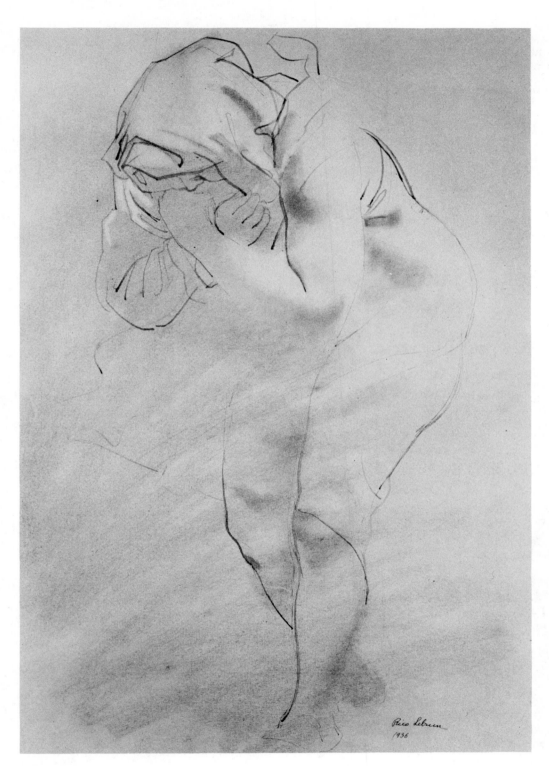

Figure 6.20
RICO LEBRUN (1900–1964)
Figure in a Dust Storm
Ink and conté crayon. 24 1/2 x 18 in.
Courtesy The Santa Barbara Museum of Art.
Artist in Residence Fund.

Figure 6.21
JULES PASCIN (1885–1930)
Reclining Woman
Watercolor, pencil, and ink. 17 7/8 x 14 9/16 in.
The Metropolitan Museum of Art.
Alfred Stieglitz Collection, 1949.

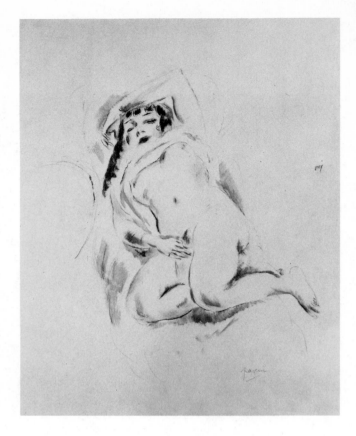

Figure 6.22
CHARLES DESPIAU (1874–1946)
Reclining Nude
Red chalk on buff paper. 23.2 x 36.2 cm.
National Gallery of Prague.

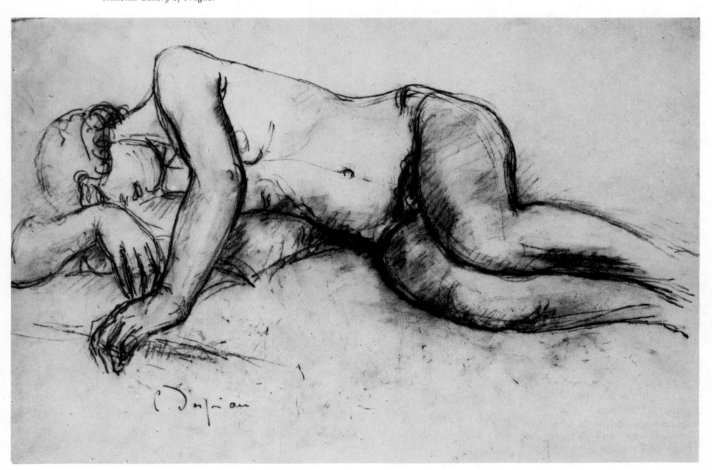

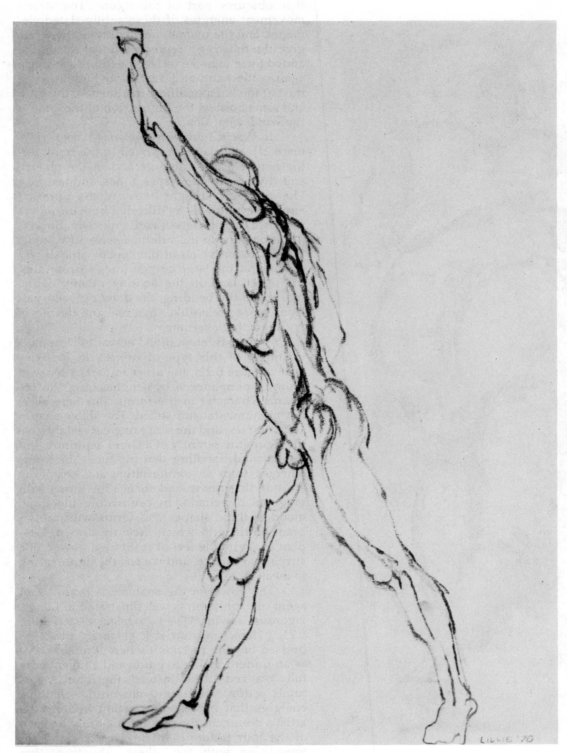

Figure 6.23
LLOYD LILLIE (1932–   )
Standing Figure, Side View
Pencil. 9 3/8 x 14 in.
Courtesy of the artist.

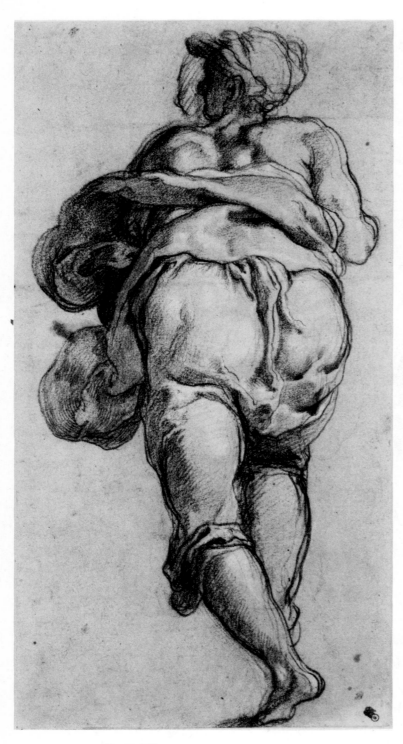

Figure 6.24
TADDEO ZUCCARO (1529–1566)
Study of a Man Seen from Behind
Red chalk, heightened with white. 34.2 x 18.2 cm.
National Gallery of Art, Washington, D.C.
Ailsa Mellon Bruce Fund:

that obscures part of the figure. The strong movement-energies of these subtly stated elements, and the overall diagonality of the forms give the drawing's representational theme the added force to make us feel the figure's struggle against the wind and dust. Note how the contrast of the harsher, linear treatment of the head and arms bolsters the impression of the force of the windswept dust.

In Pascin's drawing *Reclining Woman* (Figure 6.21), sensuality is evoked in the frank tactile nature of the contours and in the pliancy and rhythms of the shapes, tones, and textures. The very few straight lines—in the upraised arm, the eyebrows—by differing from the others reinforce their flirtation with eroticism. But it is flirtation only. In the subdued sense of volume, in the decorative air of the "open" shapes and of some of the large curved lines surrounding the figure, and in the floating quality of the figure and the bedding, the drawing's sensuality is more dream-like than real and devoid of pornographic overtone.

A very different mood pervades Despiau's treatment of this type of subject. In *Reclining Nude* (Figure 6.22), the artist imparts a sense of tranquil permanence by emphasizing the columnar character of the forms. But here all is not monumental and stilled. The stable shapes and volumes, and the sense of great weight give the figure the serenity of a Greek sculpture, but the spirited handling that produces the forms emerges from an authoritative and searching attitude that carves and shapes the forms with vigorous directness. In contrasting the quiet mood of these shapes and forms with the vibrant spirit with which they are drawn, Despiau suggests the feel of restrained power, of a striving to change; and we feel the figure trying to awaken.

The power of the anatomical factor as an agent of expression is well illustrated in Lillie's vigorous drawing *Male Figure, Side View* (Figure 6.23). Here, the artist's gestural attack is pressed beyond the point where it might serve as an underdrawing to guide and enliven more fully realized forms. Instead, the figure's gestural action, and the powerful relational energies that express that action become the artist's dominant themes. In this drawing each of the four factors is intensely active and interworking with the others. The lines that develop the structure simultaneously clarify the anatomy and, by their animated but ordered calligraphic behavior, convey an expressive design that supports the representation of a rugged but graceful figure. Lillie's penetrating sensitivity to the dynamic potentials of the figure's structure and anatomy, and the exceptionally attractive spirit of his responses, should alert the beginner to the inventive and liberating possibilities of a sound grasp of the figure's architecture and machinery.

Even when the figure is draped, anatomical considerations can continue to play an important expressive role, as we see in the drawing by the sixteenth century artist Zuccaro, *Study of a Man Seen from Behind* (Figure 6.24). The artist's interest in the figure's powerful action is strengthened by the straining action of the lower half of the body, still revealed

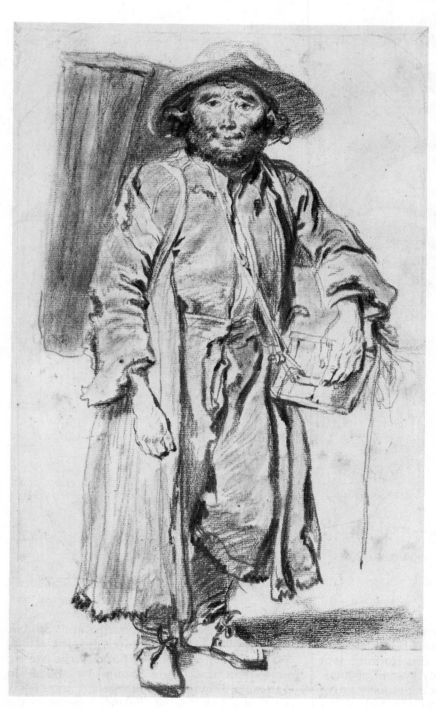

Figure 6.25
ANTOINE WATTEAU (1684–1721)
The Savoyard
Red and black chalk.
Courtesy The Art Institute of Chicago.
Joseph and Helen Regenstein Foundation.

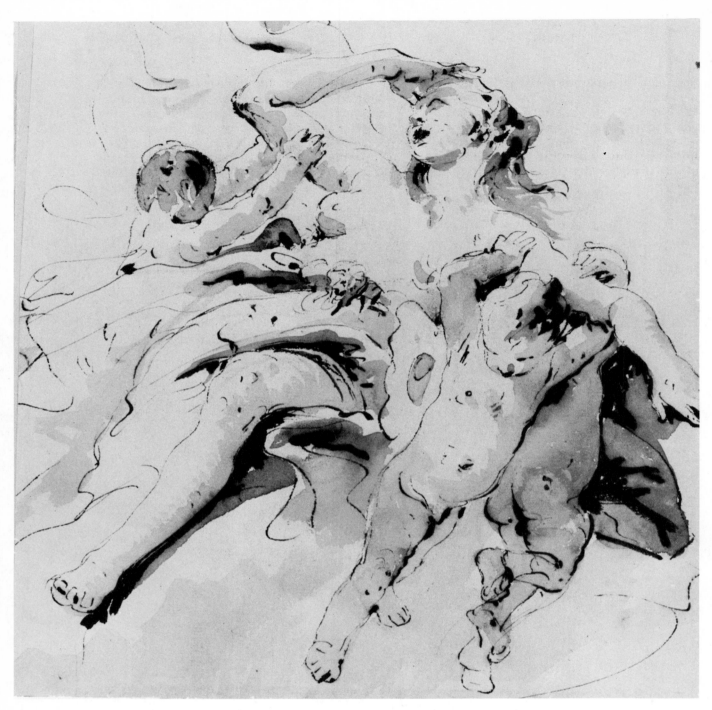

Figure 6.26
GIOVANNI BATTISTA TIEPOLO (1696–1770)
Psyche Transported to Olympus
Pen and brown ink, brown wash, over black chalk.
8 3/4 x 8 11/16 in.
The Metropolitan Museum of Art, New York.
Rogers Fund, 1937.

beneath the drapery. Zuccaro also reinforces the figure's action by establishing folds in some areas and stretching the clothing taut elsewhere. But it is the lively system of lines, shapes, and forms that, in being equally active at the abstract level, give us the *feel* of the

action. Here, everything curls and spirals, evoking a sense of the figure's turning action.

But when a stationary pose is to be shown, more than the figure should be stilled. In Watteau's drawing *The Savoyard* (Figure 6.25), the figure has paused, balanced between the

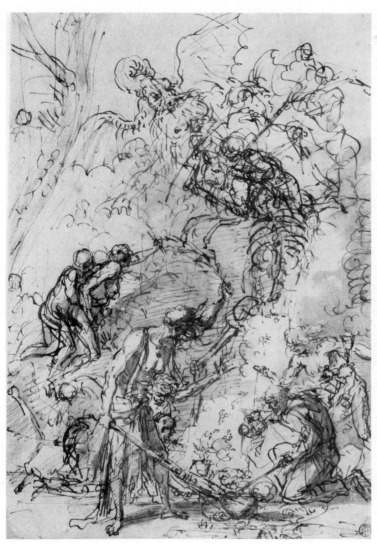

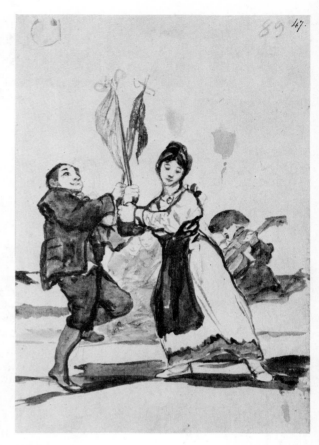

Figure 6.28
FRANCISCO DE GOYA (1746–1832)
Provincial Dance
Wash drawing in sepia. 8 1/8 x 5 5/8 in.
The Metropolitan Museum of Art, New York.
Harris Brisbane Dick Fund, 1935.

Figure 6.27
SALVATOR ROSA (1615–1673)
Witches' Sabbath
Pen and brown ink, gray wash. 10 11/16 x 7 1/4 in.
The Metropolitan Museum of Art, New York.
Rogers Fund, 1912.

case on his back and the container suspended from his neck. The stable nature of the elements —the tenuous but balanced standoff between their various movements—matches the checked action of the figure. Watteau has drawn the figure in a position that suggests the man has just stopped walking or is about to start. At the abstract level, the visual and physical weights, the cancelling out of diagonal lines, the stable and unstable shapes, the alternately vigorous and gentle handling and the fluctuations between bold and subtle tonalities, all suggest a barely maintained "truce" between

energies. They too suggest an ambiguity between actions just ended or about to begin again. By the tensions among these balanced but contradictory forces, Watteau supports a psychological tension in the figure that is summarized in his facial expression: a blend of cynicism and uncertainty, of resolution and introspection.

Because all visual relationships suggest movement, it is natural enough that the expressive meanings of many figure drawings are principally rooted in the figure's moving actions. For example, Tiepolo's drawing *Psyche*

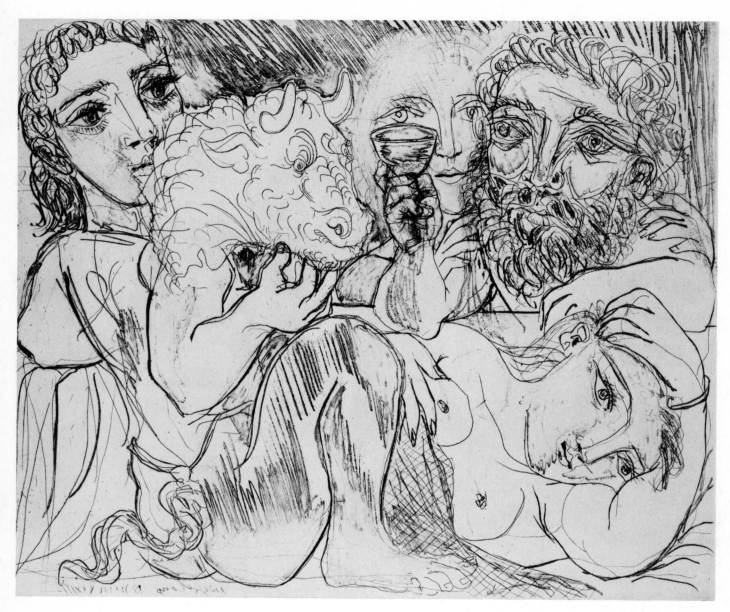

Figure 6.29
PABLO PICASSO (1881–1973)
Minotaur, Drinking Sculptor, and Three Models (1933)
Etching and aquatint. 29.8 x 36.5 cm.
Courtesy Museum of Fine Arts, Boston.
Lee M. Friedman Fund.

Transported to Olympus (Figure 6.26) is, aside from its mythological comment, an expression of figures in flight. Movement is at the heart of this drawing and each free-flowing line and tone expresses spirited action. Here, fast-moving shapes and rhythms, the sparse, but volume-informing modelling, and the drawing's diagonal "rush" across the page, help us experience these figures to be in flight, rather

than falling. Note how the configuration's main movement from the lower left to the upper right of the page is countered by an implied diagonality running from the upper left, to the lower right corner of the page.

The moving action in Rosa's drawing *Witches' Sabbath* (Figure 6.27) envelops the entire page and concerns both figures and specters. The nightmarish scene is conveyed by a serpentine coil of skeletons and beasts winding slowly upward in a mutually reinforcing blend of frenzied lines and fearful apparitions. Notice how skillfully Rosa designs the large rib cage to "urge" the spiral upward, and relates it to the curling smoke throughout the drawing.

Although less evident, the dynamic movements that animate the figures in Goya's drawing *Provincial Dance* (Figure 6.28), are of a piece with the sprightly actions of the folk dance. Goya suggests the energetic movements of the dancers and the flutter of their clothing and the flags they hold, by avoiding vertical and horizontal directions in the figures, and

Figure 6.30
MARCEL DUCHAMP (1887–1968)
Nude Descending a Staircase
Oil on canvas. 37 3/4 x 23 1/2 in.
Courtesy Philadelphia Museum of Fine Art.
Louise and Walter Arensberg Collection.

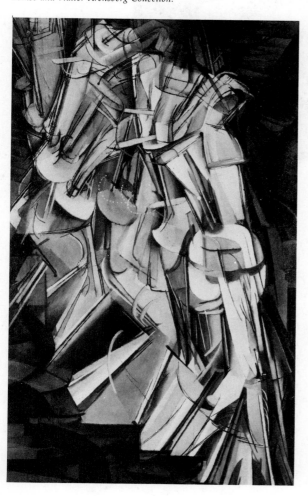

by his use of loose brushwork and reliance on ragged-edged shapes. Note how the artist, by using abrupt contrasts of value in the shapes of the background, enlists them in supporting the lively movements in the dancers.

The sense of movement among compacted forms can produce a strong feeling of constrained energy. In Picasso's etching *Minotaur, Drinking Sculptor, and Three Models* (Figure 6.29), the moving rhythms among the figures, confined arms and legs, and the artist's suggestion of their great weight impart a feeling of accumulated, dormant energy, capable of an explosive change. A similar feeling of penned-up force exists in the crowding of the five heads, in the large, bent leg, coiled as if about to spring free, and in the hatched tones that seem too vibrant for the shapes they are confined in. These conditions create strong visual tensions, intensified still more by the force and allover activity of the lines. The tactile sensuality evident in many of the contours and in the emphasis on physical weight, and the intimacy of the poses suggest a clue to the psychological nature of the heightening tensions.

Because of its emphasis on motion, Duchamp's famous painting *Nude Descending a Staircase* (Figure 6.30) serves here as a final example of the expressive power of movements that can emerge from the relational interworking of the elements. The intensity of these movements is due largely to the high degree of similarity between the directions, shapes, sizes, and locations of the figure's severely abstracted, but still identifiable, parts. Note that even in this highly subjective interpretation of human forms a sound knowledge of anatomy underlies the image: clavicles, pectoral and gluteal muscles, pelvic forms, and even a faithful set of human proportions help us to identify with the figure's energetic descent.

We have seen that a drawing's expression is revealed not only by the depictive matter, but by the intrinsic character of the elements, in the pace and temperament of their interplay, in the artist's "handwriting," and even in the uses of the medium. Expression is as much a part of the drawing's design as the design is a key to the drawing's mood.

But some intangible quality remains that eludes analysis: some spirit or state—a presence—that we sense giving life and universality to the best figure drawings, remains as mysterious as those forces that give life to the figures

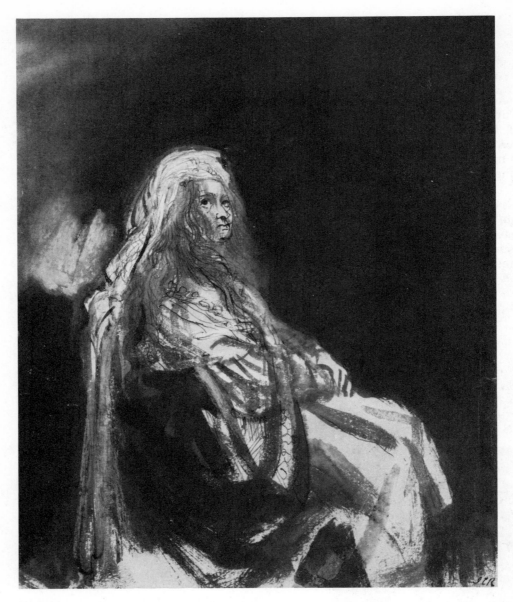

Figure 6.31
REMBRANDT VAN RIJN (1606–1669)
Woman Seated, in Oriental Costume
Brush, pen and ink. 20 x 16.2 cm.
Staatliche Museen Preussischer Kulturbesitz.
Kupferstichkabinett. West Berlin.

themselves. Perhaps it is the result of a critical degree or pitch of dynamic activity, or of a crucial blend of the artist's intellectual, intuitive, and subconscious responses; certainly it demands the interworking of the four factors we have been examining, and though indefinable, its absence in a drawing leaves the image somehow unrealized. But if this quality cannot be isolated, one fact about it is certain: no matter how faintly or obliquely sensed, an honest acceptance of our own responses and of our intent, although no guarantee of its presence, is an essential condition for achieving it.

The shadowy and moving expression of Rembrandt's drawing *Woman Seated, in Oriental Costume* (Figure 6.31), emerging from the harmony between the depiction and the dynamics, seems imbued with this impalpable quality of "rightness" and life. The drawing's unselfconscious nature, in revealing that Rembrandt's paramount concerns were to inquire, experience, and respond, suggests that approaching figure drawing with a desire to know, instead of to show, may lead to that mysterious presence that transforms knowledge and skill into art.

SUGGESTED EXERCISES

Unless otherwise indicated, there are no time limits on the following exercises, and they may be drawn to whatever scale and with whatever medium you require. Where necessary, you may combine media.

The nature of these drawings will demand your entire commitment to the depictive and abstract emotive theme concerned in each. Although summoning up feelings "on demand" is difficult, perceiving the structural and dynamic possibilities in each of the observed or imagined figures is fundamental to good drawing. Being aware of these possibilities will help you to gain insights about the subject's expressive condition and about the means to convey it. Indeed, one of the main challenges in these exercises is to have the drawing's expression come through the elements as well as the figural depiction.

1. Working from the model and using a large sheet of paper, draw some fifteen to eighteen small-sized, one-minute action poses. Using Figures 4.92 and 6.23 as rough guides, emphasize the rhythms of inner forms as well as edges, and suggest the general structural nature of the forms. Next, using these sketches as "models," make the following two drawings:

   a. Select any three or four of these action poses and combine them in a drawing that suggests battle, or some other aggressive state.
   b. Select any three or four of these sketches and combine them in a drawing that suggests flight, or any rhythmic and dance-like action, as in Figure 6.26.

2. Working from one or more models, or using a mirror, make the following three drawings of heads, in which the facial expressions are reinforced by the character and behavior of the elements:

   a. Someone shouting happily or excitedly
   b. Someone scowling or frowning
   c. Someone sleeping

3. Working from the model, make two drawings *of the same pose* that could serve as illustrations for:

   a. A mystery story
   b. A love story

4. Working from the model, make four drawings that suggest the figure's metamorphosis into:

   a. A cloud
   b. A tree
   c. A machine
   d. A rock formation

5. Working from the model, and using Figure 6.13 as a rough guide, make three comparably abstracted drawings to suggest:

   a. Melancholy
   b. Joy
   c. Conflict

6. Using Figures 6.2, 6.8, and 6.16 as rough guides, make the following, largely tonal, imaginary drawings:

   a. One figure carrying another
   b. Three figures dancing

7. Using Figure 6.24 as a rough guide, invent a drawing of a comparably draped figure performing some strenuous physical act.

8. Using Figure 6.30 as a rough guide, invent a drawing showing a ballet dancer moving.

9. Referring to the muscle illustrations in Chapter Four (or to any other source), invent a drawing of a flayed figure lifting a heavy object, such as a rock.

10. Using Figure 6.12 as a rough guide, make your own still life of human forms, not as a horror show, but to suggest Peterdi's theme or any other.

11. Using Figure 6.29 as a rough guide, invent a drawing of several figures in some comparably compacted arrangement, which suggests constrained energies.

12. Using Figure 6.27 as a rough guide, and referring to the anatomical illustrations in Chapters Three and Four (or any other source), invent a drawing that conveys your version of a "witches' Sabbath."

13. Working from the model, and using Figure 6.5 as a rough guide, make several drawings in which the elements and the handling activate passive, resting poses.

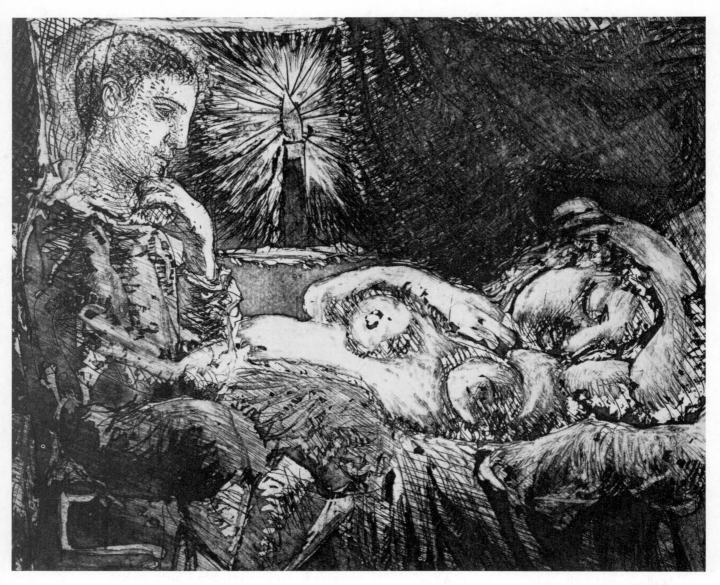

Figure 7.1
PABLO PICASSO (1881–1973)
Boy Watching over Sleeping Woman, 1935 (detail)
Etching and aquatint.
Courtesy Museum of Fine Arts, Boston.
Lee M. Friedman Fund.

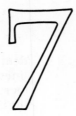

The Factors Interworking

some examples

DIFFERING FORMULAS

Throughout this book the central theme has been the high degree of interdependence and mutual support among the factors of structure, anatomy, design, and expression. We have seen that the measurable factors of structure and anatomy are as deeply interlaced with the dynamic ones of design and expression as they are with each other, and that each factor has both figurative and abstract functions to perform. As we examined each of these factors we saw some examples of how they function in their own "sphere" and how they assist the function of the other factors.

Many of the lines used to establish the structure of, say, a head, might additionally convey some salient anatomical facts which add to both the drawing's representational and design needs and its expressive meanings. Conversely, expressive-design requirements of the head might demand that these lines be plentiful in number and curvilinear in character,

thereby influencing the degree of structural and anatomical clarity of that form.

Earlier, too, we saw that each artist, according to his perceptual, temperamental, and aesthetic needs, formulates some personally necessary hierarchy of importance for the roles these factors will play in his drawings. In this section we will examine some of these "pre-scriptions" for their usage. For, we understand a drawing not only by the ways in which the factors interwork, but by their order of importance.

In Ricci's drawing *Man between Time and Death, Evoking Hope* (Figure 7.2), forms emerge from the swarm of spirited lines, the excited calligraphy "permitting" the depiction, rather than the demands of the depiction permitting some calligraphic play, as in Dürer's drawing, *An Oriental on a Throne* (Figure 7.3). Dürer insists on a precise articulation of each plane and volume, and of each tassle and jewel. Further,

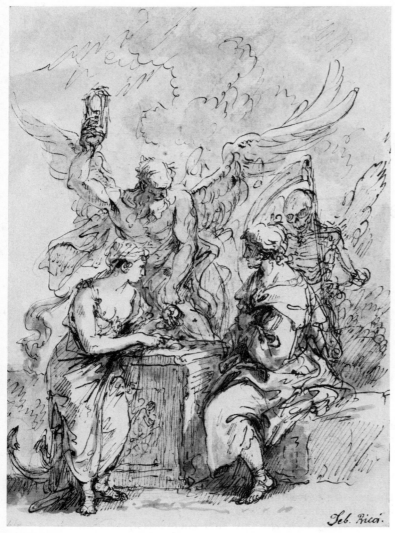

Figure 7.2
SEBASTIANO RICCI (1659–1734)
Man between Time and Death Evoking Hope
Pen and brown ink, gray wash, over black and red
chalk. 10 3/4 x 7 3/4 in.
The Metropolitan Museum of Art, New York.
Rogers Fund, 1967.

he constructs a more formal and stilled design than does Ricci. In emphasizing the subject's volumetrics, Dürer makes the structural factor dominant; in arranging them symmetrically, he calls our attention to the two-dimensional aspects of the drawing's design. The drawing's stress on structure and symmetry, however, is not developed without an appealing calligraphy of its own. Indeed, the lines are often both graceful and vigorous, qualities difficult to combine. But it is clear that Dürer's intentions

demand ranks of more structurally-oriented lines, while Ricci counts on the flutter of numerous agitated lines to reinforce the drama of the life-or-death discourse.

Although very little of the surface anatomy is directly visible in Dürer's drawing, it too is more fully explored (and more inventively stated) than it is in Ricci's drawing. But Ricci's use of anatomy, if somewhat less convincingly knowledgeable than Dürer's, is expressively compatible with the rest of the emotionally charged drawing. Hope's classical simplicity, Time's heroic ruggedness, the man's idealized head, and Death's "incorrect" but expressively effective "body" are well cast in their parts and feelingly drawn to suggest the character and mood of each of the participants in the event.

The contrasting goals of these drawings are reinforced by their very different design strategies. Ricci calls on powerful rhythms and diagonal motions, on strong figurative energies, and on a loose and urgent handling; Dürer, on a careful cancelling out of rhythms, on the stability of vertical and horizontal axes, on a motionless figure, and on a more deliberate handling. Each relies on a contrapuntal device to intensify the main emotive character of their image: the stable block in the center of Ricci's swirling forces, and the swirling sash in the center of Dürer's stabilized forces both serve to reinforce (and provide some visual relief from) the drawing's dominant expressive condition.

Although Ricci emphasizes dynamic matters, and Dürer stresses measurable ones, each drawing reveals a sensitivity to qualities in the other. We are all the more delighted in the amount of quiet, but playful rhythmic activity at work throughout the Dürer, because we see it in the context of the drawing's rigid symmetry. Likewise, we are all the more relieved to find the stabilizing forces within the Ricci, because they keep the forceful energies from "running wild." Note in the Dürer the unsymmetrical but balancing results of the long sword on the left, against the dark tones on the right. And, in the Ricci, the steadying function of the rough symmetry between the two figures in the foreground.

In a more daring abstract invention, Cambiaso's drawing *Male Nude on Horseback* (Figure 7.4) departs from his more structured and geometric approach to forms (previously seen in Figures 2.1, 2.5, 2.31, 4.80), to create a whirlwind of action. Responding to the unusual oval picture plane as well as to the forms of his subject in this action-filled scene, Cambiaso relies

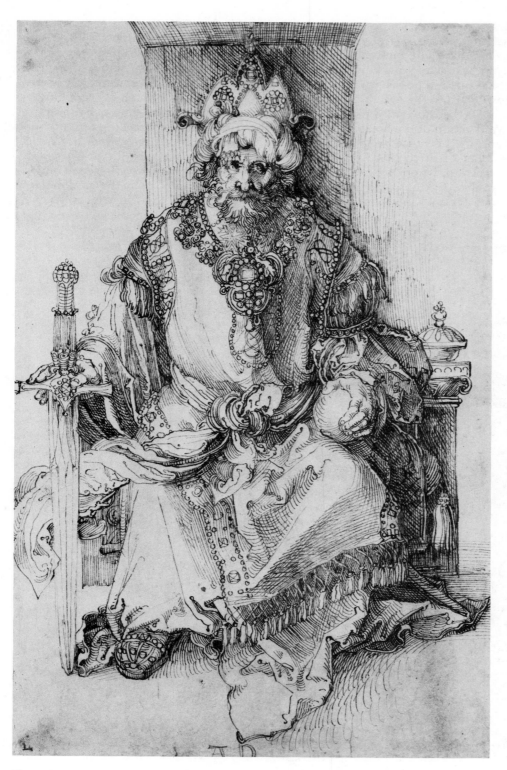

Figure 7.3
ALBRECHT DÜRER (1471–1528)
An Oriental Ruler on a Throne
Pen and black ink. 30.6 x 19.7 cm.
National Gallery of Art, Washington, D. C.
Ailsa Mellon Bruce Fund.

heavily on curvilinear lines and shapes of an animated, interweaving nature. Here, everything is in a state of turbulent motion. The drawing's equilibrium is of a tenuous kind: we no sooner react to the visual and physical weight pulling the man downward to the left, than we realize he is being wrenched toward the right side by the downward action of the horse. Led down to the meeting of the horse's legs and head, the fan-like burst of directions in that area takes our eyes upward, where we can follow any of several routes back onto the mainstreams of directional energy. The longer we examine this drawing, the greater our sense of being hurled about in a whirlpool.

The contour lines, although frenzied in their actions, are delicately stated and almost weightless. Further, the gracefully energetic rhythms that course through the drawing act as modifiers of the impression of solid masses in space. These effects, in calling our attention to the drawing's two-dimensional life, reveal the artist's fascination with the drawing's dynamics on the picture plane. These felt and sophisticated extractions from the raw material of man and horse, by their insistence on ener-

Figure 7.4
LUCA CAMBIASO (1527–1585)
Male Nude on Horseback
Pen and ink. 29 x 25 cm.
Courtesy The Fogg Art Museum, Harvard University.
Austin A. Mitchell Bequest.

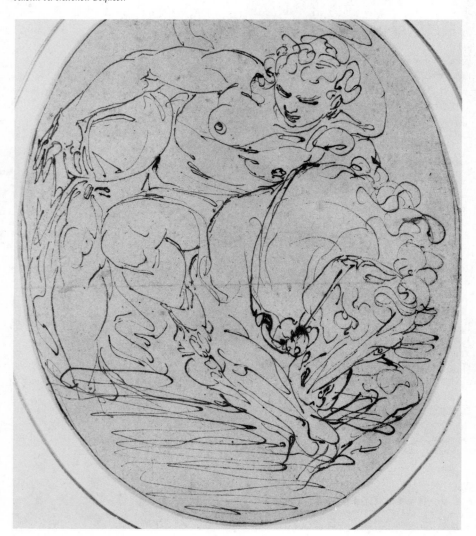

getic line and shape patterns, show the factors of design and expression to be dominant in the artist's strategy for conveying the event.

But structure and anatomy, although secondary, participate vigorously in the drawing's lively animation. To appreciate the importance of their contribution we have only to turn the drawing upside down. Now its movements, while not appreciably slowed, are more delicate than driving; they have lost the dramatic substantiality that abstract forces have when moving through known volumes and spaces. Seen this way, the fine-tuned balance between the graceful and the rugged is gone.

Notice how economically Cambiaso conveys structural conditions. His ability to summarize complex forms to suggest their more nearly geometric state helps us better understand the ovoid of the head, the cylindrical basis of the extremities, and the construction and interjoining of smaller form-units throughout both the man and the horse. These interjoinings are especially clear in the figure's arm and legs, and in the horse's head. The artist's incisive and spirited structural clues add to the drawing's energies. To have made a thorough exploration of these forms would have entailed a multitude of lines and tones that might have slowed or obscured the drawing's vibrancy, and would certainly have intruded on the airy weave of animated actions on the picture plane, a condition central to Cambiaso's visual-expressive theme.

Anatomical considerations also take the drawing's dynamic nature into account. Cambiaso "screens" these as selectively as he does the structural clues, admitting only those necessary to establish a convincing figure and to emphasize its actions. The artist's profound grasp of anatomy is evident in how much is conveyed about bone and muscle in the few lines given to these details. For example, the nine or ten lines of the figure's upper arm suggest the deltoid and its insertion point, the contour of the lateral head of the triceps as well as some of that muscle's tendonous lower portion, the olecranon process, a bit of the supinators, and the body and insertion of the biceps. Note the equally economical and informing drawing of the knees, and how clearly the anatomical differences of their differing positions are explained. Despite their anatomical function, these lines never "forget" to take part in the spirited nature of the handling and of the design. Nor does the figure's powerful musculature fail to benefit from the strong energies that

course through it, contributing to the drawing's expressive design.

By comparison, de Gheyn's drawing *Boy Seated at a Table with a Candle and Writing Tools* (Figure 7.5), is immediately more structurally oriented. Not unlike Dürer's "recipe" for using the four factors, de Gheyn's greater stress on a "warmer," more vigorous use of line and his lesser concern with details give his drawing a stronger sense of spontaneity and movement. But if de Gheyn is less precise than Dürer, he carves more insistently than Cambiaso, and does so in an appealing, tactile way, also seen in the head of the Oriental in Dürer's drawing. But, while Dürer reserves this more sensually tactile attitude for the head and some few other passages, de Gheyn models all the forms by lines that feelingly ride upon the surfaces. De Gheyn's relentless desire to experience even

Figure 7.5
JACOB DE GHEYN II (1565–1629)
Boy Seated at a Table with a Candle and Writing Tools
Pen and iron-gall ink on brownish paper.
5 5/16 x 4 1/16 in.
The Yale University Art Gallery, New Haven.

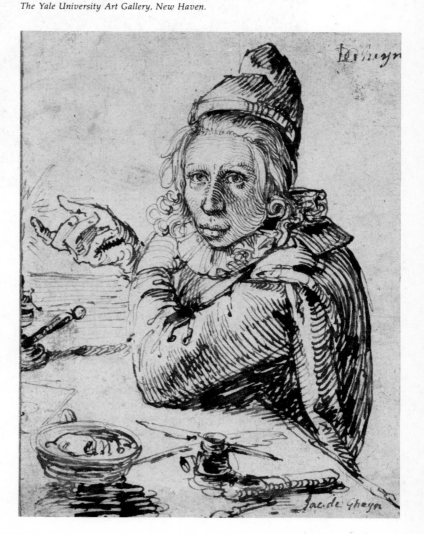

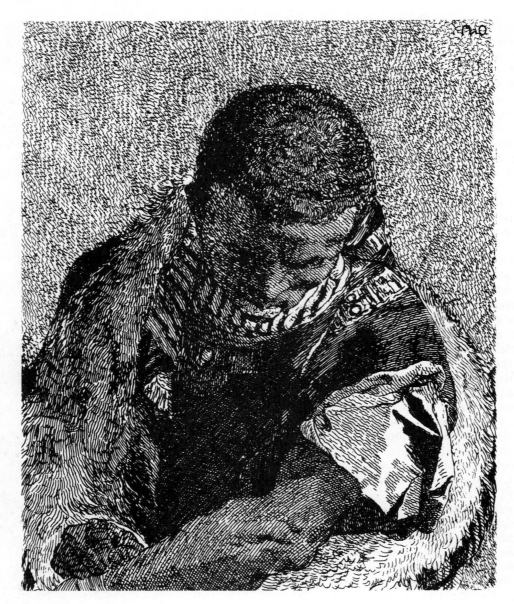

Figure 7.6
GIOVANNI DOMENICO TIEPOLO (1727–1804)
A Negro
Etching, 2nd state. 5 3/4 x 4 9/16 in.
Courtesy Museum of Fine Arts, Boston.
George R. Nutter Fund.

the figure's unseen forms is what makes him draw the figure's clothed forms in a way that convincingly suggests the presence of a torso and both arms. In the Dürer drawing, however, the artist's fascination with details of the drapery makes him occasionally lose the figure beneath it. Indeed, it is only Dürer's emphasis on a decorative formality—on an image as much symbolic as alive—that keeps the figure's oc-

casional disappearance from becoming an inconsistency in the drawing. De Gheyn is more concerned with the spirit than with the letter of a form. This is apparent when we compare the hands in both drawings. In Dürer's the hands are structurally lucid but without the enveloping rhythm and animation of the hand in the de Gheyn.

A subtle design strategy organizes de

Gheyn's drawing. In addition to the table's diagonality cancelling out the opposing diagonal of the boy's upper arm, a system of small units forms an encircling beat that moves around the page. The extended hand, the objects below it, the bowl in the lower left corner, the objects nearby, the collar overhanging the cloak, and the hat all participate in this revolving beat. Of these, the bowl in the lower left corner is an especially important component in the design. Its visual and physical weight provide that extra bit of weight necessary to keep the design from being too heavy on the right. Note, too, how the vertical fold of the cloak joins the bent arm and the gesturing hand in forming an extended M-shape whose direction moves to the left, additionally weighting the drawing on that side.

Although the drawing's emotive force is not a dominant matter for de Gheyn, the artist shows obvious pleasure in modelling the forms. The boy's gentle but energetic spirit is harmoniously interworked with the mood that issues from the drawing. These moods do not seem imposed by the artist's desire to stress either state; we feel them because the artist did, and his empathy with the subject comes across to us through the functioning of the factors.

An even stronger mood imbues Tiepolo's etching *A Negro* (Figure 7.6). Like Dürer and de Gheyn, Tiepolo relies heavily on the structural factor, but here structural lines do more than feel out the changing terrain. An overall texture of generally wavy lines, in addition to explaining the subject's topography, creates a soft, almost impressionist-like atmosphere. These lines produce tones that bathe the forms in a gentle light, intensified by the flash of bright sunlight on the sleeve of the figure's left arm.

By gently graduating values and avoiding strong contrasts between them, Tiepolo evokes a sense of hushed restraint that supports the figure's introspective mood. The overall mood of quiet contemplation is additionally reinforced by the circular movements of the design that make the figure appear to withdraw inward, even as he is actually withdrawn from the forms surrounding him. Tiepolo locates the figure at the far end of what we sense to be a cone of motion. By making the shapes, textures, and value contrasts of the cloak and arms more visually active in their overall impact and in their revolving action than the forms farther back, the artist makes us aware of the distance separating us from the young man's head and torso. Tiepolo further bolsters both the conical swirl and

the mood by reducing the value contrasts between the forms farther back. Both the tone of the background, in approaching that of the light side of the head and of the cape on the figure's right side, and the tone of the tunic, in approaching the tones of the scarf and the dark side of the head, help to strengthen the figure's physical *and* psychological retreat.

The pronounced textures which tend to muffle the structural clarity of the forms and of the surface anatomy, and the structural clarity which tends to force its way through the textural web are not conflicting ideas but mutually supportive ones. The etching's texture depends on these precise structural explanations simply because it needs something to be textured for—some reason for changing value and pattern. And, were the forms less fully realized, they would be buried under such conspicuous textural activity. Likewise, these strongly carved forms, while needing to be visible through the texture, would, if stripped of this softening atmosphere, lose their emotive character.

As Tiepolo's etching indicates, structural considerations can lead the way to quite subtle and moving dynamic states. And, as all the drawings thus far examined in this book illustrate, an understanding of anatomy is necessary for more than the ability to make economical and convincing statements about human forms; it provides a rich source of stimulating plastic responses that serve other factors. Even in Dürer's drawing, where anatomy has such a small role to play, the design of the facial forms is consistent with the design of the surrounding segments, and may even have stimulated his solution to the design of the beard and the headdress. In fact, except for Figure 7.4, all the examples thus far in this chapter show little of the figure itself. But in each (except for Dürer's necessary lapses) the drawing of the drapery makes it clear that the artist is well aware of the nature of the forms below; they continue to influence the drawing's design and expression, as well as its structure.

Again in Vespignani's drawing *Girl in Bed —Graziella* (Figure 7.7), little shows of the figure itself. But the artist's understanding of its masses beneath even these thick layers of bedding convinces us of their presence. Where we do see the forms themselves Vespignani reveals his mastery of anatomy in suggesting so much of their structure by volume-informing contours and a very economical selection of lines within those contours. In the hand the

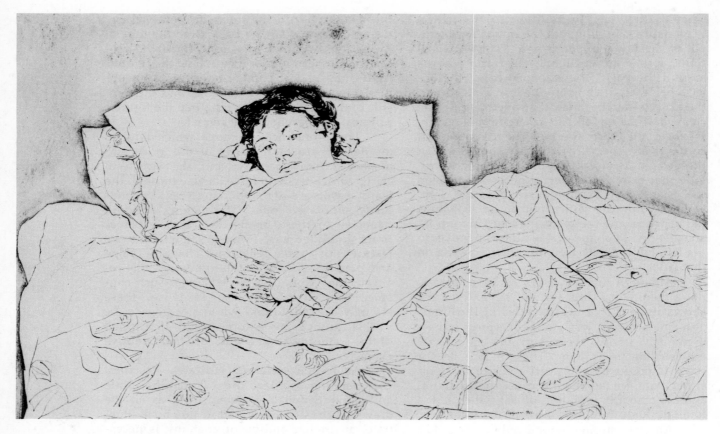

Figure 7.7
RENZO VESPIGNANI (1924–   )
Girl in Bed—Graziella (1953)
Pen and ink, washes. 20 3/4 x 35 1/4 in.
Courtesy The Fogg Art Museum, Harvard University.
Bequest of Meta and Paul J. Sachs.

only lines inside the contours are those few that describe the metacarpal heads and some folds in the fingers, and mark off important planar junctions. Even in the head, where the artist restricts his observations to the features, the contour of the face and the drawing of those features trigger strong clues about important planes of the head.

Although Vespignani's gentle drawing is expressively the opposite of Cambiaso's (Figure 7.4), they both show a similar concern with contours that sets them apart from the more structurally insistent artists discussed above. The absence of swarms of structural lines carving masses in space clears the picture plane for other visually expressive events.

In Figure 7.7 the emotive theme is the tranquility of the resting figure. Almost everything shown is in a state of surrender to gravity. The girl's limp forms accommodated to the pli-

ant bedding suggest their unseen substantiality by the mattress bending under her weight, and by the folds radiating from beneath her head and arm. The folds of the sheet and the patterned blanket "give in" to their own weight, or, where they are supported by the figure, adhere to her forms with little resistance. Only a few folds in the bedding try to hold themselves up, a half-hearted attempt that only underscores the easy yielding of the rest of the subject. Tranquility is also implied by the pearly tone and soft texture of the wall, by the emphasis on horizontality (which includes the shape of the page), and by the majestic undulations of the bedding. By giving the figure and her immediate surroundings the same white tone, Vespignani further stresses her visual harmony with the surroundings. Only the dark tone of the girl's hair breaks the visual silence of the drawing's peaceful character, and in doing so, calls attention to her gentle introspection—the psychological as well as the visual center of attraction.

Another design theme directly employs the structural considerations of the forms. If we cover all but the lower fourth of the drawing, the patterned coverlet appears to lie flat on the picture plane. When we expose only the lower half of the drawing, the arm and the mound of the legs are clearly volumetric, but are minor masses when compared to the more formidable volumes in the upper part of the drawing. By this ordered increase of forms in scale and substance Vespignani creates a uniting pattern of growth that gives each mass a necessary part to play.

Something like the same strategy guides Polonsky in his drawing *In Sleep* (Figure 7.8). Instead of forms growing more substantial as they move back in space, here they do so as they move toward the right side of the page, building to an imposing group of heavy forms on that side. Polonsky balances the drawing by the counterweights of the upper torso's block-like mass bearing down on the lower left side of the page, and by the direction of the head, lower arm, and pillows, which also aim for the lower left corner. Additionally, the figure's arm, drawn to imply ample weight, echoes the bend in the torso as it too is pulled downward and to the left.

The artist, in subtly emphasizing the sub-

Figure 7.8
ARTHUR POLONSKY (1925–)
In Sleep
Brush and ink. 22 x 28 in.
Courtesy of the artist.

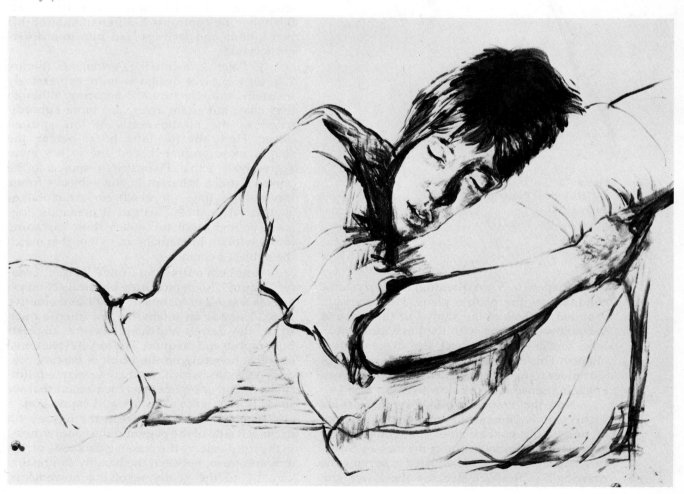

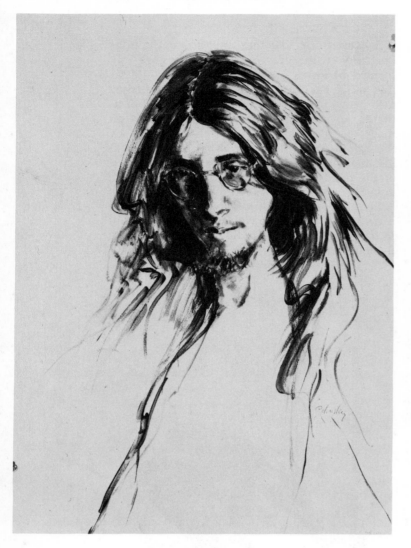

Figure 7.9
ARTHUR POLONSKY (1925–)
Portrait, J. G.
Brush and ink. 28 x 22 in.
Courtesy of the artist.

ject's shapes, calls our attention to the dynamic condition of the picture plane. Here the soft, rounded wedges of the shapes of the arm and the pillows, moving with the force inherent in long wedge-shapes, assist the expression of pliancy. This creates an image that is relaxed in surrender to weight and gravity, yet imparts an engaging sense of rhythmic action.

Note that Polonsky, like Vespignani, is led by his emotive theme of limp weight to the use of undulating contour lines that convincingly suggest the essential nature of the masses. Structure and anatomy too are enlisted in serving the drawing's expression. Because the lower arm

must suggest weight, Polonsky gives it a cylindrical simplicity and weights its lower end by bold strokes that emphasize the olecranon process; because the hand must work at gripping the pillow, he suggests the metacarpal heads and a generally more bony mass. Again, in the head, the girl's relaxed right side is simplified, but the compressed left side is more structurally stated.

As we have seen, artists who are sensitive to the total behavior of a subject's forms extract dynamic qualities in order to clarify the subject's representational condition. What they select, omit, and alter, and the manner in which they handle their marks is determined by their largely intuitive sense of what is necessary to convey their interpretation. Thus, the artist's interpretive intent determines the importance of the role each of the four factors will play. When Polonsky draws a sleeping girl, expressive design considerations only slightly overtake those of structure and anatomy; the drawing's movements and its mood are both temperate, and the handling, moderately paced. But when he confronts a different subject, his perceptions and feelings lead him to a different formula.

In Polonsky's drawing *Portrait, J.G.* (Figure 7.9), an explosive design is more expressively insistent, and structure and anatomy, although they play important roles, are more subordinated to the plastic needs of this spirited image. Here, the handling is far bolder, the shapes more animated, and the values more aggressively active. Polonsky's response to the powerful force inherent in the subject's forms leaves little time (or need) for structural or anatomical nuances. Instead it demands (logically enough) that he convey these cascading forms with an immediacy and vigor that match the subject's character.

Rothbein's drawing *Seated Woman, Leaning* (Figure 7.10) depicts little physical action yet evokes a sense of turbulent plastic and emotive force. There is an intangible but intense quality in the design and handling that suggests both repose and disquiet. The forceful relational energies hovering on the brink of balance produce tensions which, in their uneasy equilibrium, impart the same unsettled mood that we sense in the figure's gesture and expression.

There is tension between the figure's tilt to the left side of the page and the counterthrust to the right side by the massive dark tone on the arm and torso, between the harshly contrasting values and the gently revolving movements,

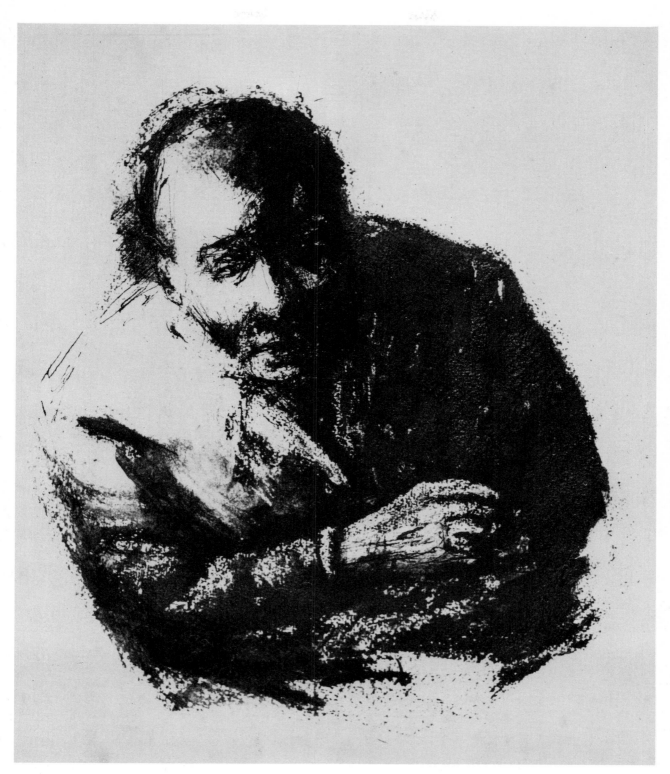

Figure 7.10
RENEE ROTHBEIN (1924–   )
Seated Woman, Leaning
Pen, brush and ink. 9 x 11 1/4 in.
Courtesy of the artist.

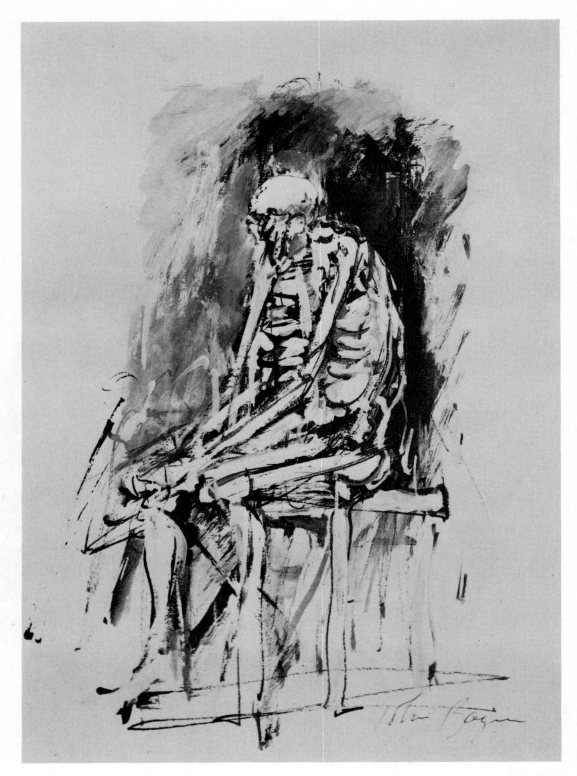

Figure 7.11
JOHN BAGERIS (1924–   )
Seated Skeleton II
Sepia and black ink, white gouache. 13 x 17 in.
Collection of Mrs. Lucy Stone, Cambridge, Mass.

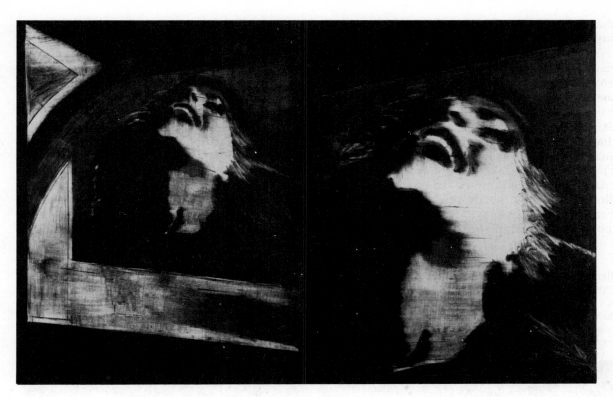

Figure 7.12
JAMES GILL (1934–   )
Laughing Woman—Closeup
Wax crayon. 28 5/8 x 45 1/8 in.
Collection, The Museum of Modern Art, New York.
Eugene and Clare Thaw Fund.

and between the alternating passages of broad and precise handling. These tensions create abstract visual sensations that reinforce the figurative ones. Both are assertive *and* tentative — the woman's enigmatic gesture hovers between reaching out and withdrawing.

These broadly conceived forms, carved by a strong light source, impart a weighty monumentality that adds force to the struggle between the physical weight on the left side and the visual weight on the right. And, in the weathered terrain of the head and hand, as well as in the knowing shapes and structure of the figure's draped parts, the artist reveals her knowledgeable control of anatomy. Although the dominant property of Rothbein's drawing is its expressive impact, it is clear that this expression emerges from an interworking of all the factors.

Bageris' drawing *Seated Skeleton II* (Figure 7.11) is a variation of the theme we saw in Figure 3.47. Here again the artist creates a frenzied but ordered swarm of dark and light strokes whose movements animate the background and chair, as well as the skeleton. These powerful spasms and strivings for change are all the more provocative because they issue from a seated and supposedly lifeless subject. Indeed, an important part of the drawing's expressive theme is the ominous energy of the subject, which threatens to explode the image, despite the several stabilizing vertical and horizontal directions, and its "still life" nature. Note that Bageris wisely subdues structural considerations to intensify the subject's abstract condition, and that he imbues each line, shape, and tone with an almost unbearable urgency. Such a bold utilization of the skeleton as an agent of expressive design requires more than a passing familiarity with its design and construction; we are not likely to see or intensify the energies and rhythms of forms we know little about.

Gill's drawing *Laughing Woman—Closeup* (Figure 7.12) uses a very different kind of rhythm. In addition to the shapes and values that, by their active and spontaneous character, support the expression of laughter, the artist repeats and enlarges the woman's head, further reinforcing the "beat" of laughter. But in the brooding nature of the surrounding tones, in the allusions to strange apertures and movements, and even in the figure's advance toward us, Gill implies an ominous undertone. Note that the throat is drawn in conformity with anatomical fact, but is illuminated in a way that produces a particularly animated shape, thus enacting the vibrating movements of laughter. Note, too, how the design strategy has the heads and their gray, window-like "containers" moving to our right, while the overall, bullet-like shape of the entire configuration rushes to our left.

Picasso's etching *Boy Watching over Sleeping Woman* (Figure 7.13), shows a complex interworking of the four factors that shifts in emphasis from a strong use of structure on the left side of the page to a more two-dimensional ordering of the forms on the right side. But Picasso takes care to make this a subtle transition, and further unifies the design by enveloping dark tones, and by rhythms, such as the C-shaped curves that relate all the arms and hands. Further, he knits the image together by arranging shapes and forms that call to each other across the page. This occurs with the

Figure 7.13
PABLO PICASSO (1881–1973)
Boy Watching over Sleeping Woman (1935)
Etching and aquatint. 23.7 x 30 cm.
Courtesy Museum of Fine Arts, Boston.
Lee M. Friedman Fund.

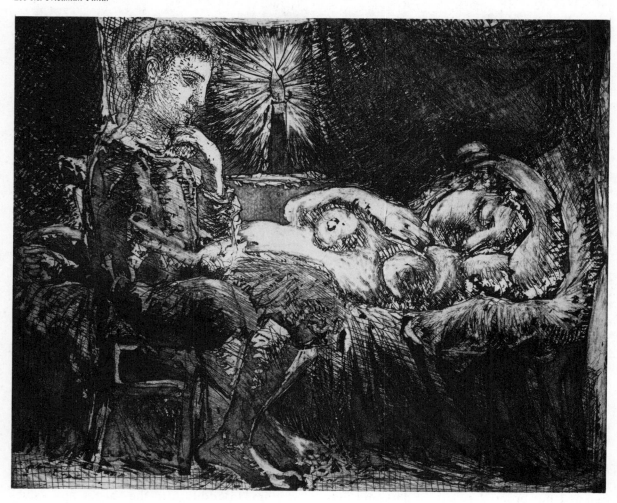

shape of the boy's head and that of the window behind him, and in their association with the spherical and blocky forms of the woman and the pillow. Picasso establishes an expressive need for this shift in emphasis from more structured forms on the left to more shape-oriented ones on the right. The boy's enigmatic but protective character is strengthened by the substantiality of his forms, just as the woman's state of deep sleep is enhanced by the rhythm of her more abstracted and shape-oriented ones.

The etching's mood is both hushed and troubled. The harsh light of the candle, the sly shifts from three- to two-dimensional stresses, and the overall level of reality all suggest a strange, dream-like state. The very active role of textures also adds to this mood. In their rich abstract play, the textures call our attention to a degree of dynamic activity that belies the innocence of the depiction. Picasso's formula results in an image that pulsates between representational and abstract "readings." We cannot disregard the unusual life in either the depiction or in the dynamic means used to establish it.

The anonymous Bolognese artist who created *Burial Scene* (Figure 7.14) reveals a similar sensitivity to the visually expressive forces that, in activating a representation, intensify its psychological meanings. He utilizes several important strategies that amplify the mood of this mysterious and fearsome event. In placing all the figures and the darkest tones low on the page, and by clarifying the structure of the lower-placed forms more than those higher up on the page, he strengthens the dramatic impact of the scene by focusing our attention on the corpse's interment. The artist emphasizes the sagging body's weight (and destination) by blending the cast shadows of the corpse and the nearby figures with the dark tone of the tomb opening, thereby adding a strong visual weight to the lowering action.

Some of the more discreet touches that add to the drawing's disquieting mood are the taut ropes which serve as a visual foil for the curvilinear and animated forms; the extended hands of the figures in the background which seem to urge the body downward; and the corpse's head, mouth open and chin upthrust— a last visual and human "protest" to the downward actions. Note how effectively the artist uses the overhead light source to emphasize some parts and hide others so as to control the design and our reading of it. The artist further stimulates the figurative and abstract actions and mood by exaggerating the curvilinear

rhythms of the surface anatomy and the drapery, giving them a nervous vibrancy.

Tiepolo's arrangement of the four factors in his drawing *Error and Falsehood* (Figure 7.15) places the bold moving actions of strong directions and rhythms ahead of even figurative energies. Not unlike Cambiaso (Figure 7.4), Tiepolo relies on a stormy two-dimensional design to activate the image. As this explorative sketch for a painting shows, most artists approach a visual challenge with a concern, not for its representational specifics, but for its dynamic essentials. And, although this is

Figure 7.14
Bolognese School, 17th Century
Burial Scene
Pen and bistre wash over black crayon.
8 7/8 x 5 7/8 in.
Courtesy The Fogg Art Museum, Harvard University.
Bequest of Charles Alexander Loeser.

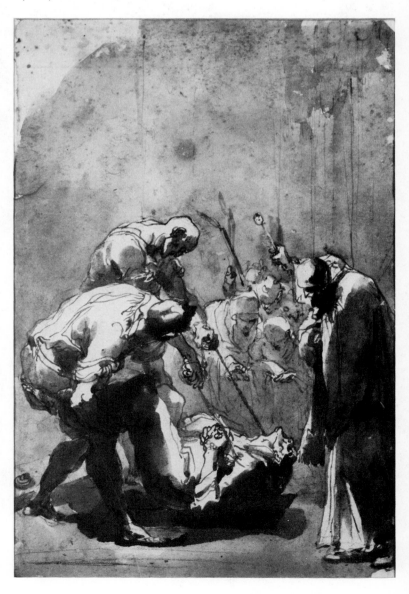

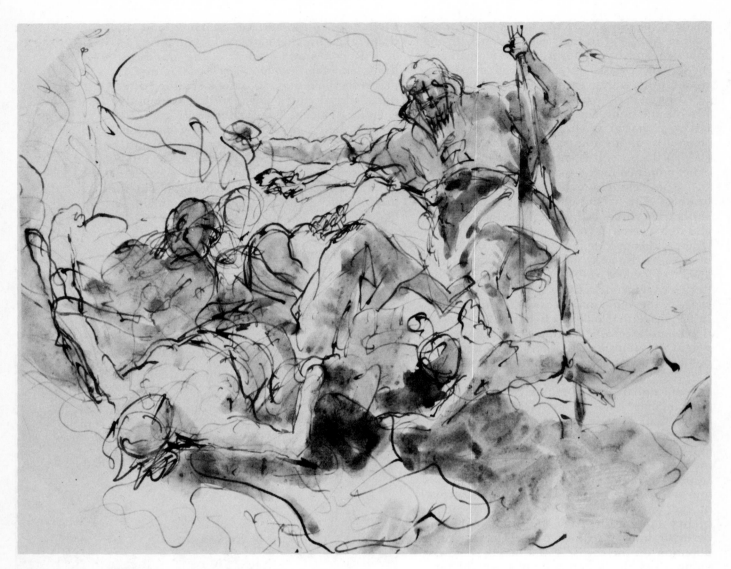

Figure 7.15
GIOVANNI BATTISTA TIEPOLO (1696–1770)
Error and Falsehood
Pen and brown ink, brown wash over black chalk.
7 5/8 x 10 1/8 in.
The Pierpont Morgan Library, New York.

a preparatory work, it is a complete graphic statement. Expressive design considerations are dominant, but structure and anatomy, their broad masses and bold surface undulations adding "fuel" to the drawing's powerful actions, are inventively interworking concepts.

Here, all the elements are in a state of strong agitation, but they compensate each other's actions to produce an orderly pattern of forces. Despite all the visual "commotion" an encircling system of arms "embraces" the

configuration and, on its periphery, encircling clouds reinforce this containing device. On the right, the vertical thrusts of the standing figure and his staff produce a needed visual weight to balance the drawing's overall movement toward the lower left corner. Thus, for all the excitation of the elements and the handling in this spontaneous sketch, the artist is in control of the image, and communicates the figures' troubled ferment.

In a similarly "busy" design, McGarrell's

lithograph *Elephant Bathers I* (Figure 7.16) creates almost the opposite emotive effect. In contrast to Tiepolo's furious calligraphy, McGarrell's lines are more deliberate and structural. Likewise, his tones are less shifting and fluid, his shapes, more sharply defined. Instead of serpentine or diagonal movements of great force, McGarrell stresses horizontal movements and, by an almost cubist-like interdicting of directions, keeps all other directions from generating any strong-moving force.

McGarrell's surrealistic theme requires these less turbulent forces and feelings. This troubled and evasive scene, half snapshot, half dream, needs the fragmented shapes and passages of ambiguity between figure and ground to impart a sense of anxiety and even of quiet terror. The artist achieves this by carefully integrating changes in perspective and scale, by concealing figures among matching values and shapes, by using subtle metamorphic occurrences, as in the animal-like head of the figure at the lower left corner, and by camouflaging interspaces separating groups with veils of

Figure 7.16
JAMES McGARRELL (1930–)
Elephant Bathers I
Lithograph. 28 x 36 in.
Courtesy Museum of Fine Arts, Boston.
Gift of the International Graphic Arts Society.

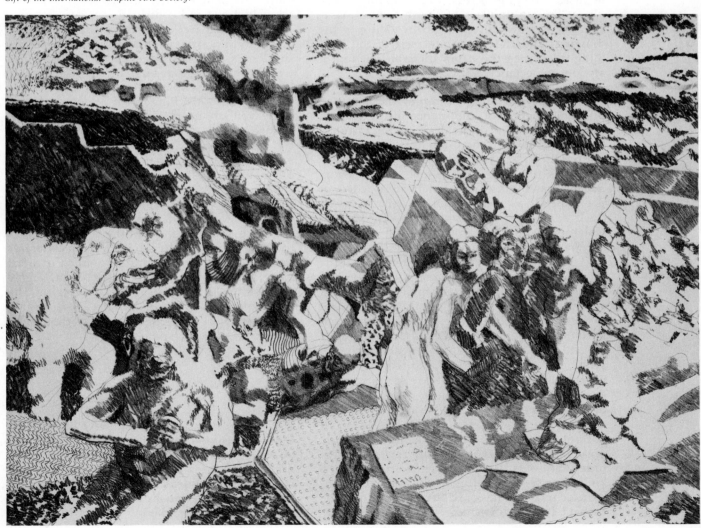

tone or overlapping and undefinable forms. The artist further merges visions with realities by teasing suggestions of figures and animals forming in unexpected places: white shapes on the table at the right suggest a small, upright animal upon a figure-like group of shapes; behind the basketball player (whose ball suggests a skull) a reclining figure appears in a textured area, which, because of the shifts in perspective, may be read as clouds or waves. Structural lines sometimes clarify and sometimes obscure forms; similarly, surface anatomy occasionally denoted objectively is sometimes distorted or obscured.

The resulting mood of this densely filled configuration in which forms are lost and found, lucid and dream-like, finds support at the abstract level of its order. The interjoining shards of small shapes and tones cancelling out strong movements; the often carefully stated textures and patterns returning us to the picture plane; the ambiguities of figure-ground associations; the overall wind-blown nature of the drawing, and the temperate pace of the handling all evince the same ineffable feeling of anxious expectancy and dread.

As the foregoing examples indicate, the differing degrees of importance of the roles of the four factors in figure drawing are virtually limitless. Although the drawings we examined are hardly an extensive sampling of such combinations of usage, they show that in every master drawing no factor is left unregarded, or is elevated to a level of importance that excludes the other factors. No drawing can bear such an isolating attention to any factor and survive as a system of expressive order.

Without the governing influences that the interworking factors impose on each other, any or all of them can be disengaged from the rest and made foreign to the image they were meant to dominate. An overconcern with structure can become a tedious fixation on measurement as an end in itself. Although an acute analytical sensibility to the structural nature of *any* form is nothing less than crucial—we simply cannot draw anything whose essential construction we don't understand—an obsessive fascination with structural matters not only excludes important aspects of form that belong within the purview of the other factors, but reveals an attitude that holds drawing to be no more than a kind of pretend sculpture. At best, a figure constructed without the contributions *and* demands that all four factors make, remains only a re-

port on the container the living figure comes in.

An obsession with anatomy quickly deteriorates into a slavish faithfulness to physiology. While a knowledge of anatomy is essential for a keen understanding of a figure's structural and dynamic possibilities, a compulsive concentration on the figure as merely a machine results only in a thorough inventory of its parts. Generally, the more successful such drawings are as catalogs of anatomical fact, the more cadaver-like and artless are the results. More than scrutiny is needed to create the graphic equivalent of life.

An exclusive interest in design soon becomes an intellectual exercise, a kind of visual chess game. Instead of the "birth" of a graphic organism which, like the real organism, has an equivalent structure, order, and temperament, the results of runaway design considerations are, at most, clever sensory entertainment. More frequently, such works seem self-consciously novel and contrived.

As noted in the previous chapter, a concentration on expression as an end in itself instead of as a necessary state of receptivity to what is actual or inferred in the subject, quickly becomes an essentially nonvisual and self-indulgent emotional fling. Such drawings do not really tell about the artist's interpretive responses to an observed or envisioned figure, but only record a kind of free-association statement stimulated by some aspects of the figure. The real subject remains the artist's psyche. But creative expression is not a retreat from reason or order. It is an attitude that, while directing what the eye should search for, is still open to receiving stimulation from the subject's objective state. Thus it is the force that both generates perceptions and, in comprising much of what constitutes the artist's "screen" of intent, largely directs the "filtering" of all his perceptions. The best exponents of figure drawing always transmit the subject's message as well as their own.

IN CONCLUSION

In the last chapter we observed that when the expressive order of a drawing depends heavily on the nature of the medium, the medium rates closely in importance with the four factors as a consideration in perceiving and responding. So we must now extend our examination of the interplaying factors to include some observations and examples concerning the role of the materials, especially when they strongly affect the image.

Here, too, we will briefly consider the needs of the emerging drawing. For in addition to the skills and interests we bring to the act of figure drawing, and beside the subject's supply of measurable and dynamic "data," the drawing as it forms makes suggestions of its own. And, finally, because we want our drawings to say what we mean them to, we will examine some drawings to see why the intent to arrive at a particular goal is the necessary point of entry into figure drawing, even though our perceptions, materials, and the needs of the emerging drawing always influence our intent.

As noted earlier, all good figure drawings show a congenial alliance between the artist's intentions and the medium's character. When a medium exerts a strong influence on the artist's handling and judgments, its value for the artist is determined by his ability to adapt the medium to his purposes or adjust his goals to take advantage of the medium's properties.

When Rembrandt uses the etching needle he accepts the restrictions it imposes on the broad, calligraphic manner of his drawing style with other media (Figures 5.1, 5.11, 5.18). But because he responds to the needle's linear precision and delicacy, the fine weave and textural

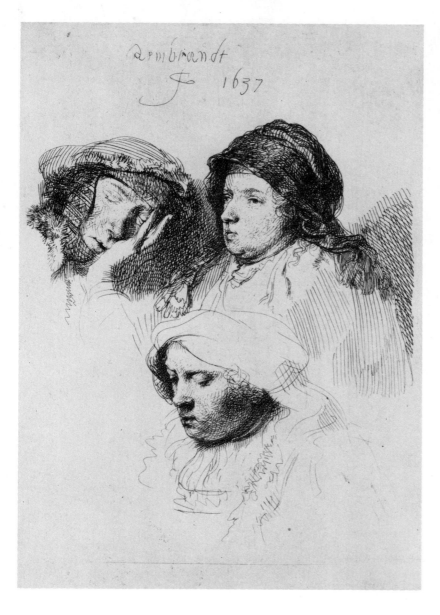

Figure 7.17
REMBRANDT VAN RIJN (1606–1669)
Three Heads of Women, One Asleep
Etching, 2nd state. 14.2 x 9.7 cm.
Courtesy Museum of Fine Arts, Boston.
Gift of the Estate of Lee M. Friedman.

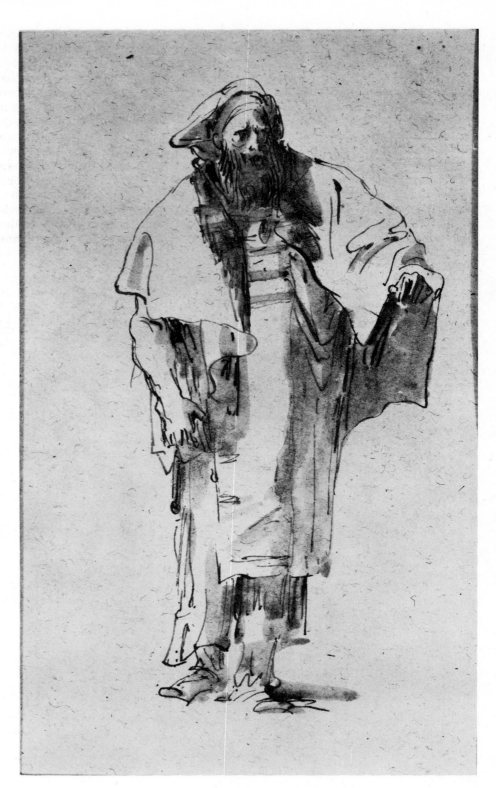

Figure 7.18
GIOVANNI BATTISTA TIEPOLO (1696–1770)
Standing Man
Pen and wash. 22.5 x 13.7 cm.
The Art Museum, Princeton University.

range of its tonalities, and even its restrictions on a more aggressive handling, he adjusts his goals away from the more painterly manner of his drawings in ink or chalk and enjoys etching's challenge to be especially resolute and precise. In his etching *Three Heads of Women, One Asleep* (Figure 7.17), although he does little to relate these three studies beyond their tasteful arrangement, he shows satisfaction in controlling the pace of the values among the heads and in conveying the gentle rhythms among the forms. Instead of the vigorously animated play between the broad strokes and bold tones of his ink and chalk drawings, Rembrandt elects to tell about subtle surface changes, textures, and light effects. He does so not as an end in itself, but as clues to the moods of the three women. For example, the sleeping head is securely held, not only by the dependably sturdy hand, but by the "cushion" of cross-hatched lines which, in completing the circle begun by the woman's hat, adds to our appreciation of the weight of the head, relaxed in sleep.

Note that even here, though an etched line is difficult to alter or remove, Rembrandt still begins to draw each figure by free lines that search out movements, rhythms, shapes, and major planes and masses. Note, too, that in drawing heads Rembrandt doesn't concentrate on the eyes, nose, and mouth, but is equally attentive to the form-units of the entire subject.

In Tiepolo's pen and wash drawing *Standing Man* (Figure 7.18), the materials assist the artist in grasping the passing gesture of the model. Although such a pose might be as successfully captured in several other media, none can move with the speed and vitality of the quill or steel pen. Nor can tones that may range from near white to pure black be as easily or quickly set down as can those made by washes of ink or watercolor. Here the speed of execution that the pen lines make possible not only reinforce the expression of the old man's subtle but sudden gesture, they convey the trembling inflections of his momentary stance and of the drapery's fluttering changes. Likewise, the immediacy of the broad washes suggests the moving nature of the action.

But these lines and tones do more. They deftly note important structural and anatomical conditions, establish textures and local-tones, and illuminate the forms in a strong light. Notice how well the line of the hat's brim explains the form of the head, how the corrugator muscles affect the structure of the forehead, and how the sinewy muscles of the lowered arm

expend effort. Tiepolo convinces us of the presence of the figure's forms beneath the heavy drapery—he even manages to tell us about the deltoids, the man's left knee, and that at the ankle the medial malleolus is higher than the lateral one.

And all this is stated with a simultaneous vigilance to the dynamic nature of the forms and to their collective action, strengthened by the fast-moving cadence of the medium. In stressing the upward expansion and growing substantiality of the figure, from its tremulous beginning at the feet to the monumental crescendo of the upper body, Tiepolo adds even greater force and spirit to the expressive gesture of the old man's head and arm.

The especially harmonious interplay between the artist's needs and the medium's character earns our immediate appreciation in Kollwitz's charcoal drawing *Self-Portrait* (Figure 7.19). Unlike Tiepolo's drawing this image is difficult to imagine being formed by any other medium. Charcoal, which is simply carbonized wood, has the sooty, velvet-like texture so necessary to Kollwitz's suggestions of atmosphere; it makes us see the figure as through a faint and unifying veil of tone. The artist's interest in a delicate modelling of powerful forms is aided by the ease with which charcoal can subtly change in value from whispered, light to mellow, dark tones. No other medium will as readily respond to such demands.

Like Tiepolo's drawing, Kollwitz's depicts a figure in action. Because the hazy nature of charcoal enables even the darkest tones to fuse with surrounding ones, Kollwitz is able to express the vigorous movements of the extended arm with vigorous movements in the broad strokes that rush up and down along it. This sudden flurry of intense activity is so expressively necessary and so well integrated in the design, that we accept it as an inventively effective strategy.

Kollwitz securely anchors this furious departure from the drawing's otherwise delicate tonal activity in several ways. At the sleeve, the vertical strokes enacting the arm's movements are blended with the tone and direction of the lower arm. All along the arm the strokes roughly suggest the sleeve's folds, and one of the strokes falls exactly at the bend of the arm, further integrating itself with the arm. Another dark stroke corresponds to the contour of the torso, and the few bold strokes on the torso relate in direction with the lighter ones all across the chest. Further, by beginning a fan-like spread of directions with the foreshortened drawing board (convincingly suggested by a single line!) that extends across the page, the broad strokes on the arm form a necessary part of that dynamic action. As "insurance," the artist defines the arm's shape in the lighter underdrawing, and even allows it to stand free of the broad strokes in the area of the elbow.

Note how easily Kollwitz moves from structural to dynamic matters. In the hand the fingers are economically summarized, the artist's knowledge of anatomy guiding the solution; but in the darkened palm, structure gives way to lines and tones that evoke, rather than delineate, the squeezing together of the muscle and skin—we feel the force of the grip on the charcoal stump.

This drawing reveals a characteristic so often seen in master drawings (as many of the

works in this book show): the avoidance of an allover sameness of structural or dynamic emphasis. Note how this drawing seems to begin faintly, reach a crescendo of activity, and then subside. Had Kollwitz continued to develop the forms of the back of the head and of the torso, not only would the drawing's present balance have been sacrificed, but its emotive force would have been dissipated. Here, the grand U-shaped sweep of the entire configuration and the developed forms of the face and hand unite to heighten the drawing's dramatic impact.

It is of course virtually impossible to point to those places in a completed drawing where lines and tones exist (or are absent) because the drawing, as it formed, demanded these conditions. The sensitive artist responds to three considerations which participate in the act of

Figure 7.19
KÄTHE KOLLWITZ (1867–1945)
Self-Portrait
Charcoal. 18 3/4 x 25 in.
National Gallery of Art, Washington, D. C.
Rosenwald Collection.

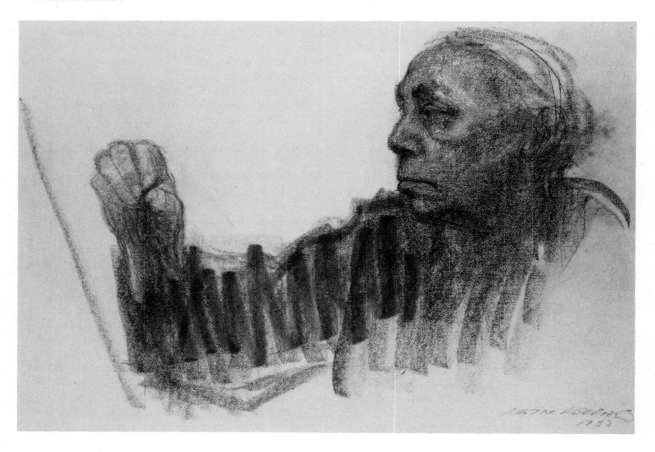

drawing: (1) his own temperamental and creative interests in general and his intentions for the drawing under way; (2) the subject's measurable and dynamic actualities and potential for stimulating creative ideas; and (3) the emerging drawing's needs for further development and integration of the four factors, and *its* creative potentialities—the hints and ideas the still malleable image suggests.

Did Kollwitz add the broad strokes along the arm because she intellectually or intuitively planned to? or because the folds in the observed sleeve suggested them? or because the drawing needed something bold to enliven it and pull it together? Perhaps these strokes exist for all three reasons. Again, did she refrain from further developing the back of the head by prior intent? or because the gray tone of her hair blended with the tone of the wall? or because the drawing's expressive order advised against it? All we can say with any certainty is that some and perhaps much of the drawing was determined by its own visual and expressive requirements.

Greuze in his drawing *A Kneeling Youth with Outstretched Arms* (Figure 7.20) accepts the general state of the model's pose and proportions, but "essays" the forms; that is, he edits out all but the essential movements and masses. No doubt the forms moved with something of the force shown, offering clues to some of the clarifying summaries of mass we see, and the clothing had more folds and wrinkles than are drawn. In making his selections and adjustments Greuze means to convey his chief attraction in the model: the graceful flow of this impassioned gesture. But, in addition to the subject's state and the artist's goal, the emerging drawing seems to have made demands of its own.

Surely the figure is posed in an indoor or outdoor setting that contains some forms and tones, some textures and a ground plane; but, except for the cast shadow extending from the legs, the surrounding environment is absent. This may well be the artist's intention—to show the pose unencumbered by surrounding forms. But if that is the case, how do we explain the cast shadow? It seems to be asking too much of the artist's ability to foresee the problems of an as yet nonexistent drawing to assume he had anticipated its overall weakness of tone without the cast shadow—or even that its shape and directional thrust would so harmoniously accord with that of the man's left arm. No, it is extremely doubtful that the cast shadow was

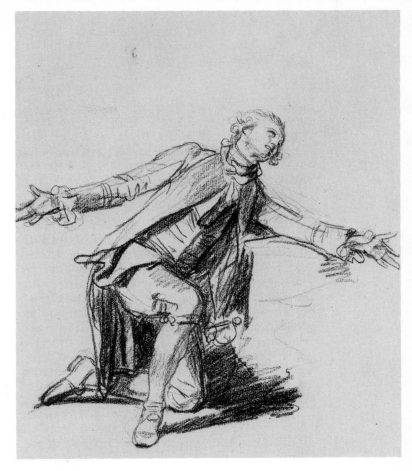

Figure 7.20
JEAN-BAPTISTE GREUZE (1725–1805)
A Kneeling Youth with Outstretched Arms
Red chalk. 14 1/4 x 11 3/4 in.
Courtesy The Fogg Art Museum, Harvard University.
Gift of Paul J. Sachs.

part of the original design plan. It is far more likely that this dark tone, in strengthening the drawing's tonal state, in echoing the arm above it, and in "imitating" the thrust of the lower left leg (thereby creating a delightful pattern comprised of the arms above and the lower left leg and cast shadow below) was a sensitive judgment by Greuze of what was needed by the drawing at that point in its development. The problem arose in the drawing, not in the subject, and the solution was determined by the state of the drawing, not of the model.

That drawings are the result of a three-way conversation between artist, subject, and drawing is of course more immediately apparent in works of a more subjective nature, or when the subject is envisioned, not observed. Figures 7.2, 7.11, and 7.13 did not appear in the mind's eye of the artists, complete in every detail and needing only to be transferred to paper, line by line. A *general* vision and intent was there, unfocused and tentative—something less than the realized drawing and more than an impulse; but, these drawings were resolved by negotiations between the artist, the subject, and the emerging drawing. And as in the Greuze drawing, such negotiations occur in objectively observed drawings made in the presence of the model. The model's needs, too, help shape the final result, as many of the drawings in this book show (Figures 1.21, 2.10, 5.4, 5.34).

Bloom's drawing *Autopsy* (Figure 7.21), done in his studio after having attended a number of autopsies, bridges the categories of subjects observed and those envisioned. Here, too, we feel the drawing was formed partly by Bloom's response to *its* dynamic needs or suggestions, as well as to his own remembered observations and intent. Indeed the harmonies, contrasts, balance, and unity of any drawing, if they are to avoid looking arbitrarily imposed or only weakly managed, must be achieved by an ongoing awareness of the drawing's strengths, weaknesses, and possibilities at every stage of its development.

The Bloom drawing also demonstrates how powerfully the nature of the abstract activities can influence our reaction to a depiction. The drawing of the cadaver, despite its dissected state, is strangely lyrical, its forms seemingly windblown. The graceful rhythms of the corpse impart a transcendental air to the forms and compete with the disagreeable nature of the subject. But there is something instantly unpleasant in the outstretched arms placed upon the cadaver. The furious rush of those arms, their claw-like fingers, and, because they end within the page, their ghostly quality, are conveyed by their directional speed, shape, and handling, all of which are *inherently* aggressive. Likewise, the forms of the dissected corpse, by virtue of their graceful flutter, gentle tonal changes, and delicate handling, seem far less forbidding than would a straightforward depiction of the subject.

In the best figure drawings the artist's intent—a blend of excitement and curiosity about the visual and expressive actualities and possibilities issuing from a particular subject—is what determines the overall character of the drawing. Although the subject and the emerging drawing provide important information and counsel, and create demands and opportunities that must be considered, their influence should serve to regulate and strengthen intent, not divert or overrule it.

Once a drawing is under way, the temptations to "alter course" are often great, especially when we attempt something that might be just beyond our reach. Sometimes we don't per-

ceive certain possibilities until the drawing is well advanced, possibilities that might be interesting (or promise a less demanding conclusion), but are far from our intended goal. Sometimes the drawing takes on unintended qualities that beckon us to some other (often hackneyed) conclusion. And sometimes the medium itself begins to dictate to us. The artist must have both discipline and faith in his original theme to steer clear of diversions. This does not mean that one cannot pursue an interesting creative possibility which might lead to a more daring result. Indeed, ideas that germinate in one drawing should be nurtured in subsequent ones, as Bageris does in his seated skeleton drawings (3.47, 7.11). But allowing the drawing or the medium to take command is a serious surrender of authority and intent, certain to produce poor results.

Bloom is faithful to his theme. The consistency of the drawing's traits and mood, the character and harmonious interplay of its elements, and its balance and unity attest to the artist's unvarying faith (and enthusiasm) in his theme, a theme conceived in an especially engaging formulation of the four factors.

As we observed in Chapter One, the frank declaration of a particular point of view is central to the art of figure drawing. It is also central to originality. Too often the beginner in search of a point of view confuses novelty with originality. Novelty *may* result from originality, but should never be pursued for its own sake. Genuine originality, the kind that makes drawings come alive, begins with the effort to respond honestly to our interests and our perceptions. And each perception increases our emotional, intellectual, and intuitive involvement with the subject, with our emerging work, and with our theme, thereby creating a state of receptivity in ourselves that enables our responses to become increasingly more personal, more insistently *ours*, and thus, original. Genuine originality is the natural result of genuine caring. As Sir Kenneth Clark has observed, "Facts become art through love, which unifies them and lifts them to a higher plane of reality. . . ."[*]

Schiele's intent and perceptual acuity are both apparent in his drawing *Seated Nude Girl Clasping Her Knees* (Figure 7.22). His candid satisfaction in the tactile experiencing of the forms *and* in the calligraphic play of the lines

*Kenneth Clark, *Landscape into Art* (New York: Transatlantic Arts Inc., 1961), p. 16.

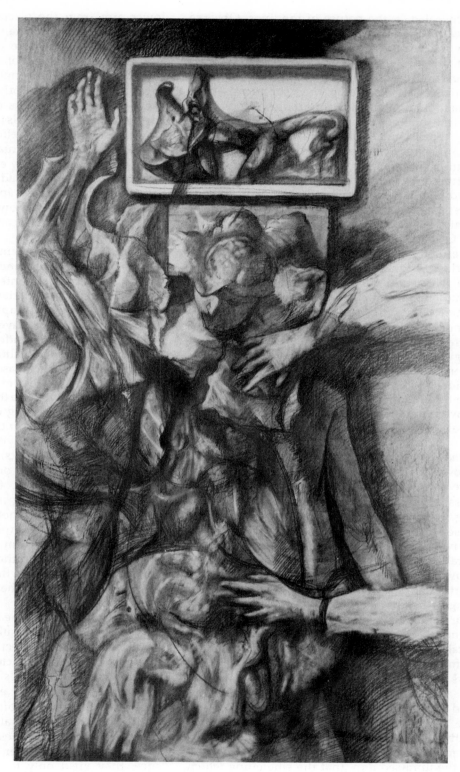

Figure 7.21
HYMAN BLOOM (1913–   )
Autopsy, 1953
Crayon. 54 1/2 x 37 1/2 in.
Whitney Museum of American Art, New York.

is revealed in the nature of the lines. Observe how the lines are equally concerned with touching and with their own abstract interplay. And not only do these interacting directions, textures, speeds, and tensions fail to conflict with Schiele's sensual theme, they support it—their visual-expressive nature amplifies the psychological tone of the artist's search of the forms.

For Matisse, in his drawing *Nude* (Figure 7.23), expressive interests are more structurally than sensually motivated, and the dynamic nature of the elements is more forcefully active in directional than in tactile behavior. In contrast to Schiele's varied and lively, but leisurely, contours, these are almost entirely comprised of C-shaped segments that race furiously on interdicting, volume-informing, and shape-enclosing functions. As in Schiele's drawing, the elements' figurative and abstract roles complement rather than compete with each other. Although these two drawings are roughly similar in their figurative sense, they are very different in temperament and theme. Both were begun and sustained by the artists' honest responses to perceptions "programmed" and guided by intent, and in both, conditions in the forming image and those set by the medium played important roles in determining their final resolution.

Likewise, Rembrandt's drawing *Study of a Female Nude Reclining on a Couch* (Figure 7.24), shows a complemental simultaneity of figurative and abstract activities among the elements. Less calligraphically active than Schiele's drawing, and less structurally insistent than Matisse's, Rembrandt's drawing nevertheless conveys qualities of calligraphic play and structural clarity that go beyond the others in economy, conviction, and the level of dynamic life. Furthermore, in embracing both of these challenges, he succeeds in an interworking of the four factors that shows each *equally* active. This is not to suggest that such a formula is intrinsically superior (though it is perhaps more demanding), but to point out that all four factors can be abundantly active at the same time.

Here, facts and inferences about structure and anatomy tell us a great deal about both, and the drawing's design and expression are alive with energies and meanings at both the abstract and figurative levels. Note, for example, in the upraised arm, that the single line which establishes the broad plane of the lower arm simultaneously performs the following additional functions: it defines the contour of the lower arm from the olecranon process to the lower ending of the ulna, explaining the bony nature of each, and also defining the base of the plane of the back of the hand; it relates, either by its position, length, or "hooked" endings, with numerous other lines throughout the drawing; and, by its energetic thrust and rugged character it reveals its own emotive force as well as the physical effort of the arm's gesture. In this drawing virtually every mark, likewise, "earns its keep" by equally advocating all four factors. Joseph Conrad's observation on the art of writing is just as applicable to drawing: "A work that aspires, however humbly, to the condition of art should carry its justification in every line."*

In these three drawings of the female figure, each artist, determined to convey his aesthetic and humanistic intent, is led to a necessarily different formulation of the factors, and thus, to an original graphic invention. Were these three artists to have exchanged models, each would have responded to a different hierarchy of perceived actualities and implications, and the result in each case would be uniquely personal. In fact, were every artist shown in this book to have drawn these three poses, we would have that many differing creative expressions. What yours would be, or can become, depends on your perceptual skills, on your temperamental interests and insights, on the intent these conditions provide, and on your recognition of the interworking nature of the four factors.

If a figure drawing is to be seriously approached as art, it cannot be regarded as an imitative, or even a simplifying, process. It is the felt ordering of form relationships which simultaneously refer to the figure and to a system of expressive order that reinforces, and is in turn reinforced by, the representational aspects of the drawing.

If we understand the term *representation* to mean the depiction of a subject's essential outer and inner self—the subject's fundamental physical and spiritual character—then unselective realism and unselective subjectivity, in failing to assert these important essentials, share a basic disinterest in the profound perceptual, dynamic, and transcendental qualities that nature and life suggest. And, these necessary qualities do not come from either scrutiny or indifference; they yield only to analysis, knowledge, order, and empathy.

*From the preface to *The Nigger of the "Narcissus."*

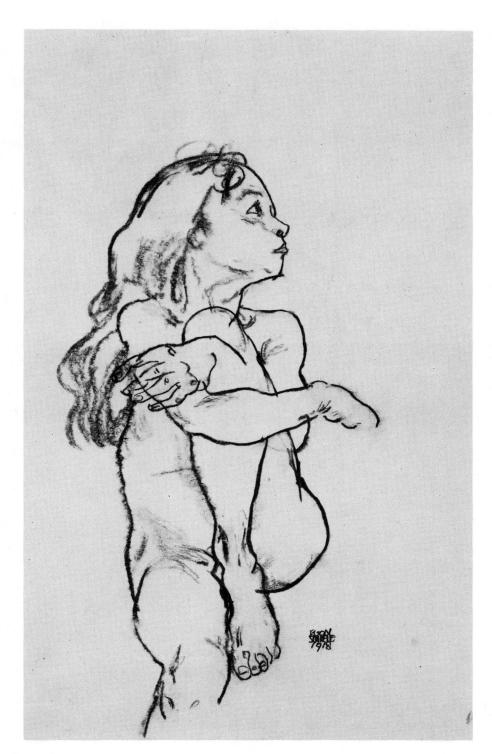

Figure 7.22
EGON SCHIELE (1890–1918)
Seated Nude, Clasping Her Knee
Charcoal. 18 1/8 x 11 5/8 in.
Worcester Art Museum, Worcester, Mass.
The Dial Collection.

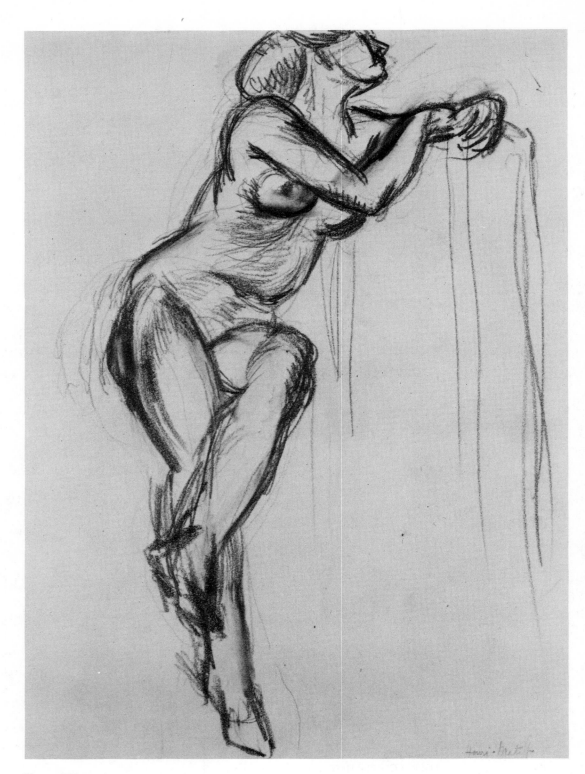

Figure 7.23
HENRI MATISSE (1869–1954)
Nude
Pencil. 12 x 9 1/16 in.
The Metropolitan Museum of Art, New York.
Alfred Stieglitz Collection, 1949.

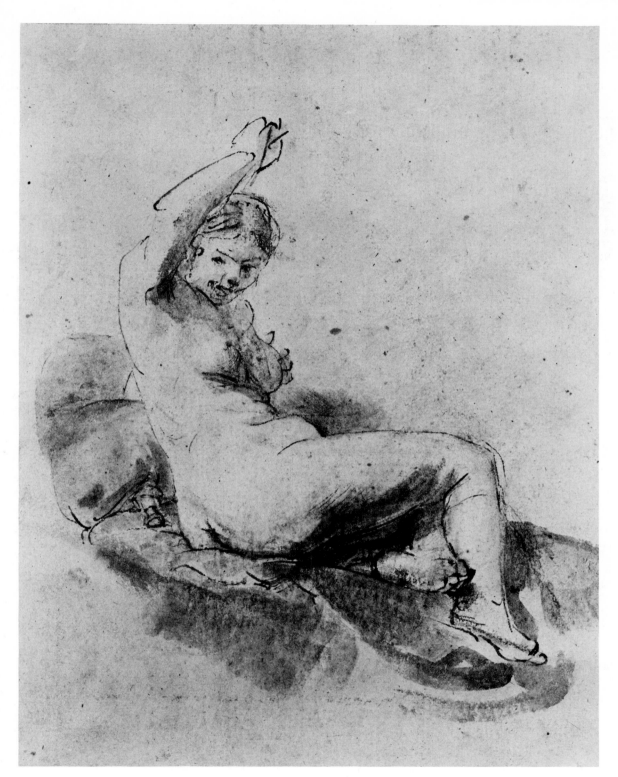

Figure 7.24
REMBRANDT VAN RIJN (1606–1669)
Study of a Female Nude Reclining on a Couch
Pen and wash. 9 1/8 x 7 1/8 in.
Courtesy the Art Institute of Chicago.
Tiffany and Margaret Blake Collection.

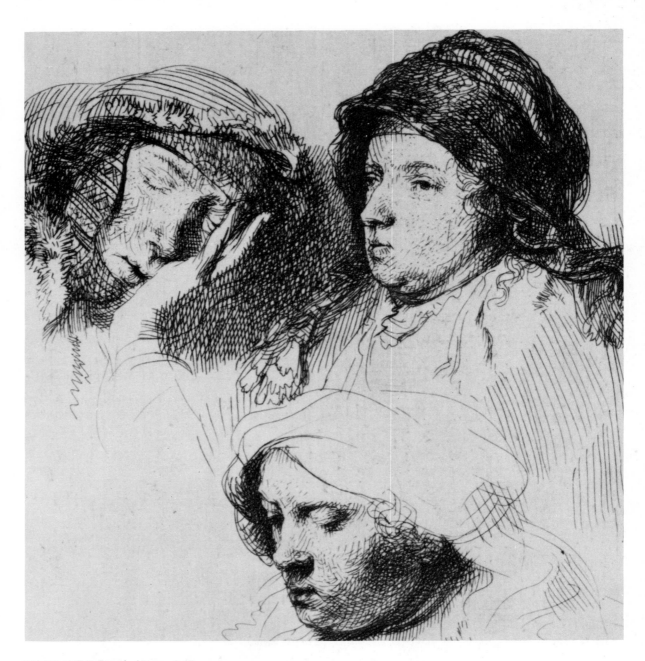

REMBRANDT, Detail of Figure 7.17

Bibliography

GENERAL TEXTS

Anderson, Donald M. *Elements of Design.* New York: Holt, Rinehart and Winston, Inc., 1961.

Arnheim, Rudolf. *Art and Visual Perception.* Berkeley and Los Angeles: University of California Press, 1969.

Arnheim, Rudolf. *Toward a Psychology of Art.* Berkeley and Los Angeles: University of California Press, 1972.

Bertram, Anthony. *1000 Years of Drawing.* London: Studio Vista Ltd., 1966.

Blake, Vernon. *The Art and Craft of Drawing.* London: Oxford University Press, Inc., 1927.

Chaet, Bernard. *The Art of Drawing.* New York: Holt, Rinehart and Winston, Inc., 1970.

Clark, Kenneth. *The Nude.* New York: Pantheon Books, 1956.

Collier, Graham. *Form, Space and Vision,* 3rd ed. Englewood Cliffs, N.J.: Prentice-Hall, Inc., 1972.

De Tolnay, Charles. *History and Technique of Old Master Drawings.* New York: H. Bittner & Co., 1943.

Goldstein, Nathan, *The Art of Responsive Drawing.* Englewood Cliffs, N.J.: Prentice-Hall, Inc., 1973.

Hale, Robert Beverly. *Drawing Lessons from the Great Masters.* New York: Watson-Guptill Publications, 1964.

Hayes, Colin. *Grammar of Drawing for Artists and Designers.* London: Studio Vista Ltd., 1969.

Hill, Edward. *The Language of Drawing.* Englewood Cliffs, N.J.: Prentice-Hall, Inc., 1966.

ON ANATOMY

Peck, Rogers S. *Atlas of Human Anatomy for the Artist.* New York: Oxford University Press, 1951.

Perard, Victor. *Anatomy and Drawing,* 4th ed. New York: Pitman Publishing Corporation, 1955.

Richer, Paul. *Artistic Anatomy,* trans. Robert Beverly Hale. New York: Watson-Guptill Publications, 1971.

Royce, Joseph. *Surface Anatomy.* Philadelphia: F.A. Davis Co., 1965.

Schider, Fritz. *An Atlas of Anatomy for Artists.* New York: Dover Publications, Inc., 1957.

Thomson, Arthur. *A Handbook of Anatomy for Art Students.* New York: Dover Publications, Inc., 1964.

Vanderpoel, John H. *The Human Figure.* New York: Dover Publications, Inc., 1958.

FOR ANATOMICAL MATERIALS

Kilgore International
172 W. Chicago Street
Coldwater, Michigan 49036

Medical Plastic Laboratory
Gatesville, Texas 76528

Ward's Natural Science Est. Ltd.
Box 1712
Rochester, N.Y. 14603

ON PERSPECTIVE

Ballinger, Louise. *Perspective, Space and Design.* New York: Van Nostrand Reinhold Company, 1969.

Burnett, Calvin. *Objective Drawing Techniques.* New York: Van Nostrand Reinhold Company, 1966.

Watson, Ernest W. *How to Use Creative Perspective.* New York: Reinhold Publishing Co., 1960.

ON MEDIA AND MATERIALS

Dolloff, Francis W. and Roy L. Perkinson. *How to Care for Works of Art on Paper.* Boston: Museum of Fine Arts, Boston, 1971.

Watrous, James. *The Craft of Old Master Drawings.* Madison, Wisc.: University of Wisconsin Press, 1957.

Index